Dramatic Discourse

C

This book is due for return on or before the date last stamped below unless an extension of time is granted

Dramatic Discourse

Dialogue as interaction in plays

Vimala Herman

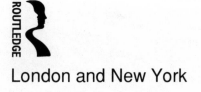

London and New York

First published 1995
by Routledge
11 New Fetter Lane, London EC4P 4EE

Simultaneously published in the USA and Canada
by Routledge
29 West 35th Street, New York, NY 10001

First published in paperback 1998

Typeset in Times by Michael Mepham, Frome, Somerset
Printed and bound in Great Britain by
T.J. International Ltd, Padstow, Cornwall

British Library Cataloguing in Publication Data
A catalogue record for this book is available from the British
Library

Library of Congress Cataloguing in Publication Data
A catalogue record for this book is available from the Library of
Congress

ISBN 0–415–08241–2 (hbk)
ISBN 0–415–18451–7 (pbk)

To my mother and father

Contents

Acknowledgements

The writing of this book was helped by various kinds of support given to me by individuals and institutions, which I gratefully acknowledge.

My thanks are extended to David Birch, Ron Carter, Bill Dodd and Bill Nash who read earlier chapters and offered invaluable advice and unfailing encouragement. Thanks are also due to the Routledge team, especially Claire L'Enfant, Julia Hall and Nikky Twyman for their understanding, patience and skilled help. To Janice Price, I owe a very special debt.

I also acknowledge with gratitude the financial support given to me by the British Academy in the form of a research grant from the Small Personal Research Grants Fund. The University of Nottingham supported me with a grant from the Humanities Rolling Project Small Grant Fund. The help given by both institutions enabled me to spend the summer of 1992 in Cambridge during a crucial period of researching and writing this book. My thanks are also extended to the staff of the Hallward Library, and the Cripps Computing Centre at the University of Nottingham, and to the staff of the Cambridge University Library, for their efficient help.

To all those scholars whose work has shaped and influenced my own thinking, either directly or indirectly, I owe a deep intellectual debt. To my family, I owe a very personal one, as also my friends for their warmth and hospitality which enabled me to put much needed distance between myself and the computer as and when the occasion arose. My students, too, have helped me test and revise both ideas and analysis by the offer of insights and critical comments of their own. Any remaining faults are inevitably my own.

Permission to use material which appeared previously under the title 'Dramatic dialogue and the systematics of turn-taking' in *Semiotica* (1991), 83, 1/2, pp. 97–121 has been granted by Mouton de Gruyter, a division of Walter de Gruyter & Co., and is gratefully acknowledged.

Acknowledgement is due to copyright holders for their kind permission to include the following material in this book:

A. P. Watt Ltd, on behalf of The Executors for the Estate of Constance Garnett, for extracts from *The Cherry Orchard* and *The Seagull* by Anton Chekhov, translated by Constance Garnett.

Conversation Piece © 1934 The Noel Coward Estate; by permission of Alan Brodie Representation Ltd, 211 Piccadilly, London W1V 9LD.

Random House for an extract from *Saved*, from *Plays: One* by Edward Bond, published by Methuen.

Arnold Wesker for extracts from *Chicken Soup with Barley*, published by Penguin.

Extract from *Riders to the Sea* taken from J. M. Synge, *Plays*, edited by Ann Saddlemeyer, 1968; by permission of Oxford University Press.

Extracts from *Table by the Window* © 1955 The Terence Rattigan Trust and *In Praise of Love* © 1973 The Terence Rattigan Trust; by permission of Alan Brodie Representation Ltd, 211 Piccadilly, London W1V 9LD.

Extract from *Look Back in Anger*, 1957, by John Osborne; by permission of Gordon Dickersea and Faber & Faber Ltd.

Extract from *Waiting for Godot* by Samuel Beckett; by permission of Faber & Faber Ltd and Grove/Atlantic, Inc.

Extract from *The Linden Tree* by J. B. Priestley; by permission of the Peters Fraser & Dunlop Group Ltd.

Extracts from the following plays by Harold Pinter are used by permission of Faber & Faber Ltd and Grove/Atlantic, Inc: *No Man's Land*, *Old Times*, *The Homecoming*, *Silence*, *The Birthday Party*.

While every effort has been made to contact owners of copyright material which is reproduced in this book, we have not always been successful. In the event of a copyright query, please contact the publishers.

Introduction

DIALOGUE AND DISCOURSE

Dialogue as discourse is characterized by a fundamental structural principle; it is interactive and interactional. It is a mode of speech *exchange* among participants, speech in relation to another's speech and not merely the verbal expression of one character or actor's 'part'. Dialogue belongs not to the sphere of the 'I' but to the sphere of the 'we', as Gadamer noted (1986a: 65). It requires, in standard cases, the agency and involvement of at least two participants who communicate through the medium of language, as the etymology of the word signifies – 'dia' – through, 'logos' – word, from 'dialegomai' – to converse. The encounter of an 'I' with a 'you' in the speech situation is itself a form of drama, as Lyons (1977) following Buhler (1934) observed, which the category of 'person' in language reflects.

> The grammatical category of 'person' depends upon the notion of participant-roles and upon their grammaticalization in particular languages. The origin of the traditional terms 'first person' 'second person' and 'third person' is illuminating in this connexion. The Latin word 'persona' (meaning 'mask') was used to translate the Greek word for 'dramatic character' or 'role' and the use of this term by grammarians derives from their metaphorical conception of a language event as a drama in which the principal role is played by the first person, the role subsidiary to his, by the second person, and all other roles by the third person. It is important to note, however, that only the speaker and addressee are actually participating in the drama. The third person is negatively defined with respect to the first person and second person: it does not correlate with any positive participant role.
>
> (Lyons 1977: 638)

In the 'drama' of speech exchange the roles of speaker and hearer are played by actual participants and the roles are exchanged during the course of dialogue. The speaker switches role to that of listener while the erstwhile listener becomes the speaker without any necessary change in place or setting, only of 'person'. The switch from attendant non-speech to speech, the change of role from listener to that of speaker, is undertaken in response to another's speech, since response is predicated by the nature of the form. The temporal progression of such alternations and interchanges constitutes the structure and course of dialogue.

The dialogic principle has sometimes been understood in profound ways. To Martin Buber, the I–Thou relationship bespoke a fundamental condition of inter-subjectivity as the basic ground for humans in contact (Buber 1923). For Mikhail Bakhtin (1981) dialogic interactiveness is omniscient and forms the basis of understanding itself, with social inter-subjectivity taking priority over solo subjectivity in questions of meaning. In fact, *dialogism* for the Bakhtin school, even in its disparateness, transcended the face-to-face scenario to take in all forms of communication, including the written forms, and, more broadly, links to an epistemology that grapples with the interconnections between mind, language, culture and history (Voloshinov 1973); and argues for relatedness and for 'a necessary *multiplicity* in human perception' (Holquist 1990: 22). In speech, the tie with Otherness which the principle affords is manifested in the form. The production of meaning is not predicated upon univocality but is always structured under the pressure of an alternative force. An *I* addresses a *you* who responds as *I* addressing *you*, who responds as *I* addressing *you* . . . and so on. The deictic tie between addresser and target addressee – the *I* and *you* of the speech situation of dialogue – ensures that face-to-face encounter is presupposed by the form. The progress of dialogue over time is, consequently, dependent on the inputs from both poles of its structuring.

Standard definitions of the form in dictionaries link dialogue to spontaneous forms of dual interaction – conversation.

> 1 a literary work in conversational form   2a a conversation between 2 or more people or between a person and sthg else (e.g. a computer)   b an exchange of ideas and opinions   3 the conversational element of literary or dramatic composition   4 discussion or negotiation between 2 nations, factions, groups, etc. with conflicting interests . . .
>
> (*New Penguin English Dictionary* 1986)

The link between conversation and dialogue posited above relates primarily to structure and not necessarily to content, function or verbal texture. But the alternating speech possibilities afforded by the form have been put to varied uses which have conditioned manifestations of it accordingly. Variations can be seen in both literary and philosophical texts in which opposing points of view, competing attitudes or intellectual positions on some question have been presented in dialogic form for exegetical or pedagogical purposes. Socrates' and Plato's dialogues, as much as Hume's or Berkeley's, are cases in point. In literature, dialogues of 'Self' and 'Soul' in poetry or *Imaginary Conversations* of the kind composed by Walter Savage Landor have surfaced from time to time in other than dramatic texts. In everyday contexts, too, variation is the norm. Dialogues in courtrooms differ from those in classrooms; social chit-chat differs from parliamentary debates. All are, nevertheless, dual or multi-speech forms entailing, in one way or another or for one reason or another, the presumption of Otherness to which One relates in patterned alternations of speech.

To linguists desirous of investigating the workings of dramatic dialogue, the conflation of conversational speech with dialogue is fortuitous since there is a body of work that has studied spoken speech as 'discourse'. 'Discourse' is a term that has many uses and encompasses, broadly, units that are larger than the basic unit of the grammar, the sentence. The concept is used in this study in its relevance to spoken speech within contexts of verbal communication, the emphasis being, particularly, on the deployments of the dialogic form as situational interaction. Instances of verbal communication actually exceed conversational contexts alone, but most studies have prioritized conversation as the exemplary genre of spontaneous, spoken speech. Before we move to a consideration of the many frameworks of analysis that can contribute to our understanding of the workings of dialogue as interaction, some preliminary remarks are necessary in order to clarify the relation between conversational speech and dramatic speech. The weight of opinion, especially in literary studies, would seem to be against any such affiliation, standard dictionaries notwithstanding.

CONVERSATION AND DRAMATIC DIALOGUE

Studies of dramatic dialogue as discourse – as a speech exchange system – are hardly in evidence, even in investigations of 'the language of drama'. The thrust of the argument has generally been to safeguard the separation of dramatic dialogue from conversation in order to preserve the latter's 'literary' quality. The relation between the two forms has been examined contrastively, as between two essences, literary and non-literary. Little attention has, therefore, been paid to connections between them, although conversation and dramatic speech share areas of commonality in being speech exchange systems, which sets them apart from poetic genres like the ode or the lyric, or narrator language in the novel. Moreover, where the relation has been confronted it has generally been confined to the uses of naturalistic speech at a certain juncture in the history of drama. Part of the reason for this bias is to do with unexamined assumptions about conversation and these focus on content or verbal texture as the point of contrast.

The differences in verbal texture, in particular, have moved critics like Allardyce Nicoll (1968) to utter uncharacteristically extreme sentiments. To Nicoll, as to many others, a playwright is 'an artist in words' (*ibid*.: 344), in a specific sense, as a poet, first and foremost. The world of drama is a 'world of emotions' (*ibid*.: 341) and Nicoll propounds on the inability of common speech to function expressively in such a world – 'everyone knows that our common speech has no power to express our passions intimately'. Conversational language, apparently, reveals us to be tongue-tied, incoherent when our passions are aroused: we splutter with rage or are stunned with grief. Playwrights who use a realistic mode are hampered by the mismatch between the force of felt emotion and the threadbare possibilities for expression of them afforded by everyday speech. Reliance on naturalistic resources in drama can have dire consequences, since it could result in dramatists being 'made mum', or worse, rendering themselves too faithful to 'the suppressions and mutterings of ordinary conversation' (*ibid*.).

Much of this invective is directed at naturalism in general as much as at naturalistic speech in particular, but subsequent developments in drama have undermined such views. Playwrights like Pinter have not only made dramatic capital out of the dramatic figures staying 'mum' in their plays; they have also revealed the force and power of conversational resources when they are used with dramatic skill.

Yet, troubling the relationship remains. The point, if not the detail, of Nicoll's opposition has been echoed by Bernard Beckerman (1970) in more sober terms. Beckerman, more reflectively, articulates a similar underlying worry regarding the lack of possibilities for emotional eloquence in conversation, since conversation operates under social constraints which generally forbid the expression of emotion or, rather, 'passion'. To quote Beckerman:

> Conversation is primarily social, that is, intended to create an atmosphere of civilization rather than reveal inner turbulence. It also resists revelation. In conversation, confidence does not readily spring forth

but must be elicited by the effort of the listener. It is not a medium for conveying passion because passion is egotistical and conversation rests on implied truce: no one is to dominate completely. . .

(1970: 123)

At first glance, there appears to be a measure of truth in this since conversation does have a social dimension and is responsive to the social norms that govern people's conduct, but it does not follow from this that norms cannot be flouted when the occasion arises. They evidently are: in quarrels, in passionate, political arguments, in expressions of grief, anger, love and so on. Beckerman appears to have in mind stereotypes of polite exchanges in 'civilized', social settings which become a prototype for all interactions. But it is hardly the case that all day-to-day interactions are always and only passionless or that for the expression of passion in any form we must have recourse to some quotation or other from a play. Moreover, the 'eliciting' of responses and the inclusion of the effort of the listener are the staples of the dialogic form. It includes a listener, who usually changes discourse role to that of speaker, which Beckerman has overlooked, as if dramatic dialogue were monologue. The efforts of both speakers and listeners are involved in the drama of 'persons' in the speech situation itself as Lyons (1977) has made clear. And as for the injunction that 'no one is to dominate completely', this is often honoured in the breach. In mixed-sex conversations, men systematically dominate women, as research has shown (Ch. 5), and inter-personal domination is more of a norm in society, at least in some contexts, for various reasons, given social stratification on grounds of sex, race, age, status, etc. than such comfortable pronouncements would have us believe.

The problem lies deeper than this, since the assumption appears to be that the relation between conversational and dramatic speech must be predicated upon reflections of surfaces and textures of the one in the other. A mirror or glass is thus inserted between the two domains without respect to the transformations that are wrought when contexts and functions of speech are taken into account. The binary divide separating the two erases the fact of commonality of underlying *interactive* processes which make both, in separate ways, instances of dialogue. It also erases the variety which characterizes speech forms in daily life which are at least as remarkable as those found in plays. For instance, an informed discussion between two academic colleagues writing a book will differ from the phatic speech produced by two recent acquaintances meeting in the street. The speech 'texts' that occur will vary accordingly. Parliamentary debates organize speech exchanges in ways ordained by convention and differ from other conventional arrangements: a board or committee meeting differs from Parliamentary debates but it also differs from a family quarrel. 'Conversation', not as social chit-chat alone, but as spontaneous speech exchange, is not the monolith of uniformity that it is projected as being. The same could be said of dramatic speech.

It is not, therefore, a question of whether dramatic dialogue is seen to mirror faithfully some real life correlate or not, even assuming that some such exists to be mirrored. Even the most naturalistic forms of dramatic speech do not quite reproduce the real life product. The mirror is not the point of reference between the two forms. Rather, it is a question of *mechanics*, in the exploitation by dramatists of underlying speech conventions, principles and 'rules' of use, operative in speech exchanges in the many sorts, conditions and contexts of society which members are assumed to share and use in their interactions in day-to-day exchanges. The principles, norms and conventions of use which underlie spontaneous communication in everyday life are precisely those which are exploited and manipulated by dramatists in their constructions of speech types and forms in plays. Thus, 'ordinary speech' or, more accurately, the 'rules' underlying the orderly and meaningful exchange of speech in everyday contexts are the *resource* that dramatists use to construct dialogue in plays. Fabricated speech in plays, however, is under no necessity to mimic some pre-given original except as a specific dramatic strategy. Even then, it is the illusion of real-life conversation that is sought which is the product of consummate art.

As Elizabeth Burns has succinctly observed, 'Drama is not a mirror of action. It is composition. . .' (1972: 33), and the fabricated activities, including speech in drama, Burns contends, need to be 'authenticated' by an audience (or reader) as credible activity in the dramatic world in which it functions. Dramatic action, broadly defined, becomes meaningful, therefore, in relation to the 'authenticating conventions' which are invoked in a play, which are drawn from the wider, social world of affairs in which dramatic activity is embedded. They imply social norms, values, modes of conduct and action which regulate how members organize their affairs, which in turn form the basis of our understanding of the speech and action of the fictional figures in the world of a play. Such a ground of commonality links playwright, actor, director, audience, reader, in a common effort at meaning, since what we encounter in plays is interpreted action, not action in the raw. In relation to dialogue, what this signifies is that it is our *communicative competence* (Hymes 1972) as much as our *linguistic competence* which is at work in interpreting 'the language of drama'. The overall conventions and 'rules' for meaningful and appropriate speech behaviour in interaction are evoked to transform the serial issue of linguistic tokens among the dramatic characters into forms of inter-personal conduct and social action as communicative activity.

The factors to be accounted for when speech is regarded as speech behaviour, exceed the limits that grammars set on it. Linguistic compet-ence as knowledge of the grammar is obviously needed, but so are other kinds. Utterances may be perfectly grammatical but may be wholly inappropriate things to say to specific others in a context. The pressures on language in context are multiple. As communication, language needs to be sensitive to a host of contextual pressures – the role and status of participants, considerations of appropriacy of speech behaviour, setting or spatio-temporal context of speech, degrees of formality or informality, how to code-switch if necessary, how to control degrees of politeness, and expressivity, whether and to whom and when to be ironical, or sarcastic, or confidential, or reserved or passionate, and the like. In communication, linguistic tokens used are functional and sensitive to such contextual pressures. As interaction, speech takes a jointly co-ordinated and managed course along a temporal path so that understanding, misunderstanding, communication and non-communication between speaker and other become actional and dynamic matters as they materialize in their specifi-cities, and contingencies, in time.

On the other hand, dramatic speech cannot simply be regarded as an extension of everyday speech into drama. There is interdependence but not identity between them, and although there are fundamental levels of commonality, there are also crucial points of difference. Drama, theatre and other performance genres like film, carnival, ceremonial ritual, etc. are embedded in social culture but as part of what has been termed 'expressive culture' (MacAloon 1984: 4), whose hallmark it is to provide forms of activity through which subjectively experienced values, prin-ciples and modes of conduct, which are naturalized in social culture, may be reflexively confronted by members of that culture and known as *other* as object. Such presentations may either undercut or endorse the assump-tions of the dominant culture. As Victor Turner has stated:

> . . . any society that hopes to be imperishable must carve out for itself a piece of space and a period of time in which it can look honestly at itself. This honesty is not that of the scientist, who exchanges the honesty of his ego for the objectivity of his gaze. It is rather, akin to the supreme honesty of the creative artist, who, in his presentations on the stage, in the book, on canvas, in marble, in music, or in towers and

houses, reserves to himself the privilege to see straight what all cultures build crooked.

(1984: 40)

This space of performance and the culturally endorsed reflexivity that distinguishes it Turner calls a 'liminal' (sometimes 'liminoid' for techno-logically advanced societies) and metasocial space, in which,

> groups strive to see their own reality in new ways and to generate a language verbal or non-verbal that enables them to talk *about* what they normally talk. They are liminal in the sense that they are suspensions of daily reality, occupying privileged spaces where people are allowed to think about how they think about the terms in which they conduct their thinking or to feel about how they feel about daily life.

(*ibid.*: 23)

The imagined and imaged worlds of drama, therefore, have a complex relation to the world of existing human affairs on which they draw for their possibilities of meaning, remaining both like and yet unlike those worlds in which they are embedded and to which they speak. Dramatic worlds, like fictional worlds in general, are not transparent to our everyday worlds, or reflections of them, but opaque to some degree, since they present alternatives, possibilities, worlds in the 'subjunctive' rather than the 'indicative' mood or mode of experience (*ibid.*: 21), worlds that could or might be, in different modalities, to some operative notion of 'what is'.

Such worlds have also been characterized as *possible worlds*, counter-factual, 'as if' worlds (Elam 1980: Ch. 4), but whose logic is accessible since taken to be similar to the world in which it is represented. The creation of such worlds draws on given, existing resources – of language, action, gesture, etc. and the conventions of use underlying these – but exploits them in order to design episodes, interactive events and situations in plays into patterns of feeling and experience of a kind that may never be felt, known or encountered anywhere but in drama. Dramatic action and speech are thus bracketed out of social reality and put into quotation marks, as it were, when they become part of stage reality where they are framed and foregrounded for heightened attention. The force of the quotation marks can either emphasize difference as in avant-garde plays, or similarity as in naturalistic plays. The conventions of behaviour, action and speech in ordinary contexts of living are made operative in the creation, assessment and understanding of behaviour in the fictional world of the play. It is the evocation of these which underlies the promise of intelligibility of the hitherto-unencountered fictional world being created through the unfolding of its interactions and actions.

The governance of convention and assumptions in questions of intelligibility and understanding cannot, however, be seen as a mechanical or compulsory mapping of a priori rules on to speech or behaviour in uniform fashion in every instance of communication or conduct either inside or outside drama. For a start, rules may be broken within the contingencies of specific situations, assumptions might have to be abandoned or the performance of our social obligations could be skilfully or clumsily executed. Social life, moreover, is not a monolith of uniformity and could involve competing conventions and norms given conflicting interests and subcultures among groups in society. A working notion of convention must allow for gaps and conflicts in interpretation, since ambiguity, bafflement or incomprehension are legitimate responses to behaviour both inside and outside drama. To quote Turner again:

> if all principles and norms were consistent and if all persons obeyed them, then culture and society would be unselfconscious and innocent, untroubled by doubt. But few indeed are the human groups whose relationships are perpetually in equilibrium and who are free from agonistic strivings.
>
> (1984: 23)

The shift of context to the 'liminal' or expressive sphere and the activation of dramatic constraints (on text and performance) which this entails brings its own set of necessities and transformations. For a start, there is the question of dramatic organization, the internal designing of the individual events and their interrelating as they unfold linearly in time. These may be overtly cohesive, cause–effect designs or they may not. Such internal designs project outwards as well, are simultaneously rhetorical designs manipulating audience involvement and response. And drama is a brief form, as Bentley noted (1965: 79), forever under the constraint of passing time – the time allotted to the whole performance. Then, there are aesthetic and expressive requirements for which, in performance, groups assume responsibility and activate the various codes of theatre as desired (Elam 1980). For this is 'framed' activity, foregrounded for attention, participation, interpretation and appreciation, with all elements in this 'bracketed' world being relevant elements in that world with multi-functions to perform.

There is, consequently, a high level of pre-formation in scripting dramatic action and speech, and pre-formance in realizing a play in its context. And if the script is pre-formed, the performance is even more so, to the extent that analysts like David Birch have argued for the notion of a separate 'text' for performance (Birch 1991: 25–33). Drama as a hybrid form leads a double life as both literature and theatre and is responsive to different traditions, but in either case the life of the dramatic tradition realizes itself and is made material and manifest through such pre-formed activities. Nor is the tradition itself transmitted through the actions of human agents acting spontaneously, but through institutionally organized forms of activity, public, collective and social. The accumulated practices of both domains are also influential.

Drama has its own history – other performances, other texts, other contexts of performance, other theatrical conventions – and its own contemporary constraints for aesthetic, experimental or social purposes. Its indebtedness to other domains of activity has also been acknowledged from time to time – the music hall, circus, mime and so on. Dramatic performances are among those which Dell Hymes has called 'authoritative' and 'authentic' performances (1975: 18), in a very specific sense, as those which materialize the tradition from age to age, as activity, practice, and in which the tradition lives, and in which the standards appropriate and intrinsic to the tradition itself are shaped, applied, tested and revised.

As far as dramatic speech is concerned, such pressures ensure that the face-to-face interactions that inform the dialogic scene are always responsible to the audience presence – however the role of the audience is assessed, as overhearers or participants – and to the necessities of presentation. Extra explicitness or expressiveness in speech may be called for to satisfy both the informational and aesthetic demands of the audience. The flow of information about off-stage and on-stage events needs to be made available or withheld as necessary, with the explicitness, inexplicitness or irony that result being products of the dramatic context itself. Overall, rhythms must be created and modulated across and within speech transactions, each interactional event providing its own form of interest while simultaneously functioning as an element in the total design. The design itself, as noted earlier, can vary, as it has done across the history of drama. The verbal component needs to integrate with the other codes of theatre with varying degrees of interrelatedness as dramatic convention or experimentation requires (Veltrusky 1941: 94–117). Moreover, dialogue and interaction are among the most immediate and accessible levels of drama, but they mediate other, more abstract levels of the genre – plot, character, thematic issues and the like. It is through the course of interactions and their outcomes among relevant participants – that is, in what the dramatic figures say and do to each other in specific situations – cumulatively, that we come to understand the kind of beings they are, the kind of events they are involved in and the nature of the world that makes such things possible.

Dialogue should, therefore, be seen more in the nature of a 'device' (Honzl 1940: 118–26), rather than as a 'reflector' in drama, with a world-creating, not a world-mirroring function. It is a complex device given that it is 'overdetermined' (Dodd 1981) in many ways when it is called upon to function in the dramatic context. Speech in drama is responsive to many of these simultaneously – to aesthetic, expressive, informational and interactional overdeterminations. The 'intentionalities' in the two domains differ as their goals differ. Such pressures have tempted some analysts to classify dramatic speech as 'deviant' but this brings its own dangers. In the first place, the problem of defining a norm from which dramatic speech is supposed to deviate can be as difficult as it has proved to be in similar debates regarding *poetic language* (Herman 1983: 99–122). Notions of deviance are often grammatically motivated, but there is little in the grammatical structures of dramatic speech which could be classified as deviant. Poetry may be a candidate case, but not all dramatic speech is poetry, not even in a dramatist like Shakespeare.

Manfred Pfister (1988: 104–5), in more complex mode, proposes a double deviance, one on the synchronic dimension, the other on the diachronic, as distinctive of dramatic speech which deviates from 'ordinary' language but can deviate, internally, from the tradition of dramatic language or styles which are in force. Instances of the former include neologisms, archaisms and highly stylized, metred language as in classical French tragedy or verse dramas written by a Fry or an Eliot. Examples of the latter can be found in Fry and Eliot, too, whose stylizations are departures from the argumentative or witty prose of a Shaw, Galsworthy or Coward. Pfister, however, has greater difficulty with dramatists who use the kind of conversational styles that had provoked Nicoll's ire. He sees these as stylistic reductions which still preserve 'an element of deviation – if only in the fact that in reproducing it they expose and clarify its characteristic stylistic features' (*ibid.*: 104). A cline, in fact, is posited, which weakens the argument for deviance since departures from norms become a question of degree, which only stylized, metred forms can uncontroversially support. The scope of the notion of deviance becomes less comprehensive.

Other aspects like polyfunctionality are also mobilized by Pfister, but such factors are available in day-to-day contexts. Radio interviews have to respect the fact that the audience has to be informed about relevant aspects of the interview, and hence the extra informational load to be communicated about participants, for example, is nearer to dramatic language in some measure than face-to-face conversation. Given that the dramatic context is one that is 'framed' as such, and, frames are cognitive and activate various knowledges of behaviours, and protocols of speech and action as appropriate to them, the issue of deviance seems to be redundant. Given the notion of a cline, the binary is not required or is unhelpful in providing us with clear-cut, unambiguous categories, in which something is to be identified in its difference from something else as if the boundaries between standard and deviant were clear-cut. There are too may overlaps for a binary division like standard/deviant to hold across the board.

This does not erase the argument for differences, since differences in the form of variation are the order of the day. It states that differences are to be sought in the constraints of context and not in features of language, for these are distributed across contexts. At any rate, binary divisions require phenomena to be classified into polar opposites – numerically, two categories. Differences as variation are many and not necessarily numerically even, to be divided into opposites by the number two. The threes and the fives and the sevens and so on cannot be so neatly organized and compartmentalized within the binary. Bits spill over, overlap and overhang. Categorizations of the binary kind are, therefore, risks, not certainties.

More broadly, the relationship between drama and life can be two-way, as Elizabeth Burns (1972: 8–11, 33–4, 98–121) has argued. If the stage is a world in its own right, all the world is equally a stage it would seem, and the 'doubling' of the metaphor has provided its own forms of illumination. Much of the modern analysis of social life uses the stage as its root metaphor – social actor, social performance and the like. So what is supposed to be deviating from what is a problem? We prefer the pragmatic and discoursal notion of *context*, which enables and authorizes arrangements and activities appropriately within it. Such a notion anchors dramatic activity within social life, but with its own specificities, with differences being sought within the play of pressures in the context of functioning. Different dramaturgies have mobilized different linguistic styles in drama's long history and the history of dramatic speech styles is both varied and complex including, as it does, poetry, formal prose, colloquial prose, phatic prose, plain and ornate speech, structurally and semantically complex as well as simple speech, fluency, disfluency and the like. The 'rules' of interaction have been put to use in highly creative and productive ways. The strength of the contextual view rests on its ability to motivate relevance for the wealth of linguistic experimentation and variety in drama as germane to its own development and functioning, as appropriate and 'authentic' activity, in Dell Hymes' sense, in a way that deviance by itself cannot do.

DIALOGUE, INTERACTION, UTTERANCE

This study focuses on the study of dialogue as interaction. With reference to dramatic dialogue this means that the perspective taken is one where the genre presupposes spoken interaction among participants in speech events. The dramatic text, as written text, addresses a context of performance which requires a change in mode of discourse – the transformation and transmutation of the written lines into the dynamics of spoken speech, which involve more than the recitation of the lines of the text by actors. Dialogue creates situations, as those jointly achieved by the participants themselves. It is as spoken speech, too, that the linguistic code which is employed in dialogue is integrated with the other codes of theatre – paralinguistic, kinesic, gestural, etc. since both verbal and non-verbal codes of this kind exploit the performer's body, including voice, which the deictic tie of speaker with speech makes available. The alternating issue of speech, as managed by the participants themselves in an episode or scene, creates the trajectory, the development in its specificity, of the situation and relationship itself as it unfolds in time. The management of the interactional dynamics of speech is thus a major aspect of dialogic art in drama.

The linguistic units of analysis appropriate to dialogue as interactional speech are *utterances*. The *sentence* is an abstract entity in linguistics, defined in relation to particular grammars, and not in absolute terms. Utterances bring back into the reckoning the contextual factors which are abstracted away by grammatical sentences. Utterances are relevant to areas of 'language-in-use', sentences to grammars. Although further complexities can be introduced, the simple distinction made above will serve for our purposes although it must be noted that there is not always a one-to-one relation between them when sentences are used in context as utterances. Utterances may be liable to false starts, slips of the tongue, be elliptical, incomplete, etc. so that it could be unclear as to which sentence analogue is being used.

Utterances do not stand alone. They are generally issued and exchanged in specific contexts, and form complex units, within wider units like *speech events*. As such they are forms of social and interpersonal action as well, and not just a collection of sentences invested with 'meaning' in the abstract. Thus, not just the meaning of what is said, but its place and function within the wider units of which it is a part, and the possible reasons for its use by users, in context, are also significant when the play of utterances is regarded as forms of action, and contextualized and particularized action at that.

The notion of 'context' has been used in various ways, but it includes extra-linguistic co-ordinates like the immediate spatio-temporal setting of speech, the roles and status of the participants, etc. Context can also refer to the cognitive context, the set of beliefs, assumptions, presuppositions, frames, which participants activate or draw on to interpret interactions. The linguistic environment within which a linguistic feature is located has also been termed the *context* of that feature, but where utterances are concerned, it is usual to refer to the *co-text* instead. The wider context of culture and the norms for behaviour required by society, or a particular subculture, exert their influence on linguistic behaviour in particular settings, or with specific social others.

Language use is, moreover, functional in contexts. Utterances are employed by speakers to others in spatio-temporal situations, for specific ends, and others respond as speakers in the change of discourse role. Sets of reciprocal utterances are cued in various ways as speech-event units. Speech is employed for various purposes between participants – to pass the time, to socialize, to communicate thoughts or opinions or emotions, to express profundities or superficialities, to share thoughts, feelings, emotions, to withhold them, to offer to do things for others, to get others to do things, to congratulate, insult, quarrel, lie, cheat, dupe, manipulate. . . The notion of 'language use' thus makes language, precisely, a tool – Bolinger called it a loaded weapon – to be exercised by users; at any rate, one that can be wielded co-operatively or coercively, or somewhere in between, for various purposes in interaction. Speech, like language, is not only descriptive; it is actional, and can be used to intervene into existing states of affairs and to create others as much as to describe them.

Whatever speakers attempt to mean and do via their utterances, their success or otherwise is dependent on how the risk of resistance is negotiated with the other or others in the situation of speech. Notions like communication and action are thus highly contingent on mutual categorizations of them among the participants involved, in particular situations of utterance. The tension generated accounts for much of the interest in the outcomes of dialogue as interaction. The patterns of strategies used, how negotiated and with what consequences, can be traced as speech takes its alternating course, in time. The dramas of dialogue are the dramas of meaning and interpretation, but also of communication, or miscommunication or non-communication, and dramas of action or inaction or stasis, as enacted in the temporal dimension, with repercussions *in situ*. They are cultural, sometimes cross-cultural, and cognitive dramas as well.

Such considerations take us well beyond the kinds of analysis which are to be found in literary studies, of whatever critical-theoretical ilk, since interaction and the dynamics of dialogic discourse are rarely the point of focus. Most of the attention has been focused on the linguistic texture of the utterances, whether poetic or 'naturalistic' or phatic, for instance, or whether speech is fluent or disfluent, and so on, but these are only a limited set of the variables to be taken into account when dialogue is regarded as discourse. The different speech styles that are exhibited across different types of drama – Renaissance, Naturalist, Expressionist, Absurd, etc. – from the perspective of discourse would still remain the exploitation of options; the forms of interaction they produce are also within the province of the conventions and rules of speech interchange employed. Performance studies are concerned less with dialogue, which is seen as literary, than with the constraints of the practices of theatre which, again, are not the central point of concern here.

Drama is more than dialogue, but, where dialogue is employed as a dramatic resource, its *mechanics* have a fundamental role to play and it is these that are the focus of this study. Thus, 'dialogue as interaction': and interactions are open to enormous variation. Participants can be mutually supportive, or mutually alienating, or separately ensconced within their own subjective worlds. Interactions can fashion or fabricate similar differences in situation and condition the kind of subjectivities that could be inferred from speech behaviour. Speakers, addressees and speech signify in different directions simultaneously – to themselves, the other, each other, the context of situation, the context of culture, the enaction of action, and in their totality they make appeals to interpreters for meaning. Where dialogue is operative in drama, speech functioning is complex with its own specificities which are different to those dealt with in the literary field. The multiple aspects, levels and conditions that affect the functioning of dialogue as spoken discourse are dealt with in greater detail in the rest of the chapters to follow.

Different frameworks of analysis are used in order to examine the multi-aspected workings of dialogic discourse. Chapter 1 deals with its *situated* dynamics, the framework derived from the Ethnography of Communication, as developed principally by Dell Hymes. Speech is never speech in the abstract, but is always 'occasioned' and encountered in relation to the specificities of persons, time and place, among other things. The broad notion of the speech event, and its influence on speech, are detailed. Chapter 2 investigates Ethnomethodological approaches to *turn-*

taking, or the mechanisms that control the alternation of speech among participants in the speech event itself and the management of the interactional 'floor'. Chapter 3 focuses on the structural organization of alternating speech, its *sequencing* procedures, since speech has a projective and a retroactive dimension to it; it calls forth counter-speech in different ways since speech alternation is not random, but structured even when spontaneous. Chapter 4 moves to the *Pragmatics* of language use and explores the 'performative' aspects of language and to the processes that underlie meaning and communication as interpersonal accomplishments, the role of inference, and to the turbulence of the space between turn and turn. The final chapter, 5 on *Gender and Language*, explores the asymmetrical workings of such normative, seemingly neutral frameworks, when the issue of sex and gender are taken into account, the issue itself being one among others like race or culture, for instance, where other forms of imbalance are also visible, but which are drawn on intermittently, not comprehensively, in this study.

Each chapter reviews the particular framework under consideration and, having set the context of terms and assumptions as appropriate to the framework to be used, explores its uses in understanding the workings of discourse in drama. The models and frameworks are presented selectively, and in a more or less integrated fashion although the scope and explanatory power of the models are continually debated in the appropriate sub-disciplines. The emphasis in each case, as in the book overall, is on issues of language as *discourse*, as interaction, from contemporary discourse – analytic perspectives, as these have been theorized in the post-Chomskyan climate of enquiry – i.e. as linguistic 'performance' – and which are delimited accordingly.

The study draws on contemporary work in the fields of 'discourse' in a comprehensive fashion, and attempts to provide the relevant concepts, vocabulary, modes of argumentation, and tools of analysis that would enable the scrutiny of dramatic speech as interaction. As argued earlier, interaction is presupposed by the dialogic form, as a multi-input form, but dialogue in drama is rarely analysed as such. It also invites a reconsideration of the notion of 'the verbal' in drama away from its traditional restrictions to patterns of syntax, imagery, metre or thematics in the name of 'language', since interaction is concerned also with speakers and addressees and the dramas of interchange of utterances in contexts. Discourse studies offer much that is relevant to performance and it is hoped that the parallels will be drawn by those interested in that field. Given that different and competing claims are often made on the drama text – as literary or performance text, for instance – one study cannot hope to encompass all concerns equally without losing its focus, and the focus here is on modern discourse frameworks for the different kinds of illumination they offer with respect to the workings of dramatic speech in plays.

As an inter-disciplinary work, the book can be approached in different ways. Those conversant with the theoretical frameworks and familiar with the analysis of conversation could well find the extension into dramatic texts profitable; those interested in the theories could well pause on these sections; those unfamiliar with or interested in both theory and application, especially in drama, or, more generally in dialogue as inter-action, could well spend time on both. And the theories offer resources which actually exceed the applications attempted which is the reason for taking the risk of including them in some detail in the book, and for presenting them on their own terms before analysing their productivities in the study of dramatic interactions. But other books could be written on dialogic discourse in its relation to performance; to specific dramaturgies, or authors or periods; or in engagement with various literary-critical theories; or in more traditional fashion to 'the language of drama'; but these directions, worthwhile as they are, are not undertaken here, although issues as they arise are addressed judiciously.

Chapter 1

The ethnography of speaking

SCENES OF SPEECH

One of the major distinctions to be made in the study of language as spoken discourse is that speech is always contextually 'situated' and occasioned: it occurs among specific participants, who use speech for various purposes, in certain settings and across various spans of time. Utterances exist and function within their *situations of utterance* which are in turn embedded in 'contexts of culture'. Utterances are thus always embedded in situations, within cultures, and are open to various social and not grammatical meanings alone. Moreover, they function within larger units like *speech events* or communicative events as they have also been termed. The co-ordinates of speech events are complex and comprise the basic prerequisites that determine speech use. The model chosen to explore the influence of such parameters on interaction comes from the sociolinguistic perspective, more precisely from the *Ethnography of Communication*. The range of factors that need to be accounted for is best summarized by Dell Hymes' (1972) mnemonic of SPEAKING. The following is a slightly revised version.

S (situation)	1. setting
	2. scene
P (participants)	3. speaker or reader
	4. addressor
	5. hearer or receiver or audience
	6. addressee
E (ends)	7. purposes – outcomes
	8. purposes – goals
A (act sequence)	9. message form
	10. message content
K (key)	11. key

I (instrumentalities)	12. channel
	13. forms of speech
N (norms)	14. norms of interaction
	15. norms of interpretation
G (genres)	16. genres

(Duranti 1985: 209)

The sixteen components characterize the complexity of factors involved in the notion of *situated speech* and provide the circumstantial and material elements that configure such events. Speech is functional in these events, and Hymes' model is but the most recent of a long line of investigation into language as a functional phenomenon, which did not focus on the grammar alone. Malinowski (1923) included magical and ritual functions of speech. Karl Buhler (1934) used the grammatical system of *persons* derived from the rhetorical grammar that preceded Plato, in which the speech *scene* was seen as a drama basically between the first person (speaker) and the second person (addressee). The third person referred to all else. Jakobson (1960) included six functions – the referential, the conative, the expressive, the poetic, the metalingual and the phatic. Hymes' model attempts to capture the insights from all these forebears since speech is multi-functional in context. The 'etic' grid was supplied for use and adaptation on 'emic' levels – to analyse the specificity of any speech event under investigation. The notion itself, it must be borne in mind, captures the components of a context of communication in abstract mode, and is a term with a reality in the analyst's descriptive framework. As Duranti notes:

> we should not expect to find speech events out there in the world, in the same way we should not expect to find sentences, predicates or adverbs in texts. We only find linguistic signs that can be classified in terms of such analytic frameworks. We do expect, however, to use the notion of speech event to make sense out of discourse patterns found in verbal interaction.

(Duranti 1985: 201–2)

It must be added that overlaps among the categories are also possible.

Speech events occur within contexts, an immediate context of situation, within the wider context of culture. The cultural load on the context of situation in which speech is used can be considerable, even if unconscious, since it includes all the 'knowledges' that native speakers may be assumed to draw upon in order to communicate and use language coherently and appropriately in the multifarious situations in which they perform (Lyons 1977: 611). The notion of linguistic or *speech community* has been invoked; a difficult notion, which attempts to ensure that language, cultural norms and modes of evaluation used are in common between or among participants in a speech event. But 'language' does not exist in uniform mode in cultural contexts, for there is usually variation in speech types and forms in any society. Dialects, accents, registers, pidgins, creoles, multi- or bi-lingualism and diglossia complicate the notion of a unitary or holistic speech community, as do international varieties of the same language with their own histories and cultures and national boundaries – British English, American English, Australian, West Indian, Nigerian, Indian English, for instance. As a general definition, Hymes proposes the following:

> Tentatively, a *speech community* is defined as a community sharing rules for the conduct and interpretation of speech, and rules for the interpretation of at least one linguistic variety.
>
> (Hymes 1972: 54)

Given, however, that there can be differences among groups regarding 'norms' as Victor Turner (1984) noted, and that problems may arise in cases where interaction is between participants who may speak the same language, but whose cultural codes for speaking are different (for example, where the language used is the first language for one speaker and a second language for the other), or that speaking rules may be similar across contiguous areas, but languages or dialects may be different, Hymes qualifies the above definition by drawing on some related notions – *the language field*, *the speech field* and *the speech network*. The former refers to the 'total range of communities within which a person's knowledge of varieties and speaking rules potentially enables him to move communicatively'. The speech network operates within the speech field, and defines 'the specific linkages of persons through shared varieties and speaking rules across communities'. Given that individuals in communicative contact may affiliate only in overlapping fashion rather than in some total fashion within and across sub-groups, Hymes proposes a more delimited scope for the notion of *speech community*:

> one's speech community may be, effectively, a single locality or portion of it; one's language field will be delimited by one's repertoire of varieties; one's speech field by one's repertoire of patterns of speaking. One's speech network is the effective union of these last two.
>
> (Hymes 1972: 55)

Speech resources are not in common even if the language is shared.

The potential for conflict is as much a reality as the potential for harmony in communication, since not every member has equal access to the speech networks or speech patterns in a community. The scale of linguistic repertoires can be limited or broad. In the cultural politics of speaking, control of speaking norms is as important as command over the rules of the grammar, in terms of access to contexts and with respect to conduct once within them. Moreover, different styles of speech can acquire affective and aesthetic values in a community, where some styles or manners of speaking are regarded as more persuasive or pleasing than others. Even quantitative characteristics like amount, duration or length of speech can be assessed qualitatively. Fluency, verbosity, pithiness, laconicity, will be differently graded as more or less desirable in different communities and even in different situations. Styles may differ according to sex – men are expected to be more voluble than women in power-driven contexts; or according to situation or formal convention in ritual speech events where discursivity may contrast with reticence; styles of performance may alternate between elaboration or sparseness, or according to status – some cultures give equal weight to valour in war and eloquence in speech in assessing their chiefs. The Bella Coolans privilege fluent, witty talk, while the democratic culture of the Gbeyas does not privilege verbal facility unduly. The value placed on witty talkers, the raconteurs, the verbal duellers, the experts of understatement or eloquence, reveals the value of the aesthetic dimension in speech in everyday use. The negative values imposed on other styles is the reverse of the same coin. Given such enormous variety and asymmetry in the use of resources, Hymes' notion of the speech community and the speech event attempts to ensure some common ground, since such is required for successful communication, without homogenizing the concept of a speech community or undermining the possibilities for miscommunication.

If the notion of speech community caters for the social resources which may be utilized in language use, the notion of speech event focuses especially on those situations whose activities are constituted by or governed by speech, where speech plays an essential, constitutive part of the activity. Speech events are distinguished from *speech situation*, which is used in a more technical and restricted sense by Hymes than would appear at first sight. It refers to situations in which speech plays a secondary role to other activities: for instance, chatting to someone while on a journey, or a bicycle ride, as opposed to a debate or an argument in which speech plays a primary role.

Hymes' 'etic' grid could be seen as static if the fact that speech events are dynamic enactments, and activity-based, is forgotten. The relationship between speech and context is reciprocal, reflexive and flexible, not unidirectional (Auer 1992). Although the kind of speech required in a context may be constrained, it is the issue of appropriate speech within it that makes the context what it is. Events are enacted, and speech both creates and is created by the context in which it functions. The relationship is a vital one. Participants use 'contextualizing cues' (Gumperz 1982) in order to make available relevant aspects of context to each other – and cues can be quite varied, including pronominal usage and address forms that frame and mark status, code-switching, prosodic variation, and non-verbal signals like gaze, body posture, etc., to signal either response or shifts of direction in interaction. These cannot be specified in advance; they belong to the contingencies of the interaction itself. Abstract social directives have thus to be enacted *in situ*, as forms of social praxis; typifications of behaviour must be made particular and interpretable within the contingencies of the interaction itself. As Auer notes, being a doctor does not mean having the relevant qualifications alone; nor being a patient being physically present in a doctor's surgery. The complementary role relationships have to be actualized through enactments of them within the incidentals of the situation itself – for instance, who the patient is, what the complaint is and how doctor and patient actually interact with each other can change from case to case. Moreover, role relationships can change – the participants can switch roles to that of being neighbours for a time, without changing the fact that the event is, basically, a medical consultation (Auer 1992: 22).

Certain things are thus 'brought along', others are 'brought about' and have an endogenous, emergent character. Presuppositions on the part of participants about appropriate behaviour, derived from cognitive *frames* or *schemata* as some term them, or what Gumperz (1992) terms *activity types*, which are conceptually typified representations of activities as sociocultural knowledges, are constantly being evoked and constrain interpretation of whatever is in progress. Interpretations of current activity can be revised, consolidated or changed as they are being enacted. Whereas sociocultural knowledge enters interactions via such *frames* or *activity types*, activity is constrained, but not determined by them (*ibid.*: 45). Such *activity constructs* enable appropriate attention to be given to the organizational requirements of speech events, but they can also be seen as members' and analysts' constructs which underwrite the generation of inferences for interpretation. The processes involved in inference generation have been comprehensively examined by Sperber and Wilson (1986). *Contexts* in the cognitive sense, therefore, are in a constant state of flux during interactions, even when other aspects remain seemingly stable.

These different facets of *context* – as space–time–participant co-ordinates that indexicalize speech, as sociocultural activity constructs, and as the space and processes of cognitive and inferential activity – come together in instances of *language-in-use* in interactions.

Of the eight major components of the SPEAKING model, the first two are concerned with the spatio-temporal setting in which speech occurs among the particular participants who are involved in the speech event, since speech does not reside in a grammar or on a page alone, but is produced by someone, for or to someone, in time and space. The others deal with various aspects of the use of speech, the medium. The component of *situation* is sub-divided into *setting* and *scene* which recognizes that verbal interaction is a spatio-temporal event and that time and place can influence speech activity. Certain kinds of speech activity are expected in bounded spaces and culturally endorsed places – in church, in court, in the drawing-room, the shop or the street. *Scene* refers to the psychological orientation and accounts for the identification or acceptance of a conventional or traditional definition of a certain occasion as itself. It also covers shifts in psychological direction when interactions change from formal to informal or when a conversation which started off as an informal chat develops into an argument or a quarrel. In plays, a change in 'scene-orientation' is required when there are indications that a time span has elapsed between the last (dramatic) scene and the current one, for instance.

The setting thus involves not only the actual physical setting, but also the psychological orientation to the activity in progress, and the cognitive uptake via inference and continuous categorization of what is going on. This is necessary since the actual physical setting can change while the verbal activity remains the same – one may keep conversing while leaving one's place of work, while driving home, and continue the conversation within the home. The physical setting can thus tightly or very loosely constrain the kind of activity in progress.

On the other hand, the activity can be varied and the setting remain the same. In shopping precincts where buskers occasionally perform, the organization of the setting is purely internal, cognitive and *scene*-orientated. A *performer* space is divided from the *audience* space which is self-selected spontaneously. Shoppers generally respect the arrangement and avoid or skirt around the performance space as they go about their own business. They rarely cut across it, although the precinct is 'theirs' as shoppers. Institutional or formal settings are far more restrictive in the kind of activity permitted. Physical setting can also signify certain functional or attitudinal requirements of participants, as when chairs are arranged in a circular pattern for a meeting or a talk. The division of space hierarchically into a raised podium and rows of chairs signifies something else about the relationship between the occupiers of these spaces.

As for the second component, *participants*, the dyadic structure of speaker–hearer related to the first and second person in the grammar is the unmarked norm. In actual fact, participant structures in speech events are far more complex than this. Goffman (1979) split the speaker or producer role into three sub-categories – since the speaker need not be the source of the message, only its transmitter – and the recipient's role into four, given that hearers may be addressees for whom the message is intended and those who are not the speaker's official or ratified targets. Levinson (1988), systematizing Goffman's insights, provides a comprehensive set of participant roles for speaker and addressee positions divided into four main categories – participant producer roles, non-participant producer roles, participant and non-participant reception roles. The producer roles are further sub-categorized according to whether the producer of the message is present in the speech event and a participant within it, whether the speaker is the source or originator of the message to whom motives and consequences for speech could be assigned, whether the form of the message is that of the speaker's, and whether the speaker is the actual transmitter of the message.

Different combinations of these decompose the producer's role in different ways. The canonical speaker is one who would have all these attributes – who would be participant and transmitter of speech to whom motive and form can be assigned. The other roles, which include those of ghostee, ghostor, spokesperson, relayer, deviser, sponsor, would vary along one or other of these dimensions. The spokesperson, for instance, could not be assigned personal motives for the speech that is transmitted; the relayer, if merely transmitting someone else's speech, does not have control over the form of the message either. If speakers in a speech event may not 'own' their speech in all cases, there are other instances in which the producers are actually not even in the speech event itself – as in chains of command, delegated speakers and the like. The recipient roles are similarly complex. The interlocutor as the canonical hearer is the one addressed and is the targeted recipient who is a participant and channel-linked with the speaker. But there may be intermediary hearers who must relay the message to someone else not in the speech event; also indirect targets of speech, overhearers, eavesdroppers and the like.

Apart from discourse roles of this kind participants assume social roles. Some of these are reciprocal and mutually defining – doctor–patient, teacher–pupil, etc. These are not the only roles available to speakers, nor are speakers confined to only one of them in an interaction. A speaker may be a teacher, colleague, mother, feminist or friend to different participants or at different times to the same person. Speakers never participate in a vacuum.

Other components of Hymes' framework – ENDS, ACTS, NORMS, GENRES – refer to the different forces that act on speech to functionalize it as inter-personal and social activity, since speech is not only meaningful but performative, actional. Speakers use speech for various ends and outcomes can be expected even when projected or desired outcomes fail. Social norms govern how speech is used and constrain the use of the repertoire of forms and the different genres that are at the participants' disposal. Across interactions or speech events, changes in KEY are possible, since this refers to the tone or manner in which speech is conducted; whether seriously or mockingly or ironically, for instance. The Key can override content and Key cues can be prosodic, or non-vocal as well – as when speech is accompanied by a wink or a smile, etc.

INSTRUMENTALITIES expand the notion of a speech event beyond the purely verbal, since this component highlights the various channels of communication that are available for use. Although speech is the major channel of communication, it is by no means the only one. Choice of medium can include 'oral, written, telegraphic, semaphore or other', the latter encompassing music, written texts, singing, chanting, and speech surrogates like drumming and horn-calling, which are used in certain communities (Hymes 1972: 53–5). Saville-Troika (1982) has attempted to expand the options further by including verbal and non-verbal, vocal and non-vocal media. Thus, spoken language, paralinguistic and prosodic features, written language, sign language, whistling, drumming, Morse code, kinesics, proxemics, eye behaviour, pictures and cartoons are all included. And there could well be others – film, smoke-signals, gestural, sign language, etc. As far as language is concerned, not only are both modes – spoken and written – included, but historical forms, specialized forms, different registers, different varieties also; even forms that are not mutually intelligible are included as resources by Hymes.

The above set of components attempts to cater for all forms of communication, including talk, as *situated* discourse. It is not confined to informal, personal interactions alone, but includes institutional and ritual events as well. A change in any of the above would change the nature of the event. But different weightings that accrue on any of the components could also influence the quality of the speech event. Hymes' ethnographic interests have made him far more sensitive to the total set of communicative resources and cues in a situation of utterance and to its more comprehensive semiotic character than analysts like Jakobson, who focus on the verbal element alone.

What is also useful to note for our purposes is that the vaunted separation between dramatic text and dramatic performance on verbal/non-verbal lines, or dramaturgies classified along the lines of greater or less emphasis on dialogue to define drama, are not quite as radical as they are seen to be. If the theatre can use the non-verbal and non-vocal codes, it is precisely because dramatic dialogue tacitly implies virtual speech events and hence permits the exploitation of the dimensions of such events comprehensively and systematically. Although it is the workings of the verbal aspects of speech events that are focused on in this study, the use of other instrumentalities is not ruled out by Hymes' model; and speech could be central or subsidiary to other activities within an event. Nor should alternative instrumentalities and media always be seen in opposition to the verbal when they make their appearance in drama, since they are formal options, which may be developed as dramatic or theatrical preferences, within differently constructed contexts of situation, as they are within everyday contexts.

DEIXIS

So far, the social and extra-linguistic determinants of speech in contexts of use have been the main focus. But there are also linguistic and verbal ties that link utterances to the context and anchor the participants within the spatio-temporal co-ordinates of speech events. This prospect is franchised by the deictic field of language, which is highly context-centred, since deictic elements take their meaning and reference from the context of situation or the co-text of a stretch of speech. Different kinds of deictic elements have been identified in the grammar: person, place, time are usually regarded as the basic ones but social and discourse/textual deixis have also been included (Levinson 1983: 54–96).

The term *language* is often used synonymously with 'the symbolic' field of language whose design features – about thirteen have been proposed (Lyons 1977: 70–85) – include the arbitrariness of the sign and the capacity for displacement, which makes it a flexible and powerful functional tool since it can be used to talk about things far removed from the person, time or place of utterance. The presence of things is not needed in the immediate environment for language to refer to them. Moreover, second-order entities, like events and processes which occur rather than exist, and third-order entities like beliefs and judgements, which are wholly abstract, are hypostatized in languages, which possibility is also credited to the displacement capacities of the symbolic field (Lyons 1977: 438–45, 657).

The deictic field, unlike the symbolic field, is deeply anchored in the context of situation and to its spatio-temporal and participant co-ordinates, in particular. Person deixis includes the first and second person pronouns like 'I' and 'you', which encode participant roles in the speech event; whoever appropriates 'I' is the speaker and whoever, either singular or plural, is addressed is 'you'. Not all languages use pronominal markers like these; Latin inflects the main verb so that there is no 'I' as part of the sentence structure, for the speaker to refer to itself (Lyons 1977: 639). The third person forms encode those who are neither speakers nor addressees. Place deixis includes adverbs like 'here', 'there' and the demonstrative pronouns like 'this' and 'that', while time deixis includes items like 'now', 'then', 'today', 'tomorrow', 'recently', 'soon', 'this or next year/week', etc. Verbs like 'come' or 'go' also use the deictic centre as the primary point of reference.

Strictly speaking, one cannot speak of linguistic terms or items as deictic, but rather of deictic *usages* of terms since the terms themselves have non-deictic uses. Social deictics can include honorifics and address forms, while textual/discourse deixis concerns the use of those items that refer to portions or propositions or elements of surrounding discourse or the universe of discourse, in the co-text itself.

The various parameters of the deictic field are generally conceptualized in terms of the speaker as origo in the deictic centre with both time and space calculated with respect to it. Thus, 'here' is a *proximal* marker, understood as near to speaker, while 'there' is *distal*, away from the speaker, while 'now' and 'then', etc. anchor calculations of time with reference to the time of utterance; similarly, 'today' as a 'shifter' will take its reference from the day of utterance, as will 'tomorrow'; 'next year' with respect to 'this' and so on, and the content of the proposition will change according to the calculations derived from the origo base point – next year being 1945 or 1995 depending on the time of utterance. So also for 'today' and 'tomorrow'. The grammatical category of tense is also calculated from the deictic centre. Verbs like 'come' and 'go' similarly orientate to the origo for directionality: towards or away from the speaker.

The body of the speaker in the deictic context is also the primary point of reference for spatial dimensions – like left, right, front, back, since these are projected from the deictic centre. The left of a tree in discourse is mapped on to it from the left/right axis of the speaker, since trees do not have intrinsic lefts and rights or fronts or backs. The front of the tree is that aspect of the tree that is visible to the speaker facing it within the deictic context, so that the face-to-face encounter with objects is the conceptual scenario that organizes fronts and backs and lefts and rights. Other fronts and backs are assigned with respect to use – the front of a cupboard is that which not only habitually faces the user but that which is functionally salient.

Thus the primary deictic scene (in English) has been hypothesized as the participant, face-to-face scenario so that objects encountered are read in relation to it (Clark 1973). The top/down dimension as one conditioned by gravity remains relatively stable, but the left/right, front/back ones are projected on to objects from the origo as the primary reference point. There are instances, however, where the origo is actually hearer- or third-person-centred, 'that', not as 'distal-to-me', but as 'that-near-you' (Levinson 1992: 12) and some languages use animals or shapes or parts of plants, etc. as reference points (*ibid*.: 8). Still others conceptualize objects in space as aligned in single file, in which case, the 'front' of the tree in English would be the 'back', as in Hausa (Hill 1982). Pointing or other gestures or gaze can accompany the use of spatial deictic terms, the *deixis ad occulus* form in Buhler's (1934) terminology. The *deixis ad phantasma* type can locate objects not in the physical space in which the speech event occurs, but in the mind or imagination of the speaker. Other conceptualizations of space as maps and journeys in descriptions of routes or apartments are also available (Jarvella and Klein 1982; Levinson 1992; Linde and Labov 1975; Lyons 1977; Potegal 1982).

SPEECH EVENTS IN DRAMA

The notion of 'situated speech' has significant consequences for understanding the workings of dramatic speech. If dialogue in drama is a representation of interaction, and interaction occurs always and only in situated fashion, it can be argued that dialogue inevitably projects situational correlates of the kind mentioned above – of participants, in various discourse and social roles, in spatio-temporal settings, with channels of contact like speech between those participating. The manipulation or exploitation of the options available is instrumental in creating different episodes, situations, etc. through which the dramatic narrative unfolds, and the fictional world of the play is concretized. What the notions of 'situated speech' and 'speech event' offer, above all, is specificity and contingency, given that it is the particularities of the components of the speech event that require attention – who participants are, where and when the interaction is occurring, what for, how it progresses, with what consequences, for whom, etc. They require multi-medial resources as well, which are used in theatre.

The above remains true even though the discourse context in which drama unfolds is more complex than that described for face-to-face interaction. The interactions in the play world among specific personae, in the 'lateral' dimension, operate simultaneously on the 'projective' dimension, towards receivers, the audience or readers. The discourse contexts of the dialogue are embedded in the performance or reception context overall. Speech events among the personae are simultaneously stage events for interpreters. And the latter exert different kinds of pressures on the design of events and the workings of dialogue within them. At its broadest, the pattern of dramatized events, the actual chronology as enacted, respects dramatic requirements like the need to create, sustain, release or heighten tension and interest for receivers. Contrasts among scenes, the distribution of smaller and larger climactic moments, the rise of the action to a denouement, if any, and even the more static patterns in which nothing much happens or cyclic patterns of repetition recur, are all dependent on the juxtaposition of scene with scene or episode with episode across the wider action of the play. The placing and relationship of a segment to the wider context will influence the overall reading which will be given to it, the dialogic segment itself being influenced by the cognitive contexts constructed by the total dialogue of the play.

Information transmission, too, is a major necessity, the double axes of character–character interaction and stage–audience reception need to be managed adequately so that background and other information is available relevantly and in timely fashion. Information necessary to the audience in the 'external', stage–audience, communicational axis may well be redundant on the 'internal' one of the stage (Pfister 1988: 40). And, conversely, information redundant to the audience may well be crucial to one or other of the dramatic figures, and the interest for the audience is then in the reactions to and consequences of that information, and the perspective or slant which the speaker gives it in the telling (*ibid*.: 41). Thus the function of information and the means adopted of transmitting it have to be evaluated in terms of both axes. Unequal distribution of significant information either between characters themselves, or between what a character knows at any point and what the audience knows, is productive of many different effects, including dramatic irony. *Discrepant awareness* is, consequently, a complex and productive dramatic technique in its own right (*ibid*.: 49–57).

The embedded nature of the discourse context and the double axis this entails are precisely the context which 'situates' dramatic speech, and to which dramatic speech is responsive. For a start, dramatic speech is usually tied to its speech–event co-ordinates rather tightly, since there is no narrator – outside epic modes, but even here, consistently, as in omniscient narrators in some novels – to give us the situational information we need. Narrators can be used as a specific dramatic device, as in Brecht's plays, or the Chorus can perform a similar function. The bulk of dramatic speech, however, works in situated fashion – with specific participants, in spatio-temporal settings of one kind or another – with interaction among relevant personae carrying the burden of unfolding the relevant situations of the plot.

Dramatic situations, if anything, highlight and heighten such co-ordinates, since the multi-mediality of drama draws on the visual and the auditory as well as the other codes of theatre. Thus, costume, setting, props, lighting, etc. often concretize and stylize such co-ordinates, which may be left abstract in the reading. Moreover, the notion of a 'deictic centre' for speech makes immediate and present within the *now* of performed (or read) utterances the contexts of utterance which are presupposed by speech. Given that the fictional interactions occur within the context of a real performance, the double deixis involved permits the audience as audience to be both 'inside' and 'outside' the contexts of utterance entailed by the speech events of the play. The deictic grounding of the audience in the overall performance context enables their anchoring as spectator-participants, in the embedded deixis of the fictional centres as they occur within the temporal and spatial axes of a play. The spatio-temporal and participant co-ordinates of the fictional world are open to shifts and change, whereas the wider performance centre remains 'constant', within performance time and place, to a greater degree. Thus each performance presupposes a different 'now', a different deictic centre, while the embedded relation of the double deixis involved remains the same. The wider performance context includes and grounds the audience in its role *vis-à-vis* the stage context, as enclosed within the 'stage event' but, conventionally, without the power to change the doings or course of affairs in the fictional world in the way dramatis personae are enabled to do.

THE PARTICIPANT FRAMEWORK

Among the major co-ordinates of the speech event are the participants; and participant structure, as we saw, is complex. The dyadic structure of Speaker–Addressee may be decomposed along both the production and the reception ends to provide complex configurations for participants and situations through the employment of different options regarding the channelling, transmission and targeting of speech. Both transmission and targeting possibilities can extend the scope of speech beyond the immediate speaker and hearer and the uses of speech in these instances have to take account of such extra options which inevitably complicate the nature of the speech event being enacted, and hence the situation itself.

The variations listed by Levinson for the producer role are the following : the author, usually the traditional incumbent of the 'speaker' role, is responsible for the form, the composition, the transmission and the motivated use of speech, and is thus a full participant in the speech event. This integrated notion of 'speaker' is the canonical one. The other roles vary along the other dimensions of participation, transmission, motive and form, and include incumbents like the ghostee, spokesperson, relayer, deviser, sponsor, ghostor. All these are participants in the speech event even if the tie between speech and its source may be weaker given that speakers may be merely relayers of another's speech or speaking themselves on someone else's behalf. There are three non-participant roles in which the ultimate authority for speech derives from another source absent from the speech event – in Levinson's terms, 'the ultimate source' can be like the general in a chain of military command; 'the principal', the one who is delegated to speak on behalf of some institutional body, and the 'formulator', the person responsible only for the form of the message, like an absent 'ghost-writer'.

These role discriminations split apart the different dimensions along which speakers take responsibility for their speech – the form, the motives, the medium, mode or manner of transmission, and the 'ownership' of speech. And not responsibility alone, but liability too, given that speech can be consequential in a communicative situation. The options for authorized receivers of speech also vary; one may not blame the messenger for the message in a way one could an empowered, canonical speaker who speaks in its own voice. Goffman's and Levinson's extended speaker roles are thus not equivalent in all respects. If a speaker cannot be deemed to 'own' its speech in the speech event, to whatever degree, and for whatever reason – not its form, content, purpose or effect – modes of response as speech activity within the speech event are constrained accordingly, as are developmental possibilities within the situation itself. The contouring of dramatic events or episodes using such options could thus be contrasted with those which are more fully interpersonal in which speaker and its speech are taken to be integrated. The different options make available exploitable resources for dramatic uses based on the kind of speaker or recipient adopted within a particular event.

Recipient roles are equally complex. The canonical 'hearer' is the 'addressee', defined as the one, and usually the only one, who is the targeted or intended recipient of speech, and who must be 'channel-linked' or within earshot of the speaker, and who is a participant in the speech event. Recipient roles can be decomposed, however, into the interlocutor, who has all the attributes mentioned above, and others who do not, in varying degrees. Indirect targets may be the ones at whom speech is really aimed, even if another in the speech event functions as the ostensible interlocutor. Intermediaries and audience make up the participant set, while overhearers, eavesdroppers and absent or present but intended recipients make up the list of those who are not in participant role with the speaker. Dramatic situations can thus be varied quite radically by the exploitation of the different combinations of this basic component of the speech event, namely, the participant framework.

The canonical or 'transparent' structure of speaker–hearer in one-to-one relation, whose roles alternate as speech alternates, is the staple of dramatic discourse, but situations which are the result of transformations wrought on this canonical structure are also to be found in drama. The messenger, for instance, is a familiar modification, whose function as transmitter of another's speech has been put to varied uses. Messengers bring other worlds and other scenarios, speech events of absent but influential speakers, into the 'now' of the deictic centre of speech, thus extending the scope of both the time and place of events or actions on-stage. Events that are understood to be simultaneous with the time of the speech event, but in a different place, usually enacted off-stage, can be described by verbal report by a speaker who speaks as 'witness' of the events as they are happening. Messengers, however, may bring news of events that are removed in both time and space. Relays of messengers arriving in succession may speed up action and express crisis, as in news of the progress of battles. Or messengers may serve to interrogate the very value of 'present' action itself as in *Waiting for Godot* (Beckett 1955). They could signify the existence of dreaded worlds, with attendant questions about the sources of speech – the ghost in *Hamlet*, as messenger – from where? – or become butts themselves of others' distraught worlds as in *Antony and Cleopatra*. The latter example also reveals another possibility, of role mixtures, when agency and responsibility for speech is awarded to those who are, in effect, denied them by their roles, on grounds of autocratic power. Conventions may differ, of course, and it may be the lot of messengers to take the brunt of the consequences of the message. But messengers can get entangled in the problems of the sources of their speech, who are their sole lifeline; those serving the wrong authority, with the wrong messages at the wrong time can come to sticky ends – witness the fate of Rosencrantz and Guildenstern as the old order and its functionaries are dislocated by the new. Or messengers themselves may take on full speech-hood, as does Kent in *King Lear* to Regan and Cornwall after his altercation with Oswald. The fate of messengers, however, can be indicative of issues in progress in the dramatic world.

The split between speaker and its speech is exploited in a different way by Wesker in *Roots* (1964). Beatie's speech is quoted speech, she acts as speaker in the role of 'ghostee' as she speaks in Ronnie's voice for much of the play. The casting off of Ronnie's mould and emerging in her own voice, and, as a consequence, 'owning', 'choosing' her own utterances as 'hers', as a sexed and independent speaker, is a mark of her freedom. A different identity is enacted in the restoration of the full deictic tie between a female, class-crossed speaker and her speech.

Other configurations can be used, as in *Twelfth Night*. Viola is in intermediary role, speaking Orsino's speech, not like Beatie, in ghostee role; but reciprocal role obligations are refused by Olivia who attempts to cast Viola as a canonical participant, as target and end-point of her own speech, and to require the same in return. She demands another voice and speech and role of Viola which she is neither authorized nor prepared to give – a risky situation given that s/he is a social inferior and a disguised woman. The embedded role difficulties are engaged in within the overall relay structure which Olivia attempts to change. It is a struggle to bring another speakerhood and its speech into existence rather than the one Viola is exercising, and with it, the links to person, identity and commitment that canonical speakerhood has at its disposal.

The possibility of such links, in which kinds of speech signify certain kinds of speakers, is exploited in *Othello* when Desdemona falls in love with the speaker of the tale, and the identity of the speaker as posited by the speech narrative, which is read as 'the kind of man' Othello is, as both Othello and Desdemona publicly testify.

Speakers use voice. It is the channel through which speakers perform as speakers. Voice, too, is the point of contact between the written mode of the text and its articulation in performance, as spoken speech, and belongs to the field of the actor, rather than the 'ghostor' dramatist, except when he or she enters the stage event as actor. The vocality of voice is thus a stage resource, not only instrumentally to articulate the lines, but to bring various potentialities of voice itself into the speech event. Regionally or nationally accented speech, 'non-standard' and standard pronunciations (and grammar), could invest the speaker with social meanings, as could male, female or children's, or ghostly voices. Volume and ranges of audibility of voice can function as dramatic signs, as in whispering, shouting, etc. Lack of voice, as in silence, can also be meaningful as could paralinguistic features like pitch, intonation, stress, tone, rhythm (Elam 1980: 79–87). It is the vehicle, too, of other instrumentalities that may be used – song, for example, or for purely vocal activities like cries, calls, screams, when instrumentalities are changed. The voice quality of the speaker, too, can be both functional and aesthetic or unaesthetic – breathy or nasal voice, etc. The specificities of vocal delivery – sexed, timbred, with variation in pitch, rhythm, intonation, etc. – can inflect the lines themselves with social, aesthetic or 'attitudinal colourings' (Elam 1984: 46; 1980: 78–83; Lyons 1977: 63–7).

The gaps, which are available in the discourse framework, are spread on a cline in what may otherwise be characterized as an expressivist and essentialist umbilical cord between speaker and speech in one-to-one relation. And different dramaturgies use the possibilities differently. Renaissance drama may have naturalized the tie between speaker, role and its speech to use speech as individually expressive especially in the mouths of tragic heroes and the like, but modern and feminist drama tend to undo the tie. Here, the theatrical metaphor, which underlies the notion of discourse role, takes on its full theatrical possibilities. The links between role and person are broken so that discontinuities are exploited. Thus, in Caryl Churchill's *Top Girls* (1982), the same actresses play different characters, all except the one who plays Marlene. The role is thus made independent of the person who is the incumbent, which is true of drama generally, but has rarely been made into an auto-reflexive, theatrical device to the same extent. Speech, in these instances, is expressive of the role and belongs to it, but it may be appropriated by 'persons' as players, in defiance of 'realism', where realism is restricted to canonical modes in the expected continuity and unique connections between speech, speaker and role. What is worth noting is that the 'realism' invoked is a convention in drama. In 'real life', such splits are not unknown, especially in public contexts where the 'role' of judge, for instance, may be filled by different people and speech is controlled by appropriateness to role and context rather than the personal wishes or desires of the incumbent.

Variation on the reception end, too, is productive of different situational configurations. 'Clandestine participation' (Elam 1984: 180) either unwittingly or strategically as in overhearing or eavesdropping can be consequential for the course of the events in a play. Elam notes ten situations of such unauthorized hearing in Shakespeare's *Much Ado About Nothing* which fuel the course of the plot, since each instance of overhearing or eavesdropping is generative of further twists in the action (1984:

180–1). But eavesdropping can have tragic consequences – Othello who misinterprets Cassio's narrative about Bianca as referring to Desdemona. Non-targeted hearers being non-participatory, misunderstandings can occur. Denied the possibility of participation and the immediate response this entails, witnessed and overheard reports can then be woven into the fabric of the play, referentially, as truth propositions, with truth effects, to impact their own consequences as they insinuate themselves into the 'reality' of the play for significant personae.

Clandestine targets are in a similar bind since indirect targets are, to all intents and purposes, deprived of response and challenge, which, if issued, can be easily rebutted. All but full addresseehood has partial, if any, participatory rights, and the deprival of such rights puts such addressees at a disadvantage, generally. Such an eventuality, however, may itself be turned to self-advantage by the withholding of speech: to note, but not to act – if there has been 'uptake', that is, by the intended party. Situations of these kinds provide the possibilities of different forms of tension or conflict which are different in their qualities and construction than the more overt ones of full participation.

The consistent rehearsal of such options in a play may not affect just the immediate speech event; they could be used systematically across speech events to such an extent as to contribute to its thematics. In Shakespeare's *Hamlet*, the canonical situation is hardly the norm. Situations in which speaking is guarded, secretive, ambiguous or mad, and hearing, illegitimate, clandestine, restricted, manipulated, are pervasive within the play. Hearing as a discourse resource can thus be exploited in different ways, since who is privy to speech can be fateful in drama, as in life. Hamlet is rarely the canonical speaker with any of his major antagonists in the play, and both Polonius and Claudius resort to modes of illegitimate hearing, as hidden, eavesdroppers, to offset this disadvantage. Hearing in collusion (between Claudius and Laertes), and confidential hearing (Hamlet to Gertrude, Hamlet to Horatio, the Ghost to Hamlet), create their own closed and dark confederacies. The mode of hearing demanded by the speech of the ghost is a question that is scarcely happily resolved. The ending of the tragedies, when resolutions are effected and secrets are disclosed, are characterized, too, by restored possibilities for open hearing and speaking after the complications evident during the course of the play.

If 'hearing' is complicated in *Hamlet*, the trials of 'speaking' run the gauntlet in *King Lear*. Speech as the mark of the ethical personhood of the speaker is a strong expectation in communication, which integrates speaker and speech, again, in canonical situations. The integrity this signifies on the part of the speaker is articulated by both Cordelia and Kent, who uphold this tie, explicitly. Both are adherents of 'plain speech'. Cordelia's inability to speak as bidden by Lear is defended on the grounds that she 'cannot heave my heart into my tongue' on demand, while Kent brings banishment on himself precisely by speaking as he feels – since 'To plainness/Honour's bound'. But in the world of the play, the exercise of this option is dangerous. The fate of Cornwall's servant issuing honest and plain speech at the blinding of Gloucester, where the provocation was great enough for intervention, by tongue and sword, signifies, too, the fate of plain and truthful speakers in their world.

Other strategies have to be found in order to speak in the play – disguise, the change of identity, being one of them. Kent never speaks in his own person again, after his banishment, at least not to Lear or any of the major players. Lear finds freedom in madness – as a deluded speaker, as does Edgar in disguise and assumed madness. Edmund assumes an identity, a mask, that is politic – to suit his own purposes – and delivers speech as appropriate to it. 'Plain' speech is open to both Goneril and Regan, but as markers of power, or in collusion – among themselves, with Oswald, or with Edmund. The simplicity and sincerity of the last interaction between Lear and Cordelia stands out in relief after the artifices and covers for speech which have been in existence throughout the play.

In the participant framework, listening, too, is a discourse resource, and different types of listening or not listening can be dramatized as necessary. Alison, in Osborne's *Look Back in Anger* (1957), uses *not listening* to Jimmy's ranting as a weapon, while Hamlet has to underscore his message to Gertrude with near-violent insistence to *listen* before she can understand what he has to say. Verbosity or monologues on the part of speakers can place a heavy burden on the listeners, since the bias is towards the speakers in these instances, and the listening can be attentive, bored, patient, impatient or hostile, which will colour the event appropriately. Acts of listening, therefore, can be made to signify character, underscore an element in the interpersonal situation being enacted, or become a process, and an event in its own right, where the kind of listening desired has to be won, or wrested, or beguiled as necessary.

The discourse roles of speaker and hearer, and acts of speaking, hearing, listening, which would seem to be inflexible 'givens' in speech events, are proven to be malleable resources, complex in their constitution and open to variation in their enactment. Speakers are characterized by other roles as well – social roles, for instance, either private or public and professional, and defined by class or social standing, sex and gender, race, age. Or speakers may be merely types or signified as pronouns in the text as 'he' or 'she'. They may be complex entities, invested with various internal properties or capacities – wishes, wants, desires, goals, rationalities, irrationalities, reflexivity, imagination, emotions, dispositions, and much else besides, which they may or may not exploit in their speech. Thus speakers are not just the sound boxes that the technology of the discourse/participant framework would have us believe, though they could be performed as such, nor is speech solely the physical emissions from sound organs, though this, too, is an option. The abstract notion of the speaker must not hide or erase the lived, historical contingencies in which both persons who speak and speech itself are implicated. The awarding of identities, personalities, internal lives, etc. to speakers through assessing their speech is a way of making them into 'persons' endowed with whatever capacities we assume to be in force in our historical or contemporary notion of 'person'.

SPEAKERS AND PERSONAE

Canonical speakers and hearers are one among a range of possibilities, as we saw, but they are the ones who enjoy the composite scope of the sub-roles and the full obligations, rights and responsibilities of participant speaking and hearing. Among all the sub-roles, it is canonical speakers who are held fully accountable for their speech. The discourse role of 'speaker' is thus but a metonym for a fuller concept of 'person' who does the speaking and listening and responding, and who is invested with rights, obligations, liabilities, for its speech. Persons appropriate or assign discourse roles to themselves or each other, in the use of pronouns, address forms, etc. – 'I', 'you', 's/he', 'my lady', 'John', etc. And 'persons' are open to more than discoursal determinations. Sex, gender, race, class, social standing, age, all serve to delineate the speaker/hearer, since they can all influence possibilities for speech and access to discourse rights. The seeming neutrality of the discourse roles in the abstract has to be socially and politically read in concrete speech events. This is certainly true of drama in which the dramatis personae are often presented not only by name, or type, but by role as well – queen, prince, nurse, doctor, etc. Social imbalances might well be written into the 'authenticating conventions' themselves which, as has been argued earlier, are constructed and circulated in social life at large, and are 'quoted' in drama.

Underlying the notion of 'person' are two metaphors, one drawn from theatre on which the notion of 'role', 'social performance', etc. in the participant framework – both discoursal and social – is based. The other is the legal one, which, as Amélie Rorty (1976b) has argued, is a second major source for our understanding of the notion of 'person'. The theatrical metaphor of person, from the Greek *persona*, is nearer that of the 'sound box' notion of the speaker in the discourse framework: *per-sonae*, literally, 'that through which the sound comes'. Greek actors played roles through their masks. The person is seen to stand 'behind the roles, to select them and to be judged by his choices and his capacities to act out his personae that is the total structure which is the unfolding of his drama' (*ibid*.: 309). The legal metaphor, on the other hand, constructs the 'person' as

> a unified center of choice and action, the unit of legal and theological responsibility. Having chosen, a person acts, and so is actionable, liable. It is in the idea of action that the legal and the theatrical sources of the concept of person come together.
>
> (*ibid*.: 309)

The construction of the concept of 'person' via the legal metaphor has its own history, and the conflation or coincidence of biological entity with legal person was a relatively late development, one effected only after the delineation of person within clan or family structures had broken down – in the West. The coincidence, even in this instance, is not total, since 'person' may well exceed the class of biological entities, and include institutions or corporations, within the scope of agency, choice, responsibility and liability. But it is to the Christian concept of divine judgement and the belief in eternal salvation or damnation, that we owe the unified sense of 'person', in the West, as a single and unique source on which judgement can be passed, on which the liabilities and responsibilities that went with choice and accountability for action can rest.

Such a notion differed from the Roman concept of person. Not all human entities were 'persons' equally in the Roman schema. Women, inevitably, and slaves had few if any legal rights, and were thus excluded from full personhood. Christianity unified the legal and theatre concepts of person in order that all human beings may be open impartially to divine judgement, since all humans were deemed to be equal in the eyes of God, which changed radically the concept of person, as much as the rule of law. Once responsibility devolved on the person as the source, the agent of action, principles to guide choices and will to carry them out were also required. And intentionality, too, to underscore the notion of agency and liability for action. History, however, has scaled things differently for classes and sorts of 'persons'. Women were impressed more with liability than responsibility. Racism, in imperialist practices, regardless of gender, not only ruled out responsibility for non-white peoples in their own affairs, when their lands and resources were coveted, but absented itself from responsibility for equality according to the theological imperative as well.

Such a turn has had abiding consequences for everyday, common-sense notions of persons or people to the extent that its historical underpinnings are often forgotten. But the concept is more complex than this, not only because it has been examined in relation to differing criteria, and linked to others like selfhood, identity, personality, subjectivity, character, etc., but also because it has undergone changes historically. Sufficient and necessary conditions, or attempts in any other guise to bring these in through the back door, do not work, since, in Rorty's view, historical changes and accretions are such that it is difficult to force concepts like 'person' into neat categories and taxonomies (*ibid.*: 302).

Instead, the variety of *vocabulary* that is used, discoursally, to trace the differing silhouettes of the concept is presented, not as a threat, but as a possibility for the enrichment of understanding. Literature is a fertile site for scrutinizing the use of such concepts since their profiles and modes of construction are more clearly visible. Thus, 'heroes', 'characters', 'protagonists', 'actors', 'agents', 'persons', 'souls', 'selves', 'figures', 'individuals' occupy different semantic and social spaces in society and fiction, with differing conditions of existence. The personhood of 'heroes', for example, Rorty argues, and the pattern of their lives is fashioned in the context of parenthood and through the deeds that they undertake – superhuman feats that qualify as acts of heroism. The performance of appropriate deeds delineates the identity of the performer as a person of valour, especially when accomplished within the grip of implacable or blind fate. The glory of the action functions as a symptom of the heroism of the agent, the necessity for such action already built in through circumstances of birth and genealogical descent.

At the other end of the scale are 'individuals' whose personhood is assembled differently, via notions like conscience, consciousness, autonomy, etc. and an inwardness that is often set against society which is seen as corrupting, in an inward/outward division. A society of individuals, as autonomous beings, invests itself with rights, inalienable rights, that cannot be exchanged or bartered – to justice, the pursuit of happiness, the promotion of the gifts or talents of individuality, and the protection of person and property. The regimes of individuality as regimes of inwardness can promote the notion of the uniqueness of individuals, which is cultivated via various technologies, as unique modes of sensibility and with differentiated perspectives on the world, integrity being seen as difference from others. Consciousness, especially of the 'conscientious' kind, becomes 'the transparent eye that illuminates the substance of social life' (*ibid.*: 317).

But such a turn has its own consequences. As perspectives on the world replace agency, and the world becomes a particular vision and version of it – in a Henry James or a Virginia Woolf – and a stranger to a collective vision, the arbitrariness of particular perceptions flattens the notion of choice. Everything in its difference from everything else, in its integrities, can be like anything else, or the same, or things could equally well have been otherwise. Unique individuals therefore operate under the threat of their own uniqueness, since

> they become obsessed with the horrors of choice; they come to see themselves as the inventors of their own principles, inventors without purpose, direction, or form. Because they are defined by their freedom, they no longer choose from their natures but choose their identities. But since such choice is itself ungrounded, they are simply the act of choosing: their attempt to submerge themselves in their choices is a necessary act of bad faith.
>
> (*ibid.*: 316)

And so, the passage from a Sartre to a Beckett and beyond, older inventions of dauntless persons battling for principles, or against fate, or social evils, giving way to 'Malloy and Malone, monologues describing the wintry endings, the fading of the northern light', or to the comic swirls of language, patterned voices, or echoes, or ventriloquisms, as history, 'Universal History' in a *Finnegan's Wake*; to death by excess, by richness (*ibid.*: 317–18).

Between 'hero' and 'individual' are, of course, other transformations, of the superordinate 'person', whose constructional criteria vary. Thus, there are diverse stories told about 'persons' across time, which contrast, compete with or complement each other. Behind any concept of 'self', or 'person', or 'individual', etc. there lies a theory and a history it would seem, since the vocabulary/discourse/constitution of 'person' and its conceptualizing never 'stands still' (*ibid.*: 301).

Trait theory (Potter and Wetherell 1989: 96) represents 'the self' as a bundle of distinct characteristics, or traits, and people are viewed as if they were the sum total of such individuating traits, which may be either deeply ingrained or superficial. Such assumptions often underlie attempts to assess 'personality' as either extravert or introvert, or some combination of the two. People are their traits, their traits explain them and their actions – they are sketched as 'honest souls' (Trilling 1974), or lazy, or miserly or Machiavellian, etc. which are their 'true' selves. Potter and Wetherell's comment that they are like the minor characters of a Victorian novel, like the Pickwicks and the Uriah Heeps, is apt, since 'Uriah Heep will continue to be underhand and obsequious whatever the situation as that is his disposition, just as Eysenck's extravert will continue to be the life and soul of the party' (Potter and Wetherell 1989: 97). They are not open to self-conflict, or self-alienation, or identity crises, and, for such types, as Rorty notes, there is no mind–body problem, since their traits fuse them into organic entities; there is no inconsistency either. Rorty sees the notion of 'character' in literature as derived from such assumptions, since character is 'known' by its characteristics. But 'characters' may find the social milieu in which they exist to be either congenial or uncongenial for the happy exercise of their traits. For instance, warrior traits would fit less happily into a social order that privileges contemplation or meditation as primary virtues. (This, however, is seen as appropriate to Dickens, etc., not Kafka, etc.) But the very predictability of this model can also be a source of pleasure in fiction.

The category of 'figure' (to be distinguished from my own more general uses of the term) which Rorty explores is similar to the trait theory entity, except that the concept of personhood is not dependent on bundles of dispositions but through its relationship to larger models which serve as prototypes, from myth, religious narratives and epics, etc. Their possibilities are constrained and defined by their place in this larger narrative – as in the pilgrim, the tempter, the innocent scapegoat, etc. in Biblical stories. Echoes of such a construction can be seen in the stock figures of fiction or drama, in allegory, hagiography, etc. whose 'ownership' of their individuating traits is weak.

Role theory (Potter and Wetherell 1989), on the other hand, focuses on self as self-in-society, as expressed in the sets of activities that social positions and appropriate roles make available, their actions usually constrained through conformity to their roles – as wives, husbands, doctors, lovers, criminals, citizens, etc. Persons, here, are not naturally and directly expressive of inner cores of themselves in unmediated fashion; they become social performers instead, and don masks like the Greek actors of old, social masks which enable adequate social performances. There is the possibility of self-fragmentation if not self-alienation here, given the multiplicity of roles that are required. 'Humanist' theories pull back from the dominantly public characterization of 'personhood' in the above and the 'social dope' depiction of the self-in-society and split the self into an inner, private and an outer, public one with 'double consciousness', the private able to monitor the public. Thus, self-reflexivity, identity crises, self-estrangement, self-ironies, are possibilities here, with exploitable tensions within the split itself. This model, however, also writes in notions of 'authentic' selfhood, which hierarchizes the split, priority being awarded to inner selfhood, which may be revealed once the stultifying or stale behaviours or necessities imposed by society or role-playing are removed. New psychic energies and directions are believed to be possible through patient acts of renovation, which are undertaken in specific therapies.

Lacanian theory (1977), on the other hand, sees the unification of any notion of the self, or 'subject', as 'imaginary' – the product of a specular relationship between the 'subjective' self and its 'reflection' in a pre-linguistic and pre-symbolic 'mirror-stage' of the child's development. The private–public dichotomy in more socially oriented theories is transformed into the relationship between the subject which perceives, acts, etc. and the object it imagines itself to be, and there is no mapping of the one on to the other or tidy demarcations between the two. The notion of agency is therefore circumscribed more radically here than in the legal metaphor mentioned above since illusion, even if a strongly motivated one, governs the notion of agency.

The feminist construction of the subject, on the other hand, attempts to grapple with tensions and dualities inherent in the lived inequalities and the desired equality among the sexes, within a community of persons. The discourses and practices and histories of rights, inner and outer identities, masks, language, history, etc. in their patriarchal constitution are open to sexed differences and are inscribed on the body of the female in such communities, but in such a way as to amount to an elision and a betrayal of differentiated rights, sexed rights having had little matriarchal or even feminist writing, discourse or law, and hardly a hearing at all. Such a position, of course, creates its own vocabulary, and narratives, but of difference – 'rights', 'agency', 'individualism', 'history', 'subject', etc. are seen as split and sexed, the concepts as split concepts still under construction, the feminine contents and boundaries of such concepts not open to generality or universality. The concept of 'sexed person' as both inside and outside the dominant patriarchal order, confined by, but also exceeding or other to, a patriarchal concept of person, still functions as the gaps in, and the unnamed and under-voiced underside of, the given, the authorized, the recorded, the necessary, the traced, and circulated, history and definition of 'persons' (Threadgold 1990).

Whatever the operative notion of the 'person' in the models briefly summarized above, in instances of discourse or action, its continuity or discontinuity across different times has also to be taken into account, and the philosophical literature on 'identity' (Rorty 1976a) attempts to do this.

Here, issues of whether 'persons' are metaphysical or moral entities are debated, as also, among other things, the question of how the connectedness of 'person' across different, 'tensed', instances of its expressions or existences or portrayals may be theorized across time. Thus, the conditions for the survival of identity are explored here, and how such survivals may be understood, across different 'person-stages' in time. To exemplify some of the issues – if a crucial inter-personal battle is to be fought between you and your employer, and you wonder about its outcome, is there a continuity between you, now, at the time of wondering, your past, yourself at the time of wondering, and the identity you have when you have won, and the identity you have if you have lost? And what if you wound your employer for the reason that God directed you to do so? Is this 'you'? – 'I' to yourself? Is 'fission' in identity possible, or 'fusion', which involves a notion of two or more identities somehow related to each other, negatively or positively? Are there 'tensed' identities, and if so, how do 'fused' or 'fissured' identities relate to 'tensed' identities and 'tensed' identities square with 'identity'? Are 'tensed' identities equivalent? Can memory be seen as a link? And how do we counter the threat of 'over-population' of identities? And is it a threat at all? Is it the body that survives across time? If so, are you the 'same' body or self when you were twenty and when you are sixty? Is it rights invested in you as body-person by your society, and if so, what happens when your body together with your memories and your identities are seen as discontinuous (or Other, if you translate into a Martian or a fly, or a 'subnormal', or a schizophrenic) in time?

Whether 'person' is seen as a subject, or figure or character, with a self or identity or soul, and as constituted by internal essences or cores, or as a set of social roles, or as intersections between private and public, precipitated by desire, or responsibility, it is not the case that such disjunctions necessitate mutual exclusions among these concepts.

Rather, overlaps, blends, traces of one in another, nostalgias for dis-preferred or historically discarded concepts, and paradox or even conflicting concepts may be mobilized to explain 'persons' in particular instances. It is not unknown for comments like 'She was very rude to me, but then she is not herself these days' to be made in response to behaviour, which reveals the daily construction of the self, in the present instance, as split between 'herself' and 'not herself' in relation to some particular form of behaviour. More crucially, in the violence which followed the anti-apartheid protests to the Springboks rugby tour of New Zealand in 1981 (Potter and Wetherell 1989: 112–15), the behaviour of the police as much as the protesters was called into question. When questioned, onlookers, not involved in the violence, drew on specific models of 'the human' and 'self' in their narratives and three different narrative constructions emerged from the interviews.

As far as the police were concerned, they were regarded as 'only human'; 'human nature' seen as basically brutish, but this brutish core, although quiescent in 'normal' circumstances, could surface under provocation. The model of self drawn upon excused the police since they were 'swept' or 'carried along' with the force of circumstances. Protesters' selfhood and 'human nature', on the other hand, were split into two kinds – those with 'genuine' motives and those without them. The 'ungenuine' ones were regarded as impelled by the love of violence and aggression for its own sake. Although 'human nature' is accepted as basically violent, there were subtle differences in how the violence of the police as opposed to the violence of the sub-categorized, 'ungenuine' protesters was judged; human nature used to excuse the one as responding under provocation, and to condemn the other as enjoying violence and aggression. 'Meanings' of 'violence' varied. The 'genuine'/'ungenuine' split was designed to solve a problem for the interviewees who believed in the right of democratic protest but not violent protest. The protesters were thus categorized as 'troublemakers' and 'stirrers', the constructed selfhood serving to erase the political issues behind the protests.

Even in the more openly combative dichotomies like the private and the social constitution of 'person', connectedness or interconnectedness can apply, though not always happily or equally. Adorno's discussion in *Minima Moralia* (1974) of the individual and individualism traces the different dependencies that hold between the individual and society even where they would seem to be in acute and mutual opposition. The very independence and autonomy that defines the individual as individualistic, in relation to the social as *polis*, if taken to its logical conclusion, does not merely undermine the *polis*, but is in danger of destroying individualism itself (Adorno 1974:149). Definitions of individuality as freedom from society actually seek to negate the conditions for the existence of that self-same freedom. The individualistic impulse to transcend society only bespeaks the interconnection.

And it is this form of traffic among concepts that is productive. The abundance of definitions and concepts makes available the different sorts and conditions of 'persons' that have contributed to the details of our knowledge or understanding of the concept itself, but 'persons' may also be seen as fluid, dynamic, 'tensed' but open to change, within and across time. In drama, these have been exploited in the different modes and styles of characterization and presentation of the dramatis personae – allegorical types, personifications, psychologically full figures, stock figures, psychologically reduced figures, figures with or without memories, or identities, or names, and so on. Different types are often used in the same play.

Dramatic figures, however, are primarily, if not uniquely, presented as *speakers*. And their speech behaviour is a more immediate point of access which enables the more mediated or complex constructions of them as 'persons'. They have no existence that is verifiable or falsifiable except within the bounds of the language of their construction in the text (or script) which may be variously interpreted by interested parties. Moreover, their construction is dependent on their actions, interactions and behaviours with others, in varied participant patterns, in particular situations and speech events. In participant configurations, figures may play leading or supporting roles, or be cast as major or minor characters, and particular figures may be present in some configurations, and absent in others across a play. This 'gapped' mode of characterization in drama, via sequenced, speech event 'showing', inscribes interpreters more actively in the business of creating a personhood for the figures than might be the case in 'telling' modes either of novels or of epic narrators in drama. If dramatic figures bring themselves into existence in speech, the resources of the linguistic medium itself are involved in their creation. Psychological interiority or disposition, usually seen as cause of subjecthood, becomes instead the product of inferences made by interpreters (Herman 1989). Participant behaviour in interactional settings provides the contingent 'grounds' on which self-formation and evaluations of selfhood are constructed or supported. On the basis of assumed grounds for our beliefs we make subjects of the speakers we encounter.

Both the theatrical and legal metaphors are invoked in the linguistic constitution of person, since speakers are held to be accountable and liable for their speech, even when speech is tailored to social masks. Notions of agency are operative, since they are functional in techniques of characterization in drama, in the structural and other relationships that are forged between character and plot, or between character and action, if the character is presented in canonical mode. From the linguistic point of view, too, agency and action are linked, especially intentional action, again, in canonical instances. But intended actions may not succeed, or a speaker's investment in its own powers of intentionality may be weak or absent.

But there are options even here in the descriptions of persons. Persons can be described statically as entities, through attributing properties to them, by relating them to some state-of-affairs. The dynamic mode, on the other hand, focuses on potentiality for action or interaction. For instance, a thing can be described statically with respect to a physical property like 'hardness'. It can also be alternatively and dynamically portrayed as having the capacity to resist pressure (Lyons 1977: 482). The dynamic characterization of persons would thus see them as agents, those entities, in other words, that are capable of operating on other entities and attempting to effect changes on them (*ibid.*: 483). And it is the dynamic notion that is used in drama, of personae as agents who attempt things, even if they fail or their attempts are weak. In theories of action, the conditions for performance of actions include 'a being, conscious of his doings, who intentionally brings about a change of some kind in a given context' (Elam 1980: 121), the constitutive elements of action being agent, intention, act/act-type, spatio-temporal setting, purpose. Actions or events brought about through the mediation of agents in this sense can be distinguished from others which are also to be found in drama – 'natural' disasters, deaths, interventions of *deus ex machina* and the like, which are not dependent on human agency.

On the macro-structural level, there are long-term consequences, since higher order actions installed as a series on the level of *szujet* are interpreted at the level of the *fabula* as related and, hence, consistent; since a series of such discrete actions 'are understood to form coherent *sequences* governed by the overall purposes of their agents' (*ibid.*: 123). The teleological presumption also affects drama's dynamism, in Shakespearean drama, at any rate, since the knowledge of the full purpose and the total consequences across the play of such acts is delayed or suspended and thus constantly projected into the future in terms of whether the intentional projects of agents is to be successful or not, so that 'every distinct act is replete with global result' (*ibid.*: 125). Higher order actions, including negative actions – where agents refrain from doing something intentionally; actions with more than one agent, complex actions, co-ordinate actions, etc. can fall within the scope of intentional actions (*ibid.*: 120–6). The power of directed action to effect changes can, of course, be scaled along a spectrum of possibilities, both negative and positive.

Different dramaturgies can subvert the possibilities for human action defined in this way by changing the conditions for their existence and by adopting different discourse strategies. The strong version of action is truer of the Renaissance and the heritage of the Renaissance across drama, but the notion of consequence and change in situation via human action and speech can be overturned, so that its distance from the other possibility may be gauged. Motives for action may be obscure as in Pinter, or change may not be possible as in Beckett, or the very situations in which speech occurs may not lend themselves to inter-personal fullness of contact and continuity as in some 'expressionist', *I-dramaturgy* plays (Szondi 1987: 63–5). Or speech may not project towards some future but concentrate on the past instead, as in Chekhov. Where speech has to carry the burden of producing such effects, the manner in which the multiple co-ordinates of the speech event are utilized and the manner of response that speech evokes, as much as the linguistic quality of the speaker's speech, are involved.

Participant role options, however, remind us that notions like agency and liability can only be ones of degree. From the standpoint of participant structure, too, the role of speaker, however crucial, is only one of the roles in a speech event, and is dependent on the responsive or reactive work done by the second person(s), the addressee(s), for the drama of speech to be effected. Social roles of the participants, and the power rights which define them in relation to each other in situations in which they are cast, will also influence the course of 'purpose' and 'goals' in speech. This is not an argument against the notion of agency in speech, but an observation that in interaction such factors can blunt, curtail or distort an agent's effectiveness in a speech context. It must be stressed, too, that speech or language here does not signify speech in the abstract, or in some auto-expressive mode, but in its uses in communication, and in situations – within the pressures and constraints that the presence of the 'other' imposes on the uses of speech, in its transindividual employments.

PARTICIPANT CONFIGURATIONS AND DISTRIBUTION IN DRAMA

The participant framework can also be used to order the events in such a way that various dramatic figures are prioritized or given stronger or weaker dramatic profiles, as necessary. If speech events are omnipresent in drama, the patterning of configurations of participants in scenes, the inclusion or exclusion of figures, physically as well as interactionally, in successions of scenes can condition the extent of their participation in the events of the play, as well as their dominance in its world. Large casts of dramatic figures crowding a scene can expand the sense of 'life', or make it into a spectacle, or emphasize its climactic character, especially if the speech events are crucial and of a public nature, with formal complexity and ceremonial dignity as elements in their making – the deposition of Richard II, Othello's accusation and vindication in the Venetian senate, the play within the play scene in *Hamlet*, Caesar's murder at the Capitol, and the like (Brennan 1986: 40). Some of the dramatic figures may be foregrounded through speech, action and consequence, others may be backgrounded as backdrop, or minor figures, or yet others may be no more than animate stage props. Although length of time spent on stage in participatory mode – as participant in events – need not be an infallible guide to dominance, a longer span of 'stage life' (*ibid*.: 105) is certainly one way of achieving magnitude and import. On the other hand, familiarity can breed boredom, and limited access to central figures can intensify interest in their fates and themselves – as in the 'rest' periods, usually provided in Act 4, for Shakespearean tragic heroes (*ibid*.: 107). In the romance genres, the separation of major characters, the lovers, is a necessity, thus the stage life they can share is limited. The parsimonious use of love scenes, as in *Romeo and Juliet*, serves to keep fresh the quality of love expressed by limiting access to the lovers as participants and disallowing a shared stage for them as much as possible (*ibid*.: 105–28). The designing of the participant framework scene by scene, and its modifications within scenes – who is present with whom, who speaks to whom, who is not spoken to, etc. – is thus a necessary aspect of the dramatist's art.

VERBALIZING SPACE

The notion of 'situation' in Hymes (1972) is constituted by spatio-temporal parameters as well as by 'scene' – i.e. shifts in the above, or their psychological designation. Time and place deixis are the grammatical co-ordinates that ground speech in the speech event in progress.

Time and space are fundamental categories in drama and are differentially delineated in languages. And this is true not only for the fictional world but for the audience as audience, too. Performances take place in bounded spaces; theatres, usually, but also in less formal venues – the street, for instance – which for the duration of the performance becomes 'scene-wise', a performance space. As far as a play is concerned, stage space is generally the arena for the fictional representation of appropriate spaces and places in the world of the play. As an authenticated space for fictional representations, various transformations are possible.

Localities in plays can either remain static and 'closed' or be open and extended. Often, when space is expanded through the inclusion of different localities in scenes, time may be extended, too. Shakespeare's *Henry VI* trilogy spans a period of about forty years, and includes constant changes of locality. This 'open' technique is functional given the historical setting and has the effect of creating an exhaustive backdrop for a comprehensive world. As Pfister notes,

The succession of different locales is used to present a vast tapestry of images in which public and private locales, interiors, and scenes in towns and open countryside, aristocratic and plebeian environments, England and France are constantly being contrasted. After sequences of scenes from the battlefields, which seem to cover the whole of England and France like a topographical net and emphasize the horrors of war, the scene always returns to London, where the changed constellations of power are ratified ...

(Pfister 1988: 255)

On the other hand, a play like Beckett's *Endgame* uses the 'closed' option, its setting restricted to a small, claustrophobic space, even if seen as a refuge, in which time moves slowly and heavily, if at all. The speech event structure does not signify radical changes in situation, and 'other' times and places are intimated only through narratives of memory within a fundamentally static 'present' – i.e. 'here' and 'now'. Sumptuous interiors as opposed to shabby bedsits give off their own social meanings, while the location of participants systematically in public places like railway stations or roads with the attendant renunciation of any stable, personal space, for one reason or another, can colour how we are to view the participants themselves. In feminist plays, setting can become an issue. Women in male spaces, like the inn in Arden's *Sergeant Musgrave's Dance* (1960), are confined to the roles that such spaces allocate them – as servers of food or sex to their male clients. The authorized space for black women in white homes is usually confined to the kitchen, while class can be symbolized by the division of spaces in upstairs/downstairs mode in a play (Issacharoff 1989).

Settings may also have symbolic or contrastive value, especially in relation to other settings that precede or follow them. In the *Henry VI* plays, in Shakespeare, garden settings are used as a point of contrast, which, in their order and harmony, are set against the background of war and political chaos, and serve as a reminder of what the body politic should be like under good government. And then there are those settings that are symbolic, not of public but private matters, which serve to intensify the turmoil of the internal world of a figure – Lear on the heath, for instance, or those that create atmosphere – Belmont in the moonlight in *The Merchant of Venice*. Contrasting or antithetical settings of court and country could be used, as in *As You Like It*, or *The Two Gentlemen of Verona* in which the troubles of the urban, everyday world are resolved in the green shades of the Forest of Arden, or the Forest near Mantua – a world of innocence and regeneration.

Such patterning of scenes can be done systematically in a play. In *A Midsummer Night's Dream*, high symmetry is used so that the scenes in the wood are set centrally between two scenes set in Athens which precede and follow them (Pfister 1988: 260). The time in the wood thus serves as the central point of transformation after the fleeing from Athens and before the return to the 'ordinary' world. Such contrasts also serve another function; of distancing the audience from the realities presented in their settings, or of involving them more nearly. Far off places are places of romance – France, Italy, Greece, Illyria – whereas London in particular remains a setting for satire. In *Every Man in His Humour* Ben Jonson transferred the setting for the Folio edition from Florence to London, to sharpen his point. Such distancing provides the dramatist with opportunities for greater licence under the guise of 'foreignness' than would otherwise have been the case (Styan 1987).

Settings can also integrate with the participant framework and function with semiotic charges of their own since some contexts, especially institutional ones, define the participant roles that are appropriate to them. A judge functions as judge only in the context, the spatial and institutional context, of a courtroom, in which his or her utterances are invested with institutional power. Ad hoc arrangements can be made at times of crisis, like the assassination of a President, but these are 'scenic' shifts, and usually confined to critical cases. A goalkeeper performs as such only within the field and for the duration of the game. Such instances can be multiplied. Many roles are not so strictly confined, spatially, but are typically or sometimes stereotypically associated with certain settings – parents with children in the home, cooks with kitchens, teachers with classrooms, doctors with surgeries, etc. Some roles in such settings bring reciprocal roles with them – doctors and patients, judge and jury. Settings in plays can therefore raise expectations about speakers or participants who occupy them, and about behaviour, and can have silent signifying functions of their own. Access to such places and rights to stay or visit can also colour our views of the figures. Social meanings can be cued regarding class, social standing, gender or race via such means.

Participant or figure movement, too, can be used to signify space. Exits and entrances, as threshold spaces, can bring intimations of places and spaces outside the deictic centres and areas of speech, especially if destinations or departure points are named in the speech of outgoers and incomers. Many figures converging into the same space can make it a focal point and significant – for instance, in Wesker's *Chicken Soup with Barley* (1964), Sarah's basement kitchen becomes the focal point for the Socialist view of events since it is a common space for all the major politically involved figures. It is there that they meet and plan and remember and hope. Participant perspectives on individual experiences of a setting or place can be used to present contrasting viewpoints and hence a more varied and modulated representation of some particular locality in the dramatic world.

Localizing techniques in drama can be divided into those that exploit visual or other non-verbal means usually provided in the secondary text or stage directions supplied by dramatists, and those that are dependent on the dialogue. Verbal presentations of the spatial context, or localities, abound in Elizabethan drama and serve to complement the conventional economy of the visual methods adopted, whereas later drama, as in the nineteenth century, manifests a preference for the visual, given the possibilities of more complex methods of staging. Verbal techniques may exploit the deictic field, thus foregrounding the immediate spatio-temporal context, or draw on the resources of the 'symbolic field' of language in order to bring spaces and places, persons, events, objects and times not immediately in view, or temporally concurrent with the utterance, into the 'present', the deictic context of speech. Both options could also be combined in any fragment of dialogue (Issacharoff 1989).

Verbal resources include deictic usages and the co-ordinates of the origo whether speaker, hearer or other-centred, for the up–down, left–right, front–back dimensions, as noted earlier. Non-deictic resources include lexical resources like compass locations of east, west, north, south, although these can vary culturally, and are not as standard in languages as one might believe. In some Austronesian languages, terms like 'seawards'/'mountainwards' or the direction of monsoons do the job, or, as in Walbiri, 'West' is designated by a tangent on the North/South line. For Tzeltal speakers among the Mayan Indians of Tenejapa owing to the terrain in which they live, 'south' is 'uphill', and 'north' is 'downhill' (Levinson 1992: 14–17). Other fixed points include the stars, the constellations, the rising and setting of the sun, prevailing winds, places, landmarks in the environment and the like, which may serve as reference points. 'Absolute' systems thus locate objects via fixed points, whereas 'relative' systems like the deictic system use the body or some primary reference point as 'Ground' and fix the 'Figure' or other points or objects relative to it. Since space is an abstract it is configured often in terms of spatial relations among objects with respect to reference points.

Prepositional resources in languages, as locatives, are a major asset in the grammar for localizing space. Objects may be located either statically or dynamically. Prepositions like 'in', 'on' and 'at' delineate positional locations, whereas 'into', 'out of', 'from' and 'to' involve movement from a 'source' to a 'goal'. Where dimensionality is concerned, objects may be conceptualized and cognitivized as located on a line or a surface as is the case in 'on' or as 'within' an enclosure when volume is implicated (Lyons 1977: 690–703). Pragmatic or real world knowledge is also often involved in many instances in interpreting locative expressions – in 'the cat is sleeping under the bush', the cat would be understood as located at ground level, not under the roots (Herskovits 1986).

Verbal painting in drama was not just a necessary way of filling in gaps in stage technology. Such descriptions usually served some other dramatic function as well. In the opening scene of *Hamlet* different devices are used to transform the stage into the kind of place that would provide the right setting for the critical event of the appearance of the ghost, as a dark place. That it is very dark is clear from the behaviour of the dramatic figures, especially their inability to identify each other during the changing of the guard, although within audible distance of each other. Deictic time references mark the passage of time – *"Tis now* struck twelve. . . ' and the deictic object reference to 'yon' star, at a spot in the heavens 'where *now* it burns' (which has the added function of signalling the imminent appearance of the ghost), underscore darkness, as do other deictic references – to the ghost, 'What art thou that usurp'st *this time of night*. . . ' and later while discussing its recurrent appearance, 'Thus twice before, and jump *at this dead hour*. . . '. And finally, the personal perspective of a participant in the setting – Francisco: '. . . 'tis bitter cold,/And I am sick at heart', locates the setting as in the dead of night, and suffused with dark and cold, so as to create the appropriate physical and psychological landscapes in which the fearful events of the night can be enacted.

The scene ends with the break of day, which is brought into the stage context by Horatio's word painting of the actual physical dawn, which signals the break up of the watch.

> . . . But, look, the morn in russet mantle clad,
> Walks o'er the dew of yon high eastward hill;
> (1.1.166–7)

Scene painting strategies used include not only the obvious personification of the dawn, but localizing strategies that make it relevant to the dramatic, deictic context, an aspect of the dramatist's skill which a purely literary analysis might well ignore. In two short lines, Shakespeare has used some of the major strategies available in language to inscribe the sunrise deictically into the context of utterance. The imperative 'look' introduces the first light of morning into the visual field of those present at the time and place of utterance, to be understood, in Gricean fashion, as 'look now'. The later 'yon' sustains it. The directional field between observers and observed is specified in relation to the compass – 'eastward hill' – but oriented in line with the direction of the gaze of the speaker, and in the description itself, the top–bottom spatial axis invoked in the use of 'high. . . hill' expands the domain of light lifting it and spreading it accordingly. The choice of the dew on the mountain as the external point of reference for placing the emerging and expanding 'russet' light, as it is being reflected, adds visual as much as spatial interest to the description.

Such strategies are not confined to Shakespeare or earlier drama and are to be found wherever localizations of various kinds are required in plays. An instance, very similar to the above, but in modern dress, can be found in Thornton Wilder's play *Our Town* (1962) in the opening scene and in the speech of the Stage Manager who appears as a character in the play, in epic mode. Time on stage is dawn, and is represented verbally and deictically. After the aural signal as before, of the crowing of the cock, the Stage Manager refers to the fact that the sky is beginning to show streaks of early morning light behind the mountain bordering Grover's Corners, 'over in the East there'. The speaker also refers to the morning star in the scene which appears to get brighter just before it is extinguished by the expanding light of day. The deictic 'over. . . there', the compass direction 'in the East', the portrayal of the distant, external location of the dawn light by using the mountain as the reference point, with the direction of the gaze oriented towards the 'streaks of light', and the reference to the morning star, all provide parallels to the earlier instance.

The point of the long monologue is to transform the almost bare stage space into the appropriate setting for 'Our Town' and a wide variety of localizing strategies are used. The only stage props are two sets of table and chairs which are placed symmetrically downstage left and downstage right; a low bench (left) is to represent the space of the Webb's household. A varied repertoire of verbal strategies is used in order to effect the transformation of performance space into Grover's Corners, New Hampshire. After introducing the play and mentioning details of author, producer, director and actors as relevant, the Stage Manager first locates the town non-deictically by using numerical, cartographic references, invoking as analogue an atlas or a globe, thus authenticating the existence of the town as a place on the planet. Grover's Corners is precisely situated across the Massachusetts line, with its own numbered details of latitude and longitude. The inclusion of meticulous particulars of journey time, calculated according to the number of minutes it takes to traverse the space from the Massachusetts line to the town, is another locative device. By the end of his speech, the speaker in *Our Town* has accomplished the spatial transformations needed through using a high density of mainly, deictic references. Physical aids on stage, according to Wilder's stage directions, include the back wall of the stage which is used deictically for locating other places. The major resource, however, is the speaker's body for left/right, near/far, up/down, etc. orientations as the topography of the town unfolds in speech.

Grover's Corners, as created by the Stage Manager's speech, has all the trappings of a 'real' town. It has a Main Street, post office, jail, railway station, schools, churches, houses and gardens, and is bordered by a mountain in the East while a river runs through the town down in the valley. The geographical scale that has to be inferred is that of a typical small town, since it is generalized as such, but made specific as 'Our' Town. The method of its creation, however, is anti-realistic. In the Preface to the play, Wilder notes that the basically nineteenth-century 'box-set' and its conventions of realism stifled the life of drama and smothered the rich possibilities of theatre (Wilder 1982: 11–12). Hence, the non-scenic set and the use of the epic, verbal mode to paint in the rich details of the town. Wilder's choice was apt and his reliance on verbal resources enabled him to ground spatial calculations deictically in the actor's body in space and then to locate the 'figure', other objects, places and spaces in indexical relation to it, via gesture, gaze, movement. Given the scale of the town, the strategy allowed him to transform stage, auditorium and the space beyond into fictional spaces, with language being used as a dynamic device of theatre itself. This mode of transformation also brought his own practice nearer to Shakespeare and the Japanese Noh plays whose fluid and imaginative modes of space depiction Wilder admired. Neither rendered dramatic space 'realistically'.

The Stage Manager begins by locating the Main Street which is *up here*, i.e. where the body of the actor is at the time of speech, while gesture places and expands the spatial scope of the street as running in parallel with the 'back wall' of the stage, as the stage directions enjoin. The space gestured to thus forms the Main Street. Once this deictic mooring is secured, secondary points of reference are used for further placements, with gesture, movement, gaze, used as directional cues and supplements. Connective lines, therefore, radiate away from the body of the speaker and link spaces and places into the complex spatial web which is the town. The railway station is located *way back there* away from the speaker, distal, in the far distance, in deep space, directional orientation given by gesture, gaze. The tracks go *that way* (distal marker, plus gesture probably), and once the tracks are 'placed', verbally and deictically, other locations are positioned relative to it: Polish town's *across* the railway tracks. All the churches are placed to the *left* of the speaker according to the stage directions, so that the speaker's body orientation would change accordingly towards the relevant vector of space. The Catholic Church is *over beyond*, possibly some distance along the same tracks, the Congregational and Presbyterian churches are *across* the street, while Methodist and Unitarian are simply *over there*; only the speaker's gesture and gaze in the deictic centre of speech could give the directional cues which would locate where they are in any performance. The Baptist church is *down* in the valley, the up–down deictic dimension drawn on to portray the hilly nature of the terrain, with Mr Cartwright's house *up* on the hill. Both are thus deictically distal to the speaker but are then placed non-deictically via secondary reference. Distal references locate the Public School as *over yonder* with the High School *still farther over* in relation to it, in the far distance and in deeper space.

Proximal, near-to-speaker, *here* type deictic referencings put into place the town's various other amenities – the Town Hall and Post Office in the same building with the jail in the basement; the grocery store and Mr Morgan's drugstore, and the row of stores, with hitching posts and horse blocks in front of them, presumably all along the Main Street, which has been the speaker's *here*. By far the greatest number of deictic references are of the 'index finger' type, since only general positions near the speaker or away from the speaker can often be gauged without the directional and positional guidance of gesture. But even these vary from the specificity of enumeration of the contents of Mrs Gibbs's garden in which each item is pointed to and listed, or can be, to the relative indeterminacy of *way back there*, or *way yonder*, where directionality rather than specific locations are provided. The near-the-speaker places too vary – from *here, this*, to *up here, right here, these very steps*. The 'big butternut tree' is delineated by speaker place, *right here* (centre stage) and the gaze (he looks upward), its height dependent on how far up the up–down dimension the limit is set by the incline of the head and the gaze of the speaker. No great poetic or descriptive virtuosity is used although there is great linguistic skill. The setting is portrayed deictically in the main, with the effort directed at representing the town topographically rather than pictorially.

Localizing techniques can also be used to describe settings which are offstage, and out of visual range, somewhere else, so to speak, but still part of the fictional world. This is the case in *A Midsummer Night's Dream*

when Oberon, having been refused the changeling and a reunion by
Titania, plots revenge. The setting for her undoing is her bower, described
by Oberon to Puck.

> I know a bank where the wild thyme blows,
> Where oxslips and the nodding violet grows
> Quite over-canopied with luscious wood-bine,
> With sweet musk-roses, and with eglantine:
> There sleeps Titania sometime of the night,
> Lull'd in these flowers with dances and delight;
> And there the snake throws her enamell'd skin,
> Weed wide enough to wrap a fairy in:
> And with the juice of this I'll streak her eyes,
> And make her full of hateful fantasies.
>
> (2.1.249–58)

The setting is located not as something seen, but as a place known and
remembered by the speaker – 'I *know* a bank. . . ' Its placing uses the
category termed *deixis ad phantasma* by Buhler (1934), in which 'the
memorable absent' is located in the domain of 'the constructive imagination', but what is physically absent is made present in context to the mind's
eye. The symbolic resources of the language come into their own in the
evocative naming of the absent objects – and the bank itself is located via
the objects in it, 'where', i.e. the place in which, all these flowers grow.
Where exactly in the locality it is to be found is left unspecific. No
directional or other information is given, so that the sensuous quality of
the place itself, its lush and scented character, is foregrounded.

A secondary form of location designates it as Titania's place, her place
of rest, the present tense making it her habitual place of rest which brings
it into the time span of the present fairy action in the fictional world even
if removed in space, which Oberon duly notes in his anaphoric and deictic
use of 'there' – 'There sleeps Titania'. The bridge between the two spaces
– Oberon's 'here' in stage space, of the context of utterance, and Titania's
'there' is formed by the resolve to squeeze 'the juice of this' into her eyes
(there) when she is asleep in her bower. The implied movement between
the two places expands both the actual terrain of the wood as well as its
fairy character. Oberon's description includes an unexpected use of the
demonstrative 'these' – 'Lull'd in *these* flowers. . . ' where one would
have expected the anaphoric and distal 'those'. The reading of 'these' as
a proximal, deictic, marker of place affords the intensification of its
'phantasma' function – the proximity being not physical, but in imagina-

tion, the scene vivid in the mind of the speaker, which invites audience identification accordingly.

Prepositional resources are used in abundance as a means of delineating the fairy world. In the above, Oberon knows a bank *whereon* various things grow. The preposition enables the conceptualization of a spatial surface with objects on it, in two-dimensional mode. In Puck's speech, a variety of prepositional resources are used to configure space, the iconicity of the clausal 'spacing' being read as a journey, albeit a 'wander,' through terrain which is made explicit in the last line.

> Over hill, over dale,
> Thorough bush, thorough brier,
> Over park, over pale,
> Thorough flood, thorough fire,
> I do wander every where. . .
> (2.1.2–6)

'Over' as a preposition signifies surfaces, and is two-dimensional, whereas 'thorough' delineates enclosures, the interiors of things, conceptualized in three-dimensional mode. The nouns undulate the terrain – hill and dale – and are relatively solid, whereas bushes and briers can pragmatically be inferred to be less so in terms of density, and fire and flood are openly 'gaseous' and 'liquid' and thus unbounded. 'Every where' expands space in indeterminate directions. The space traversed is thus given different textures and the terrain itself is enlarged.

Miniaturizing techniques are also used to give the fairy world its particular character. In the following, the preposition 'in' evokes the interiors of small objects referred to by the nouns and locates activity or objects inside them or in tiny parts of them:

> The cowslips tall her pensioners be;
> In their gold coats spots you see,
> Those be rubies, fairy favours,
> In those freckles live their savours.
> I must go seek some dewdrops here,
> And hang a pearl in every cowslip's ear.
> (2.1.10–15)

A very different and rather interesting space strategy is to be found in Titania's first long speech to Oberon, in which she describes, for Oberon's benefit and for the audience's, the consequences of their quarrel – the parlous state of affairs in the human world, of which they are custodians.

> And never, since the middle summer's spring
> Met we on hill, in dale, forest or mead,
> By paved fountain, or by rushy brook,
> Or in the beached margent of the sea. . .

$$(2.1.82–5)$$

The time reference which projects backwards from midsummer, or the middle summer's summer as the time of the play, to 'the middle summer's spring', expands space as well since the localities mentioned are outside the present context of the play of the wood in Athens. However, what is located are absences, things not there, as it were, beside or on, or in, the primary references of the objects listed, so that the absences themselves become presences in their absence and absence is animated.

Localizing strategies can be used for other purposes than to provide representations of place alone. In *Macbeth*, King Duncan arrives at Macbeth's castle where he is to be murdered. His description of the place on arrival manipulates the different levels of knowledge of what is to occur and the 'discrepant awareness' between the audience and the speaker and is thus productive of dramatic irony. There is unconscious irony, too, in Banquo's response. Both speakers use deictic anchorings, thus underscoring the presence and context of the place.

> DUNCAN   This castle hath a pleasant seat; the air
> Nimbly and sweetly recommends itself
> Unto our gentle senses.
> BANQUO   This guest of summer,
> The temple-haunting martlet, does approve
> By his lov'd mansionry that the heaven's breath
> Smells wooingly here: no jutty, frieze,
> Buttress, nor coign of vantage, but this bird
> Hath made her pendent bed and procreant cradle:
> Where they most breed and haunt, I have observ'd
> The air is delicate.

$$(1.6.1–9)$$

Deictic usages in discourse can signal a dramatic figure's psychological distance or involvement in the events in which it is embroiled. After the murder, Macbeth is distraught, while Lady Macbeth, having returned the daggers to the scene of the crime, attempts to calm him and get him to take control of the situation. A knocking is heard, which makes composure urgent. The use of deictics in this scene is highly strategic.

> MACBETH   Whence is that knocking?

How is't with me, when every noise appals me?
What hands are here? Ha! they pluck out mine eyes.
Will all great Neptune's ocean wash this blood
Clean from my hand? No; this my hand will rather
The multitudinous seas incarnadine,
Making the green one red.
                    [*Re-enter* LADY MACBETH]
LADY MACBETH   My hands are of your colour, but I shame
To wear a heart so white, – [*Knock*]
     I hear a knocking
At the south entry; retire we to our chamber.
A little water clears of this deed;
How easy is it, then!. . .

                                        (2.2.58–68)

Macbeth's deictics anchor both the knocking, 'that knocking', and his hands and the blood on them – 'this blood', 'this my hand' – into the present context of utterance. Such signifying intensifies his consciousness of salient aspects of his situation, by making intense and present to himself (and to us) his startled awareness of the *sound* of the knocking, and his horror at the *sight* – the visually immediate evidence – of what he has done, the focus being very particular, on blood and his hands, in close, visual range. Lady Macbeth, on the other hand, locates the knocking non-deictically, compass-wise, 'at the south entry', although she, too, hears it. She thus distances it both in her consciousness and from the immediate context. She is similarly non-deictically descriptive of her hands, even if she were to use a gesture simultaneously. The blood, too, is more euphemistically and abstractly referred to as 'this deed', rather than as 'this blood', the deed itself having been conducted elsewhere and not in the context of utterance.

Deictics may relate to character feeling or attitude in other ways. In Chekhov's *The Seagull* (1923), Sorin's annoyance with his steward, who has threatened to resign because of the impossible demands made on him to supply horses, results in the use of deictics for emphatic, emotive purposes; here, a temporary intensification, a 'flaring up', under the pressure of the moment, as notified in the stage directions '. . . bring all the horses *here this* minute!' (Chekhov 1971: 23, emphasis added).

Unfolding some critical event in a scene by accentuating the use of deixis can make tangible the enacted or performed rhythm of the action as in the first scene in *Hamlet*. On the final appearance of the ghost, Bernardo and Horatio attempt to attack it.

BERNARDO	'Tis here!
HORATIO	'Tis here! [*Exit* GHOST]
MARCELLUS	'Tis gone. . .

(1.1.142–4)

In this instance, the physical action of striking the ghost keeps pace with the deictic references to its location in the scene. Word and action are closely integrated, and the speed of the changes in deictic referencing is iconic of the speed of the movement of the ghost, and the reactions of the dramatic figures to its movements.

Other aspects are also open to dramatic exploitation. Deictic referencing means that the proper referent has to be found, or located in context, and can be made actional, in discourse time, and this fact can also be capitalized on for dramatic ends. Proximity and presence are other possibilities afforded by the use of place deixis, all of which are exploited in the banquet scene in *Macbeth*. Specifying location in the actual physical setting, via deixis, rather than through non-deictic reference, compels Macbeth, when invited by Ross, to locate the fateful chair in which he is to be seated within the immediate speech environment, and on finding it he stumbles upon its unwelcome occupant as well. Such a mode of discovery dramatizes the horror of the moment and focuses interest on Macbeth's reactions, while such unexpected physical proximity deepens the menace in the confrontation between Banquo and his discomfited murderer. Both serve to heighten the deadly and perturbing ironies in the visible/invisible tensions attendant on the ghost's presence in the situation.

ROSS   Please't your Highness
To grace us with your royal company.
MACBETH   The table's full.
LENNOX   Here is a place reserv'd, sir.
MACBETH   Where?
LENNOX   Here, my good lord.
What is't that moves your highness?

(3.4.45–8)

TIME IN LANGUAGE

Time and space are intimately related in languages. Many temporal expressions are locative in underlying structure so that spatial expressions are often used to delineate linguistic time. Many temporal expressions are also derived etymologically from spatial ones, and places, dimensions and even shapes may be used to characterize time in languages. The temporal system interacts with other systems, too, like modality which is used (in English) to express the future, but has functions independent of temporal uses. Numeration, too, can be used for temporal purposes (Traugott 1979).

There are different bases on which the measurement of time and the location of events in time are calculated. They vary from the natural rhythms of the seasons and the revolution of the sun, or phases of the moon, and the like, to more culture-based notions of calendrical and clock time – the Gregorian, Indian or Chinese calendars, or Greenwich Mean Time. Certain events may also form reference points for time calculations, like the birth of Christ, or the founding of Rome (753 BC), the Russian Revolution, American, Indian, etc. Independence, and the like.

Linguistic time is not in any sense 'time itself', whatever that might be, but a representation of how experience of time is conceptualized in the languages of the world. Unlike space, which is three-dimensional, time is generally conceptualized as uni-dimensional, and spatially, as a straight line on a horizontal plane. In English, the basic distinction is made between the past and non-past and is calculated deictically from the time of utterance at the deictic centre. There are, to be sure, other representations and conceptualizations of time, from astronomy and physics to philosophy and theology, and differently in other languages, but it is linguistic (English) time which concerns us here. Different languages may grammaticalize time differently, or they may not use the morphological system and use aspect, or some other means instead (Comrie 1985), but there are two basic ways of representing time in languages – deictically and non-deictically. Deictic frames of reference have recourse to the time of the utterance, which functions as the zero point from which past and future are calculated. The crucial grammatical category of *tense* is, therefore, deictic. Aspect is not. Conventional elements with deictic uses include 'now', 'then', 'today', 'tomorrow', 'yesterday', 'this year', 'next year', and so on, which are anchored to speaker time in the context of speech, so that the specific day or time referred to will vary according to the time of the utterance at the zero point of the deictic centre.

However, given that modern technology has enabled persons separated in space and time to maintain contact, via written communications or by telephone, or when pre-recorded materials are broadcast at a later date and so on, a difference has to be made between Coding time and Recipient time, and with it decisions as to which is to function as the deictic centre. Languages, however, are indifferent to such practical, scientific and technological benefits and still behave as if the face-to-face scenario and the zero point of the deictic centre were central. There are apparently no known languages which provide two words for 'now' – one for coding time and one for recipient time. Shifts of deictic centres and deictic projections, as 'point-of view' projections, do the job instead, 'now' being coded appropriately by coder or recipient as needed (Lyons 1977: 677–90, 703–18; Levinson 1983: 54–96).

Non-deictic possibilities include lexically composite items, like 'three o'clock on Friday 1 April' or 'for two hours', 'during the rainy season', etc. which specify time, either punctually or durationally, independently of the deictic centre, and which are by far the largest class, and also potentially infinite. Other resources include the aspectual character of verbs, which characterize the internal constitution of actions, events, processes, activities, their duration, instantaneity, completion, momentariness, etc.; the temporal uses of prepositions, adverbials, etc. and serializing or iterative elements (Lyons 1977; Comrie 1976). Once a situation is located in time, further locations can be made via the use of secondary tenses like the pluperfect, which is generally acknowledged as signifying the 'past in the past', or by recourse to these other resources. Thus different situations can be related to each other relative to a primary reference point.

TIME IN DRAMA

Dramatic interactions are oriented to the deictic centre, the time of the speech exchange, and therefore, 'the present' of speech is the unmarked time of the dramatic speech event. Dramatic requirements, however, involve other aspects of time – both past and future. Much expository information is committed to giving background information and to filling in the gaps, by providing a past for dramatic figures and, often, a history for events, thereby increasing the temporal scope of the fictional world. The future, too, is a significant dramatic dimension, since current dramatic situations project other possible events, whether resolutions or non-resolutions, as the plot or sequence of events unfolds. The future, like the past, is calculated from the imagined time of the fictional speaker's utterances in the deictic centres of its speech.

The chronology of events and the fictional time scale presupposed by plays have to be communicated within the real time of performance, and the time structures or duration of the fictional action in plays can vary greatly, from a span of a few hours to a range of historical periods or the history of different generations. Dramatic time is a complex phenomenon and different temporal organizations have been noted (Pfister 1988). 'Primary' time relates to the whole of the action, whereas 'secondary' time originates from 'the point of attack' – the selected situation or incident at some point in the story from which the enacted action begins in a play – and includes the time of the 'hidden' action, between scenes, which is not staged but presumed to have occurred. Chekhov's plays are generally regarded as having late points of attack, so that the future is foreshortened and the burden of the past bears heavily on the action. And, finally, there is 'tertiary' time which includes 'secondary' time but incorporates other times presupposed by background information and projections into the future given in the speech of the dramatic figures.

Generally speaking, succession is the principle that organizes events, situations, temporally in the fictional world, the standard convention being that the succession of events as enacted is the succession of events in the story. One event or incident follows another, but where the time-scale established within the fictional world of the play exceeds performance time, time gaps have to be filled either by overt references or by inference, pragmatically. This is especially the case in 'open' structures where the fictional time stretch can be quite extensive, as in plays based on historical events or where time itself is made thematic, which could cross generations, if not whole centuries. The past is, however, constructed or reconstructed in the present, from within the deictic anchorage of the utterance, via reference, or report, through memory narrations, or by some other means.

Future-orientated 'genres' and speech acts like predictions or forecasts, or commitments on the part of the speaker, can point forward in time, establishing a tension with the present in relation to anticipated outcomes – witness Macbeth and the witches in the first act of Shakespeare's play. At any rate, the 'present' of the speech event contains these other dimensions of time. Representations of the past or future can vary in language. So can the present. Neither past nor future is uniquely represented linguistically; in other words, there is not a one-to-one relation between linguistic – grammatical or lexical – elements and the characterizations of time. Both secondary tense and the aspectual character of verbs and pragmatic, real-world knowledge can complicate unilinear relationships among these various spans of past, present and future.

Various degrees of chronological precision can be achieved or dispensed with as the necessity arises. In Shakespeare's *A Midsummer Night's Dream* both types are available. Precision of chronometric references characterizes the passing of time in the human world, whereas events in the wood take place in a mode of indeterminate time or timelessness. The time span of the play is organized within a strict scale, a future event, the marriage of Theseus and Hippolyta, which we are informed in the opening scene of the play is to occur in four days' time. The sequence of events in the various sub-plots are bounded by this event and reach their termination at this point. Hermia is given till the nuptials to bend to her father's will and to marry Demetrius, or to live in 'single blessedness', which precipitates her flight to the woods. Lysander advises her to 'steal forth thy father's house tomorrow night', the deictic time adverb fixing the time of the arrival in the wood quite precisely. Being informed of the fact, Demetrius follows and Helena follows him. The Mechanicals' play rehearsal is directed to the wedding festivities – 'to play before the Duke and his duchess on his wedding day at night' (Act 1, scene 2), and they decide to 'meet in the wood tomorrow night by moonlight'. The duration of the fairies' visit to Athens is to last till the wedding, and the wood is their natural home (Pfister 1988; Elam 1984).

The time span in the wood is much less distinct. The strategies used vary: deictic, referential and contextual. Most of the action occurs at night. Owing to the previous deictic reference, we know that when we see the lovers in the wood, it is the night of the next day. The duration of events here is indistinct; there are unclarities regarding the durations of the different characters' flights from each other. The second night is ordered by Oberon to stop the confused lovers getting into trouble and everybody sleeps. Meanwhile, Titania, too, is released from her spell, and Oberon announces that the blessing of Theseus' house is to occur at 'tomorrow midnight'. The arrival of the hunting party, on cue, after Puck's 'I do hear the morning lark' makes clear that it is indeed the wedding day, which is deictically confirmed by Theseus and Egeus in Act 4, scene 1.

In Act 4, scene 2, the Mechanicals wait for Bottom and we learn that the triple wedding has taken place – 'the duke is coming from the temple and there is two or three lords and ladies more married'. In Act 5 the wedding festivities are in progress, for a period of three hours ostensibly, but of course, actual time is shortened. The chronometric marking of time in Theseus' 'The iron tongue of midnight have told twelve' in scene 2 is the cue for the festivities to end, and the fairies arrive around midnight to bless Theseus' house as they had come to do.

The foreshortening of time is explicitly undertaken in Marlowe's *Dr Faustus* ([1616] 1966), with explicit references to clock time to speed up the passage of time and to infuse the last hours of Faustus' life with subjective urgency and panic. In Shakespeare's *Romeo and Juliet*, three days are all that the lovers are given. Time references are marked variously in the text. Capulet informs Paris that he is to wed Juliet on Thursday – the 'today' of the time of speech being 'Monday'. In the face of Juliet's reluctance, Capulet changes his mind to 'Wednesday' which is repeated. Folk calculation of time is used in the crowing of the cock to signify that it is morning. All of this in twenty minutes' playing time, as Styan notes (1971: 48).

The elasticity of fictional time includes in its option near concurrence of the performance time with audience time, although not totally. This is the case in Albee's *Who's Afraid of Virginia Woolf?* ([1962] 1989). The action of the play is actually located at a later time than audience time, but fictional time once set, the duration of the action could well coincide with the time of the performance. At the beginning and the end of the play, time anchors are laid down, bounding the time span between two in the morning, and just before the break of dawn. Punctual references like George's 'It's two o'clock in the morning', and a few lines later, 'It's past two o'clock', as well as references like 'It's late', 'It's very late', set the time at the beginning. At the end, 'nearly dawn', 'go to bed', the departing guests wish their hosts 'good night' and the exhausted couple decide to 'go to bed', too. All references are in the present tense and mark time deictically, in the implied 'now' in the utterances.

In Handke's *Offending the Audience* ([1969] 1971) total concurrence between performance time and audience time is attempted. Present tense predominates and deictics are used. The address is directly to the audience, they do not address each other, thus the person resources used are wholly deictic, first person singular or plural to you, second person, singular or plural. Stage event and speech event coincide. Yet, the 'frame' of performance paradoxically remains, the audience still in the traditional position, and unable to intervene or change the course or character of the address events. Their role in the stage event is to be the recipients of the dramatic 'insulting' of the utterance and speech events that are in progress on-stage.

The strength of the convention that events occur successively along a time line can itself be flouted for dramatic effect. Instead of the past being represented by report, it can be given scenically, shifts in time being presented on-stage, so that the time line is distorted in the deictic pattern adopted for speech. This is the case in J.B. Priestley's *Time and the Conways* (1948) in which Act 1 is set on an autumn night in 1919, on one of the character's – Kay's – birthday. Act 2 takes place in 1937, eighteen years later, and Act 3 returns to 1919 as a continuation of the same autumn evening in which Act 1 ended. The doubling back of the time scheme allows contrasts and ironies inherent in the gap between hopes and achievement in time to be made explicit. The earlier time is characterized by verbal references in the dialogue to events contemporary with 1919 – the war that has ended, to the nationalizing of the mines, to Lloyd George, or to a character's age – the stranger Ernest is introduced to Kay, and told that the occasion is Kay's twenty-first birthday, or Kay is referred to as a budding writer. In the second Act, setting shows a difference, the decor of the room being relevant to the later time.

The physical appearance of the characters, too, shows the passing of time – Priestley notes in the stage directions – 'Kay and Alan are not quite the same, after nearly twenty years. Kay has a rather hard, efficient, well-groomed look, that of a woman of forty who has earned her own living for years. Alan, in his middle forties, is shabbier than he was before. . . .' The dialogue punctuates and underscores references to age, change of personal status, address forms, memory of events as located in the past, and references to events in the deictic universe of discourse in contrastive mode. It is Kay's birthday, and she announces to Alan that she is forty, while Alan responds with the information that he is forty-four. Change of status for characters also signals that time has passed – Joan is married and with children. Mrs Conway is referred to as Granny Conway. Other references and information keep the fact of time that has passed in mind – Carol as dead for sixteen years, the fall in the value of the house since the First World War, since they are 'now' at the brink of the Second. In Caryl Churchill's *Top Girls* (1982) the chronology of events is presented in reverse fashion. Earlier events come towards the end of the play which is evident especially in the age gap of Angie who is a young adult when first introduced, but a child when the play ends.

If time lines can be wrenched or reversed or presented in diverse patterns of this kind, on the linear, 'horizontal' or successive plane, the 'vertical' one of simultaneity can also be exploited. Participant structure is a useful resource here. In relation to the presentation of time, the role may be historical or pertinent to a remote time, while the speaker is entrenched in or anchored to the 'present' of the deictic centre of speech, within the contemporary time of the audience. Such an integration animates the past, either as a present representation of the past itself, as in the history plays of Shakespeare, or as elements in a participant time collage in which past and present speakers or addressees have equal status within the deictic centre of speech. Such is the case in Thornton Wilder's *The Skin of Our Teeth* (1962) in which temporally bounded roles are sifted out of their time-constrained contexts and mixed in with others which, historically, are out of their time. The time-cocktail of the dramatis personae, as participants in the deictic centres of the speech events of the play, thus makes present different layers of time simultaneously present, so that time cannot easily be viewed solely, in linear fashion, with acceptable divisions between the past, present and future, except in the order of presented action.

The past/non-past distinction is a fundamental one in the tense system, and calculations of time are undertaken in relation to the speaker-centric time of utterance in the deictic centre of the speech event. Aspect deals with the internal constitution of a temporal situation and is non-deictic, given that tense locates a situation on a time line, deictically. Apart from the conceptualization of time on a time line, events or situations or states of affairs may be delineated punctually, conceptualized as a point in time or durationally as within a stretch of it. Tense and aspect together can delineate time in various ways in languages and are an invaluable resource for representing time in dialogue. The options here are extensive, and the following very brief summary is taken from Leech and Svartvik (1975: 62–82).

The present tense is the unmarked tense in the deictic context – anchored to the speaker's time of utterance. Yet the present tense is not confined to rendering present time alone. It has other functions; for instance, the present tense is used to signify a series of habitual actions continuing across time – as in 'He walks to work (every day)', where the time span referred to has an originating point at some time in the past which continues into the present, and can be interpreted as continuing past the 'now' of the utterance. On the other hand, events which are co-referential with the moment of speech can also be referred to in the use of the present tense, in instances of immediate report and commentary (Lyons 1977: 678), as in 'I declare the meeting closed', or 'Seles grunts again as she serves'. The present tense sometimes expresses the future as in 'The shop closes at ten'. The present progressive forms stress the aspect of duration, temporary or limited, of events – 'She is sleeping in the conservatory', 'They are living in a rented cottage' as opposed to 'She sleeps in the conservatory' or 'They live in a rented cottage', the latter signifying greater permanence than the former examples.

The past can similarly be characterized in complex fashion grammatically via tense, secondary tense and aspect. Simple past tense forms locate situations in a definite time in the past, they are 'then' forms in relation to time, with a gap between the past situation and the present. 'He lived in a cottage' – i.e. at some definite time in the past, but not now. The present perfect forms on the other hand can bring the past up to and into the present – 'I have known her for years' or 'He has applied for a number of jobs' and the like. The present perfect progressives deal with temporary states, events, etc. up to the present time – 'She has been telephoning all day' or 'I have been waiting for ages'. The past progressive instils duration, though not necessarily completion, to situations in the past which are characterized as still in progress at the time denoted by the verb. 'I was trying to tell her that it was alright, but she left'; 'We were closing the front door when the lightning struck the tree'.

The past perfect, on the other hand, signifies 'the past in the past', where a past event is characterized as in a remoter past than another one which serves as its reference point. For instance, in 'When Jane left Crete, Brian had gone to Tuscany', Brian's departure for Tuscany is in the past of the event of Jane leaving Crete, which is itself located in the past in relation to the time of speaking. Similarly, in 'The house had been derelict when we bought it', the time span of the derelict state of the house precedes the time of our buying it, which is in the past relative to the time of speech. Such a form locates one event in the past using another already located as its reference point, so that a remoter past is located by an event in a 'nearer' past relative to the time of speaking.

The future is also open to different forms of representation, depending on the options available, which include the 'will/shall' forms which are used for neutral predictions, although with first person forms they could also signify intention. The 'be going to' forms indicate 'the future as a fulfilment of the present' and as resulting from intentions in the present, or from causes in the present – 'I'm going to be an astronaut when I grow up'. The present progressive suggests the near future, or indicates the fulfilment of plans or arrangements made in the present – 'We are coming to America'. The modals like 'will/shall' with the progressive can indicate the future as a matter of course – 'I will be working next week'. Forms with the modal + perfect indicate the past in the future, while a future can be implanted into the past by putting some of the future forms, like 'be going to' or 'be to/be about to', in the past tense, although these usually mean that the action anticipated did not occur – 'He *was going to* emigrate, but he was given a promotion'. On the other hand, 'was/were to' and 'would' characterize a future that is fulfilled in the past.

Given such options in the grammatical system, they are obviously open to use in highly discriminate ways in the portrayal of time in plays via dialogue. And variation among characters has discourse functions to perform. Yet very little attention has been paid to this aspect of dialogue or of linguistic time. The 'past' or 'the future' are generally seen as blocks of time rather vaguely located before or after the 'present' of the speech event with respect to a time line. Linguistic portrayals of time are obviously a large area of investigation. Some examples given below may illustrate the uses made of some of the available options in selected instances, but with no pretensions to exhaustiveness.

The transmission of expository information where such is available in plays designed to include them is obviously crucial for their effectiveness, and such information can be communicated to the audience through the external, projective axis while being embedded in the internal, interactional one. In the opening scene of Shakespeare's *Hamlet*, various linguistic options trace time differently as situations are located as near or remote in time to the 'present' of the watch on the battlements. Clock references set the time of the beginning of the scene as at midnight. By the time the ghost appears, within forty lines of the opening of the scene, it is about one o'clock. The scene thus begins with the focus on the present in punctual mode, in the clock references. On the change of the watch Marcellus enquires, 'What! Has this thing appeared again tonight?' The deictic 'tonight' stretches the time span but within the span of the night, up to and including the present. The 'has. . . appeared' as a present perfect form sees the event of the possible appearance of the ghost within a very recent indefinite past, within the duration of 'tonight' itself. Bernardo's response, 'I *have seen* nothing', continues to bound the event again, within the recent indefinite past, its relevance taken up to the time of speech. The location of the ghost's possible appearance here is as an event in a larger span of time of present duration. Its absence so far, of course, invests both the present and the future of the night with apprehension and dread. Frequency references – 'twice seen of us', 'what we two nights have seen', 'if again this apparition come' – inform us that it has been a repeated event within the span of two nights. As the time arrives for the ghost's appearance, deictic forms take over.

> Last night of all,
> When yond same star that's westward from the pole,
> Had made his course t'illume that part of heaven
> Where now it burns, Marcellus and myself,
> The bell then beating one –
>
> (1.1.36–9)

Ostensibly the situation being described is one that happened 'last night', but the deictic 'yond same star' 'where *now* it *burns*. . . ' repeats the same situation 'now', with the star as it burnt 'then' burning likewise in the present 'now' of speech, which collapses time to the ominous *moment* of appearance – 'now'.

The second appearance of the ghost has to be prepared for again in order that the dramatic momentum may not be lost. And this is done not by a focus on the present time span of the night, but by switching attention to remoter pasts which are narrated by Horatio. The relevance to present occurrences is also referred to, given that this section has an expository function as well. The simple past or past perfect forms are used in that part of the narrative that tells of the doings of Hamlet senior and the elder Fortinbras – 'Our last king. . . was. . . ' (by Fortinbras of Norway)'. . .

dared to the combat./ Our valiant Hamlet did slay. . . Fortinbras. . . who. . . did forfeit. . . / A moeity competent was gaged by our king. . . ' When the story shifts to speaker's time of narration, and to the actions of the young Fortinbras, the overall tense forms shift to the present, including the present perfect.

> Now sir, young Fortinbras
> . . . Hath in the skirts of Norway, here and there,
> Sharked up. . .

(1.1.95–8)

The second speech which immediately precedes the ghost's second appearance moves to a remoter past, to the time of Julius Caesar, and the past tense and the past perfect are used, both of which enable gaps to be effected between the present and the past. Since only listening is required, in the deictic centre, and the load on listening is heavy given the complicated syntax and length of the speeches, the present is obscured as attention is distracted by the past which is brought into focus by the narrative. The narrative ends, however, with relevance drawn between past events and the present, on which cue the ghost appears again. The scene closes with the verbal painting of the dawn as noted earlier, the coming of which is also indicated, folk-wise, by a reference to the crowing of the cock. Psychological closure, too, of 'dark' and 'dread' is instituted in Marcellus' references to a symbolic time, not in the 'present' of the enunciation, but with reference to a timeless time, a hallowed and sacred time, of hope and redemption.

> Some say that ever 'gainst that season comes
> Wherein our Saviour's birth is celebrated,
> The bird of dawning singeth all night long;
> And then, they say, no spirit dare stir abroad;
> The nights are wholesome; then no planets strike,
> No fairy takes, nor witch hath power to charm,
> So hallow'd and so gracious is that time.

(1.1.158–64)

In Shakespeare's *King Lear*, the time gap between the division of the kingdom and the emergence of Lear's difficulties with Goneril is left unspecified. At the end of the scene of the succession, in Act 1, scene 1, Lear's departure to the home of the elder of his newly rewarded daughters is indicated and the length of his alternating sojourns with each of them. The time of departure is projected as the deictic 'tonight' and then, the change of residence is located deictically as 'next month'. The time span for the action to follow is thus drafted verbally as to be calculated from the moment and present situation of speech.

GONERIL   . . . I think our father will hence tonight.
REGAN   That's most certain, and with you; next month with us. . .
(1.1.285–6)

That Lear has departed is confirmed by Gloucester in scene 2 (23–4) in the use of the past tense for Lear's departure within the scope of the deictic 'tonight', which indicates that the time of speech is later that same day.

GLOUCESTER   Kent banish'd thus! And France in choler parted!
And the king gone tonight! prescrib'd his pow'r!. . .

By scene 3, we learn from Goneril's speech that there is trouble brewing between herself and her father, though we have little idea as to how long Lear has been living with Goneril, except that it is, perhaps, under a month. Shakespeare, however, does not give us objective, chronometric references to time in this instance. Instead he locates it subjectively in Goneril's cumulative experience of Lear's behaviour at the time of speech, in the use of the present tense in its habitual or iterative sense, where time is measured by successive repeats of the same events, but without a definite origin or end for such repetition.

GONERIL   By day and night he wrongs me; every hour
He flashes into one gross crime or other
That sets us all at odds. I'll not endure it.
His knights grow riotous, and himself upbraids us
On every trifle. . .
(1.3.4–8)

The Knight, too, uses the same strategy, but from a different perspective, since he presents his own observations of the habitual discourtesies which he feels have been and are continuously directed at Lear. His speech is in the present tense.

KNIGHT   My lord, I know not what the matter is: but to my judgement, your Highness is not entertained with that ceremonious affection as you were wont; there's a great abatement of kindness appears as well in the general dependants as in the Duke himself also and your daughter.
(1.4.56–61)

Lear responds that the Knight merely reminds him of what he himself has noticed. But his speech is cast with the present perfect predominating:

LEAR   Thou but rememb'rest me of mine own conception: I have perceived a most faint neglect of late, which I have rather blamed as mine own jealous curiosity than as a very pretence and purpose of unkindness. I will look further into't. But where's my fool?. . .

(1.4.66–70)

The present perfect forms, 'I have perceived', 'I have. . . blamed', do not signify the continuity in time of habituality, rather they make relevant, in the present, events or states which have occurred habitually in the past. Lear sees the point of the Knight's observations because he has been aware of them himself but the awareness is not presented as continuous or unified as in the other two speeches. The awareness, although it endures into the present, is more intermittent than that portrayed in the habitual sense of the present tense used earlier. The sense of 'often' seems to be relevant to Lear's speech, whereas Goneril's, in particular, would seem to have 'always' in mind. And Lear needed to be *reminded* that he actually has such a 'conception'.

Time could also figure as a potentiality or possibility from a viewpoint in the past, in relation to a 'future' located at the time of a past event, which may not have been realized. The 'future in the past forms' are thus valuable and interesting when they are used, which is not often. From the perspective of the 'present' of the utterance, the possibilities not realized 'then' could be traced or indicated with the hindsight afforded by the distance in time 'now'. Such situations have their own poignancy as is the case in Terence Rattigan's play *Table by the Window* (1985).

ANNE   No, John. Let me stay just a little while longer. May I sit down?

JOHN   Is that a way of reminding me of my bad manners? I know I shouldn't sit while you are standing –

ANNE   [*Laughing gently*] You're so bristly. Even bristlier now than before. [*She sits down*] Your manners were always very good.

JOHN   You used to tick me off about them often enough.

ANNE   Well – only sometimes – when we had silly conventional people at the flat who didn't understand you as I did.

JOHN   [*With a faint smile*] I think if I'd been given time, I could have predicted that answer.

ANNE   [*With an answering smile*] Oh dear! Tell me, did you always find me so predictable – even at the very beginning?

JOHN   Yes.

ANNE   Why did you marry me then?

JOHN   If it pleases your vanity to hear my answer once again, you shall. Because my love for you at that time was so desperate, my craving for you was so violent, that I could refuse you nothing that you asked – not even a marriage that every prompting of reason told me must be disastrous.

ANNE   Why did it so necessarily have to be so disastrous?

JOHN   Because of class mainly.

ANNE   Class? Oh, that's nonsense, John. It's just inverted snobbery.

JOHN   No. I don't think so. The gulf between Kensington Gore and the Hull Docks is still fairly wide. I was one of a family of eight, as I must have told you many a time, and my views of a wife's duties must have been at least a little coloured by watching my mother sacrifice her health, strength and comfort and eventually her life to looking after us children, and to keeping the old man out of trouble. I'm not saying my demands on a wife would have been pitched as high as that. But they would, I think, at least have included the proper running of a home and the begetting of children.

ANNE   [*Hotly*] About children, I did make it perfectly clear before our marriage –

JOHN   Yes. You made it perfectly clear. A famous model mustn't gamble her figure merely for posterity. I accepted the bargain, Anne, the whole bargain. I have no complaint.

ANNE   [*Angrily*] You have, John. You know you have. Your real complaint is still the same as it always was – that I didn't love you when we got married –

JOHN   Oh God! Do we have to go into that again?

(1985: 106–7)

The conversation is between a divorced couple who meet again and go over the past in this conversation. After pleasantries in the present tense, Anne's reference to John's prickliness 'now' as 'before' loops into the past into memory narration. Time references point to habitualities, to repetitions of similar actions in the past, forming a pattern for the past, the repetitions in time forming the identities, the selves that they 'were' (ANNE 'Your manners were *always very good'* ; JOHN *'You used to* tick me off. . . *often* enough'). These are occasions safely located in the past, as the main clause tense forms reveal. But the reconstruction of a shared life on grounds of patterned habitualities is indulged in up to John's answer to Anne's 'Why did you marry me then?'. The past safely and distantly located as past is brought into the present and the closures of the past are opened up by John in the change in tense – 'If it pleases your. . . ', i.e. now. Tense changes vary a lot in this passage and are used differently by the two characters as discourse resources: Anne, on the whole, locates difficulties in the past, and contrasts them with the present. John's usages are more complex – modalities project futures in the past from the point of view of the present of the context of utterance, signifying the recognition of roads not taken 'then', things not understood or articulated 'then', but with traces still present in the situation of utterance, 'now' – 'I would have. . . ' It is Anne who creates the link between past and present as a continuous time line, and thus projects the continuity of past and present, and of nested, tensed, identities from the past into the present – 'You *have*, John. You *know you have*. Your real complaint *is still* the same as it *always was* – that I *didn't love* you *when* we *got married*' (emphasis added).

Since time, as an abstract, is configured spatially either as a point, punctually, or as a line when movement is being represented durationally, the tension between these spatial representations can also be exploited. The uses of deictic terms like 'now', 'then', etc. often invoke encyclopedic knowledge and pragmatic inference in order to clarify their time scope – as in 'Pull the trigger *now*/I'm *now* working on a PhD' (Levinson 1983: 74). The elasticity of time, even with respect to the present of coding time in the deictic centre, is exploitable. In Handke's *Kaspar*, the initially autistic Kaspar, after personal and protracted agonies with grammar, use and inter-textuality, begins to speak.

> After I came in, as I see only
> now, I put, as I see only now,
> the sofa into disorder,
> whereupon, as I see only now,
> the wardrobe door with which
> I, as I see only now, played as
> I see only now, with my foot,
> was left open, whereupon I, as
> I see only now, ripped, as I see only
> now, the drawer out of the
> table, whereupon, as I see only
> now, I threw over another
> table, thereupon a rocking
> chair, as I see only now, also
> turned over, as well as a further
> chair and broom, as I see only
> now, whereupon I walked
> towards, as I see only now, the
> only chair still standing (as I

see only now) and sat down. I
neither saw anything nor heard
anything, and I felt good. *He
gets up.* Now I have got up and
noticed at once, not just now,
that my shoelace was untied.
Because I can speak now I can
put the shoelace in order. Ever
since I can speak I can bend
down to the shoelace in normal
fashion. Ever since I can speak
I can put everything in order.
. . .

(Handke [1967] 1972: 31–2)

The deictic form 'I see only now' punctuates times of mental awareness especially of past actions, as they occur in the 'now' of present speech. Speech has also given Kaspar the privileges of symbolic displacements in the deictic centre, and the ability to represent action which happened 'then' in the 'now' of speech. The succession of 'nows' contingently stills the moving line of time in the deictic centre momentarily, into punctuated points, but the moving line moves, points constitute a line. The temporal 'now' as a spatial point is forever erased at the moment of enunciation, the spoken 'now' vanishing in the very breath of articulation as already the past since overtaken by the breath of speech. The speech extract dramatizes linguistic *development*, as movement between stages. The graphological presentation 'moves' from spoken language modes and their articulatory and acoustic dis-órders of voice, into a written language, graphemic, discrete order, marked by full stops and capitals and other indexes of written, standard language normativity. Expressive control over time can be seen in the uses of both the symbolic and deictic fields of language in the variations among the 'after', the 'ever', the 'where-upon', the 'thereupon' and the paced repetitions of 'now', and the 'I see only now' and the 'now I can. . .', and in the complex cognitions of 'not just now'; in the shifts in tense and modality; and in the punctuated, overt clues to and implicit interrogations of syntactic iconicity. The whole compresses, merges and streamlines into a questionable and ironic confidence in the ability to put 'everything' into 'order' via language or discourse; the very regard for language and discourse consolidated in the grasp, in *spoken* speech, of normative, power-driven, literate, written language forms, as a mark of the properly 'human'.

Chapter 2

Ethnomethodology and conversation analysis

In an earlier section it was argued that certain underlying *rules* and regularities operative in day-to-day exchanges are at work as 'authenticating conventions' which are also enabling conventions in the interpretation of dramatic dialogue. The specificities of interaction in any segment of a play among the dramatis personae can be seen to be the product of the manipulation and exploitation of such 'rules' and conventions by dramatists for dramatic purposes. Segments of action are shaped through the employment of such resources within the alternating course of dialogue. If this is the case, some understanding of these resources should prove useful in analysing dramatic dialogue and it is to the work done recently on the mechanics of conversation itself that we now turn.

The term 'conversation' in the framework of *Conversational Analysis* can be misleading if it conjures up visions of trivial social chit-chat alone, and for our purposes, it is best regarded as a technical term covering a variety of forms of spontaneous social interaction in a speech community. But analysts vary in their definitions and delimitations of the scope of the term. Levinson opts for the narrow definition:

> *conversation* may be taken to be that familiar predominant kind of talk in which two or more participants freely alternate in speaking, which generally occurs outside specific institutional settings like religious services, law courts, classrooms and the like.
>
> (Levinson 1983: 284)

Such restrictions have not been adhered to, in the main, since talk in institutional settings like courtrooms and classrooms and boardrooms has also been investigated by analysts. The problem is compounded by the division in the field between *Conversation* and *Discourse* analysts both of whom investigate spoken interaction with different methodologies. The 'Discourse Analysts' of the Birmingham school (Sinclair and Coulthard

1975) base their work on classroom interaction, excluded by Levinson. Moreover, even from the Ethnomethodological viewpoint, which Levinson supports, talk in institutional settings like courtrooms and surgeries have been analysed. Our own preference is for a more inclusive if looser definition which covers all forms of spontaneous spoken interaction with due attention being paid to differences that arise from the constraints or special arrangements that condition institutionally located talk.

A word about the different branches of investigation into conversation and their differences is in order at this point. First, there are the *Ethnomethodologists* originally, a break-away group of sociologists, of whom Harold Garfinkel and Harvey Sacks were perhaps the most influential, whose dissatisfaction with methods of traditional sociology led to the formulation of alternative methods and aims. Questioning the value of traditional methods of investigation – the use of questionnaires and the like – as drawing the analyst away from the lived stuff of social reality they proposed closer scrutiny of the methods used by social actors themselves in managing their affairs inter-personally. The common-sense or lay methodologies used in actual social interactions became the focus: its study known as *Ethnomethodology*. In the analysis of conversation the data used are recorded interactions from everyday life which are scrutinized for the regularities that occur and the mechanisms that underlie such regularities. 'Rules' to account for the orderly and co-ordinated nature of spontaneous interactions are constructed. These rules are seen as those which actors themselves are using to order their interactions and to make sense of their interactive activities.

The *Discourse Analysts* of the Birmingham School are more influenced by modes of argument and methodology derived from linguistics and there are different frameworks around that attempt to extend research into the workings of stretches of discourse – units larger than the sentence. Discourse research in general (Brown and Yule 1983) has led to the scrutiny of different kinds of issues than the descriptions of interactions in institutional settings, like classrooms or courtrooms. Text analysts (Halliday and Hasan 1976; de Beaugrande and Dressler 1981) have also probed the modes of organization that make various stretches of written language coherent. Among Discourse Analysts, yet another emphasis can be detected in the work of Labov and Fanshel (1977) who have attempted to incorporate speech act theory into the workings of interaction.

None of the work mentioned above is fully adequate as offering comprehensive tools for the analysis of dramatic dialogue. Each offers insights but there is contention rather than consensus on which framework or methodology is best suited to the study of spoken interaction. Future research will adjudicate amongst them. The Discourse Analysts of the Birmingham School have a complex set of concepts but these are directed piecemeal work on specific areas of interest as mentioned above. The efficacy of the model when dealing with data outside the classroom is as yet unclear. The rank–scale model closely links the constituent levels of analysis such that lower level units realize higher ones and the hierarchy itself is complex – acts constitute moves which constitute exchanges which make up transactions, which together enable a speech event like a lesson to function as such. Of these, the lower ranks of Act and Move have caused problems and revisions. Deirdre Burton (1980) has adapted the Birmingham-based, Sinclair–Coulthard framework for the analysis of dramatic texts, but the analysis reveals both the strengths and weaknesses of the framework. While permitting a high degree of classification of the various constituent elements, there is also a danger of overclassification for its own sake, the descriptive machinery being as finely discriminating as it is. Also, in cases where a dramatic character's speech is composed of a large stretch of talk, the minute classifications required by the framework of small, one-clause, phrasal or lexical units, while exhaustively coding all aspects of talk, work better on short fragments of speech and prove cumbersome and counter-productive in larger stretches. Yet, this model is among the more principled and explicit available since it overtly seeks a degree of objectivity and replicability. Our own preference is for the Ethnomethodologists, whose proposed categories and 'rules' may be more ad hoc, but the framework itself permits greater flexibility which allows more attention to the fluidity of interaction. The insights offered by this framework are summarized below.

THE SYSTEMATICS OF TURN-TAKING: GENERAL

Central to Conversational Analysis is the concept of *turn-taking* which organizes the distribution and flow of speech between the two poles of interaction thereby keeping speech, generally, continuous. Turn-taking has been described as a process in which 'one participant A talks, stops; another, B, starts, talks, stops; and so we obtain an A–B–A–B–A–B distribution of talk across two participants' (Levinson 1983: 296). Yet, the co-ordination itself is achieved with some rapidity – the time gap between one person stopping and the other starting being just a few fractions of a second and the turns are appropriated in orderly fashion. Overlaps can occur, though it is estimated only in about 5 per cent of the interaction, but even here, there is a level of systematicity involved. Moreover, turn-taking regularities are observable in instances where more than two participants are involved, and in cases where participants are not face-to-face, as in telephone conversations.

The organization of conversation in day-to-day settings, it has been hypothesized, must be controlled by some kind of mechanism which facilitates the orderly distribution of turns and governs the progress of talk in a variety of contexts and for a variety of purposes. The description of such a mechanism has been the objective of a considerable amount of effort, and one such, proposed by Sacks, Schegloff and Jefferson (1978), has gained priority, as set forth in their seminal review of the *systematics* of turn-taking in conversation.

The informal conclusions arrived at after examining a wealth of data were the following:

> First, the fact of turn-taking and that it must be organized, was something that the data of conversation made increasingly plain: such facts as that one party talks at a time overwhelmingly, though speakers change, though the size of the turns varies, though the ordering of turns varies; that transitions seem finely co-ordinated; that there are obviously techniques for allocating turns that are used and whose characterization would be part of any model that would describe turn-taking materials; that there are techniques for the construction of utterances relevant to their turn status that bear on the co-ordination of transfer and on the allocation of speakership; in short, a body of factual material accessible to rather unmotivated inquiry exposed the presence of turn-taking and the major facets of its organization.
>
> (Sacks *et al.* 1978: 9)

Any serious model of conversational exchange, they contend, should be capable of accommodating various 'grossly apparent' facts of conversational behaviour summarized as,

1. Speaker change recurs, or at least occurs
2. Overwhelmingly, one party talks at a time
3. Occurrences of more than one speaker at a time are common, but brief
4. Transition from one speaker to a next with no gap and no overlap between them are common. Together with transitions characterized by slight gap or slight overlap, they make up the vast majority of transitions
5. Turn order is not fixed but varies
6. Turn size is not fixed but varies
7. Length of conversation is not fixed, specified in advance

8. What parties say is not fixed, specified in advance
9. Relative distribution of turns is not fixed, specified in advance
10. Number of parties can change
11. Talk can be continuous or discontinuous
12. Turn-allocation techniques are obviously used. A current speaker may select a next speaker (as when a current speaker addresses a question to another party); parties may self-select, in starting to talk
13. Various 'turn constructional units' are employed. Turns can be projectedly 'one-word long' or, for example, they can be sentential in length
14. Repair mechanisms for dealing with turn-taking errors and violations are obviously available for use. For example, if two parties find themselves talking at the same time, one of them will stop prematurely, thus repairing the trouble.

(Sacks *et al.* 1978: 10–11)

The variety of data on which such observations were based led them to claim that the turn-taking mechanism must be abstract enough to be context-free – i.e. not tied specifically in its organization to any one context or set of participants, but capable of operating in context-sensitive fashion so that the mechanism 'can, in local instances of its operations be sensitive to, and exhibit its sensitivity to, various of the parameters of social reality in a local context' (*ibid.*: 10). Attention is thus directed to the *invariant* aspects of the system and its generalities although the level of invariance must be constructed in such a way as to make it capable of respecting the local variations to which it is subjected and which are observable in actual use.

Generalizing over all of this, they propose a turn-taking system composed of two components – a turn constructional component and a turn allocational component and a set of rules to facilitate their workings. Turn units are composed of turn types which may be clausal, phrasal or lexical, such units being characterized by their *projectability* or predictability of their closure as a unit. The end of the unit is the place where speaker change can occur and the turn may pass to another speaker, thus keeping the progression of turns in motion. Such a juncture of transition has been labelled a *transition relevance place*, the structural significance of which participants appear to respect since the switch to next speaker is accomplished, in the majority of cases, without gap or overlap among turns.

The turn allocational component regulates turn change and its sequential unfolding among participants on an alternating, turn-by-turn basis, and comprises a set of rules for the allocation of the next speaker's turn in such a way that the transition is smooth. Techniques for allocation follow certain rules which are ordered and may be recursively applied, and operate at the appropriate transition places of each turn.

The rules given below are taken from the slightly modified and simpler version of Sacks *et al.*'s formulation as described by Levinson (1983). Following Levinson, C = current speaker, N = next turn, TRP = Transition Relevance Place. The rules are basically of two kinds, those by which the current speaker selects the next speaker and the next speaker self-selects at TRP. Where neither option is used, the turn lapses, but the rules can operate recursively so that one or the other option could be used again till the turn passes to the next speaker. The rules provide for three options, including the failure option. Current speaker selects next, next speaker self-selects, or the turn may lapse and the lapse(s) incorporated into the current turn as *pause(s)* till turn change occurs via one or the other two options. According to Levinson,

Rule 1 – applies initially at the first TRP of any turn
  (a) if C selects N in current turn, then C must stop speaking, and N must speak next, transition occurring at the first TRP after N-selection
  (b) if C does not select N, then any (other) party may self-select, first speaker gaining rights to the next turn
  (c) if C has not selected N and no other party self-selects under option (b), then C may (but need not) continue (i.e. claim rights to a further turn-constructional unit)
Rule 2 – applies at all subsequent TRPs
  When Rule 1 (c) has been applied by C, then at the next TRP Rules 1 (a)–(c) apply and recursively, at the next TRP, until speaker change is effected

(Levinson 1983: 298)

The rules and their ordering serve to explain the facts observed in the regulation apparent in day-to-day talk. They ensure, in any one conversation, that only one speaker speaks at a time and they remove the clash potential in the two sets of techniques available for turn change – current speaker selects next/next speaker self-selects. Moreover, 'the first speaker has rights' provision; (Rule 1 (b)) ensures that when conflicts occur and simultaneous starts happen among the different parties, the first starter maintains the turn and the competing other starter must drop out. Where this rule is not respected, the underlying potential for conflict and competition is intensified, since the rights of the first speaker are actually being flouted. The provision for transfer at TRP means that the rest of the turn is freed from gaps, overlaps, etc. since these are localized at TRP, generally, at the end/beginning of turns where possibilities for competition or error are greatest. For instance, next speaker may mistakenly assume that the turn has been completed, say, after the use of address forms, tags, or even at the end of a clause; or seize opportunities for the turn at these junctures. Overlap at any other point would generally be regarded as an interruption. Orderly speaker change is thus facilitated by the rules, and recurs in the course of talk.

The third option states the conditions under which turn change may not occur, but then, as noted above, the rules are applied recursively. Given such options, turn change is not automatic or mechanical. It is not obligatory for the current speaker to use any one option alone. The fact of a TRP predicts change and even if the next speaker's turn lapses for one reason or another the current speaker has the option to continue and attempt to relinquish the turn at the next TRP.

As far as turn order is concerned, the system generates different options again. Current speaker may select next by name, gaze, by pointing, or whatever. This may well be the previous speaker, creating an A–B–A–B alternating pattern. On the other hand, the next speaker need not be the previous speaker, someone else could be selected and a different order, A–B–C–B–A–. . . could ensue. Self-selection may also occur and the rules provide possibilities for different turn order patterns as each participant in the pool of available participants takes a turn, the unmarked norm in social intercourse being equal rights to the floor. These norms are, of course, culture specific and can vary across cultures. Which options are actually used and which patterns are created are left to the interlocutors themselves, locally, within the specificities of the speech events in which they are involved. Thus, although there are general rules, the turn-taking system is a *local management system*, left in the charge of the users themselves to manage within the contingencies of their talk.

As far as *turn units* are concerned, their length, linguistic complexity, etc. can vary. Different lengths of input are possible – clauses, phrases, one-word turns and variability in turn size can be quite extensive. In all cases, however, the system is one of differences, of options, and is not characterized by the either/or of syntactical organization or the judgements of grammaticality or ungrammaticality that it calls forth.

The pool of participants who may converse cannot be fixed in advance either, and again local management comes in. Where there are more than two parties, pressure is exerted on the system in the expectations of floor rights. If current speaker wishes to hold on to the floor special measures have to be taken, for floor hogging would be assessed as rude or bump-tious. In story-telling or when relating anecdotes, it has been noted that bids for extended turns are made by the prospective story-teller to gain the requisite floor rights, which must be ratified by others for the bid to succeed. If a speaker wishes to select a specific other, this must be done in a way so as not to allow the turn to pass to someone else at next TRP so strategies have got to be found. Moreover, at large gatherings, multiple and self-contained turn-taking systems could come into existence among independently self-organized groups. If a speaker wishes to counteract such *schisms* and keep open the maximum number of possibilities active measures have to be taken and the situation may have to be re-negotiated. The enactment of the rules becomes fluid and flexible and highly sensitive to the contingencies of the interactive context itself.

Although much of all this appears to signify that conversation is continuous talk with marvels of split-second timing suturing up any threat of discontinuity or silence, it need not be. Options to talk, when used, create continuity of speech, but the refusal of such options is also permit-ted and has the effect of generating a kind of semantics of silence in which instances of non-speech are interpreted according to the expected poss-ibilities for speech and as a negative product of the system itself. In the first place, the fact of turn change at TRP ensures that the silence of listening becomes a productive one for non-speakers, especially for the attendant non-speaking participant(s) as intending turn user and possible next speaker. Silence thus has a structural place in speech exchange as responsive activity. But there are other kinds of silences. Sacks *et al.* distinguish among different kinds of non-speech – lapses, pauses, gaps – which are assessed according to their placement in the turn and the exchange. At TRP if current speaker stops and none of the options for next turn is used, there is a *lapse* of a turn. The use of such a non-speech option makes the silence of a lapsed turn an *attributable silence* – attributable, that is, to the lapser as his or her silence. Intra-turn speaker's silence, not at TRP, is generally not expected to be filled by another speaker and is a *pause*. Silence at the end of a turn which is delayed is a *gap* when filled by some speaker and thus minimized, but where nobody picks up the turn and the silence extends itself it can function as the gap of closure of the segment of interaction or the interaction itself. But an erstwhile gap can be made into a pause by the speaker incorporating it into the current turn and projecting another TRP.

SEQUENCING OF TURNS: GENERAL

Another set of mechanisms explored in the literature has to do with the sequential organization of turns in a protracted stretch of talk. Turns call forth other turns and the sequencing mechanisms involved have received a fair measure of attention. The minimal unit of interaction is an exchange of at least two turns, a pair, through which the reciprocity of interaction is enacted. Although there is some degree of latitude in respect of what may follow what within the contingencies of an exchange, there are also regularities and expectancies and the notion of the *Adjacency pair* has been posited to account for next-turn constancies which underlie the linear structuring of talk.

Adjacency pairs, of which question–answer (QA), greeting–greeting (GG), comment–comment (CC) are instances, are tied pairs of utterances and ordered such that the issue of the first part in a turn sets up an expectancy that the other will follow in the next turn. The use of a question presupposes or requires an answer, the use of a greeting raises expectations of a reciprocal greeting, and so on. Such pairs are interactively consequential in that they constrain, in unmarked cases, the interlocutor's response. The absence of the second part of the pair when the first has been used is thus both noticeable and noticed given their conventional tie. They are also, as a consequence, a kind of provisional norm by which interactional units can achieve closure in default ways, as the expected and unmarked option through which inter-personal relationships may proceed untroubled and without hitches.

But interactional troubles, confusions, etc. are also a fact of life and are empirically certified in the research. Strict, linear adjacency is observable but so are structures in which it is not, so that expansions of the two-part form are also evident as are various *insertion sequences* that can complicate the structure of the basic pair through embeddings of various kinds. In contrast to a structure of basic QA adjacency pairs as in the following:

Q   What time is it?
A   Six fifteen.

We can also have others which involve various depths of embedding, as in the example given below.

Q1   May I have a bunch of flowers, please?
Q2   Which one?
A2   The yellow roses.
A1   Here you are.

The longer sequence in the second example protracts the QA structure into a QQAA structure so that the original Q1 is completed by its relevant A1 via another adjacency pair Q2A2. The original QA pair thus holds over another in its own right, and the interactive business takes on a more extended course. Different linear patterns can be constructed depending on the depth of embedding that occurs which also display the tangible path that interactions take in their specificities, in their turn-by-turn construction. In these cases, the adjacency tie does not disappear, since *conditional relevance* is said to hold across the intervening turns till the second part of the pair is performed. It groups together intervening parts as belonging to the *same* interaction even though more turns are expended than strict adjacency pairing would permit. Others of this kind have been noted. A slightly less ordered form of insertion is available in Gail Jefferson's (1972) *side sequence* in which, in her data, a misapprehension or error has occurred, and enacted and displayed as such, and the drift of the talk is deflected into a sub-sequence which is used to rectify matters before the conversation resumes again. Here, the embedding is not within the two parts of the adjacency pair as in an insertion sequence. As Coulthard (1986: 75) has pointed out, the sequence begins on a statement, which is not the first part of a pair nor are subsequent turns projected by it. The sequence is negotiated as is the resumption of the original course of talk, but the issues of break as well as resumption may well be authorized on semantic or topical, rather than purely structural, grounds, although there are structural consequences. In Jefferson's example, the detour begins on a *questioning repeat* which is understood and displayed as a problem and then subsequent turns are used to set it right. Consider the following, taken from an occasion when children were getting ready for a game of *tag*.

STEVEN   one, two, three, [*pause*] four, five, six, [*pause*] eleven, eight, nine, ten.
SUSAN   Eleven? – eight, nine, ten.
STEVEN   Eleven, eight, nine, ten.
SUSAN   Eleven?
STEVEN   Seven, eight, nine, ten.
SUSAN   That's better.

Other forms of sequential organization deal with a different set of procedures in cases where the second part of the adjacency pair bifurcates, as it were, to provide options in its own right. In such instances, a unique second part is not available. Instead, ordered options provide alternatives, as in offers or invitations which may either be accepted or refused. The *preferred* option for an invitation would be the acceptance which is both socially desirable and linguistically simpler in design. The *dispreferred* option, the refusal, is a socially negative act and is also more complex in its realization, including delay features like 'well. . . ', or hedges, or elaborations in the form of excuses or reasons for refusal and the like. Similarly, if comments call forth comments, and where comments are assessments, the second part may either agree or disagree with the first part and disagreements are complex in their construction. Given such facts, *preference organization* has had a fair share of attention. The exception to the rule that *dispreferreds* are to be avoided is in cases of negative or disparaging self-assessments where disagreement with the content of the first part of the pair is the preferred option. The performance of such options can be quite complex and need not be confined to two or even three turns.

Other kinds of sub-organizations have also been investigated. *Openings* and *closings* of conversation may be undertaken across many turns but are structured as types in their own right. Openings present a particular interactional problem since entry into conversation has to be managed by participants; they do not just happen. Work done on telephone conversations has led researchers to posit a three-part structure to openings – Summons–Answer–Reason for Summons. Summons can be non-verbal, like the ringing of the telephone, or a tap on the shoulder, or they may be verbal, including polite markers like 'Excuse me' or the use of names and address forms. A familiar instance would be:

A   John.
B   Yes.
A   I'm just going out for some milk.

The Summons–Answer sequence is an initiating device, a preamble to something else to come, which serves to bring the interactive and responsive structure of conversation into being. Other kinds of preambles include Pre-requests and Pre-invitations which serve to check out if the right conditions obtain before requests or invitations proper are made. Closings of talk have their own characteristic structure and since talk has to be *brought* to a close, it has to be interactively achieved with both parties agreeing to close talk and entering a process of disengagement. A four-part structure has been proposed comprising a pre-terminal pair before the conventional leave-taking pair like Bye/Bye or some such is undertaken. The pre-terminal pair signals the oncoming closure, but also provides opportunities for any unfinished business to be attended to if necessary before talk is concluded.

Such anticipatory structures also reveal the contingent and collaborative nature of interaction in conversation. The abstract rules create different structuring possibilities but which of these will be realized *in situ* is left to the contingencies of the particular situation and the participants actually involved in interaction. The course of interaction is also left to participants to manage jointly and locally, and its course can be plotted turn by turn.

Collaboration and co-operation do not mean that troubles of various kinds cannot make their appearance in conversation. They obviously do, but there are *repair mechanisms* for dealing with them. These, if anything, serve to strengthen the claim that conversations are co-productions of meaningful activity, which, when threatened, can be attended to jointly in order to produce mutual satisfaction. Repair mechanisms serve to check and monitor that the interaction is working as desired and that errors in production or problems with comprehension are being countered.

A   If Thatcher is challenged at the Tory party conference that'll liven things up.

B   Who. . . ?

A   Major, I mean.

Turn repairs may be undertaken economically as in the above, but they can also stretch across many turns, since the structures described are composed of *slots* and not necessarily turns in adjacency. Repairs may either be self-generated, or other-generated, and accomplished with or without prompting from an interlocutor and undertaken by self or other. Others repairing speaker's errors could create offence or signal power imbalances, and thus self-repair is preferred to other-initiated, other-repair in the interests of social equilibrium (Levinson 1983: 339–42).

Repair sequences of this kind, sometimes also called *clarification sequences*, are small-scale troubles that can be dealt with and the interaction can move on, but full-scale misunderstandings and conflicts are also possible in which proper remedial action has got to be undertaken, if desired, in order to restore the breach in interactive harmony caused by some impropriety or the other; by sins of omission or commission. Various possible structures have been examined and one such is the Reproach–Account–Evaluation of Account sequence, such that an Account follows a Reproach, and an Evaluation follows the Account (Cody and McLaughlin 1985: 51). A breach having occurred, the offended party may reproach, which calls for a reciprocal remedy in turn, which has to be accepted as such. The first and last slots are filled by the offended party, the medial one by the offender. Different strategies have been investigated for playing the sequence. If the rules of the sequence are not observed, recyclings may occur as remedy is insistently sought, by extending the Reproach slot. Or Accountings may be protracted by offering repeats that attempt to strengthen the case when an Evaluation is not positive.

Different typologies have been constructed for playing the sequence: different kinds of Reproaches, for instance, or Accounts and the manner in which one constrains the other. Thus, the first slot can project a *concession* ('Aren't you sorry you did it?'); or project an *excuse* ('Were you stuck in traffic?'); or project a *refusal* ('Don't try to pretend you didn't see me'). Reproaches may also be assessed along a continuum of aggravation–mitigation in which aggravating tactics can escalate conflict if they are returned by aggravating responses, and mitigating reproaches could decrease the temperature if responded to in the same spirit (Cody and McLaughlin 1985). Situational factors of various kinds can influence how the sequence is conducted and the construction of the turn itself – degree of intimacy between the interactants, severity of the alleged offence, importance awarded to maintaining *face*, and so on. Such aspects are generally not attended to in the more structurally oriented ethnomethodological work which has been the major focus of this review.

Extensions of these formal structures are possible as we have seen. It is not the case that all remedial episodes are played in three sequences or even three slots, since the sequence can be aborted. If the turns revolve around recyclings of Reproach and Accounting slots without arriving at an Evaluation, the conflict is left unresolved, since the Accounting remains rejected. Expansions are possible through recyclings and re-runs of some particular aspect or aspects or parts of the structure, and not with conflictual or hostile results either. According to the machinery for offers, preference organization provides either an acceptance or refusal as second part. But as Davidson (1984) has shown, offers and other similar *firsts* like invitations or requests may be revised in the light of a post-proposal rejection or a rejection-implicative *second*. Re-offers or re-invitations can be issued which may not again be accepted and the initiator can try again and the sequence can go on till some jointly acceptable closure is achieved. Expansions of talk within an episode can also occur via embedded structures or side sequences, repair sequences and so on.

Such structures also reveal the built-in, collaborative nature of interactions. Collaboration, in the guise of joint management, does not mean that talk is always harmonious and necessarily predicated on convergence of interests, since participants collaborate in conflicts as well, when interests diverge. The rules of the turn-taking system create different possibilities for structuring interactions but which possibilities are to be realized is left to those interacting. The course of interactions is also left for participants to manage locally which can be plotted turn by turn. In actual talk, therefore, the options can be regarded as *resources* which are available for strategic employment within the contingencies of a situation. Participants enact their engagement with each other. As each talk turn is produced, the option is open for the interlocutor to either link with what has gone before, to depart from it, to continue or close the interaction. The progress of talk in its turn-by-turn construction offers itself as its own evidence for how each contribution has been produced and interpreted in the light of what has gone before, and in relation to how talk was actually managed. The place of a turn in a sequence can be significant in how it is interpreted, given its retrospective and projective linkages.

Apart from structures and sub-structures of this kind, some attention has also been paid to the means by which participants achieve and sustain various forms of orientation – to each other, and to the business in hand. For co-presence alone is not sufficient to establish participation in an exchange. Work has to be done in order to establish mutual orientation as a pre-condition, as shown above in how openings are achieved. Where normal processes of initiation like partner selection by name, gaze, etc. fail to get the attention of the addressee, specific actions have been noted – re-starts, pauses, etc. – in order to achieve the desired counter-orientation. Once mutual orientation has been established, it has to be maintained and displayed and communicated as such. 'Back-channelling' strategies, and 'minimal responses' – like *uh*, *ah*, etc. – are often given, as markers of attention and orientation, but gaze, nods, body posture can be used as well. Where more than two participants are involved, spatial arrangements can be significant: face-to-face arrangements can be indicative of those actually in interaction, while side-by-side patterns evince mutual orientation with respect to a third party. Apart from the actual language used, gaze, spatial arrangements, body posture, 'back-channelling' and minimal responses etc. could also play a role in the display of orientation.

Interactants display other forms of orientation – to the reality of the unfolding sequence of talk in progress. In the flow of talk, embeddings or nestings or separated units are possible without the threat of dislocation, as noted earlier, but interactants may specifically signal their imminent departure from the current topic or focus of talk through the use of 'misplacement markers' and prefaces of various kinds to alert the interlocutor to the fact that what is about to be said must not be linked to the immediately preceding turn – the use of phrases like 'by the way', etc. Breaks in discourse coherence are attended to by both participants and the collaborative work of talk proceeds. Other interactive cues may signal alignments with another's point of view in the use of special forms of endorsements which display a speaker's sympathetic alignment with another's speech. Thus interactive support can be made a reality by the use of forms of endorsement, convergence, alignment, etc.

Talk can be organized around some common focus to which participants orientate, like *topic* (Brown and Yule 1983; Craig and Tracy 1983). The notion of topic is a complex one and open to grammatical, pragmatic, cognitive and discourse levels of investigation. There is little consensus on its description nor, as yet, a unified account of the phenomenon. In grammatical analysis, the notion of topic relates to the unit of the sentence and topic–comment relations have been analysed with respect to grammatical relations like subject–predicate. Here, the topic may be the subject noun phrase and the comment, the expansion of the topic in the rest of the sentence. In conversational analysis, topics are what users construct via their formulations within a discourse context, which they maintain via mutual orientation to a common point of reference to which utterances contribute. Members' formulations have been examined for the features or reference strategies which display such a focus – lexical items, for instance, which refer to common objects, events and the like. Members' talk identify and orientate to common points of focus in such a way that their joint and alternating formulations fit together, turn by turn, to construct the topic itself. Topics are a rich resource for conversationalists and may be chosen from the immediate context of utterance, from memory, from the preceding part of the conversation, from other conversations and so on. Talk can also focus on itself, reflexively, on the terms of its own production in *metalinguistic* or *metacommunicational* mode. Once chosen and ratified, the focus on topic has to be maintained jointly, and where topics are to be closed or changed, negotiated accordingly.

Topic introduction in a conversation generally assumes that it is *newsworthy* or 'tellable'. As Sacks (1971, in 1967–72) has pointed out, contributions are analysed in terms of 'Why that now and to me?', and where the criterion of 'tellability' is not met, talk can *fall flat*. Restrictions on topics are well known since some may be taboo in a particular situation. What not to say when and to whom requires equal attention. Talk may drift from topic to topic in *stepwise* transition without threat of dislocation. But talk can also be competitive via topic conflict. The development of topic can be pulled apart when competing aspects of the *same* topic or even different topics are attended to independently by the participants. Turn clashes against turn with the common focus being lost. Each participant connects with the content of his or her own turn while ignoring that of the interlocutor. Such instances of *turn skip* are not uncommon and *skip-connecting* procedures can be used to propel a speaker on a self-chosen path.

The emphasis in all of this is on talk-internal, micro-levels of analysis in which talk is seen as a dynamic, contextualized and particularized accomplishment undertaken and achieved by those involved. Cross-context generalities are made, but the interest, on the whole, is on the particular achievements and their specificities. All those aspects that generalities abstract out are brought back into the reckoning in this form of analysis. The turn-by-turn organization of some particular activity, under the constraint of mutual accountability, traces the course of its making, a course which builds both the 'architecture of intersubjectivity' and the specificities of situation as they are being constructed. Participants enact their engagement with each other via the turn-counter-turn pattern of exchanges which may be scrutinized for how participants manage themselves, each other and the situation within the contingencies of its making. In the effort, the study of dialogue goes further than the content of the linguistic turn alone. Turn change, turn distribution and turn sequencing, together with the environment of other turns, are as important as content when dialogue is considered as interaction.

DRAMA AND THE SYSTEMATICS OF TURN-TAKING

The dramatic text usually sets out the turn-taking options used by drama-tists to structure dialogue in the order of names or other indices attached to turns. The conversational floor is thus 'given', yet it is the product of strategic ordering and patterning. The order of turns and the sequencing patterns adopted point to the communicative situation which will be realized on stage by actors. A significant aspect of dramatic art is to be found precisely in the choice of interactants and in the strategic patterning of turn rights and turn distribution within a segment or scene. Who has rights to the floor in the pool of possible participants, and the configura-tions created by the dramatist through spoken interaction like who speaks to whom, who is not spoken to, the ratio of speech apportioned to a character relative to others (Alter 1979: 254–5), the course of the interac-tion and the outcomes jointly achieved, could all be significant. Nor is the appearance or co-presence of the dramatis personae on stage by itself sufficient for drama. Characters appearing on stage during the course of a scene have to be integrated into the turn-taking dynamics already in motion, and this applies not only to new arrivals but to those on-stage already. Floor rights have to be awarded and accepted by a speaker before speech is possible for a character – before, that is, he or she can take a turn. Similarly, a character's disengagement from speech has to be managed within the flux of speech in motion. Once the required interactants (dramatis personae) are brought into relation through speech the ensuing speech must be distributed and sequenced between them in such a way that the speech business undertaken contributes to the evolution of the situation itself, in its moment-to-moment course, turn by turn. Floor creation and floor management options are foundational aspects of dialogic, dramatic art, since they control how speech itself may function in an episode, segment or scene.

Although the purely verbal aspects of dramatic dialogue have generated much interest in the analysis of drama, the genre is basically an actional one as has been noted from Aristotle onwards in the Western tradition. The verbal dimension, although important in its own right, does not stand in isolation but contributes to and participates in the construction of the dramatic action. It is shaped in particular ways to do so, which the dialogic form, as drama's major mode of discourse enables it to do. The verbal element cannot be confined to its literary aspects alone, which though influential are not primary, for it is speech that we are dealing with, even as poetic speech, and in relation to counter-speech in the main. The dialogic scene predicates face-to-face verbal, communicative collaboration, though collaboration itself is a matter of degree. Within speech events, the exchange of speech keeps dialogue in motion, but response can be silent or non-verbal – a speaker and a listener, an addressee, are the basic components. When the *exchange* of speech is undertaken, the exchange aspects are manipulated and shaped in various ways to create the required situations. The shaping of dramatic speech in its actional and interactional mode is not dependent on literary quality alone, or even on language alone, but also on the more basic mechanisms that regulate turn change, turn order, distribution of turns, sequencing and the like, as dealt with above. The various exploitable resources of the turn-taking system and their motivated use in creating different forms of interaction are part of a dramatist's scene management strategies, interaction management contributing to the formalities of scene management in plays.

TURN CHANGE OPTIONS

Turn change can occur by current speaker selecting next, next speaker self-selecting, or the turn may lapse, in which case the speaker may incorporate the lapse as a pause and either of the earlier options can be used to relinquish the turn at the next TRP. Overlaps and gaps are to be avoided, but can occur. At first glance it would appear that the exploitation of this option is of limited significance in drama, since dramatic speech is generally regarded as tidied up speech, and smooth turn change would be the required norm, given that stage speech needs to be audible to the audience. Moreover, multi-party speech rather than two-party speech would be required, it would seem, for a dramatist's floor and interaction management skills to be properly exercised. This is not necessarily the case, although multi-party speech management offers the dramatist greater scope but greater risks as well. In dyadic interactions, the A–B–A–B. . . alternation would be the expected and unmarked pattern, which would most easily satisfy the presupposition of equal rights to the floor. Yet, variation is possible even here. Turn change must occur for dialogue and interaction to come into existence at all; but given the options for change, even this necessary and functional aspect of the form can be exploited. The option actually used and how the next speaker responds can structure the ensuing interaction in dramatically significant ways.

For instance, in the following extract, taken from the opening scene of Pinter's *The Homecoming* ([1965] 1978), two participants, Max and Lenny, father and son, are in the living room of their home. It is a domestic context, with the participants in family roles. Lenny is busy with the paper; Max comes in and initiates the interaction.

MAX   What have you done with the scissors?
    [*Pause*]
I said I'm looking for the scissors. What have you done with them?
    [*Pause*]
Did you hear me? I want to cut something out of the paper.
LENNY   I'm reading the paper.
MAX   Not that paper. I haven't even read that paper. I'm talking about last Sunday's paper. I was just having a look at it in the kitchen.
    [*Pause*]
Do you hear what I'm saying? I'm talking to you! Where's the scissors?
LENNY   [*Looking up quietly*] Why don't you shut up, you daft prat.

The turn pattern employed attempts the A–B–A–B–. . . or Max–Lenny–Max–Lenny alternation we would expect, but Lenny's turns are dominantly constructed on the turn-may-lapse option, rather than one of the speech options. The form of interaction that ensues introduces the audience without preamble into an inter-personally hostile world. With every *pause* in the text, a TRP is projected by Max, to which Lenny fails to respond. The resulting silence is thus an 'attributable' silence, here, to Lenny, which is taken as such by Max who re-initiates over and over again, incorporating Lenny's lapses into his turn, as pauses, in order to get a response from Lenny. Max's re-initiations are metacommunicative as well. He speaks about what he is doing, which is obvious to both Lenny and to us – for example, 'I said. . . ' – or about communicative conditions that obviously obtain – 'Did you hear me. . . ', 'Do you hear what I'm saying. . . ' – thus emphasizing by cues of this kind his own awareness of Lenny's intentional, non-responsiveness and the fact that the interaction is blocked. Lenny's turn lapses are part of his interactive strategy with Max, which he uses to ignore Max, the turn lapses constituting one kind of Pinter's famous silences. He communicates non-availability for speech with Max in this instance. Max's strategy is to override the fact that Lenny's silently communicated wish is to be left alone. He continues to extend his turn by repeated attempts to get a response from Lenny in defiance of the opt-out of talk displayed by Lenny. Moreover, Max's turns contain questions, with the normative expectancy of response built in. But none is forthcoming. After one grudging concession, Lenny makes explicit his rejection of Max, with speech, this time. Their interactive strategies do not *other-orientate*. Lenny attempts to coerce Max into the silence he desires; Max, in reverse, attempts to coerce Lenny into speech. Speech and counter, lack-of-speech play out mutual provocation.

This opening segment structured through systematic choices sets the tone for the general tenor of relationships in the play. By these and other means the drama of communicative frustration is foregrounded, and the responsive sharing of subjectivities remains both unrealized and undesired across the play. The inter-personal reality created in this opening segment is reinforced by other instances in which options to speak or not to speak, to respond or not to respond, and speech itself, are used to humiliate, undermine, coerce, insult and exploit others in other segments of inter-action.

Intra-turn pauses, in which speakers break the flow of their speech by punctuating the turn itself with brief silences, are also possible. Some pauses are filled with *erms* and *ers*, and lengthened syllables and the like, but some are not. Hesitation, for instance, is an example of an intra-turn pause, but such pauses have different functions. Intra-turn pauses create ambiguities since they may be misjudged as TRPs or used by another speaker to grab the floor. Long pauses by a speaker place a burden of tolerance on the listener and could create uncertainties especially when the pause is respected as not a TRP and part of the speaker's turn. Chafe has argued that pauses and other kinds of disfluency are production strategies which reveal the speaker's attempts to bring together thought and language, or memory and language. If memory can be regarded as a vast store of information and experience, salient aspects of it can be activated, brought into consciousness and into speech for some communicative or interactive purpose. Hesitation pauses can be interpreted not only as attempts to find the right focus for what to say next but also how to say it. As Chafe notes,

> A speaker does not follow a clear, well-traveled path, but must find his way through territory not traversed before, where pauses, changes of direction, and retracing of steps are quite to be expected. The fundamental reason for hesitating is that speech production is an act of creation.
>
> (Chafe 1985: 79)

In dramatic speech, especially in long turns in which the character relates events of the past, pauses can be used to signify thoughtfulness or attempts to recall or focus on relevant aspects, or even a kind of privacy or self-enclosure as if lost in memory, or lost in thought. Even if the text does not supply such pauses, an actor may well introduce them if such effects are desired. Similarly, where self-deliberation is enacted as in some Shakespearean soliloquies – Hamlet's 'To be or not to be. . . ' speech, for instance – the introduction, lengthening and shortening of pauses across the soliloquy could serve to create the fiction that the rhythm of the thought process itself is being realized. Many of Chekhov's characters incorporate pauses in their speeches which add to the sense of an 'internality' in the characters that is not fully expressed – especially as the talk often tails off mid-sentence into a pause – and left unfinished for the others to infer the rest. Much is said, but much remains unsaid which these strategies make clear. The pauses in these instances often also give the appearance of characters enacting the disjointedness of thought as well, as if responsive more to the internal workings of their minds which has to be brought into relation with the demands of external life. The said and the unsaid thus modulate each other in communication. As Walker notes, thinking and speaking are generally seen as separate activities and mutually exclusive, so that those who are supposed to 'think on their feet' are objects of admiration (Walker 1985: 56). Pauses can signify the gaps between the two activities and dramatize the toil of speech to express the movement of thought. Pauses may also signal uncertainty, lack of confidence, or may be used by a speaker to create suspense, or to highlight something about to be said. As production strategies they refer to the speaker, but their use interactively is important, since how respondents react and take up or drop the implications of such speaker strategies is important and will affect and slant the course of the dramatic business in hand.

Unlike intra-turn pauses, gaps in speech are often to be found between the boundaries of turns, and, according to the turn-taking rules, gaps are to be minimized if possible. Because of the distribution of gaps at turn boundaries and also because in duration they can appear more like pauses than lapses, they have also been called *switching pauses* and there can be difficulties in working out who 'owns' the gap, whether it is the first or second speaker. Different qualities can enter the interaction in the introduction of these elements, especially when second turns begin after a gap. For instance, if Cordelia's response of 'Nothing' when Lear demanded her to speak of her love for him had been accomplished with the usual split-second timing between the end of his turn and the beginning of hers, her reply could be assessed on an ascending scale from certainty to arrogance. A gap before speaking could mitigate – signify reluctance to speak, or her own sense of the inevitability of her speech. The personality that we create for characters through the inferences we make about their behaviour would certainly be affected by these elements, as would our assessment of the situation itself. Cordelia would be viewed far more sympathetically in the second instance rather than the first, especially if intonation were used to underscore the effect of the gap. A gap before speaking in response, especially in cases where the first turn constrains the second as in commands or requests, could signify defiance or refusal, or even politeness. At other times, gaps could enact the 'think before you speak' maxim, thus making the response more deliberate.

The gap, when not filled in any way, can bring a segment of interaction to a close, but since silence in all these instances is interrelated with speech, it is often interpreted within the environment of the speech in which it occurs. In Chekhov's *The Cherry Orchard* (1923), towards the end of Act 2, the conversation moves into profound topics of life and death and notions of progress and failure, a little after which all conversation comes to a close. The stage directions instruct that 'All sit plunged in thought. Perfect stillness. . . ' The atmosphere of the previous section of speech spills over into the silence which makes it a communal silence filled with individual thought. The Act had opened in similar fashion with characters sitting plunged in thought, and, as the second silence approaches, Trofimov ends a long speech declaring that serious conversations and talk in general are empty, since nothing gets done, and that silence is better. The quality of silence that follows is coloured by the sentiments expressed earlier, and by the intensity of listening and interactive attention that have been demanded, while the unsaid implications of all that has been said leave their mark communally and individually. The silence looks forward, too, since the wayfarer arrives and a sense of threat with him, which is made sharper by contrast with what has gone before. Its placing colours its functions.

The closure aspects of gaps can be used to dramatize the limits or impossibilities of communication itself via speech as often in Pinter. In *Silence*, the following interaction occurs:

BATES Will we meet to-night?
ELLEN I don't know.
 [*Pause*]
BATES Come with me to-night.
ELLEN Where?
BATES Anywhere. For a walk.
 [*Pause*]
ELLEN I don't want to walk.
BATES Why not?
 [*Pause*]
ELLEN I want to go somewhere else.
 [*Pause*]
BATES Where?
ELLEN I don't know.

            (Pinter [1969] 1978: 205–6)

Pinter's *pauses* in this extract can function as *gaps* which disjoint the flow of interaction and divide it into different interactive segments. But the time duration of the textual *pause* in performance is important, whether intra-turn or not, when it takes its place within the stream of speech, and there is no clear definition of it. Pauses, as significant lack of phonation in discourse studies, are seen to be meaningful from about 10 milliseconds, but more recently .5 second has been considered, although .1 second has also been used (Walker 1985: 61). This does not include pauses that use fillers of various kinds. In the above extract, if Bates were to re-initiate within a minimum time span, the whole interaction would seem more directed, cohesive and integrated than if the time span were lengthened and the instruction to pause were used as gaps to punctuate and separate the different segments of interaction. In the first case, Bates could seem to be more insistent, and Ellen as more actively disinclined to accept Bates' advances or as more evasive. At any rate, the interaction could be performed as if both characters are more personally and inter-personally involved.

Lengthened gaps or medial closures between segments of the interaction after an exchange make the longer silence that follows differently meaningful. Each initiation seems blocked, so that the silence can be interpreted as a planning silence on the part of the initiator attempting to cope within the contingencies and tension of threatened closure of talk itself as displayed by the addressee. The effort to maintain even minimal contact through speech gets foregrounded, since alternative strategies have to be found, not only to get talk off the ground, but to maintain even a vestige of direction or development. The timing and duration of the gaps can dramatize the afflictions of speech when initiation and response are such arduous, time-consuming labours.

The silences are jointly produced, and shared, but different meanings accrue depending on whether the silence is attributed to Bates or to Ellen. When Ellen is in focus the silences she claims within the adjacency pairs of invitations and so on can signify a kind of letting go of the effort itself; her responses are mostly refusals. When Bates re-initiates, the silence becomes 'his' as well, which retrospectively makes it a time of ordeal and uncertainty for him, resulting in yet another effort being undertaken again. The slow motion rendering of initiation and response reveals the rickety or tremulous state of inter-subjectivity in speech which is generally hidden from view when split-second alternations are accomplished.

Silences, in the guise of gaps and lapses, can be used for conflictual purposes, as we saw in the case of Lenny's turn lapses in the extract from *The Homecoming*. Deborah Tannen, in her analysis of Pinter's *Betrayal*, has shown that silences occur at points where information to be given can be explosive. It can also be used to diffuse potential conflict as she also shows when analysing a passage from Mattison's *Great Wits* (Tannen 1990: 260). In all these cases, silences are not seen merely as the negation, or absence, of speech. They function as communicative and meaningful elements in interaction and as resources to be used. Within speech events there is the silence of listening, or the silence of participation as in a Quaker meeting, and active silences as in inferencing procedures used in communication.

Thus, there are, as Saville-Troika (1985) notes, different ways of assessing silences in speech, since they are inter-dependent. On the one hand are those that depend on the previous utterance for their meaning: silences in response to greetings, questions, offers, etc. are 'fraught with propositional meaning' (*ibid.*: 6). So also are those that are played in response to 'speech acts' as sequels, so that silence can be used to 'question, deny, warn, threaten, insult, request, command. . .' (*ibid.*) with both illocutionary force and perlocutionary effect. (See Chapter 4.) Silences in delayed responses to questions or in the use of pauses in institutional settings like a trial are often assessed as possible evidence of lying or vulnerability, although there are contradictory points of view on this, since advice given to witnesses by own lawyers is 'think before you speak', but on the other hand, hesitation in speech can be interpreted negatively (Walker 1985).

The timing of silences, and their meanings, are, therefore, highly variable and context-dependent. Tannen (1985), in her analysis of New York (Jewish) speech, reveals the misperceptions that result when different conversational styles are used by participants. A fast pace of speech, swift turns, shifts in pitch and amplitude, jumping from topic to topic, preferences for narratives of personal experience and for overlapping speech characterize styles favoured by the New Yorkers under scrutiny. Silence in these circumstances is an enormous threat, although the question of whether silences used are too little or too much is assessed in relative terms. Added to this are cultural values associated with fast or slow speech which includes pauses and silences – with speakers being assessed not in relation to their own privileged styles but in relation to those of the assessors. Whereas non-New Yorkers adjudge the pace and preferences of New York speech to be 'crowding' and domineering, faster speakers could adjudge their opposite numbers to be unco-operative, sullen or stupid. What is or not a pause, a gap, etc. would be assessed in relation to expectations derived from the normative modes of performing them in the sub-group or group of which the participants are members, and not absolutely.

There are also genres of silence which presuppose mental or emotional activity like prayer and meditation, of religious ecstasy, madness, outrage, etc., when words are said to *fail*. Proverbs and idioms encapsulate folk wisdom about a culture's attitudes to silence. One may be seen but not heard, and silence is golden, but words could also be taken out of one's mouth. There are silences that are deafening in their absences when something expected is not forthcoming from an interlocutor. And there is the silence of endings when nothing more is possible – in plays or in life when contact is cut, and the parting of the ways is ensured. Cultures have institutionally located places for silence, like libraries and churches. Groups may have membership silences if they have taken vows of silence, and taboo silences operate in some communities so that direct communication with certain members like chiefs, or mothers of wives, is forbidden. Silence can signal deference, status, attitude and the like (Saville-Troika 1985: 16–17).

Interactions can also be structured along the other options of the turn-taking system. In multi-party speech, the options available for speaker change can be exploited in dramatically significant ways. The norm of equal rights to the floor may either be respected or flouted with differing consequences. In the case of flouts, imbalances can accrue, since speech is a form of dramatic life for characters and the privileging of one or the other through the use of turn change options will inevitably exclude some other character. How and why such imbalances are created and how they are managed can be of interest in a scene.

Such is the case in Synge's *Riders to the Sea* from which our next extract is taken. Maurya is waiting for confirmation of the death of her son Michael on the sea. The two sisters, Nora and Cathleen, have hidden the clothes of a man that have been washed up by the sea and which they have not had time to examine in order to determine whether or not they are indeed Michael's. The possible death of Michael leaves Bartley the youngest and last-remaining son and he is determined to take the horses to Connemara like his father and brothers before him. Maurya, having lost husband, elder and middle son to the sea, does not wish him to go. The extract enacts the confrontation between mother and son before his departure. The turns have been numbered for easy reference.

NORA   [*looking out*] He's coming now, and he in a hurry.

1. BARTLEY   [*comes in and looks round the room; speaking sadly and quietly*] Where is the bit of new rope, Cathleen, was bought in Connemara?

2. CATHLEEN   [*coming down*] Give it to him, Nora; it's on a nail by the white boards. I hung it up this morning, for the pig with the black feet was eating it.

3. NORA   [*giving him a rope*] Is that it, Bartley?

4. MAURYA   [*as before*] You'd do right to leave that rope, Bartley, hanging by the boards. [BARTLEY *takes the rope*] It will be wanting in this place, I'm telling you, if Michael is washed up tomorrow morning, or the next morning, or any morning of the week, for it's a deep grave we'll make him by the grace of God.

5. BARTLEY   [*beginning to work with the rope*] I've no halter the way I can ride down on the mare, but I must go now quickly. This is the one boat going for two weeks or beyond it, and the fair will be a good fair for horses I heard them saying below.

6. MAURYA   It's a hard thing they'll be saying below if the body is washed up and there's no man in it to make the coffin, and I after giving a big price for the finest white boards you'd find in Connemara. [*She looks round at the boards*]

7. BARTLEY   How would it be washed up, and we after looking each day for nine days, and a strong wind blowing a while back from the west and south?

8. MAURYA   If it isn't found itself, that wind is rising from the sea, and there was a star up against the moon, and it rising in the night. If it was a hundred horses or a thousand horses you had itself, what is the price of a thousand horses against a son where there is one son only?

9. BARTLEY   [*working at the halter, to* CATHLEEN] Let you go down each day, and see the sheep aren't jumping in on the rye, and if the jobber comes you can sell the pig with the black feet if there is a good price going.

10. MAURYA   How would the like of her get a good price for a pig?

11. BARTLEY   [*to* CATHLEEN] If the west wind holds with the last bit of the moon let you and Nora get up weed enough for another cock for the kelp. It's hard set we'll be from this day with no one in it but one man to work.

12. MAURYA   It's hard set we'll be surely the day you're drown'd with the rest. What way will I live and the girls with me, and I an old woman looking for the grave?
[BARTLEY *lays down the halter, takes off his old coat, and puts on a newer one of the same flannel*]

13. BARTLEY   [*to* NORA] Is she coming to the pier?

14. NORA   [*looking out*] She's passing the green head and letting fall her sails.

15. BARTLEY   [*getting his purse and tobacco*] I'll have half an hour to go down, and you'll see me coming again in two days, or in three days, or maybe in four days if the wind is bad.

16. MAURYA   [*turning round to the fire, and putting her shawl over her head*].   Isn't it a hard and cruel man won't hear a word from an old woman, and she holding him from the sea?

17. CATHLEEN   It's the life of a young man to be going on the sea, and who would listen to an old woman with one thing and she saying it over?

18. BARTLEY   [*taking the halter*] I must go now quickly. I'll ride down on the red mare, and the grey pony'll ride behind me. . . The blessing of God on you. [*He goes out*]

19. MAURYA   [*crying out as he is in the door way*] He's gone now, God spare us, and we'll not see him again. He's gone now, and when the black night is falling I'll have no son left me in the world.

20. CATHLEEN   Why wouldn't you give him your blessing and he looking round in the door? Isn't it sorrow enough is on every one

in this house without your sending him out with an unlucky word behind him, and a hard word in his ear?

(Synge [1968] 1980: 5–6)

Nora's turn on which the extract begins functions both to close the previous interaction and to prepare the audience and the characters for Bartley's arrival, and is a 'noticing' conversation-wise. On his arrival, Bartley self-selects his turn and initiates himself into the family group.

The turn-taking patterns from now on are constructed along basically two options – current speaker selects next, and next speaker self-selects. On the current speaker selection/non-selection axis turns the management of this critical encounter among the family members. Across the extract, the three siblings select each other by name and gaze, and the turn passes among them. On the whole, Maurya self-selects – in fact, more than self-selects, she turn-grabs, since she initiates herself into the interaction, unlicensed, against the rights of previously selected speakers. In the central section, Maurya and Bartley interact briefly, but though Maurya selects Bartley by name, appropriate pronoun or gaze, he never names her for selection. He speaks to all present, generally, when he has not nominated one of his sisters.

The first three turns in the segment form a round of speech among brother and sisters from which Maurya is excluded. Bartley selects Cathleen, who responds and selects Nora, who responds and selects Bartley. It is only in turn 4 that Maurya speaks, cutting across what is legitimately Bartley's turn. Having taken the turn, she addresses Bartley, and holds the floor in alternation with him for two more exchanges. In turn 9 Bartley chooses Cathleen, but Maurya turn-grabs again and in turn 10 addresses Bartley. Bartley does not reciprocate, but chooses Cathleen in turn 11. Maurya turn-grabs again and addresses Bartley; again Bartley does not respond, but chooses Nora in turn 13, to which Nora responds. In turn 16, Maurya's self-selection is a kind of self-defeat, since she addresses no one and withdraws from interaction by turning her gaze to the fire and away from Bartley, whom she addresses as the 'overhearer' of her speech by using the third person form – 'a hard and cruel man' – instead of some more direct or personal address form. Cathleen self-selects to protest to Maurya. Bartley self-selects and departs on a blessing to the family in leave-taking. Although Maurya speaks next, it is not to close the adjacency pair; it remains a 'noticeable absence' and the extract ends with Cathleen taking issue with Maurya on her omission. The unfinished leave-taking on Maurya's part forms a poignant contrast since the right to the second part of the pair is wholly hers as mother to her departing son, which she voluntarily lets go. By comparison with the effort expended in having her turn earlier, her denial to herself of this right to respond to Bartley is highly marked. No one picks up the omission for her, and Cathleen in the post-sequence explicitly foregrounds the omission.

The basic conflict is between mother and son, but the turn-taking options adopted delay bringing the two into contact. If contact is achieved, it is not through Bartley's initiative, since speaker selection strategies adopted reveal that Bartley does not willingly engage with his mother at all: he never selects her as he does his sisters. All the effort is on Maurya's side, at some cost to herself. She turn-grabs and will have her say, but there is little responsiveness or reciprocity on Bartley's part, which contrasts with his collaborative interactions with his sisters. This reduced engagement with Maurya has the effect of diffusing the emotional explosiveness of the scene – it is played out in a much more muted but fateful key. Against the protective wall of speech which the sisters build around their brother, Maurya stands isolated, with the force not only of the sea but of tradition ranged against her, played out in the sisters' acceptance, without counter, of their brother's decision. Only once does Bartley overtly counter Maurya, in his taking the rope against her stated wish (turn 4), but even this is non-verbally performed and simultaneously with her speech, since she continues with her turn.

Topic management is another interactive variable used in this extract with dramatic relevance. Joint orientation to topic can bind together sequences of turns and interactants towards a common purpose, but this does not occur in the mother–son exchanges in the extract. Bartley's topics have everything to do with his impending departure. His speech focuses on the rope, the halter, the wind, the farm business to be looked after in his absence, and the boat he must shortly board – the sequence of topics forming a pattern that reinforces the certainty of departure. Maurya's focuses on Michael's body being washed up, the coffin to be made, rituals to the dead, derision at the idea of Cathleen taking his place, the possibility of his drowning. Neither orients sympathetically to the other's concerns. When Maurya engages with Bartley's topics, it is usually in order to invert what he says, since she partly repeats his speech but changes it to suit her own purposes by turning the drift of the talk away from the course on which he has set it. For instance, to Bartley's 'the fair will be a good fair for horses I heard them saying below', she responds with 'It's a hard thing they'll be saying below if the body is washed up'; and again, to Bartley's 'It's hard set we'll be from this day with no one in it but one man to work', she counters, 'It's hard set we'll be surely the day you're drown'd'. Maurya's turns also include questions, which are not answered by Bartley, since he generally chooses someone else in his turn. His strategy is to let drop Maurya's topics and stick to his own. Consequently, Maurya's attempts to create any form of interaction with Bartley that can be meaningful to her are frustrated by his blocking and deflecting strategies. Each, on the whole, skips the other's turn and creates coherence on the content of his or her own. Each set of turns develops unilaterally, especially Bartley's, rather than enmeshing with the other's speech. Speech and counter-speech, in effect, play out mutual isolation.

Both turn strategies and topic management strategies reinforce the alignments that have been noted among the characters – the three children in one camp, with Maurya in another, in a youth versus age conflict – but they also provide a situation jointly created by all of them, which is important for our understanding of the play's overall concerns. What such a contrast brings to the fore are two sets of 'realities' which are also two conflicting aspects of the same situation. The conflict is sustained here because Maurya alone articulates one reality of the situation which the others leave unsaid: the issue of death – especially the reality of Bartley's possible death, which she makes her reality. She speaks in the role of mother whose sole concern is her only remaining son. Bartley, however, plays not only the role of the son, but also that of the 'man-of-the-house' (Beckerman 1970: 64–8), indeed, the only remaining one, and the conflict is resolved between the two roles by him playing the latter in such a way that the former has no place and is closed to negotiation, his reality being the necessity to carry on with the responsibilities of the household like his father and brothers before him. Bartley's turns focus on business to do with his departure, having nothing at all to do with the personal risks he is also taking. Maurya's turns deal with the personal fear of his death, and have nothing at all to do with his departure. In this, she refuses to accept his other role as he refuses to accept the legitimacy of hers. Her enacted reality is put into sharp focus with a question to him which no one answers, and which makes him opt out of interaction with her altogether – 'If it was a hundred horses or a thousand horses you had itself, what is the price of a thousand horses against a son where there is one son only?'

The sisters play out their supporting roles to the brother as 'man-of-the-house'. The only time Cathleen uncharacteristically butts in is to challenge Maurya and to simultaneously articulate the reality that they too have been enacting: 'It's the life of a young man to be going on the sea, and who would listen to an old woman with one thing and she saying it over?' This counter-reality has been given added weight by the non-verbal stage activity which Bartley attends to as well. The business of the rope which initiated the interaction has also taken its course in the action of the segment; his taking the rope, making the halter, changing his coat, collecting his tobacco and pouch and the halter, enact along another dimension the impending loss of her son under Maurya's very eyes, as the son's role is negated in the upsurge of activities of the man-of-the-house. The ragged leave-taking refuses any easy resolution to the conflict, since the two realities are yoked together – the stark economic necessities *of* their lives and the personal costs of these necessities *in* their lives. There is no resolution here, which dramatizes, with tragic force, the conditions of living of the Aran islanders who had inspired Synge's drama.

Dramatic interactions use such options with creative skill and with great variation. Turn skips or poor or perfunctory topic orientation to another's turn can create monologic effects, and effects of isolation or non-communication which are often used systematically in Beckett, and post-Beckett drama. Options create their own dynamic which can be varied to create very different dramatic episodes and segments and it is this creative aspect of their use which is being focused on here. A very different type of interaction and a different dramatic effect is achieved by exploiting the use and the consequences of turn-taking options in the extract given below. And it is a different dramatist.

In Act 1 of *The Cherry Orchard*, a segment is about to close since some of the dramatis personae are about to depart. Lyubov begins the departure sequence.

LYUBOV   [*kisses her brother, then* VARYA] Well, go to bed. . . You are older too, Leonid.
PISHTCHIK   [*follows her*] I suppose it's time we were asleep. . . Ugh! my gout. I'm staying the night! Lyubov Andreyevna, my dear soul, if you could. . . tomorrow morning. . . 240 roubles.
GAEV   That's always his story.
PISHTCHIK   240 roubles. . . to pay the interest on my mortgage.
LYUBOV   My dear man, I have no money.
PISHTCHIK   I'll pay it back my dear. . . a trifling sum.
LYUBOV   Oh, well, Leonid will give it to you. . . You give him the money, Leonid.
GAEV   Me give it him! Let him wait till he gets it!
LYUBOV   It can't be helped, give it him. He needs it. He'll pay it back.
(Chekhov [1923] 1971: 77)

Turn change, topic and pause strategies are all involved in constructing the action in the extract. The segment begins ostensibly as a closure to the action of the day and managed by Lyubov who extends concern to Leonid. The action of the segment, however, is hijacked by Pishtchik and his concerns about the roubles to be paid. Turn change is effected as in the previous section by self-selection or turn grabbing, or current speaker selecting next. Self-selection and turn grabbing dominate as the more effective strategies. But the management of topic is the most effective, and it is Pishtchik's exertions that accomplish this. His first turn is a grab since Lyubov had selected Leonid/Gaev. But since her own turn had a double focus – the business of going to bed addressed to Varya and Leonid and then the topic of Leonid's appearance addressed to Leonid – Pishtchik semi-legitimizes his turn by orientating to the first topic of going to bed, and then changing the focus in his own turn to himself and his gout, and finally brings in the topic he wants addressed, and this time by choosing Lyubov by name. The response from Lyubov is delayed because of Gaev's self-selected intervention and Pishtchik's second self-selected turn that follows. Pishtchik's quick second turn across what is Lyubov's right to speak brings the topic of his need for the money to the foreground again. The detail is repeated, especially the sum needed, and the risk that the stage business would go off in its previously set direction is countered. His topic is thus firmly anchored and becomes everybody else's topic as well. A brief exchange occurs between Lyubov, who finally takes her delayed turn, and himself, with his affairs as the focus. She refuses, but on yet another appeal Lyubov *passes* the turn and the responsibility for executing her own decision to Leonid/Gaev whom she selects by name and the two interact about Pishtchik in his presence but make him the bystander.

Turn distribution among all of them is more or less equal, except for Gaev who has only two, shorter turns by comparison with the other two. Yet the responsive structure is fractured by the turn grabs, especially at the beginning. Pishtchik is the disadvantaged participant, since not only is the stage business set on a different course, but his own affairs are risky and personally face-threatening since he needs money. By the end of the segment, not only has he got his affairs to the foreground, but he has got the money, too. Yet, he is not overtly dominant. Apart from the brief exchange in the middle of the segment with Lyubov, he is not addressed directly. He talks, but nobody talks to him. He is the talked-about in his presence rather than the one talked to. Gaev in his first turn sidelines him by the use of the third person. At the end, both Lyubov and Gaev refer to him in the third person. His turn style, too, is hesitant, pause ridden, elliptical. His pauses, however, re-focus his speech strategically – to get the topic of money into the foreground, to minimize the debt, to cue rather than state his need. The verbs are left out in his request, but the detail of the exact sum of money needed is repeated across his two initial turns. For all this, his turn grabs had got everybody's attention on to his affairs. And even when he is not the speaker or the spoken-to, it is his affairs that are central. His topic becomes everyone's topic and his affairs are attended to and concluded by others, but to his satisfaction. Even if he does not dominate as speaker, his affairs do, precisely because he had played the resource of topic and the collaborative possibilities it entails, which the others carry through. Turn change possibilities do not allow him to dominate as they did Bartley in the previous section. His strategies are more like Maurya's in turn grabbing, and he is like Maurya, too, in being sidelined by others' turns; but, unlike Maurya, his topic is shared by all, so that his stage influence in the interaction and the course it takes is greater.

Other options at TRP include forms of behaviour which bring interactants into competition for the floor and these include interruptions and overlaps. The overall convention in these cases is that one speaker speaks at a time and, therefore, the other(s) must drop out. Who interrupts whom in plays, who drops out and who preserves and maintains the initiative can be significant, for such choices create forms of inter-personal drama in their own right. The outcomes of such competition in favour of one or another character may also set the course of events along one path rather than another. Such conflicts over the right to speak may also involve opposing forces and points of view about dramatically significant matters. Whose will prevails can influence the course of action in a play.

An instance of this kind can be seen in the division of the kingdom scene in *King Lear* in the interaction between Kent and Lear (1.1.119–66). The context of this scene is well known. Lear has cast off Cordelia, disclaiming 'all my paternal care/Propenquity and property of blood' – with 'thou my sometime daughter'. Kent self-selects and intervenes, first formally:

KENT   Good my liege –

which Lear interrupts:

LEAR   Peace, Kent!. . .

Lear then holds the turn in a long speech commanding Kent to 'Come not between the dragon and his wrath. . . ', reaffirming his banishment of Cordelia and bestowing all on his daughters and sons-in-law. Given the one-speaker-speaks-at-a-time rule, Kent has to remain silent while this turn (of about eighteen lines) takes its course. At the end of this, Kent re-cycles his intervention and claims the floor again:

KENT   Royal Lear,
Whom I have ever honour'd as my king,
Lov'd as my father, as my master follow'd,
As my great patron thought on in my prayers –

which Lear interrupts again. Kent's turn here is a preamble – a kind of preparatory pre-sequence – establishing his credentials to speak on contentious matters to come, but he is not allowed to get far, since Lear cuts him short.

LEAR   The bow is bent and drawn; make from the shaft.

At this, Kent, refusing to be silenced any longer, launches into and holds his turn in a long speech denouncing Lear's folly.

KENT   Let it fall rather, though the fork invade
The region of my heart. Be Kent unmannerly
When Lear is mad. What wouldst thou do, old man?
Think'st thou that duty shall have dread to speak
When power to flattery bows? To plainness honour's bound
When majesty falls to folly. Reserve thy state;
And in thy best consideration check
This hideous rashness. Answer my life my judgement:
Thy youngest daughter does not love thee least;
Nor are those empty-hearted whose low sounds
Reverb no hollowness.

Lear hears him out for the first time, but makes explicit in his turn that Kent is an unlicensed speaker and cautions silence.

LEAR   Kent, on thy life, no more!

which Kent rejects and counters pointedly:

KENT   My life I never held but as a pawn
To wage against thine enemies; nor fear to lose it,
Thy safety being my motive.

There follows a brief exchange when Kent is not only forbidden to speak but commanded to remove himself from the scene of speech participation itself, which is then 'negotiated', contended over.

LEAR   Out of my sight!
KENT   See better, Lear; and let me remain
The true blank of thine eye.

LEAR   Now by Apollo –

a King's turn which Kent interrupts:

KENT   Now, by Apollo, King,
Thou swear'st thy Gods in vain.

which provokes Lear to apoplectic rage.

LEAR   O vassal! miscreant!
[*Laying his hand on his sword*]

This causes Albany and Cornwall together to self-select with turn overlap
to intervene:

ALBANY
and CORNWALL   } Dear Sir, forbear.

Kent, however, takes his turn, regardless:

KENT   Do:
Kill thy physician, and the fee bestow
Upon the foul disease. Revoke thy gift,
Or, whilst I can vent clamor from my throat,
I'll tell thee thou dost evil.

Lear responds in a long speech of about fourteen lines accusing Kent of
treason and banishes him from the kingdom. Kent accepts this with a
farewell to Lear, bestows a blessing on Cordelia, delivers a parting shot
at Goneril and Regan and exits on a general polite leave-taking of the
assembled company.

The extract shows turn change in variation, effected after competition
and struggle for the floor, or in smooth transition, in the middle of the
extract, though interruption occurs again towards the end, this time
initiated by Kent. Lear's refusal to allow Kent to speak in the interruptions
at the beginning has its corollary in Lear's refusal to listen once Kent does
speak. The interruptions, as well as Lear's monopolizing of the floor in
his own turn, deny Kent any speaking rights at all. When Kent finally wins
the floor, the very resistance he has encountered adds to the force of his
speech, since Kent not only speaks, but speaks out. Although the turn
change proceeds without interruption, Lear does not license him as an
interactant. Kent has to speak and continue speaking, against the grain of
Lear's resistance.

It is interesting, too, how turn length is manipulated between these two
in the mainly K–L–K–L–K–L–. . . alternation. Lear had begun in domi-

nance, not only in having the upper hand through office and occasion and in his control of floor rights, but also in the length of his turns. Once Kent gains equal rights to the floor the ratio of speech length changes, for Kent's speech presence is the stronger as he denounces Lear in his own longer and shorter speeches. Lear's own turns are basically one-clause turns at this point, but make very clear his explicit refusal to license Kent as interactant, to deprive him of speech itself on this occasion. The interruption of Lear by Kent is, of course, a highly charged option to have used at that point in the sequence. It flouts accepted protocol, is a personally insulting form of behaviour and so on, and becomes the pretext to raise the temperature of the interaction in such a way that a swift closure becomes desirable and possible. The segment does close soon thereafter, but not before Lear asserts his dominance once again in his long speech of banishment.

Lear's overall interactive strategy is characterized by overt and covert attempts to frustrate Kent's right to the floor or to speech. Three strategies are used: he interrupts Kent, which Kent forbears more than once; he uses long turns which stop Kent's access to the floor; and he explicitly forbids Kent to speak, characterizing him as an unlicensed speaker, and thus speaking 'out of turn'. Kent, in response, first lets the interruptions pass, and gives up any claim to the floor when Lear is speaking in the long turns. But, finally, he takes the floor and holds it, explicitly unlicensed though he is, even at the cost of getting Lear off the floor by interruption. Lear, as King, is in control of the turn-taking system in force in this scene. It is he who had nominated the order of turns for the sisters, and others, before Kent's interruption. For this is a formal scene with crucial matters of state – the succession – being enacted. Kent's challenges to Lear on speaking rights, as much as what he says, are highly marked behaviour, and are doubly conflictual. The battle over the right to speak is also a battle over two versions of the 'truth' of what is being enacted, Kent's and Lear's, one of which can be said and the other cannot. Kent's is precisely the version that Lear does not want spoken as the tussle for the floor dramatizes, and, when spoken, will not hear. It is the speaking itself as much as what is spoken to which Lear objects; for Lear, here, brooks no dissent. Agreement or silence are the only possible responses which, as King, Lear will permit.

Coercive interactions can be the product of other strategies. In the handkerchief scene in *Othello* (3.4.35–96), topic is the resource used. Here, Othello sticks, turn after turn, to the subject of the whereabouts of the handkerchief which he had given Desdemona, rather than responding to the subjects she initiates, in order to force Desdemona to give him the speech he wants – a confession of her presumed adultery. The double bind operative in such coercions is evident here, since either she speaks as Othello wants her to or she does not speak at all. His strategy attempts to force her to use her turn rights to do his speaking for him, to channel her speech into his mould rather than her own.

Interruptions, however, are a useful resource for the dramatist. They are a potentially conflictual form of turn change, and structuring a dialogic segment through the use of this option can bring opposition, conflict and tension into the interaction and the dramatic action with great economy. On the other hand, how the character who is interrupted deals with it is equally important, since inter-personal tension or harmony is jointly produced by those interacting. For instance, a character who is constantly interrupted by others but who does not make a counter-bid for the floor can be interpreted as the weaker character. 'Talk, talk, talk' may be a source of pleasure in drama, but it can also be a form of power, and speakers who accrue to themselves the rights and privileges of speech may be the more dominant characters. By the same token, those who consistently have speech wrested away from them will be seen as in unequal relation with the more masterful ones (Bentley 1965). How interruptions are handled may also be significant, since inter-personal battles can be won not only by force, but also by irony, humour or by some other means. The tables could very well be turned on the interrupter by the interrupted, the responsive dimension in dialogue being as integral to the situation as it is. For instance, the use of metacommunicative devices can bring the interlocutor's interruptive style itself into the talk as the topic, which could be conflictually, co-operatively or comically negotiated.

Forms of simultaneous speech like overlaps and interruptions are used judiciously and economically in drama, given the audience's need to follow what is being said. They also count among the more dispreferred forms of turn change, given the one-speaker-speaks-at-a-time rule. Yet, even such risky options may be used systematically as a dialogic device, as Caryl Churchill does in her play *Top Girls* (1982), especially in Act 1. Her notes in the play inform the reader of the turn-taking strategies she has chosen to adopt, with examples. Two of the three kinds she mentions are turn-change strategies; the other has to do with orientation to topic. Generally, turn change is smoothly achieved, and sequencing follows the expected pattern, turn relating to previous turn; but characters may also start speaking before the other has finished. Such instances are notated with/in the text, and constitute interruption and partial overlap. In addition, characters may continue speaking right through another's speech so that the marked option of continuous simultaneous speech is used without one party dropping out. And finally, speech follows on, not from the preceding turn but from the one before; a character's turn skips the previous speaker's and orients not to the prior turn but to one earlier in the co-text, either one's own or someone else's. This last option creates *schisms* in the talk with two sets of interactions going on simultaneously, or provides a kind of monologic style within the dialogues through continued self-orientation across others' contributions.

The characters are drawn from different periods of history and from different cultures, and are both fictional and historical: Lady Nijo, a thirteenth-century courtesan in Japan who became a Buddhist nun after losing the Emperor's favour; Pope Joan, who disguised herself as a man and became Pope in the ninth century; Dull Gret, a Dutch female warrior, who was painted driving out devils from Hell; Isabella Bird, a Victorian explorer; Patient Griselda, from Chaucer's *Canterbury Tales*; and a modern business executive, Marlene. The characters meet in a contemporary restaurant to celebrate Marlene's promotion. Churchill's variations on turn transitions and speakers' orientation exploit the less used options of turn-taking, with intriguing, interpretative consequences. Self-oriented turn skips could symbolize the fact of alienation from each other in women's history, and the singularity of a 'top girl's' life in her own time given their exceptional careers and the lack of a tradition into which various 'top girls' could be inserted. Competition for turns could be read as the negative side of such isolation, the inability to establish contact in equality with others of like kind – for the women are cast as egotistical speakers who manifest the inability to *listen* to each other in these instances and to make a reality of co-operative reciprocity in speech, since attentive listening is an interactive resource. But overlaps are sometimes also used to signal the reality of attentiveness and eagerness to contribute to the other's speech, and to signal solidarity. On the other hand, simultaneous speech also makes a reality of different strands, or narratives, of women's experience across time, merging or blending together to produce, from a listener's point of view, noise, a babble of voices (women's talk, in male parlance), not discourse, or speech, though each strand is shaped as and in language, and 'owned' by the women as their meaningful speech. The stories they tell have common themes of exploitation and deprivation, spanning a time scale from the ninth to the twentieth century, and within the contexts of history, art, literature, mythology, all in the contemporary setting of a luncheon party in a modern restaurant in a cosmopolitan city. The simple but original device of exploiting the lesser-used mechanics of the turn system itself enables the symbolization of women's history and its reception in complex and dramatic fashion.

Overlaps – either partially, as in interruptions, or as in the issue of simultaneous speech across whole turns – need not signal conflict. They may manifest sympathy or attentiveness, particularly when they are characterized by other- rather than self-orientation. In such cases, overlaps may occur because listeners anticipate the speech of another and display it, and signal their affiliation by making an interactive reality of attentiveness in listening. In Shaw's *You Never Can Tell* we get the following instance of simultaneous speech. Mrs Clandon is being pressed by her children to tell them who their father is, since their ignorance of the fact is interfering with their lives – issuing luncheon invitations or accepting proposals of marriage become difficult when lineage is vague.

GLORIA   [*inexorably*] We have a right to know, mother.
DOLLY   Oh! Gloria, don't. It's barbarous.
GLORIA   [*with quiet scorn*]   What is the use of being weak? You see what has happened with this gentleman here, mother. The same thing has happened to me.

MRS CLANDON		
DOLLY	[*all together*]	What do you mean?
PHILIP		Oh, tell us!
		What's happened to you?

(Shaw [1898] 1984: 225)

Here, overlaps among turns, where three speakers spontaneously self-select to take one next turn in various ways, still orient to Gloria's and project her jointly as next speaker. Such a strategy heightens interest in what she has said and what she has to say, and awards her and her turns high interactive and dramatic value. Overlaps can be used for other effects: for instance, in *Othello* (1.3.56–60). Brabantio has learned of Desdemona's elopement and marriage and has accused Othello of sorcery just prior to this scene, in which the Duke is in council over the threat of the Turkish fleet, and in which Othello and Brabantio, among others, are present. The Duke and the Senators are ignorant of what has transpired, but are glad nevertheless for Brabantio's presence in their midst in this emergency. Brabantio, however, indicates that his presence is owing to personal causes. The following interaction ensues:

DUKE   Why, what's the matter?
BRABANTIO   My daughter! O! my daughter.
ALL   Dead?
BRABANTIO   Ay, to me;
She is abus'd, stol'n from me. . .

(1.3.56–60)

Here, Duke and Senators overlap with the same inference – that Desdemona must be dead – in one next turn, in response to Brabantio's, which is also a performance cue for the actor playing the part to emphasize force of distress felt, even though the turn is short and devoid of all but bare, essential information. It is impressed with expressive force, however, since ostensibly all concerned independently come instantly to the same conclusion and respond relevantly. This personal mini-drama has the effect, too, of bringing Brabantio's affairs into prominence in a context where dire matters of state were the original focus of concern; thus, such matters may now, temporarily, be laid aside, while the contention between Othello and Brabantio is enacted.

TURN CONSTRUCTIONAL STRATEGIES: DISTRIBUTION, ORDER AND LENGTH

Turn-change strategies bring relevant characters into interaction with each other in various ways. Participant roles of speaker and targeted or untargeted addressee(s) are given by the order of turns in a text. Floor management strategies involve more than order; distribution, length of turns, etc. are also included. Especially in multi-party speech, how turn rights are distributed in the who-speaks-to-whom, who-is-not-spoken-to dimension, can be consequential. Where the pool of possible participants in a scene is larger than two, characters must be brought to speak with relevant others as required by the design of action in a segment or scene. Given that whatever appears on stage will be assessed as dramatically motivated by an audience, how the dramatist manages the pressure on the floor for turns is of interest, since respecting or rejecting a character's turn rights will be significant. Turn distribution patterns can consistently exclude a character, as analysed earlier in the Synge extract (see pp. 99–105), but it can also create configurations among groups of characters in terms of exclusion or inclusion, and alignments in sympathy or antipathy among those who are co-present in a scene.

An instance of exclusion of a character who is made to wait for a turn is to be found in the opening scene of Shakespeare's *King Lear* (1.1.1–26) with Kent, Gloucester and Edmund on stage, but floor and participation rights are confined to Kent and Gloucester who converse for eight turns before Edmund is invited to join in. Awaiting a turn by itself does not signify exclusion; later on Cordelia has to wait to speak till nominated by Lear, but the turn-taking system in force in the latter case is a formal one, based on order of precedence from oldest to youngest and in the control of the King. In the former case, the option to include or exclude Edmund is open from the beginning, but not used, and the delay is played out in such a way that the co-present Edmund is doubly excluded – by the distribution of turns and by the talk itself. Edmund figures as 'the bastard' son excluded from legitimate familial bonds by his father's ribald talk to Kent, and also cast as 'third person' in his presence in the talk. Dramatically, our first introduction to Edmund is as the 'outsider' and under erasure as a character, so to speak. The two-versus-one pattern predicated by the distribution of turns allows the silent and marginalized Edmund to cast his own enigmatic shadow in the scene. How the actor, on-stage, playing Edmund aligns himself physically to the other two can also colour the event, given the visual resources of the stage; the effect would differ depending on whether the physical stance was one of powerlessness, with head bowed and gaze averted, or some such, and at the mercy of the exclusion, or if the excluded character were to lounge about carelessly with a smirk on his face.

Drama and performance analysts quite often examine groupings among the characters for their visual or spatial appeal, but rarely touch on what may be called the auditory configurations which speech alignment patterns make possible (Styan 1987). In the opening scene of Shakespeare's *The Tempest*, given the setting of a storm at sea, the Boatswain has tried to keep the royal party down below, but they insist on talking to him and getting in his way. Initially (1.1.6–31), the turn-taking alternates between the Boatswain and members of the royal group, the self-selected turn distribution pattern being Alonso–Boatswain–Antonio–Boatswain– Gonzalo–Boatswain–Gonzalo–Boatswain. The Boatswain is central to the segment, all turns being addressed to him although all present take a turn. The Boatswain's presence dominates as a consequence since he is the focal point of all others' speech. So does his official role to the extent that it overrides all other considerations since his interactive behaviour shows scant respect for his passengers' social ranks. His centrality in turn distribution, as well as his manner of engagement, become indicative of the crisis at sea.

Further on in the scene, the pattern changes. The Boatswain's fight to save the ship has failed and a realignment of turns occurs in a one-versus-three pattern – played out differently. To the Boatswain's 'What must our mouths be cold?', there is no reply and the turn distribution pattern passes from the self-selected Gonzalo to Sebastian–Antonio–Gonzalo–Antonio– Sebastian–Gonzalo. In Antonio's first turn, the Boatswain is addressed, but Gonzalo turn-grabs and sidelines the Boatswain who never speaks again in this scene although he is spoken about in third person form by the others. The Boatswain is erased from interaction, attention and importance once matters have come to the extremity of the inevitable shipwreck.

Groupings among characters can be created via turn distribution patterns which can intensify some particular property of a segment. In Pinter's *The Birthday Party* the Goldberg–McCann alliance inflicts a form of sadistic coercion on Stanley in a two-versus-one configuration. In the earlier part of the scene Goldberg and McCann collaborate in order to get Stanley to do what they wish – to sit down, for instance. Goldberg gives the orders and McCann complies and gets Stanley to comply as well, although against his wishes. The turn pattern does include Stanley even if in reduced degree, and the possibility for some form of counter-response and negotiation is still left open to him. As the scene proceeds, however, even this is eliminated by the turn order adopted.

GOLDBERG	Where is your lechery leading you?
MCCANN	You'll pay for this.
GOLDBERG	You stuff yourself with dry toast.
MCCANN	You contaminate womankind.
GOLDBERG	Why don't you pay the rent?
MCCANN	Mother defiler!
GOLDBERG	Why do you pick your nose?
MCCANN	I demand justice.
GOLDBERG	What's your trade?
MCCANN	What about Ireland?
GOLDBERG	What's your trade?
STANLEY	I play the piano.

([1976] 1980: 2.61)

The threats, insults, comments and questions in the alternating turns of the other two are actually addressed to Stanley, but although adjacency pairs are used, he is not permitted to answer. His speaking rights are projected but removed simultaneously by the other two men, their playing of turn order squeezes him out. As their accusations pile up, their discourse about him manufactures a 'Webber' figure over the form of the actual Stanley which he is powerless to rebut. Lack of speech here is also a loss of identity.

Turn distribution and order can split groups of characters in symmetrical fashion and arrange them two versus two for playful or antagonistic purposes. In Shakespeare's *The Merchant of Venice* (3.2), after the caskets have been opened, Portia and Bassanio declare their joy and acceptance of each other. This is followed by Nerissa and Gratiano expressing joy at the others' good fortune and revealing their own, which augments the romantic aura of the whole segment. Turn order can also be used to bracket off one set of characters in collusion or co-operation within the interactions of a larger, public scene as happens, for instance, in *King Lear* when Goneril and Regan voice to each other alone their own private thoughts about Lear's actions after the banishment of Cordelia.

The turn constructional component also regulates the speech composition of the turn unit itself – its linguistic texture, length, size, etc. – none of which is specified in advance and are left to participants to manage locally. And this aspect has been explored most fully in literary studies when the linguistic texture of the turn is scrutinized for its poetic or stylistic qualities as 'the language of drama'. The range of speech styles used is enormous and includes choral speech, metred speech, the symmetrical balancing of speech in stichomythia, poetic speech, dialect, colloquial prose, formal prose, conversational speech, phatic speech and the like. Different styles are privileged in different eras as different speech resources are favoured by one or other dramaturgy. And 'code-switching' in plays is also evident when 'high' characters in Shakespeare speak in poetry and 'low' characters mostly in prose. The linguistic texture of the turn can also incline to monologue, as in the use of soliloquies, or to monodrama, either consistently or intermittently as much as it can to the fully interactive dialogue. Speech may be constructed to resemble the written mode of discourse in its grammar, phonology and lexis, or spoken features could be preferred, in the use of non-standard syntax, enclitics, disfluency, etc. Declamatory or conversational modes of the delivery of speech can also be turned to dramatic ends when necessary. Analysts have created different typologies of dramatic speech. Bentley (1965) offers four kinds – naturalistic speech, rhetorical prose, rhetorical poetry and poetic dialogue, while Fischer-Lichte (1984) rings the changes on different combinations along an oral–literary cline of communication.

Speech for a character, however textured linguistically, and whether the style is explicit or inexplicit, is essential if its dramatic potential is to be fully realized, especially in plays where the full resources of the medium are drawn upon. On the one hand are the personal and expressive possibilities afforded by speech; we may learn about a character's thoughts, motives, feelings, opinions, emotions, about others or itself, or the events in the world of the play. We may take pleasure, too, in a character's linguistic virtuosity. Speech with others affords possibilities for a character to be brought into a variety of relationships with other characters and to achieve a high or low degree of participation in the events and actions that occur within the play. Shakespearean heroes interact with a wide variety of characters in different inter-personal roles and are involved in a host of situations. Turn distribution strategies privilege them greatly; so do turn style strategies, since not only are they awarded great poetic qualities of speech, they also control a variety of verbal styles and resources, so that varied modes of participation are open to them, which enhance their dramatic profiles accordingly.

As far as turn size is concerned, participatory proportionality would be the unmarked norm in order to maintain the inter-personal balance among characters in speech interchange. In fact, in everyday contexts, when extended turn rights are required, as in story-telling, bids are made by the current speaker for the extension of floor rights, which, when ratified by others, permits the speaker to proceed as desired. Often, 'back channelling' tokens and other forms of behaviour like attentiveness, gaze, nods, vocal signs like 'uhuuh', 'ahmm', etc. are returned as co-operative signals. But such norms are often breached since inter-personal equilibrium is not the most functional of options in dramatic worlds. Hyperdominant speakers who claim time and extended speech rights put pressure on the floor, disproportionately, on their own behalf and at the expense of other participants. The expenditure of time, too, is crucial, since drama's element is time. Speech size, therefore, can be used as a coercive tool to dominate, and as a sign of power, since proportion and balance are not always desirable in drama and the 'rightness' of speeches to situations in their dramatic motivations might well require disequilibrium and disproportion among the participants. The receptive dimension, however, has to be borne in mind, since quantity alone is insufficient for dominance. Long turns, as noted earlier, block another speaker's access to the floor as effectively as explicit forbiddings can do. Other markers of the exercise of power in a speaker's speech include greater volume, fast speech, loud speech, fluent speech, and the use of privileged or varied lexical styles. Control of the various aspects of the turn-taking system itself, like the initiation of speech, topic control, the right to interrupt or to keep the turn on interrupting, are also relevant.

Apart from power, super-speechmanship can bring other values into the interaction. It can create an intensely private space of intimacy when thoughts, feelings, emotions, anxieties, etc. are disclosed. Such an eventuality gives access to a character's internal life and psychological fullness to the role. Shakespeare's and Chekhov's plays abound in such instances; Shaw's characters, on the other hand, often use turn length to reveal their argumentative and intellectual dexterities. Although turns of this kind can function interactively, they could also have other forms of existence which are not highly participatory. Long speeches can be used to fulfil what Beckerman has termed a 'reactive' tendency in drama, when a character's speech is not goal-directed and targeted at another, but purely experience-directed, in order to dramatize moments of sustained emotional release. Such is the case in Euripides' Electra's long speech of grief at Orestes' supposed death on the reception of the urn from the disguised Orestes himself. The development of the intensity and desperation of grief within the speech itself provides its own internal movement which reaches its climax through a process of sheer accumulation of emotion (Beckerman 1970: 80–3).

Explicit verbal adequacies have also been used for more rational and argumentative functions; to develop or justify a point of view or philosophical position, as in Shaw's plays, or in Greek drama, to reveal verbal dexterities of argument, debate, disquisition, propaganda or persuasion which are their own reward. On the other hand, excessive and egotistical speech on the part of a character can also create parody, unnecessary verbosity, self-evasive self-rationalizations or defensiveness when too much protesting is done. In these latter instances the claim on the floor gives rise to negative effects, but effects nevertheless, which are significant in drama.

Long or multi-clause turns in a context or co-text of other turns can be coloured by the reception they are given – either in the kind of listening signals that are displayed, which would cast the speech as riveting or boring, for instance, or in the kind of attitude to it that is displayed by next turn. Content alone is not sufficient in interaction. In Shaw's *You Never Can Tell* Philip and Dolly yet again attempt to broach the subject of the family secret with their mother. After a preamble, a pre-sequence, Philip takes the plunge.

PHILIP   Well, there are certain matters upon which we are beginning to feel that you might take us a little more into your confidence.

MRS CLANDON   [*rising with all the placidity of her age suddenly breaking up into a curious hard excitement, dignified but dogged, ladylike but implacable: the manner of the Old Guard*]   Phil, take care. What have I always taught you? There are two sorts of family life, Phil: and your experience of human nature only extends, so far, to one of them. [*Rhetorically*] The sort you know is based on mutual respect, on recognition of the right of every member of the household for independence and privacy [*her emphasis on 'privacy' is intense*] in their personal concerns. And because you have always enjoyed that, it seems such a matter of course to you that you don't value it. But [*with biting acrimony*] there is another sort of family life: a life in which husbands open their wives' letters, and call on them to account for every farthing of their expenditure and every moment of their time; in which women do the same to their children; in which no room is private and no hour sacred; in which duty, obedience, affection, home, morality and religion are detestable tyrannies, and life is a vulgar round of punishments and lies, coercion and rebellion, jealousy, suspicion, recrimination – Oh! I cannot describe it to you: fortunately for you, you know nothing about it.   [*She sits down panting*]

DOLLY   [*inaccessible to rhetoric*] See Twentieth Century Parents, chapter on Liberty, passim.

(Shaw [1898] 1984: 223)

The response undercuts the seriousness of the passionate sentiments expressed and makes it a comic episode, whereas the content of the speech by itself would make it a serious one. Contrasts in lengths of speeches can be patterned in symmetry or asymmetry. Formal symmetries are to be found in certain speech styles like stichomythia in Greek drama, flyting in medieval drama, the formal lament found in Shakespeare's early plays, repartee and duels of wit, and the music-hall patter of Didi and Gogo in Beckett's *Waiting for Godot* (Kennedy 1983: 13). Speech equilibrium can thus provide balance but also stasis. Contrast, as in the above, can be used for a number of effects like alienation, irony, disinterest, or more positively to signify interactive success when succinctly accomplished. Hyperdominant speakers may be counter-challenged with equivalent hyperdominance or they may merit no more than short, laconic replies. A mixture of long and short turns can be used to vary the rhythm, interactive weightings, dramatic presence, etc. of characters in a scene. How speech is given and how taken, together, define the situation.

Long speeches necessitate long spates of listening on the part of addressees and listener respondent or back-channelling behaviour may itself colour the situation either negatively or positively, as we have seen. The atmosphere and concentration of attentive listening in a segment can be used to contrast with another as was the case with Horatio's long narrative in *Hamlet* when the calmer atmosphere of the long speech is used as a foil to intensify the electrifying engagements with the ghostly visitor on the battlements. Where a succession of long, informative speeches follow each other, as when Prospero relates his past history to Miranda in the second scene of *The Tempest*, Shakespeare has catered for the load on the audience's attention span by including 'back channelling' turns from Miranda. Prospero, in monitoring her attentiveness, jogs the attention of the audience as well.

Short turns like one-clause or even one-word turns can speed up the tempo of the interaction in a segment to signify panic, fear, etc., as turn follows upon turn in quick succession. But such patterns have been employed at different times for very different effects. Compare the rhythm of the following extract from *Macbeth*, which signifies urgency and panic with that of the extracts quoted earlier:

LADY MACBETH   . . . Did not you speak?
MACBETH   When?
LADY MACBETH   Now.
MACBETH   As I descended?
LADY MACBETH   Ay.
MACBETH   Hark!

                                        (2.2.15–20)

In the episode quoted below, from Pinter's *No Man's Land*, short turns serve to animate the lack of common focus on the content of speech in the mismatches in understanding in attempted communication, since the interaction is based on repairs. The motivation and dramaturgy are very different.

HIRST   It's a long time since we had a free man in this house.
SPOONER   We?
HIRST   I.
SPOONER   Is there another?
HIRST   Another what?
SPOONER   People. Person.
HIRST   What other?

                                        (Pinter [1975] 1986: 83)

In the *Waiting for Godot* extract which follows, the speed of turn change in the use of short turns promotes the collaborative language game of symmetrical, oneupmanship, and a kind of jouissance in abuse which the interactive energies invested in it make available. Quick turn change enhances the interactive verve in the game.

VLADIMIR   Moron!
ESTRAGON   Vermin!
VLADIMIR   Abortion!
ESTRAGON   Morpion!
VLADIMIR   Sewer-rat!
ESTRAGON   Curate!
VLADIMIR   Cretin!
ESTRAGON   [*with finality*] Crritic!

                                        (Beckett 1955: 75)

Chapter 3

Turn sequencing

TURN SEQUENCING IN DRAMA

If turn change and turn distribution options can be used as a dramatic resource, the mechanics of sequencing can be made dramatically relevant as well. For any stretch of dialogue to be brought into existence at all, turn change must occur. In the course of the play different dramatis personae are brought into relation through interaction to construct various speech events. Each segment of interaction has its place and function within the whole design. As turn succeeds upon turn, the character-to-character communications that ensue articulate in their linear structuring the emergent and emerging course of the inter-personal action as it develops turn by turn. A dramatist's turn sequencing strategies are thus of interest since they shape the contours of a situation within the immediacies of its making and by those involved in it. The initiation of speech calls forth other speech, which, in turn, calls forth further speech, till the interactive business required is accomplished. Characters are thus implicated in what happens, their management of the responsive dimension of dialogue making them personally and jointly responsible for the course and outcomes of their actions.

Different kinds of structuring options have already been noted. To recapitulate: adjacency pairs like Question–Answer, Greeting–Greeting are paired utterances such that the use of the first part of the pair sets up expectations that the second will follow. In the absence of the second part, *conditional relevance* is said to hold across the intervening turns till the concluding part is used, thus embedding the structure of the intervening turns into the adjacency pair. Where such a second part is not used, its absence is noticeable and noticed. Preference organization orders the dual options that are available in some pairs, like offer/acceptance–refusal, in such a way that the unmarked alternative is the *preferred* one, socially, with the *dispreferred* pair part being linguistically more complex in design. Pre-sequences may serve to check that the desired conditions obtain before the main sequence is initiated. Post-sequences may be used after a closing sequence in order to attend to unfinished business, or to firm up business already concluded. Opening and closing sequences initiate and terminate sequences. Side sequences and embedded sequences can protract the main business in various ways. Remedial sequences can rectify a breach. Repair and metacommunicative sequences can serve to monitor the state of the interaction in progress. Topic control and topic development can suture together a chunk of exchanges through orientation to what is being talked about. Overall, however, even where sequencing is not strictly adhered to, the turns may be scrutinized for what their *adjacency relationships* (Schegloff 1988) reveal about how participants themselves are structuring and constructing the situation they are enacting through their talk.

Interactions evolve in time, and as talk proceeds other things develop as well – personal relationships, social relationships, contours of character, situation and event. A developmental path is created as turn succeeds upon turn in which relationships may be forged, sustained, damaged or destroyed. A dramatist's sequencing strategies enable the progress of the evolving inter-personal dynamic to be charted in its smooth or conflictual course, given a turn's orientation to other turns. And this is the case, even when such orientations are absent, when normative requirements are flouted, since specific sequencing choices structure the interaction and influence its inter-subjective quality. Inter-personal states are constantly in flux as talk proceeds – those in harmony may be estranged, those in conflict reconciled, intimacies may be exchanged, or frustrated; existing relationships consolidated, power or dominance exercised or resisted, and so on. A whole cline of relations, situations and realities can be made to unfold through the alternating course of talk.

Segments of interaction have their own internal shape but function also as a part of the overall design of the play. Characters cannot talk at random or talk themselves out (Bentley 1965: 80), except as a specific dramatic tactic. The path taken by interactions must lead to dramatically relevant outcomes, or to the frustration of the very expectation of outcomes, as required. The flow of interaction in a larger dramatic unit like a scene or an act must be organized into sub-rhythms of its own – rhythms of intensification and descrescence (Beckerman 1970: 62). The build-up to a major climax can be achieved through the manipulation of minor cruces (*ibid.: 74–7*). Situations which are highly conflictual or tension-ridden may be followed by those in which dramatic and emotional intensity is low, or vice versa. Other patterns – of stasis, in which the pattern of climax or closure to the action is refused – are also possible. Cyclic patterns can bring the course of the evolving action back to square one. The tenor of individual segments will contribute, in one way or another, to wider considerations.

Dramaturgical conventions influence the larger design and these have changed historically. The role and place of dialogue as an element of drama has also varied. The strongly inter-personal kinds which were developed in the Renaissance defined the sphere of the 'between', the inter-human or inter-subjective as the most significant for displaying various forms of the human condition. Speech was associated with will, decision and the disclosure of personality (Szondi 1987: 7). The role of dialogue, as the vehicle that best transcribes this sphere, is primary. Modulations that inhibit the fully inter-personal aspects of the form are still evident in later drama, while in more recent drama dialogue is more likely to be employed to dramatize inarticulacy and alienation, the failures of speech and the gaps between people as states more truly representative of the conduct of human affairs. Whichever option is chosen, the dialogic *trajectory* or path of development may be examined in order to determine *how* a situation is achieved in the sequential organization of turns.

Among the sequencing options we have considered are those in two-part form, like adjacency pairs, that permit the closure of interactive business with high economy. Others, like embedded sequences, facilitate a protracted course for interactions. Expenditure of turns is expenditure of time and has to be dramatically justified. The choice of economy or elaboration in sequencing some interactive section is thus both strategic and significant.

In order to explore how sequencing options and patterning contribute to interaction management and the creation of situations we will examine an extract from Arnold Wesker's *Chicken Soup with Barley*. The extract is taken from the opening scene of the play and is a two-party exchange in which turns alternate between Sarah and Harry Kahn, husband and wife. The setting is a domestic one, their home in a basement flat in the East End of London. Wesker's stage directions describe Sarah Kahn as 'a small fiery woman, aged 37, Jewish and of European origin. Her movements indicate great energy and vitality.' Harry Kahn is described as '35, and also a European Jew. He is dark, slight and rather pleasant looking and the antithesis of Sarah. He is amiable, but weak.' For the reader of the text, the 'antithesis' is given a priori, but the relevance of this statement will be assessed only in terms of how the dialogue and the interaction enable the enactment of the antithesis. The static description has to be made dynamic via the management of the interactive possibilities of the dialogue. The role of sequencing strategies is examined in the extract given below. The turns are numbered for convenience.

1 SARAH   [*from the kitchen*] You took the children to Lottie's?

2 HARRY   [*taking up book to read*] I took them.

3 SARAH   They didn't mind?

4 HARRY   No, they didn't mind.

5 SARAH   Is Hymie coming?

6 HARRY   I don't know.

7 SARAH   [*To herself*] Nothing he knows! You didn't ask him? He didn't say? He knows about the demonstration, doesn't he?

8 HARRY   I don't know whether he knows or he doesn't know. I didn't discuss it with him. Hey, Sarah – you should read Upton Sinclair's book about the meat-canning industry – it's an eye-opener. . .

9 SARAH   Books! Nothing else interests him, only books. Did you see anything else outside? What's happening?

10 HARRY   The streets are packed with people, I never seen so many people. They've got barricades at Gardiner's Corner.

11 SARAH   There'll be such trouble.

12 HARRY   Sure there'll be trouble. You ever known a demonstration where there wasn't trouble?

13 SARAH   And the police?

14 HARRY   There'll be more police than blackshirts.

15 SARAH   What time they marching?

16 HARRY   I don't know.

17 SARAH   Harry, you know where your cigarettes are, don't you? [*This is her well-meaning but maddening attempt to point out to a weak man his weakness*]

18 HARRY   I know where they are.

19 SARAH   And you know what's on at the cinema?

20 HARRY   So?

21 SARAH   And also you know what time it opens? [*He grins*] So why don't you know what time they plan to march? [*Touché*]

22 HARRY   Leave me alone, Sarah, will you? Two o'clock they plan to march – nah!

23 SARAH   So you do know. Why didn't you tell me straight away? Shouldn't you tell me something when I ask you?

24 HARRY   I didn't know what time they marched, so what do you want of me?

25 SARAH   But you did know when I nagged you.

26 HARRY   So I suddenly remembered. Is there anything terrible in that?

[*She shakes a disbelieving fist at him and goes out to see where the loudspeaker cries are coming from. The slogan* 'Madrid today – London tomorrow' *is being repeated. As she is out HARRY looks for her handbag, and on finding it proceeds to take some money from it*]

27 SARAH   [*she is hot*] Air! I must have air – this basement will kill me. God knows what I'll do without air when I'm dead. Who else was at Lottie's?

28 HARRY   [*still preoccupied*] All of them.

29 SARAH   Who's all of them?

30 HARRY   All of them! You know, Lottie and Hymie and the boys, Solly and Martin.

[*He finds a ten-shilling note, pockets it and resumes his seat by the fire, taking up a book to read. SARAH returns to the front room with some cups and saucers*]

31 SARAH   Here, lay these out, the boys will be coming soon.

32 HARRY   Good woman! I could just do with a cup of tea.

33 SARAH   What's the matter, you didn't have any tea by Lottie's?

34 HARRY   No.

35 SARAH   Liar!

36 HARRY   I didn't have any tea by Lottie's, I tell you. [*Injured tone*] Good God, woman, why don't you believe me when I tell you things?

37 SARAH   *You* tell *me* why. Why don't I believe him when he tells me things! As if he's such an angel and never tells lies. What's the matter, you never told lies before I don't think?

38 HARRY   All right, so I had tea at Lottie's. There, you satisfied now?

39 SARAH   [*preparing things as she talks*] Well, of course you had tea at Lottie's. Don't I know you had tea at Lottie's? You think I'm going to think that Lottie wouldn't make you a cup of tea?

40 HARRY   Oh, leave off, Sarah.

41 SARAH   No! this time I won't leave off. [*Her logic again*] I want to know why you told me you didn't have tea at Lottie's when you know perfectly well you did. I want to know.

[*Harry raises his hands in despair*]

I know you had tea there and *you* know you had tea there – so what harm is there if you tell me? You think I care whether you had a cup

of tea there or not? You can drink tea there till i comes out of your
eyes and I wouldn't care only as long as you tell me.

42 HARRY   Sarah, will you please stop nagging me, will you? What
difference if I had tea there or I didn't have tea there?

43 SARAH   That's just what I'm saying. All I want to know is whether
you are all of a liar or half a liar!.

44 HARRY   [*together with her*]   . . . all of a liar or half a liar!

(Wesker [1959] 1985: 13–16)

The interaction begins smoothly enough with Sarah initiating the conversation and Harry responding in a series of three QA sequences in
adjacency pairing. From turn 7, however, the sequencing pattern gets more
complex and varied. As far as the overall design of the scene is concerned,
the extract may be informally re-cast according to topic and the interactive
business in hand. Basically, the QA pair predominates and chains into
larger segments. These contrast with other types of sequences – a side
sequence, repair sequences and a remedial sequence. The types of questions also vary, and project different types of responses on the part of the
interactant.

Turns 1–6: Series of three co-ordinated and satisfied QA pairs with
topic orienting off-stage, outside the immediate setting.

Turns 7–8: Repair sequence initiated by Sarah. Harry's turn 6, 'I don't
know', motivates the inward turn of the dialogue in a discourse-internal
move as Sarah checks out whether the right conditions obtain for Harry's
answer to pass muster. Turn length expands to three consecutive questions, to which Harry responds with three consecutive answers. Harry's
attempt to change topic fails, being rejected by Sarah.

Turns 9–16: Topic orients to the off-stage world again, and comments
are followed by supportive comments, the rhetorical question in Harry's
turn being assessed as a comment. Questions are followed by answers till
the repeat of Harry's turn 6 – 'I don't know – in his turn 16.

Turns 17–26: Side sequence in mostly QA form and oriented dis-
course-internally. Sarah makes Harry expand on what he knows and does
not know. Harry attempts a counter-question once, but Sarah maintains
the initiative. At the end of the questioning drill Harry provides the
withheld answer, thus contradicting his erstwhile profession of ignorance.
The sequence does not end here although it could; Sarah initiates a
postsequence which endorses her own performance and reviews Harry's.
Harry's responses to her questions include counter-questions, and the
segment ends with Sarah's non-verbal response of her shaking of her fist
at Harry.

Turns 27–30: After initially orienting to the immediate context of the basement flat, Sarah's turn resumes her questions on discourse-external matters, like who is coming to the march. Harry's vague 'all of them' in turn 28 triggers a repeat of the repair strategy as Sarah questions him again for a more precise answer.

Turns 31–44: The topic switches to tea and orients to the immediate setting and the stage business in it initially, but the bulk of the sequence is discourse-internal as the focus moves to the ground rules on which interaction is being conducted by them, and which are conflicted over. After an initial QA pair, normative sequencing patterns are continuously broken. Sarah challenges and rejects Harry's questions. Harry attempts the first part of a *reproach* sequence, to which Sarah responds with a counter-reproach so that the sequence cannot proceed to the accounting and evaluation slots as required for the remedial effort to be successful. The issue of who has the right to reproach whom is itself contended over. The aborted remedial sequence protracts instead into a metacommunicative drama as the participants play out the lack of consensus on the rules of interaction itself, which exacerbates the conflict. The sequence ends on an overlap of turns, an ironic conclusion here, since anticipatory overlap of this kind usually signals supportiveness and collaboration, both of which have been missing in what has gone before.

The sequencing choices used are strategic in many ways. They enable various dramatic tasks to be fulfilled simultaneously. In the first place, such choices vary the progress of the dramatic action and tension across the whole extract. Segments of relative harmony contrast with others which enact minor or major conflict, and a pattern of intensification-descrescence is built up as a consequence. Turns 1–6, 9–16, 27–8, 31–3 are either harmonious or project mutuality, but they get very brief towards the end. These sequences not only create interactional co-operativeness – questions are answered, comments are followed by comments, and so on – they also function as an informational device to tell the audience, economically, about off-stage events and characters that have a bearing on future events. They have an expository function as well. We learn that Sarah and Harry have children, that a march is imminent, that the children have been taken elsewhere, that some of the characters referred to will probably be involved in the march, that violence can be expected, and so on, all through Sarah's desire to know what is going on in the outside world.

The discourse-internal sequences focus on the interaction itself, and these move in the direction of greater and greater conflict as the sequences expand, from brief forms of repair, to indirect confrontation when Sarah shows Harry up, to open conflict at the end. As the dialogue focuses internally on the interaction itself, the informational function falls away and the drama of speech and its exchange takes over. In fact, turn time is taken up disproportionately by the personal sequences so that the dramatic quality of this extract is dependent on the course taken by the conflicts between the characters to which the other kind of sequencing forms a contrast. The two types of sequences are related in that it is Harry's insufficiencies as an interactant from Sarah's point of view that motivate the inward focus of the dialogue into conflictual matters. The rhythm of the extract is modulated, too: quieter sections are contrasted with the more volatile ones. Among the trouble-laden sequences, a pattern of gradually accumulating tension can be noted which, in its progress across repeated conflictual sequences, builds up towards the explosion at the end.

If the overall, general pattern of sequence segmenting across the extract is strategic in its composition, the internal design of individual segments is equally so. Strategies used here regulate the responsive structure of turn alternation which manifests the particular course of the inter-subjective dynamic of the segment. In the satisfied QA pairs, the rules are observed and mutually accepted, and harmony ensues. In the conflictual sections, various negotiations are engaged in, and asymmetry arises in how turns are given and how taken, till some consensus is reached, with Harry usually deferring to Sarah. At the end, the lack of consensus regarding the rules themselves is dramatized and inter-personal harmony is completely fractured.

The first *failure event* occurs, as we saw, in Sarah's turn 7, in response to Harry's turn 6 – 'I don't know'. Harry's reply should have closed the pair, but Sarah re-initiates in order to repair the previous response to her own satisfaction. After a display of irritation, 'Nothing he knows!', she checks out whether Harry's response can be taken at face value: 'You didn't ask him? He didn't say? He knows about the demonstration, doesn't he?' and the turn expands into three successive questions. Only after she is answered accordingly and satisfied does the interaction proceed. A similar repair of Harry's 'All of them' occurs later when she re-initiates again to get full details as to whom 'all' may refer to. Both are *other-initiated* forms of repair as far as Harry is concerned, but he complies with them immediately. Checking strategies of this kind not only cast Harry as an incompetent interactant, from Sarah's point of view, they fracture the norm of equality that underlies conversational exchange, since, in normative cases, a person's profession of ignorance should be believed and talk would proceed having taken the fact into account. Displaying suspicion as to whether another's word suffices would create conflict, since it calls into account both the ethical and social demeanour of the interactant. In this instance, Sarah's assumption of such a right upsets the initial equilibrium between them and awards her a greater degree of dominance, especially as her move is not counter-challenged by Harry. Other options reinforce this impression. Sarah interrupts Harry more and she maintains topic control when Harry attempts to change it, to which Harry gives up his right to the floor and lets drop his own topic and defers to hers.

The side sequence uses other strategies, again triggered by Harry's repeat of 'I don't know'. The sequence moves laterally, at Sarah's initiation, into establishing what Harry knows and does not know. Sarah uses questions dominantly, but they are, as it were, double-edged. They are not requests for information but the kind that Labov termed A–B events, which are played out as B events. Sarah and Harry both know that Harry knows that Sarah knows the answers. But the adjacency organization does enable the triviality of what Harry knows, as compared with the significance of what he does not, to be played out in slow-motion fashion. Sarah's turns pattern repetitively – 'You know. . . ', 'And you know. . . ' 'And you also know. . . ' 'So why don't you know. . . ', the *punch-line* coming at the end, the sequence displaying a *poetics* of its own and creating its own form of suspense. Her monitoring style of questioning resembles that of a teacher to a pupil, a style also used by Pinter in *The Dumb Waiter* (Burton 1980: 71–99), which signals her dominance again.

Harry's interactive style, in response, is first to comply and answer, then to attempt resistance with a counter-question, which Sarah ignores, and then to attempt an opt-out, and finally to come out with the withheld answer about which he had professed ignorance. Sarah's strategy is to continue against the grain of his countering strategies till she gets the response she wants, which she pursues relentlessly. Once successful, her review of their interactive performance, in metacommunicative mode, focuses on the rights and responsibilities of participants in interaction – 'Why didn't you tell me straight away? Shouldn't you tell me something when I ask you?' which appears very much like a colloquial version of the adjacency pair rule. Instead of playing by the normative rules expected of him, Harry blatantly uses the responsive structure to give plausible but untrue replies of which both are aware. The sequence establishes him as a liar, which enters the universe of discourse of the play and contributes later to the precipitation of the conflict at the end.

After a repeat of the Repair sequence, the final sequence is initiated by Sarah on the business of tea. The segment begins again on a relatively harmonious note. Harry displays his approval of the prospect of tea on which she has embarked, which becomes, in turn, the basis for her seemingly innocent question – as a Q projecting an A – 'What's the matter, you didn't have any tea by Lottie's?' The ensuing course of the interaction, however, establishes it retrospectively as an A–B type questioning event. Again, Harry's denial – he takes it as a straight question – should have closed the pair, but Sarah challenges the turn with an insult – 'Liar', thus initiating a Reproach which requires redress.

From now on, neither respects the response projected by the other's turn. Harry attempts to initiate a deflecting counter-reproach using Sarah's prior turn as the basis for his 'injury' and casts Sarah in the role of the accounter and redresser of injury – 'Good God, woman, why don't you believe me when I tell you things?', which requires a concession from Sarah. This she rejects, by yet another aggravating tactic, since she throws the role of accounter back at Harry, thus negating his pose of injured innocence and his right to assume the role of reproacher in the first place – '*You* tell *me* why. . . ' Thus, who is the injured party and who has the right to the role of reproacher and who should account are conflicted over. In the rest of her turn, Sarah's anger spills over into a series of barbed, sarcastic comments, the content of her turn displaying her understanding of Harry's underlying, pragmatic, calculations (see Ch. 4). The turn focuses on the inferences she was supposed to draw from his interactive pose, which are rejected. Unable to counter Sarah's direct challenge to his indirect strategy, Harry finally moves to the Account slot, thus admitting Sarah's right to reproach, and yet again admits to the opposite of what he had maintained earlier, and acknowledges that he had already had tea at Lottie's. He does so, not as a confession, or as an attempt at redress, but as a weary, co-operative gesture on his part, which is designed to give *her* satisfaction – 'All right, so I had tea at Lottie's. There, you satisfied now?' – which, cast in question form, attempts to pre-empt and constrain her response in the direction of agreement with him.

Instead of agreeing, Sarah again rejects this ploy, by re-interpreting and categorizing his turn as, precisely, an admission of guilt which, moreover, she was aware of, and the sequence moves into metacommunicative mode as she articulates her understanding of the rules of the game he has adopted. She focuses specifically, on the deeper, manipulative calculations she infers are his from his behaviour – 'You think I'm going to think. . . ' Her evaluation of his accounting is wholly negative. Since the tactic of a reproach and the pose of co-operativeness has failed, Harry attempts an opt-out, to close the interaction – 'Oh, leave off, Sarah. . . ', which Sarah again rejects with an unmitigated refusal, and an explicit dispreferred 'No! this time I won't leave off. . . ' She then concludes her turn with a direct demand to him that he gives her an accounting of his total behaviour, Sarah claiming the role of the reproacher that she has wrested from him, and tightly constrains his next turn in response to hers, by underscoring with repetition her requirement for redress – 'I want to know why you told me you didn't have tea at Lottie's when you know perfectly well you did. I want to know.' Harry does not comply but 'raises his hands in despair'. Sarah re-runs her Reproach, this time, spelling out, in metacommunicative mode, the grounds on which her complaint is based. She makes explicit the terms of the tacit, communicative contract that underlies inter-personal communication in society, and her sense of her right to have it respected, especially, in Gricean terms (1975), respect for the Quality Maxim, which enjoins that speakers commit themselves to the truth of their utterances – '*I* know you had tea there – and *you* know you had tea there – so what harm is there if you tell me? You think I care whether you had a cup of tea there or not? You can drink tea there till it comes out of your eyes and I wouldn't care only as long as you tell me.'

Harry does not reciprocate as Sarah has demanded. Instead, he tries another opt-out and counteracts her referencing of him as a *liar* with one of his own, of her as a *nag*. Thus the evaluation of each other's utterances becomes the drama. He provides his own mode of pragmatic, counter-reasoning and provides a counter-logic to hers. What difference does it make whether he tells her or not? Thus he makes out that the giving of information is the issue, not the speaking of the truth as she had contended. He, in effect, splits the normative tie that links the two, thus separating the two issues. To this, Sarah claims the counter-point as *her* point, as part of *her* reasoning, but the split is recast into the issue of whether he is 'all of a liar or half a liar'. His overlap with her turn at this point is one more attempt to turn the tables on her: his correct anticipation of what she is about to say implies that he has heard it all before, and hence that *she* is the nag. Such a conclusion to the segment also releases the tension of the conflict, since it concludes on a note of humour.

The sequencing strategies described above display their mutually negative orientations based on the *lack* of common ground or agreement about communicative rules themselves. Even the first QA pair turns out to be inter-personally defective, if structurally sound, since Harry's denial about having had tea turns out to be a lie. Only after challenge from Sarah does the truth come out. Sarah's interactive style is constructed of mostly negative moves – insults, challenges, counter-challenges, counter-reproaches, rejections, demands and the like – with rejections of Harry's responses predominating. In fact, Sarah's choices are mostly *disprefer-reds*, and played in unmitigated and direct fashion, which signifies direct confrontation and heightens conflict. Harry's interactive style is composed of mainly illicit moves. He initiates *reproach* when he has no right to it, claims innocence when he is guilty of Sarah's charges, denies and then has to admit that something is the case and so on. He plays out a tissue of *seemings*, covert flouts of the rules which are not displayed as such, but are exposed by Sarah.

Moreover, there is no consensus about what the interactive rules themselves should be in this situation. They are, in effect, perspectivized. To Sarah interaction requires full, honest and open engagement. To Harry interactive rules of Sarah's kind are a game to be manipulated, which Sarah finds unacceptable and deeply provocative. Thus, much that is taken for granted in normative communication is contended over, and the ground rules – social and ethical – have to be established over and over again, usually by Sarah. Sarah's rules are the normative ones: that you answer a question in adjacency pairing if you have the information; that the convention of truth or evidence, at least, underwrites statements; that the underlying calculations on which inferencing is based must not be manipulative; that if one reproaches, the precondition of a right to re-proach must exist in the first place for the reproacher; and so on, none of which Harry honours. When she, in turn, claims the right to reproach after establishing her credentials to the role, the move is not ratified by Harry. Points of view clash. The Reproach–Account–Evaluation of Account structure protracts, as the first slot itself is re-run across many exchanges since claimed equally by both of them. The Account is dragged out of Harry, but does not proceed to the remedial Evaluation, since the Evaluation given by Sarah is negative, and the structure loops again to Reproach which Sarah claims and then aborts. Thus inter-personal harmony cannot be restored and the conflict remains unresolved.

Nor is there agreement on the nature of the issues being enacted either. There are 'double referencings': each categorizes the other and the other's performance in different ways – as *liar* and as *nag*. There are double logics; each uses a different premise about what is supposed to be going on and comes to different conclusions as to what is important in the interaction – giving information or speaking the truth. Thus, goals for speech differ. Harry wants to be left alone; Sarah wants talk. As the consensus on ground rules is fractured in this way, conflict issues through the cracks. It behoves the audience in the end to decide where its sympathies lie, and whose is the more acceptable form of behaviour given the enacted terms of the performance. But the performance itself is constructed in the clash of points of view, the reality of the situation is doubly aspected and perspectivized and enacted accordingly.

Sarah's interactive style across the extract is authoritative. She is in control of many of the variables of the turn-taking system, and her relational playing of her turns with Harry establishes her as the dominant partner. The use of questions, as noted earlier, is a foregrounded feature of this extract, and it is Sarah who is mostly cast in the role of questioner. The right to initiate exchanges is dominantly hers. Questions constrain the content of the next turn as an answer, thus Sarah is able to determine the scope of Harry's turns in her role of initiator of discourse. Her question types vary including those which are requests for information, the AB events which are used as B events, in which mutually known information is still the object of questioning, and rhetorical questions as in the last section, which do not tolerate dissent, all of which constrain Harry's performance. Harry, of course, does not play by her rules, but is made to, since challenged successfully, and her initiating performances and his responsive ones function as indices for the evolving course of the situation between them, and the subjectivities displayed and consolidated in the course of their talk.

Sarah's dominance is furthered by the fact that not only does she initiate talk and constrain Harry's responses, it is she who decides in most instances what does and does not count as an answer, adequate information and the like. Harry uses his turn to say something, but Sarah evaluates it in terms of her own standards of satisfaction. She decides, too, which topic will be the focus of their interaction, to which Harry, on the whole, complies. Sarah is given the one successful interruption in the whole extract. She successfully uses strategies against him to further her goal of showing him up to be trivial in his concerns and a liar, and makes him accountable *to her* for his performance. It is generally in her control whether talk will cease or not since Harry's attempts to opt out of talk are dismissed repeatedly and talk takes the course she has set it on. It is her will that drives the direction of the talk; her requirement that talk should be characterized by full open and honest encounter, accountability and respect for the terms of the communicative contract itself as given by society that changes the nature of the encounter to one of conflict and contention.

Harry's interactive style is more compliant, but not wholly so. He is mostly cast in the role of respondent and his strategies are minimalist in this discourse position. He takes his turn when she relinquishes hers, but uses it to give the minimum of response that would allow him to pass muster as an interactant. If Sarah's question types are highly constraining, his own more limited repertoire of questions is less so. He uses tag questions which mitigate the force of his assertions, especially in his displayed desire to opt out at critical moments. Thus, 'Leave me alone, will you, Sarah?' where the onus falls on Sarah, which she rejects. There is a rhetorical question about the police during the QA session at the beginning, to which Sarah concurs, but most of his questions are of the *defective* type, where he has broken the rules and has to defend his performance – 'Why don't you believe me. . . ?' when he knows full well why not, and 'There, you satisfied now?' when the basis for satisfaction is missing. Occasionally, there is an attempt to counter-question Sarah, as in 'So?', but usually he replies first before choosing to counter-question, as in 'I didn't know what time they marched, so what do you want of me?' and again, 'So I suddenly remembered. Is there anything terrible in that?', which being 'defective', plays the game, but remains non-serious, i.e. flouts the Sincerity Condition (see p.169) on his speech acts. The few instances in which he attempts to grab the initiative – as in changing the topic to the books he has read, or by attempting to play the role of reproacher of Sarah, or counter-questioning Sarah – she re-establishes her authority by either successfully countering his moves, or by plainly ignoring his attempts and continuing with her own, as in the questioning drill in the side sequence.

Open challenge to Sarah's interactive authority does not get him very far. Harry resorts to illicit, covert, games of his own that systematically flout the basic communicative agreements in relation to which interactions in ordinary life achieve their precarious success. This is his strategy of defence against Sarah, but it only embroils him in more trouble. He plays two, self-contradictory answers to her questions, but finally capitulates to Sarah's pressure, having displayed himself as a liar *en route*. He carries through the letter but not the spirit of the communicative contract, which is adjudged as inadequate and dishonest by Sarah, and it is her point of view which prevails. His turn overlap with Sarah at the end succeeds, but only indirectly, on grounds of irony and as a deflective tactic. His tactics, however, undermine Sarah's dominance by refusing to play by her rules since her concerns are constantly ignored or treated as a game by him.

Interaction is thus conducted against the grain of resistance, overt and covert, between them. There is no common ground, and neither fully appreciates or accepts the other's point of view, which is dramatized at the end in the mutually contradictory claims as to what is said, what is meant, what the interaction is supposed to be about, what inferences are legitimate, what role is appropriate to whom, whose goals are licensed and so on. The fundamental and mutual otherness of those in contact through dialogue, and the incipient potential for divergence and separation in conversation which the co-operative rules of interaction attempt to counter, is played out in this section, and with it, the failure of the mutuality of interaction and the limits of negotiation on which they are based.

Thus, speech with Sarah becomes a bondage for Harry, and speech with Harry a chore for Sarah. The extended sequences play out, enact, the expenditure of effort she needs in order to get interactive satisfaction from him. He pays lip-service to interactive rules. Sarah attempts repair over and over again. Harry deflects, plays fast and loose with normative rules. The interaction, however, is sustained by their joint strategies. Harry's goals in interaction are to be left in peace; language is thus used to obstruct. Sarah's goals are to know, and she demands her rights of co-operation in her dialogic encounters with him; language is a tool for her for sharing. Joint management of talk, however, based on separate ground, plays out the alternation of evasion and aggression which generate each other as a consequence of the lack of fit between them.

The inter-personal realities enacted have overall thematic consequences. The dispute between them arose precisely because of Sarah's need to be informed about the happenings in the outside world. Harry's feckless, evasive responses downgrade the importance of these external events, as Sarah's QA drill about the relative importance of different types of detail in Harry's knowledge makes clear. Harry either will not say, or does not know, about events in the immediate, external world which are Sarah's concern. Either way, his disinterest is communicated. Yet, this is a family of politically committed, Socialist, East European Jews, living in the overtly racist quarter of London, the East End, with the threat of violence hanging over the whole imminent event of an anti-Fascist demonstration, which even Harry acknowledges is a reality and in which members of the family and close friends are involved. If, character-wise, Sarah's interactive performance casts her as relatively dominant, it also reveals her as involved in and concerned with the political events in which they are implicated. Harry's performance casts him as pliant, self-seeking and indifferent. His lack of involvement and general fecklessness may seem *amiable* as Wesker indicates but it also makes him a type in relation to the other types of erstwhile Socialists with their post-war accommodations which are contrasted in the Trilogy. His weaker character is underscored by his dependence on Sarah by the end of the play, when he is physically enfeebled and ill. But across the Trilogy, this direct, baiting, interactive style between them plays out repeatedly the mode of inter-subjectivity displayed in this opening scene, which normalizes it as their habitual and preferred marital mode of interaction. It colours their domesticity in the play world and gives it specificity.

Sequencing strategies have thus facilitated the structuring of the course of the action in this extract in various ways. Intensity in the extract is varied as a consequence of the different types of sequence pattern. Conflict itself is systematically and cumulatively managed across the whole extract. Speech deportment and interactive management have established the power relations between the two characters as basically asymmetrical, with Sarah being given the interactive edge, but not wholly so. The management of speech, too, has given the audience background information and a glimpse of the kind of characters they are, and an insight into their fictional identities.

Conflict situations have high dramatic value since they are productive of tension and generate suspense and involvement of the audience in outcomes. Yet, each has its own specific mode of achievement, since context-bound variables like who the characters are, the co-textual environment, the actual path of interaction and so on can give a segment specificity. The linear path of development of a segment can realize different degrees of responsiveness along its course which could vary its emotional colouring. Inter-personal intensity, affectivity and degrees of mutuality can be manipulated within the give and take of speech. In contrast to the above, therefore, we will examine another situation of conflict to analyse how changes in sequence design and the responsive patterns adopted can create differences in situation accordingly.

Our second extract is taken from Edward Bond's *Saved*. The setting is a house in South London in which Pam and Len live and which they share with Pam's father, Harry. The extract is given below. Harry and Len are already on-stage and Pam comes in with her hair in a towel and a radio which she tunes and re-tunes from time to time while drying her hair.

LEN   [*to Harry*] 'Ow about doin' my shirt?

[*He laughs.* PAM *finishes tuning. She looks around*]

PAM   'Oos got my *Radio Times*? You 'ad it?

[HARRY *doesn't answer. She turns to* LEN]   You?

LEN   [*mumbles*] Not again.

PAM   You speakin' t' me?

LEN   I'm sick t' death of yer bloody *Radio Times*.

PAM   Someone's 'ad it. [*She rubs her hair vigorously*]. I ain' goin' a get it no more. Not after last week. I'll cancel it. It's the last time I bring it into this 'ouse. I don't see why I 'ave t' go on paying for it. Yer must think I'm made a money. It's never 'ere when I wan'a see it. Not once. It's always the same. [*She rubs her hair*] I notice no one else offers t' pay for it. Always Charlie. It's 'appened once too often this time.

LEN   Every bloody week the same!

PAM   [*to* HARRY] Sure yer ain' got it?

HARRY   I bought this shirt over eight years ago.

PAM   That cost me every week. You reckon that up over a year. Yer must think I was born yesterday.

[*Pause. She rubs her hair*]

Wasn't 'ere last week. Never 'ere. Got legs.

[*She goes to the door and shouts*]

Mum! She 'eard all right.

[*She goes back to the couch and sits. She rubs her hair*]

Someone's got it. I shouldn't think the people next door come in an' took it. Everyone 'as the benefit a it 'cept me. It's always the same. I'll know what t' do in future. Two can play at that game. I ain' blikin' daft. [*She rubs her hair*] I never begrudge no one borrowin' it, but yer'd think they'd have enough manners t' put it back.

[*Pause.*

She rubs her hair]

Juss walk all over yer. Well it ain' goin' a 'appen again. They treat you like a door mat. All take and no give. Touch somethin' a their 'n an' they go through the bloody ceilin'. It's bin the same ever since –

LEN   I tol' yer t' keep it in yer room!

PAM   Now yer got a lock things up in yer own 'ouse.

LEN   Why should we put up with this week after week juss because yer too –

PAM   Yer know what yer can do.

LEN   Thass yer answer t'everythin'.

PAM   Got a better one?

HARRY   They was a pair first off. Sent me back a quid each. Up the market. One's gone 'ome, went at the cuffs. Worth a quid.

LEN   Chriss.

([1965] 1977: 88–90)

Although there are three participants in this extract, the turn-taking system actually brings Pam and Len into contact most of the time and it is the interaction between them that constitutes the interest of this extract. Harry's contributions are minimal but provide a pertinent display of lack of interest in interacting with Pam, which contributes to the frustration of her attempts to impress herself upon the situation. Len, on the other hand, interacts; he alternates his turns with Pam's, but the management of his responses plays out his ostensible disinterest more elaborately, since his strategies attempt to disqualify her speech as defective interactively, through overt evaluations of her performance as not worth attention at all. Pam's turns contain *firsts* of questions and an initiated remedial sequence, which projectively constrain Len's turns, but he refuses the normative path set by her and provides instead his own mode of response, which undermines hers. No interactive support is forthcoming from either of the men. There is some similarity in strategy adopted by the men against her as in the previous extract, but there are differences as well.

The extract opens with Pam initiating herself into the conversation between the other two with a question, first to Harry who lets his turn lapse and so does not open himself up to interrogation. When this fails, Pam chooses Len, who responds, but not with an answer to her question. In fact, the question remains unanswered across the extract; nobody admits to taking her *Radio Times*. Len's response displays, instead, negative orientation, boredom with her questioning. Like Harry, in the previous extract, he exhibits that he has heard it all before. What she has to say is categorized by him as lacking *tellability* and thus disqualifies itself from a hearing. Pam picks up on his displayed lack of orientation, both in what he has said and in his manner of saying, since he 'mumbles', his speech lacking audibility as well – 'You speakin' t' me?' Again, Lenny does not answer, but re-iterates rejection, explicitly, of her topic and her speech – 'I'm sick t' death of yer bloody *Radio Times*.' Not getting anywhere on the QA strategy Pam moves into another sequence, a *Remedial* one, casting herself in the role of Reproacher and, thus, in possession of a grievance. Her turn expands into a long list of complaints and inconveniences that beset her when her *Radio Times* is not to be found when she wants it, and she threatens to cancel the subscription. Len does not play the second part of the canonical sequence: no accounting or redress or remedy is offered or suggested, nor any reaction to her threat. He sticks instead to classifying her new strategy as even more boring.

Pam's attempts to get Len to take her performance seriously having been thwarted, she chooses Harry again and questions him. Harry lets her topic drop completely and initiates a wholly unrelated one, on his shirts, as if she hadn't spoken. He uses the turn passed to him by Pam but not to further her concerns. Pam next re-initiates 'grievance' and launches into a long speech on how people treat her and her magazine. She pauses, i.e. she projects turn change, but no one picks up the turn, so she is obliged to go on – and on. After a second pause, when neither of the men claims the turn she is forced to proceed with further grievances in her turn. She finally provokes Len into interrupting her, since the men had failed to silence her by their previous strategies. Len takes the turn with a counter-reproach, not an account – 'I tol' yer t' keep it in yer room' – thus attempting to turn the tables on her. Her displayed grievances are interpreted as her own fault and, therefore, disqualified, since they are not grievances at all. Pam, in response, incorporates his statement as reason for a further grievance, Len attempts to take the reproach slot by providing a grievance of his own – 'Why should we put up with this week after week juss because yer too –' which Pam interrupts with a rude counter-suggestion instead of an account, which Len counters, and Pam counters in turn. Harry's wholly irrelevant intervention on a self-selected turn breaks the developing quarrel between Len and Pam but also deflects attention away from Pam and on to Harry, as Len swears in disbelief at Harry this time.

In most of this extract, Pam's attempts to attain interactive equality and reciprocity fail. Her questions are never answered, and her projected next turns either lapse or she gets a response she has not bargained for. Even the off-stage Mum does not bother to reply. When she moves into *grievance* mode, there is no support, nor any reaction to her threats. Pam re-initiates repeatedly on her original initiatory moves, but given no reciprocity on the part of the men, this strategy only compounds her ineffectuality. Her interactive style attempts control – she initiates, she introduces topics, she interrupts, but control fails to come off. The men do not play to her initiations, and so her will cannot prevail. In fact, the men pointedly ignore or undermine her performance. Both use male strategies – Len does not focus on what she has said, the content of her turn, but on the manner of saying it, which he evaluates as boring. Len's style is also deflective; it chokes off development of her concerns. He counters successfully – not only does he refuse her projected role for him in her turns, he continually evaluates and references her performance as defective, since she tells what is not worth listening to, complains when she has no right to, etc., which attempt to disqualify her from speaking. Her topics, too, are not developed or oriented to by him, except in disagreement.

Pam sticks by her questioning strategy and her grievances, and her topics, ignoring their reactions, but on her own, and in defiance of the non-co-operation displayed by the two men. In the absence of interactive reciprocity, Pam takes the floor, in long and sustained turns, which she finds difficult to relinquish, since they do not want the floor or interaction with her. The men remain unimpressed and unco-operative since every time she provides an opportunity for turn change nobody responds. Her assumed role of reproacher is neither ratified nor acknowledged by them and the sequence does not proceed to redress for her from them. She achieves speech dominance by her long turns and her claim on the floor, which she uses in such a way as to force them to respond, but this does not provide her with interactive dominance in this segment.

By contrast, Sarah, in the previous extract, shared speech more equally with Harry, yet managed to get him to respond as she had wished for most of the time. Her questions are answered, for instance. When Sarah does not achieve satisfaction, she moves into repair, or into metacommunicative mode, to expose and deal with the very strategies Harry used to frustrate her, and to his discomfiture. No such possibility is given to Pam, who repeats failed strategies, the length of her turns only emphasizing her ineffectuality. Thus, Len and Harry, here, prove a stronger counter-force because of their ability to frustrate Pam, which she is ineffectual to counter. They undermine her by not listening or responding inappropriately, or negatively categorizing her attempts. Pam acts in defiance of this resistance and continues to do so, but she cannot dominate as Sarah was able to do in the previous extract. Pam does, in the end, achieve a measure of interactive equality in getting Len to exchange turns with her, but even this is short-lived, since Harry successfully intervenes with his irrelevancies. Both extracts use the aborted remedial sequence, but this enables the conflicts to be sustained.

Sequencing in general, and adjacency pairs in particular, can be used in more complex ways since there are many options that cluster in the turn change gap as much as in the mode of response. In the following extract, from Shakespeare's *Hamlet*, the QA pair is played in such a way that different modes of answering are used. Turn change options are mobilized to vary the playing of response.

The variation in patterns contributes to the construction of situation and to a reading of character, especially the contrast between 'ALL' (Horatio, Marcellus and Bernardo) and Horatio. It also accentuates the quality of the initiator's – Hamlet's – concerns in a specific way as the information required is played out detail by detail through chaining multiple QA pairs. The extract is part of a larger segment in which the three principals communicate the fact of the ghost's appearance on the battlements to Hamlet. He questions the others on its appearance and its demeanour.

HAMLET	. . . Hold you the watch tonight?
ALL	We do, my lord.
HAMLET	Arm'd you say?
ALL	Arm'd, my lord.
HAMLET	From top to toe?
ALL	My lord, from head to foot.

HAMLET   Then saw you not his face?
HORATIO   O yes, my lord; he wore his beaver up.
HAMLET   What? look'd he frowningly?
HORATIO   A countenance more in sorrow than in anger.
HAMLET   Pale, or red?
HORATIO   Nay, very pale.
HAMLET   And fix'd his eyes upon you?
HORATIO   Most constantly.

(1.2.224–34)

Hamlet initiates the QA sequences, which are played in short, one-line turns. The answers are equally brief, to the point, so that the tempo of this segment is rapid, although gaps could be inserted to give it a more speculative or thoughtful feel, especially on Hamlet's part. But the sequencing follows the rules and economy of QA adjacency which contributes to the sense of significance in the detail required. There is variation on the mode of playing answers. Although in adjacency, Marcellus, Bernardo and Horatio overlap and speak in unison in a single turn which is used jointly in answer to Hamlet's questions. Horatio is also given sole control of his turn. Two modes of conviction and certainty about the information communicated are provided: an affective one in the emotional urgency displayed in the triple-voiced mode of response within a single turn in the collaboration of the overlaps; authority in the more measured solo turns of Horatio, person and voice integrated to attest to the truth of the statement.

Comparisons in sequence design among segments reveal the different interactive strategies and their responsive dynamics which help to create situational differences. Such comparisons may also enable a greater appreciation of the creative and imaginative ingenuity of dramatists since a sense of déjà vu is rare in drama even in instances where similar situational types recur – like conflict scenes, recognition scenes, trial scenes, persuasion or debate scenes, love scenes and so on which are common types in plays. Comparative analysis can also make available the different interactive strategies employed by a character and how outcomes are managed in the various situations in which he or she is embroiled, in order to enhance or diminish a character's effectivity or fullness of realization.

INTIMACY SEQUENCES

Situations of many kinds make their appearance in drama and not all of them are conflictual or quarrelsome. The design of situations may change, action may move to a climax, conflicts may be resolved, or they may be left open or unresolved, but these outcomes are to be assessed within the structure of the duality or multiplicity of input through which such achievements are constructed. Among the variety of situations are those at the opposite end of conflict – the creation of intimacy. These have their own rules and trajectories like conflicts do, and are open to variations of degree and kind and are produced by the exploitation of normative rules. The creation of affiliation, intimacy, support among characters can be valuable dramatically and these, too, are interactive processes. Where intimacy and informality are already in existence among characters they have to be suggested or communicated to an audience and sustained in a scene through turn-taking and sequencing displays. Where they do not exist, but are needed for some dramatic end, they have to be created. At any rate, mutual reciprocity, inter-personal closeness and interactive harmony are equally matters to be achieved through the employment of speech in drama. They are, in other words, products of interactive work, which counter the threat of separation and self-enclosure of individuals. How effects of this latter kind are produced are open to analysis.

Among the most intimate of situations must be those in which charac-ters affectively disclose personal feelings of mutual regard for each other, and such declarations need to be sequenced. Degrees of mutuality, inten-sity and reciprocity need to be displayed and accepted. These situations, like others, are created reciprocally. The strategies dramatists use to build up intimacy segments in which interactants display openness or the desire for union with another, show their own creative variation, even though at first glance it may appear that happy interactions, like happy families, must all be alike. There are, too, different kinds of intimacy – romantic and non-romantic – and sequencing strategies used must be flexible enough to permit a great deal of variation, given the many kinds of positively affiliated, mutually supportive or enhancing relationships dramatists have created in plays.

A strategy that has been explored in the literature for the creation of intimacy is that of reciprocity of various personal resources, among them, in turn-taking terms, self-disclosure (Jefferson *et al.* 1987; Dindia 1985). Offering intimate information to another invites intimacy reciprocally, and if returned in like measure, mutually creates it. Subsequent turns may either disengage from proceeding with such a sequence, or sustain it, or escalate its affective quality, or refuse it. The degree of intimacy achieved or essayed can also vary as a consequence. In *Othello* the strategy is used to colour the relationship between Desdemona and Othello when they meet again after the latter's return from the wars in Cyprus. Othello's expression of the depth of his feeling for his wife in his turn is reciprocated in hers, and their mutual confessions and ratifications of love build up the sequence.

> OTHELLO   O my fair warrior!
> DESDEMONA   My dear Othello!
> OTHELLO   It gives me wonder great as my content
> To see you here before me. O my soul's joy!
> If after every tempest come such calms,
> May the winds blow till they have waken'd death
> And let the labouring bark climb hills of seas
> Olympus-high, and duck again as low
> As hell's from heaven. If it were now to die,
> 'Twere now to be most happy; for I fear
> My soul hath her content so absolute
> That not another comfort like to this
> Succeeds in unknown fate.
> DESDEMONA   The heavens forbid
> But that our loves and comforts should increase
> Even as our days do grow!
> OTHELLO   Amen to that, sweet powers!
> I cannot speak enough of this content;
> It stops me here; it is too much joy.
> And this, and this, the greatest discords be,
>   [*They kiss*]
> That e'er our hearts shall make!
>
> (2.2.179–96)

The exchange is a brief one – in five-part form and in alternation. The intensity of feeling expressed by Othello in his long turn is reciprocated by Desdemona, if briefly, which is in turn ratified by Othello. Emotional intensity is deepened chiefly by Othello in his long turns, which he uses to elaborate on his feelings but its evolution is dependent on Desdemona's return of feeling in her turn.

Reciprocity of this kind, when personal disclosures of love lead to the return of disclosure of similar kind, knits characters together in emotional bonds, but not all intimacy sequences need to succeed. Mismatches in feeling or intensity can display love relationships that misfire, with the intimacy desired by one partner not accepted or reciprocated by the other. Such asymmetries need to be unfolded through the management of turn sequences. In Act 1 of Chekhov's *The Seagull*, at the beginning of the play, we have an instance of the latter kind when self-disclosure initiated by Medvedenko is not reciprocated by Masha, which affects the interpersonal situation accordingly.

MEDVEDENKO   Why do you always wear black?

MASHA   I am in mourning for my life. I am unhappy.

MEDVEDENKO   Why? [*Pondering*] I don't understand. . . You are in good health; though your father is not very well off, he has got enough. My life is much harder than yours. I only get twenty-three roubles a month, and from that they deduct something for the pension fund, and yet I don't wear mourning. [*They sit down*]

MASHA   It isn't money that matters. A poor man may be happy.

MEDVEDENKO   Theoretically, yes; but in practice it's like this: there are my two sisters and my mother and my little brother and I, and my salary is only twenty-three roubles. We must eat and drink mustn't we? One must have tea and sugar. One must have tobacco. It's a tight fit.

MASHA   [*looking round at the platform*] The play will soon begin.

MEDVEDENKO   Yes. Miss Zaretchny will act: it is Konstantin Gavrilitch's play. They are in love with each other and today their souls will be united in the effort to realise the same artistic effect. But your soul and mine have not a common point of contact. I love you. I am so wretched I can't stay at home. Every day I walk four miles here and four miles back and I meet with nothing but indifference from you. I can quite understand it. I am without means and have a big family to keep. . . Who would care to marry a man who hasn't a penny to bless himself with?

MASHA   Oh nonsense! [*Takes a pinch of snuff*] Your love touches me but I can't reciprocate it – that's all. [*Holding out snuff-box to him*] Help yourself.

MEDVEDENKO   I don't feel like it. [*a pause*]

MASHA   How stifling it is! There must be a storm coming. . . You're always discussing theories or talking about money. You think there is no greater misfortune than poverty, but to my mind it is a thousand times better to go in rags and be a beggar than. . . But you wouldn't understand that, though. . .

(Chekhov [1923] 1971: 3–4)

Turn-taking alternates between them regularly and from the first initiating question, Medvedenko's turns focus on personal and intimate topics – her dress, her family, his salary, his family commitments and his opinions and feelings for her. Topic is the resource he uses to invite intimacy from her in return and his speech casts him as an intimate of hers:

he talks about personal details in her life as well as his own, and of his desire for a deeper attachment. Masha, however, after her first self-disclosing answer about her unhappiness, refuses to continue in this vein. No matching self-disclosures are forthcoming from her in return. Her second turn sticks to generalities, while her third turn actually changes topic. Intimacy invited by Medvedenko is blocked or deflected since Masha's responses do not permit development of the sequence beyond the level of intimacy permitted of friends rather than lovers. In fact, her topics do not even orientate towards him affectively or intellectually. Even his declaration of love for her and his disclosure of his misery in unrequited love misfires since she responds factually with a low-key statement of her inability to love him and offers him a pinch of snuff instead. At the end of the extract, she changes topic again by initiating a more intense disclosure of her own thoughts, which are in direct contradiction to his, but breaks off midstream, declaring him an inappropriate recipient. Emotional intensity is exceedingly sparse in this extract since the development is one-sided, on Medvedenko's part alone, and is not permitted to escalate by Masha. The emotional environment created by the exchanges is one of mutual familiarity, the affective register restrained and muted through lack of developmental support.

Non-romantic intimacies of various kinds, in friendships or in the sharing of close, personal bonds of one kind or another, also make their appearance in drama. If characters are cast as friendly, supportive, open to each other, these too have to be created and sustained via interaction and sequencing. The relationship between Celia and Rosalind in *As You Like It*, and between Juliet and the Nurse in *Romeo and Juliet*, and Horatio and Hamlet, are cases in point. Occasionally moments occur when drastic changes of state are called for when participants cast basically as non-intimates, as strangers, have to be made to realize very different levels of inter-personal possibilities, which have not been available owing to various obstacles. In *Twelfth Night*, Sebastian and the disguised twin Viola offer and re-offer to each other personal and intimate family information, and personal expressions of grief at the supposed death of the other twin, which in the sharing and reciprocation enacts the process of bringing them closer together in new realizations of who they are.

Intimacy and affiliation may be invited not only by affective displays and by choice of personal topics, but also, paradoxically, by the use of rude or crude socially 'improper' talk. As Jefferson *et al.* note,

> . . . it is a convention about interaction that frankness, rudeness, crudeness, profanity, obscenity, etc. are indices of relaxed, unguarded,

spontaneous, i.e., intimate interaction. That convention may be *utilised* by participants. That is, the introduction of such talk can be seen as a display that the speaker takes it that the current interaction is one in which he may produce such talk; i.e., is informal/intimate. Further, the introduction of such talk may be, not only a display of perception by one party of the status of the interaction, but a consequential, programmatic action. By introducing such talk, a speaker may be initiating a move *into* intimate interaction from a status he perceives as non-intimate so far. Speaker may be offering an invitation to his co-participants to produce talk together whereby they can see themselves as intimate; together they will be constructing intimacy.

(1987: 160)

The possibilities for exploiting such an interactional resource are high. Tokens of rudeness, when exchanged and sequenced as responsive, affiliative play, can be seen as not only displaying intimacy but affection as in the interactions between Jimmy and Cliff in Osborne's *Look Back in Anger* (1957). Rudeness with Cliff is Jimmy's dominant interactional ploy but the resource itself functions dually – as banter and affiliative with Cliff, and as rudeness pure and simple with Alison. Again, the response is important since Alison does not reciprocate with such tokens as Jimmy does, so that she is read as the victim of them, whereas Jimmy exchanges rudeness quite amicably with Cliff. In the extract given below Cliff is reading a paper which Jimmy uses as the topic of his first sally against Cliff.

JIMMY   Why do you bother? you can't understand a word of it.
CLIFF   Uh huh.
JIMMY   You're too ignorant.
CLIFF   Yes, and uneducated. Now shut up will you?
JIMMY   Why don't you get my wife to explain it to you? She's educated. [*To her*] That's right isn't it?
CLIFF   [*kicking out at him from behind his paper*]   Leave her alone, I said.
JIMMY   Do that again, you Welsh ruffian, and I'll pull your ears off. [*He bangs Cliff's paper out of his hands*]
CLIFF   [*leaning forward*] Listen – I'm trying to better myself. Let me get on with it, you big, horrible man. Give it me. [*Puts his hand out for paper*]

(Osborne 1957: 11)

With Alison the same strategy has different consequences. Alison does not respond to Jimmy's negative assessments of her so that she does not use the option to transform them into the play of intimacy with Jimmy. Jimmy's turns can only be evaluated as rude as a result. Moreover, Jimmy returns to the same strategy and pursues a response from Alison as he continues to bait her. His attempts are interpreted as bullying by Cliff, too, who intervenes more than once to stop him.

The creation of intimacy, informality, etc. is thus an interactive matter in which the concerned parties are involved and which they create through their speech. Speakers may invite intimacy but the extent to which it can become an inter-personal reality is dependent on its relational development among interactants themselves and is open to negotiation. Jefferson *et al.* (1987) have noted several negotiatory options that those invited to participate in the *improper talk* strategy can use. Recipients of such talk may affiliate, decline to respond, disattend, appreciate, escalate, and different combinations of these can structure a sequence. Disattention may follow appreciation which could lead on to failure to respond or appreciation escalated in return. In the above extract, Jimmy and Cliff could be interpreted as sustaining and appreciating intimacy through improprieties, while Alison usually disattends and thus blocks any further progress. Both verbal and non-verbal tokens like laughter as intimacy devices are also examined in Jefferson *et al.*'s (1987) data.

More complex forms of negotiation are also possible in which conflict may arise in instances where intimacy offered by a speaker may be desired, but not the terms involved: the exchange of some specific kind of improper talk. Such an instance can be seen in the following extract from *Othello* between Cassio and Iago when Iago initiates a sequence of obscene talk about Desdemona.

CASSIO Welcome Iago; we must to the watch.

IAGO Not this hour Lieutenant;' tis not yet ten o'clock. Our general cast us thus early for the love of his Desdemona; who let us not therefore blame. He hath not yet made wanton the night with her; and she is sport for Jove.

CASSIO She is a most exquisite lady.

IAGO And, I'll warrant her, full of game.

CASSIO Indeed, she is a most fresh and delicate creature.

IAGO What an eye she has! methinks it sounds a parley of provocation.

CASSIO An inviting eye; and yet methinks right modest.

IAGO And when she speaks, is it not an alarm to love?

CASSIO She is indeed perfection.

IAGO   Well, happiness to their sheets! Come Lieutenant, I have a stoup of wine. . .

(2.3.12–27)

The interest of this segment is in the management of the intimacy drive. Cassio does not respond to the invitation to collude with Iago in the exchange of such talk but he does not break off talk with Iago either. He responds, but uses a specific strategy – in Jefferson *et al.*'s (1987) terms, Cassio 'disattends it while responding to an innocuous aspect of the carrier utterance'. In fact, he reciprocates comment with comment in partially affiliative mode but re-interprets and re-formulates Iago's obscenities as compliments to the absent Desdemona, which he escalates in his own speech and which he sustains across the interaction as Iago escalates and sustains the tenor of his speech in his turns. Cassio preserves his relationship with Iago while simultaneously maintaining his own loyalty to Desdemona against Iago's attempts to dislodge it.

Intimacy, friendship, closeness, these qualities also bring with them inter-personal and social values like trust as appropriate to them. Intimacy strategies, as a consequence, leave room for manipulation of others since the default values signified could be abused. And this is precisely what Iago does in his transactions with Othello. Iago initiates intimacy sequences over and over again, protesting to Othello about 'the love and duty I bear you' and other such disclosures of personal regard. He also offers many impertinent, untrue, personal disclosures to Othello regarding Desdemona in the guise of the 'honest' friend and confidant, who has Othello's interests at heart. He reinforces the pose with other protestations of concern at Othello's state of mind at his own disclosures about Desdemona. He uses a wide range of strategies. Othello takes the seeming trustworthiness of such intimate offerings and Iago's performance at face value and the damage is done. Collusive interactions with Roderigo are also sprinkled liberally with markers which assume intimacy on Iago's part. The intimacy offered by Iago is wholly a means to get his victims off-guard. It also encloses them within the restricted circle of participation he has created for them with himself, and is used for manipulative purposes and for power.

ALTERNATIVE SEQUENCES

Sequences enact the path of action as if on the wing, and the resources mobilized to construct their course employ the basic, projective and retrospective orientations of turns. Abstract social directives become concrete and time-bound in their sequenced enactments while involving the participants themselves in their dramatic destinies. But interactions need not develop into anything. They need not have a linear, developmental path, a teleology, or result in outcomes of any kind. They may plod the same relational space with characters unable or unwilling to develop any meaningful or directed form of action via speech or construct any meaningful form of inter-subjective relationship. Thus phatic exchanges, which involve the give and take of routine social tokens which are only feebly inter-subjective, if at all, may be the staple of interactions, with sequencing requiring no particular inter-personal involvement or effort, resulting in the set of the interaction following no particular direction. The speech channel is open, turns are taken and alternate but only very basic tokens of contact are achieved. There is much redundancy in speech with little new information attempted and, even if given, this is done only after a round of phatic talk, as Deirdre Burton's (1980) analysis of Pinter's *Last To Go* reveals.

Within such exchanges, embeddings, like repair sequences, may occur to protract the course of these styles of talk. But difficulties are encountered even in the reduced engagements that dialogue enacts. Basic difficulties are enacted, like hearing properly or attending properly to the speaker's speech. Interactions lengthen, as turns and time are expended in securing attention, or fixing reference, or clearing or creating a ground for interaction so that the prerequisites for communication, which are taken for granted in normative talk, become the matter and focus of interaction itself. What should be communicational givens, and are generally used as such in plays that exploit the full communicative potential of the verbal medium, become metacommunicative uncertainties and matters for extended, dramatic engagement.

Modern drama, in particular, with its suspicion of the efficacy of words as instruments of communication and its distrust of the notion of communication itself, creates situations in which problems of communication and the inability to orientate or relate to the other in speech are privileged above notions of evolving inter-personal realities in which interactions actually achieve something consequential for those involved, or in the world of the play as a whole. Interactions proliferate, in which nothing in particular is done. The pointlessness itself is dramatized by the exchanges, turn by turn and in time. Or speech is used merely to depict empty lives or the absurdity of situations in which people are involved, or to portray the basic isolation of people from people. Instead of structures of inter-subjectivity, which are designed to develop or change through talk, we get structures that display blight of various kinds via miscommunication or non-communication, as the major forms of inter-personal truth.

Even where communication is successful, it can often be ensconced in worlds where character interactions create situations which, from the point of view of our familiar social world, are irrational, closer to dream or nightmare, productive of void rather than meaning, which are accepted and ratified as *normal* in those worlds through interaction. Yet, such effects have to be structured and sequenced, within the evolution of turns, as they are; characters are made jointly responsible for such displays in the speech events of their participation; speakers contribute to the creation of these situations by their speech uses, and in ways credible to the participants and to the audience. Mutual acceptance of such forms of interaction on the part of the fictional characters serves to authenticate and stabilize such exchanges within the play world and enables, too, the reflexive confrontation by an audience of its own assumptions of the nature or value of communication in its own. The basic principles on which speech exchange is based remain the same, even when they are called into question, and even if their strategic employment varies.

Dialogic incongruities of various kinds proliferate in modern drama. Many are owing to motivated, semantic or pragmatic, or sometimes theatrical, 'infelicities', but others are brought about by various distortions of the rules of the turn-taking system and its sequencing procedures. Dina Sherzer has examined various strategies employed especially in the drama of the Absurd. Among them are sequences of unrelated turns, inappropriate answers which are uttered sequentially 'without overt transition or presupposed causality' (Sherzer 1978), story-telling sequences in which the back-channelling devices required are not only not forthcoming but the interlocutor behaves as if the story had not even taken place. To quote Sherzer,

> Story telling conventions are manipulated: details irrelevant to the story are mentioned. . . ; the events are not topics worthy of telling. . . and the reactions of the listeners are out of proportion.
>
> (1978: 275)

Sequence structure is also wrenched out of place and shape. What would normally be regarded as a pre-sequence, and usually a brief sequence, can become protracted to function as the main business itself. In Ionesco's *The Bald Soprano* (1965) the pre-sequence prompt to a story becomes the main interaction while the *story* itself is about the speaker seeing a man on the street tying his shoelaces, which delivers the effect of bathos. In the same play, husband and wife exchange information as if they were strangers and ignorant of the details of each other's lives. Styles of speech can also be mismatched: a conversation between husband and wife conducted as if they were reading a manual for learning a foreign language.

REPETITION

Speech used by participants can itself provide the means for sequencing some part of an interaction through the use of repetition – by speakers re-duplicating and re-cycling bits and pieces of their own or others' previous talk. Repetition in discourse has a variety of functions although, as a rule, it is evaluated negatively, as indicative of lack of involvement or creativity in speech, and generative of effects like boredom and tedium when used. Yet, much of language is already *pre-packaged* as Bolinger (1961: 381) has observed:

> At present we have no way of telling the extent to which a sentence like *I went home* is a result of invention, and the extent to which it is a result of repetition, countless speakers before us having already said it and transmitted it to us in toto. Is grammar something where speakers 'produce' (i.e. originate) constructions, or where they 'reach for' them, from a pre-established inventory. . . ?
>
> (Bolinger (1961), quoted by Tannen 1989: 37)

If specific forms, like *I went home*, are used and re-used in similar situations or for similar communicative purposes, the repetition of form, of syntactic form, even as an abstract, is even more pervasive. Moreover, pre-patterned forms like idioms and proverbs are to be found in many languages, which are often repeated in different contexts and by different speakers as the need arises. Poetic form depends on the use of repetitive patterns – of stanzas, rhyme and rhythm, but also of syntactical and lexical patterning. Jakobson's (1960) contention that the poetic principle is a principle of *equivalence* which projects the axis of selection on to the axis of combination endorses the creative use of repetition as parallelism of forms, and as a device for foregrounding and de-familiarizing in poetry. Oratory, too, is highly patterned speech. In day-to-day settings, routinized and formulaic speech forms (Coulmas 1981) often serve to lubricate social relationships: in fact they are expected in some cultures as part of social behaviour and their omission could be read as a dereliction of social obligation (Tannen 1989: 38–44).

Repetition, therefore, has very different functions to perform, from the phatic to the poetic. In interactions, speakers may use pre-patterned resources like proverbs, idioms, etc., but speakers also 'reach for' already-used speech within the speech events in which they are engaged. Or they may use speech that was issued in other contexts, by quoting or mimicking it. Within the contingencies of an evolving situation speakers may re-use recently produced speech as an immediately available resource. The uses of repetition of this kind have various interactive consequences, and have been the object of recent study (Johnstone 1987; Norrick 1987; Tannen 1989).

Two kinds of repetition can be distinguished: self-repetition, and other or allo-repetition. Words, phrases, clauses or longer stretches can be repeated, or part repeated. Self-repetition can function as a production strategy for the speaker, to minimize pauses or disfluency, or as a means of transition when working out how to proceed with one's own turn. It can facilitate comprehension when speakers repeat themselves to clarify what they mean and to ward off ambiguity, to summarize and paraphrase and so on (Norrick 1987). In longer turns, or texts in general, repetition can also have a cohesive function as Halliday and Hasan (1976) have noted, since it can stabilize both reference and topic across a stretch of discourse. But it may also have an evaluative function, and thus signify speaker attitude, when something is repeated for emphasis or invested with an iconic function which may weave in emotional overtones to a description, while making the description itself more vivid. For instance, 'She has blue, blue eyes' makes the blue eyes bluer while indicating the speaker's positive attitude to the colour of the eyes. Similarly, 'It was a long, long, long journey' lengthens the journey with each repetition while telling us something of the sense of endurance felt by the speaker. A series of repeated utterances can create its own paradigm and set up expectations which could be undercut for various reasons. Tannen gives the following example:

1   *And he knows* Spanish,
2   *and he knows* French,
3   *and he knows* English,
4   *and he knows* German,
5   *and He* is a GENtleman

(1989: 50)

in which the sudden change of the pattern reinforces the cumulative regard that had been built up by the repetitions.

A series like this can be undertaken interactively as well, and for more coercive purposes, as we have already seen in the Sarah–Harry interaction (see p.125) in Sarah's 'You know. . . , You know. . . And also you know. . . So why don't you know. . . '. The repeat of the question, dealing item by item with details of Harry's knowledge, binds Harry again and again to the tie of the answer, even though both know the other knows the information requested. It functions, as the dramatist indicates, as a means of showing Harry up to himself. Matoesian's (1993) study of a rape trial reveals a similar strategy being used by the defence lawyer against the female victim. His questioning lists her actions one after another in such a way as to form a paradigm in order to create and reinforce inferences in the jury's mind that the victim invited the rape.

Allo-repetition can perform many interactive services. Repeating or part-repeating what the previous speaker has said may signal merely a desire to hold the floor, especially if performed with contextualizing cues like stress on some word and with gaze averted. Without special stress and intonation and with gaze focused on the previous speaker, it could signal a return of the turn to the speaker (Norrick 1987: 249). Interactively, repeats can have strongly affirmative functions. Questions can be answered merely by repeating what was asked in reply. Or repeats could be a means of displaying rapport in interaction as giving evidence of attentive listening; or they could signal acknowledgement of the other's speech and agreement with the speaker. Often, speakers, temporarily at a loss for the right word or phrase, may use the speech proffered by another, co-operatively, and integrate it into their own speech.

D   . . . it is going to tarnish quite severely –
P   some of the FBI
P   – some of the FBI.

(Norrick 1987: 251)

Shadowing another's speech even before the speaker has finished his or her turn is another device of participation. Tannen gives the following example:

DEBORAH. . .
8   because there's no word
9   that expresses *body and soul together*
     CHAD   Body and soul together.

(Tannen 1989: 60)

Repetition is thus a handy means for performing positive interactional tasks like displaying listenership or making participation tangible. Expansions of some repeated previous utterance and even reluctant or 'grudging' concessions or agreements (Norrick 1987: 251) can display degrees of supportive ratification of another's speech. The 'matching claim' repeat

(Keenan 1977: 132) can signify alignment but also competition, with the addition of contrastive stress alone, as in 'I'm fat/*I'm* fat', spoken in succession by two different speakers. Other affiliative uses include the creation of humour and play as Tannen reveals in the following extract from her data, which she labels *savouring*: repetitions of this and other kinds constituting a *poetics* of conversation in their use.

1 DAVID   That because you have a –
   /arcane/view of reality. [*laughter*]
2 DEBORAH   Cause we're sensitive. [*laughing*]
   [*laughter*]
3 SALLY   Cause we're *ladies*.
   [*laughter*]
4 STEVE   Ladies. . . Ladies. [*laughing*]

(Tannen 1989: 64)

Disagreement and competition may also be realized by the use of this device. Norrick lists four or five major types with some sub-types from his own data. In adjacency pairs, repetition can be used to question a prior statement, in the form of questioning repeats of the kind noted by Jefferson (1972). Within the statement/disagree pair, allo-repetition can assist in the expression of disbelief or surprise, facilitate competitiveness via a matching claim, contradict or correct the previous speaker by a counter-claim, or mockingly imitate another. Repetition can also be used more neutrally to think aloud by re-playing another's speech or to re-broadcast someone's speech as in a classroom situation when a teacher repeats a student's question for the benefit of the whole class. The varied effects cited above are not accidental since they are of the class of significant repeats that perform some operation on a previous utterance and not the random instances with which they are often confused (Norrick 1987: 246).

As a dramatic strategy, repetition in a stretch of dialogue is particularly fruitful given the range of possible uses to which it could be put. The poetic and aesthetic aspects of the device are perhaps the strongest witness to its value, especially in dramatic poetry, whether as expressive, self-repetition in single lines, as in Macbeth's 'Tomorrow and tomorrow and tomorrow. . . ' or Hamlet's antithetical 'To be or not to be. . . ' with its orientation set towards the speaker; or in longer stretches that interlace repetition with variation in tight or flexible fashion, to enhance its poetic texture and effect. Dramatic genres like stychomythia are constructed of parallelisms across turns, and repetition can be used to stylize or ritualize speech to give it communal rather than individual import as in T. S. Eliot's *Murder in the Cathedral* (1935). Poetic, speaker repetition can have manipulative or persuasive uses in public settings when addressee-orientated, when the aesthetic is mobilized for political ends. It functions as oratory, and as a hypnotic, political tool in the mouth of Mark Antony at Caesar's funeral oration. Instances can be multiplied and these conventional types of repetition derived from poetic, dramatic and rhetorical traditions have a long history and have been noted extensively in traditional literary studies.

Repetition in dialogue, as a discourse strategy, as mentioned above, uses the speech resources at hand, and is generally not backed by a traditional rhetorics or poetics, although it may well create contingent poetics or rhetorics within an interaction. Repetition in conversational discourse is a kind of interactional *bricolage*, constructed within the pressures of the moment and with the means at hand, and derives both meaning and value from within the interaction itself. Repetition of this kind diminishes interest in the content of speech, an exigency which is generally responsible for its negative evaluation, since its automaticity seems to signify limitations of various mental, expressive and communicative kinds on the part of the speaker. No new information is forthcoming when a stretch of talk uses and re-uses the same language and its contents. Consequently, a speaker's topic or idea or thought or argument or perspective or the expression of emotion, etc. is not open to development when speech is employed in this way. Moreover, repetition depletes the resource of time in drama and in life. And, further, it has to operate against the expectation of *tellability* when assessed on content lines.

But the furthering of explicit content is not repetition's function. It focuses attention instead on the mechanics of discourse and interaction. It is a turn constructional strategy – whether as self- or allo-repetition – and as such it can direct the course of talk, often by inhibiting development and colouring the situation itself. Repeated references to some item can make it matter for attention within the fictional universe of discourse which the talk constructs, or foreground it as an unfinished topic or concern among the participants on-stage which awaits closure or outcome, which may or may not ensue. Repeats of talk in direct quotation or parody, or of items of talk from previous speech or even previous contexts of talk, can form a cohesive link bridging separate and disjointed scenes in time and space or placing them in juxtaposition in the present context of speech via memory or narrative. The functions are many, and are made more various by the exigencies and pressures that operate to produce repetition in any specific interaction. The use dramatists make of repetition is equally prolific, if not more copious since all sorts and conditions of persons in fictional situations, different dramaturgies and historical conventions of language use further complicate dramatic uses.

The exploitation of the tension between the forward, linear, dynamic thrust of talk, as that which evolves in time, turn by turn, and the stasis presupposed by repetition, is one among the many areas that has produced variation in the way dramatists have mobilized and patterned repetitive talk to furnish distinctive situations. Given that the development of content or idea is not the leading principle that motivates repetitive strategies, other functions of interaction take priority. Repetitive speech, when it plods the same interactional space, could be seen as the death of language in drama. But this is the case only when *language* is assessed, as it often is, as synonymous with those instances when it manifests the full weight and significance of its symbolic, deictic or figural capacities. But it must be borne in mind that this eventuality is but one point in a spectrum of uses, and not to be identified with all of it. As speech, its 'negative' possibilities are as rich, a fact which is made more visible in its manifestations in interaction. The whole range of the interactive potential of language use is, of course, what dramatic dialogue mobilizes.

In the following extract, both self- and allo-repetition are the resources used to structure the situation. Participants re-cycle either their own or others' speech. The situation is taken from Edward Albee's *Who's Afraid of Virginia Woolf?* and from a sequel to confidences that had been exchanged among the men earlier about their wives. The participants are in the roles of hosts–guests, late at night, at a drunken, post-party party. Interaction is a series of deadly games which Martha and George, the hosts, play. In the extract it is the game of *Get the Guests* initiated by George who is also the leading player and takes the managing role by using the confidential information given to him by Nick, the young guest, about the first, false pregnancy of his pregnant-again wife, Honey. George initiates the story of 'How They Got Married' in the unsuspecting Honey's presence.

1 GEORGE   How They Got Married. Well, how they got married is this. . . The Mouse got all puffed up one day, and she went over to Blondie's house, and she stuck out her puff, and she said. . . look at me.

2 HONEY   [*white. . . on her feet*] I. . . don't. . . like this.

3 NICK   [*to* GEORGE] Stop it!

4 GEORGE   Look at me. . . I'm all puffed up. Oh my goodness, said Blondie. . .

5 HONEY   [*as from a distance*] . . . and so they were married. . .

6 GEORGE   . . . and so they were married. . .
7 HONEY   . . . and then. . .
8 GEORGE   . . . and then. . .
9 HONEY   [*hysteria*] WHAT?. . . and then, WHAT?
10 NICK   NO! No!
11 GEORGE   [*as if to a baby*]. . . and then the puff went *away*. . . like
  magic. . . pouf!
12 NICK   [*almost sick*] Jesus God. . .
13 HONEY   . . . the puff went away. . .
14 GEORGE   [*softly*]. . . pouf.
15 NICK   Honey. . . I didn't mean to. . . honestly, I didn't mean to. . .
16 HONEY   You. . . you told them. . .
17 NICK   Honey. . . I didn't mean to. . .
18 HONEY   [*with outlandish horror*] You. . . told them! you told
  them! OOOOHHHH! Oh, no, no, no, no, no! You couldn't have
  told them. . . oh, noooo!
19 NICK   Honey, I didn't mean to. . .
20 HONEY   [*grabbing at her belly*] Ohhhhh. . . nooooo.
21 NICK   Honey. . . baby. . . I'm sorry. . . I didn't mean to. . .
22 GEORGE   [*abruptly and with some disgust*] And that's how you
  play Get the Guests.

(Albee [1962] 1989: 89)

The content of George's narrative is quite simple; most of it is mentioned in his first turn – 'The Mouse got all puffed up one day, and she
went over to Blondie's house, and she stuck out her puff, and she said . . .
look at me. . . I'm all puffed up'. The other parts of George's narrative,
like 'Oh my goodness, said Blondie. . . and so they were married... and. . .
the puff went *away*... like magic; pouf' are dispersed among the repetitions. The rest of the action in summary is equally simple – Nick says that
he didn't mean to and is sorry but Honey is outraged that he had told them.
In its dialogic delineation, as construction of the inter-personal situation,
these seven basic clauses are rendered in twenty-two turns, and expand
threefold in length. Pauses and gaps between turns extend the performance
of the situation, as repetitions do. In fact, the last third of the extract – eight
turns – is devoted to enacting Nick's regret and Honey's sense of outrage
and betrayal.

  George's pauses could be interpreted in different ways, but in his first
two turns, it would appear to be a strategy to produce a deliberate delay
to gain attention for maximum effect, which he achieves. His repetition
in turn 6 of Honey's '. . . and so they were married. . . ' shadows her turn

confirming her knowledge as his. His next repetition of her turn, '. . . and then. . . ', again shadows Honey's, but returns the turn to her and forces the initiative for the rest of the narrative on her as a ploy to bait her, lead her to humiliate herself, to force her to tell his tale, to speak in his voice and tone. Honey's speech then shadows George's. She extends the unfinished clause, 'and then, WHAT. . . ?' with presumably rising intonation and volume, and throws the turn back to him, and insists on an answer from him. He repeats on her extension and answers her WHAT – with his knowledge of her false pregnancy. Honey repeats the phrase '... and the puff went away...' repeating George's pauses as well, but the function changes. From her mouth it makes present to her and to us her remembrance of the time, and a possible mixture of emotions for the pregnancy that never was.

His delays accumulate a sense of the inevitable, with Honey in his power. She merely repeats what he has said, the cruel register of his speech imprinted on her tongue and brain. She responds in automatic fashion, as she enacts her internalizing of his crude and brutal perspective on her which her shocked and diminished self is unable to counter. She speaks his proffered speech about her, and her pregnancy. The repetitions of their own turns between Honey and Nick enact the remoteness of the emotional and inter-personal freeze into which George's revelation has led them. Honey cannot move out of the humiliated, emotional outrage into which she has been led; she can only repeat and repeat it; and the gaps and pauses in her speech merely extend the emotional load of her felt situation in her speech. Nick can only escalate and intensify his regret through his repetitions, his pauses and his gaps, since there is nothing else he can say, but he is hardly heard by Honey. Nick's self-selections during the course of George's baiting of Honey fall ineffectually into the interaction – George ignores him and skips over his interventions.

OPENINGS AND CLOSINGS

A dramatist's floor management strategies have to attend to the boundaries of interactions. Relevant characters have to be brought on-stage and taken off it; thus, incoming and outgoing personae have to be either incorporated into the speech already in progress, or be disengaged from it. New arrivals on-stage can create pressure on the floor and have to be integrated into speech and turn-taking. Different sequencing patterns and re-alignments among those present are also made possible. The identity of newcomers has to be established for the audience and their place in the scheme of things indicated. In earlier drama, specific, stylized dramatic devices were incorporated into the dialogue. For instance, the *behold and see* type of introduction of one character by another, or self-introductions directly to the audience, were among the means used in medieval drama. In later drama, arrivals were integrated through the use of more naturalistic means and in these instances the sequences that appear at interactional boundaries have proved useful. Thus greetings, introductions, summons – be they knocks on the door or other non-verbal attention-getting devices – open up interactional spaces for the newcomers, as do *checking* sequences – 'Who goes there?' and the like – which enable characters to identify themselves to the audience and to enter interaction by answering the query of another.

Incorporation of arrivals into the dialogue and the scene has to be negotiated as do leave-takings and departures. A conversational convention states that those who enter occupied spaces usually speak or initiate interaction first, usually by stating their reasons or business. But these requirements could be played variously. In Shakespeare's *As You Like It* (Act 3, scene 2) there are many entrances and exits and different strategies are used to bring characters into association with each other. Orlando enters an empty stage to pin his verse on a tree, provides a commentary on his own actions and exits on the pretext that he has to pin verses on all the trees in the Forest of Arden. Corin and Touchstone enter next, already in conversation, as a twosome, but they keep who they are at the forefront since they name and categorize each other via address forms like 'Master Touchstone' or 'shepherd'. Just before Rosalind's entrance, Corin's turn prepares us for her arrival on-stage, through the use of a *noticing* turn and he identifies her as well – 'Here comes young Master Ganymede, my new mistress' brother'. Rosalind is too engrossed in reading the verse on the paper, which she reads aloud, thus speaking first, but not to the others. She is incorporated into interaction by Touchstone's mocking comments on the quality of the verse which targets her, and which brings them into a sequence of banter.

Celia enters reading a paper, too, her arrival being noticed by Rosalind who clears a space for her. After the reading aloud of the verse, Celia requests that Corin and Touchstone leave, which they do and a long interaction ensues between Celia and Rosalind about the problem of Rosalind being Ganymede in the face of Orlando's love for her. Orlando is about to enter with Jacques, which Celia observes, another *noticing*, but since the talk is about Orlando as is their interest in his behaviour, they slink away in order to 'note him', which clears the stage for the next twosome. Orlando and Jacques are in conversation already, thus introduced *in media res* as they make their entrance but it is not a very amicable one, they indulge in combats of wit at each other's expense, which Jacques terminates, and takes his leave and so exits. These latter forms of introduction are a useful dramatic device since characters already in talk signify prior acquaintance, and talking together provides its own evidence of *knowership*, in the use of the right to exchange speech with another. Such talk also has other functions: as an *unmarked beginning* it projects and authenticates continuity with another time, off-stage, and provides its own form of cohesion. It also removes the need for greetings, or access rituals of some kind to be performed each time characters appear on-stage, which could become tedious.

Rosalind has to be brought into interaction with Orlando, who is alone, so she uses a Summons to attract his attention – 'Do you hear forester?' – to which Orlando responds in the conventional fashion which creates interactive space for her. She responds with the third slot, with a 'Reason for Summons' turn with a request for the time of day, which is regarded as inappropriate by Orlando, this being the Forest of Arden after all. After their exchanges, their exit is prepared for by the interaction itself since Orlando has agreed to woo Ganymede as if 'he' were Rosalind at 'his' cote and has to be shown the way, which Rosalind offers to do, and invites Celia to go with them. This is the only instance, too, in this extract when the formal Summons–Answer–Reason for Summons structure is used. *Noticings* are used which, while targeting incomers and making space for them, also serve to close the current stretch of talk. Departures are requested or self-initiated, but with reasons built into the dialogue itself. In this scene, Shakespeare manages to keep his characters on the move, and brings only a small proportion of them into interaction at any one time, thus dispensing the resource of the floor in piecemeal fashion.

In crowded floors, as in Shakespeare's *Timon of Athens* (Act 3, scene 6) where a state banquet is about to begin, diverse Lords, Senators, servants and others fill the stage but speech is exchanged only by the three Lords who either introduce or greet each other, thus bringing relevant others and themselves into contact, and discuss matters of state. All other characters are backgrounded at this stage. The turn-taking is thus parsimonious and used to counter the threat of overloading the floor, but also to provide necessary information economically for the audience and to leave the bustle and drama till after Timon's arrival.

Functional slots like greetings, summons, etc., which bring characters into interaction, can be made material for drama in their own right. Omissions of the second parts of pairs at boundary sequences would make them noticeable absences, as would a lack of greeting when one is expected – on the arrival of a character into a household, for instance. In

Osborne's *Look Back in Anger* (1957), Alison returns after losing her baby. Helena does not reciprocate her 'Hello'; Jimmy takes a turn, but addresses Helena and passes the turn to her – 'Friend of yours' – and exits. The playing of the small boundary sequence in this way dramatizes Helena's discomfiture as well as Jimmy's hostility, with the access ritual also initiating the new situation that Alison's arrival has brought about for the other two. In Pinter's *The Homecoming* (1978), Max's refusal to greet or be introduced to Ruth or even to reciprocate to his long-absent son Teddy's greetings protracts the greeting sequence into one of insult and violent rejection – especially of the woman, who is labelled a whore and is incorporated only as one into his household at the end of the play. The terms of 'family' integration for Ruth are thus dramatized in the way the first boundary sequence is conducted.

Exits require characters to leave the stage. Before exits can be performed, characters have to disengage from interaction. Closings are usually more complex in structure than openings, and there are slots for concluding unfinished business before the final closure of leave-taking. In drama, such disengagement slots may be used to prolong departures as a measure of love or regard for the departing character, when the post-closure sequence takes on a dramatic life of its own. The rules are open to variation, even in one play. In Chekhov's *The Seagull* (1923) before tragedy strikes, Nina's departure is prolonged by Madame Arkadin and Treplev who issue protests at her leaving and request that she stay a little longer, to which she responds with displays of reluctance to go but with assertions of family necessities that require her departure. Intense or polite inter-personal regard is thus manifested by all parties concerned. At the end, a similar pattern occurs between herself and Treplev, except that Nina's self-projected departures are overridden by herself much more as she continues her story across her own initiations to leave, and finally leaves mid-sentence. The necessity for a speedy departure from the house is there, but she plays through her inability to go and the state of her divided mind by protracting the closure sequence in the way she does.

The leave-taking sequence has also been used to begin a scene or as a ruse to introduce a character – Ophelia in *Hamlet* is introduced to us for the first time saying farewell to her brother. The leave-taking terminal pair may also remain unconcluded, as was the case in the Synge extract examined earlier (see p.99) which brought appropriate tensions into the scene. When characters agree among themselves to leave, they usually leave, but this, too, can be flouted, as in the well-known instance in Beckett's *Waiting for Godot* – 'Let's go' [*They do not move.*] – which concludes the two acts of the play.

This chapter has attempted to explore the possibilities offered by the turn sequencing system. The alternating course of speech dramatizes the course of the evolving situation as it is being developed turn by turn. In general, various interactive paths are possible. The normative rules are those that maximize on co-operation and harmony in talk, but the rules can be manipulated to create other situations – of conflict, isolation, separation – since these are also potential realities of inter-personal communication and talk. The paths taken and the effects achieved are also owing to the strategic use of the system. The variety and creativity of the uses of the turn-taking system are legion, since each segment in a play creates its own specificities of situation and character through the enacted patterns of participants' talk.

The Ethnomethodological sequencing options are basically structural ones. The issues of content and meaning and the inferences that are often needed to establish cognitive linkages between turn and turn have been left unanalysed, where these were not authorized by the structural and contingent, joint management aspects of the retrospective and projective mechanisms of the turn-taking system itself. It is to issues of these kinds that we now turn.

Chapter 4

Pragmatics

PRELIMINARIES: GENERAL FRAMEWORKS

The mechanics of the turn-taking system, as we saw, can be used to construct the specific architecture of an interactional speech event in the evolution of turns. Structural analysis of this kind left out of account issues of content and meaning and the use of the utterance itself as a means of communication. These were left unanalysed and treated as transparent. Yet issues of this kind are not simple. Meaning in dialogue is not meaning in the abstract, nor univocal, but that constructed with respect to the other in discourse, and is thus often negotiated. Moreover, it is meaning to be conveyed to another across the barriers of singularity and separateness of those involved in discourse; it functions as and within a context of communication. And meaning is often constructed in the spaces between turn and turn. The business of communication is a drama in its own right within the immediacies of the give and take of speech exchange. Such dramas construct all manner of communicative events as inter-personal events, including those based on miscommunication or non-communication since these, too, are enactions with a process and dialectic of their own.

When language is used in contexts for the purposes of interaction, the meaning we are concerned with is that produced by speakers for recipients within situations. The linguistic turn thus points in many directions simultaneously – to the speaker, to the addressee(s) and to the context, at least. In such instances, the linguistic code and semantic meaning can be radically underdetermined in relation to meaning conveyed. Often, the linguistic tokens used function only as cues, for other processes to take effect. The propositional contents of utterances delimit, but do not determine, meaning completely. The burden of meaning falls, not solely on the code, but on *users*, on participants, and the assumptions and inferences they bring to bear within communication. The nature of the operative processes and procedures are under investigation within the domain of *Pragmatics*, which, in Charles Morris' (1938) well-known semiotic'triad, is that area which deals with the relationship of language to users; syntactics deals with the relationship of signs to signs and semantics with the relationship of signs to the world, independently of issues of use.

The term *Pragmatics* has a very wide scope and its delimitation is a problem (Levinson 1983: Ch. 1), and many of the topics dealt with previously in this book could also be regarded as included in it as pertinent to its widest interpretation as 'language-in-use'. But for the purposes of this chapter, we shall confine ourselves to two major strands of exploration in the field: that pertaining to speech acts and illocutionary force derived from the work of J. L. Austin and his followers; and the concepts of the Co-operative Principle, the maxims of conversation, and the notion of implicature, and its revisions in the work of Paul Grice and Griceans. Even within this restricted scope, the range of studies is extensive. The preliminary review is expanded to include some of the major investigations, not only the work of J. L. Austin, J. R. Searle and H. Paul Grice who set the future directions of Pragmatics of this ilk on course, but some of the later studies like Bach and Harnish's (1982) study of speech acts, Sperber and Wilson's theory of Relevance (1986), and the enquiries into politeness phenomena in the work of Brown and Levinson (1987) and Leech (1983). Insights from these studies are used in the 'Pragmatics and Drama: General' section to follow (see p.196).

To take each of these in turn, we shall concentrate on speech acts first. The importance of this concept is to be found in the fact that language, generally regarded as descriptive of a given, pre-existing world, can be examined from a contrary point of view – language as action. It was J. L. Austin (1962) who first alerted us to the fact that language may be used not only to describe things but to do things as well. Focusing on the declarative, which has been the primary, statement-making and, hence, truth-bearing of all the major syntactic forms, Austin made clear that there were, precisely, declaratives in the language that could not be assessed in relation to truth and falsity, but more in relation to 'felicity' conditions for the successful or 'happy' performance of the acts they named. He had in mind sentences of the form 'I bet you five pounds it will snow at Christmas', 'I name this ship the *Queen Elizabeth*', in which the verb performs an act rather than describing a state of affairs – here, acts of betting and naming respectively. He termed such utterances 'performatives', to distinguish them, initially, from truth-bearing utterances, or 'constatives', a strategic distinction he was to erase in the interests of a comprehensive theory of *speech acts*, in which the constative was subsumed under the performative. This move has had multiple, sometimes contradictory, consequences – either to regard all speech acts as propositional and truth functional, and hence as semantic-like phenomena, which is the strong version (Allan 1986); or, in a weaker version, seeing considerations of truth as not outside the realm of language in use (Schiffrin 1994; Sperber and Wilson 1986; Blakemore 1992); or to see all speech acts as social-functional and, hence, as socio-pragmatic phenomena (e.g. Levinson 1983; Mey 1993).

Performatives were characterized by the fact that they were in first person, present tense, indicative active form, and had to pass the *hereby* test. Verbs that could co-occur with 'hereby' were informally regarded as being performative verbs – hence, I (hereby) bet you. . . ', I (hereby) name. . . ', etc. For the successful performance of the act so named, certain conditions had to be fulfilled of the kind given below, which is a more succinct version taken from Levinson.

A. (i) There must be a conventional procedure having a conventional effect
   (ii) The circumstances and persons must be appropriate, as specified in the procedure
B. The procedure must be executed (i) correctly and (ii) completely
C. Often, (i) the persons must have the requisite thoughts, feelings and intentions, as specified in the procedure, and (ii) if consequent conduct is specified, then the relevant parties must so do.

(Levinson 1983: 229)

In other words, only an authorized speaker in the relevant situation may perform the act of naming. If someone other than the authorized person within the relevant situation and procedure were to throw a bottle of champagne at a ship and attempt to name it, the action would probably be regarded as one of vandalism; at any rate, the ship would not be named. Thus, the execution of performatives can be unsuccessful or 'infelicitous' in various ways – they may misfire, be void, or there may be abuses of the conditions, all of which would affect the happy performance of the act in negative ways. What is to be noted, however, is that it is not considerations of truth that would affect their performance. They do not relate to an existing state of affairs in the world, and are not immediately open to truth evaluation; rather, such acts bring about new states of affairs when they are felicitously performed.

Speech acts are constituted in complex fashion by sub-acts. They are: the locutionary act – the utterance act, with more or less determinate sense and reference; the illocutionary act – the act done in the saying; and the perlocutionary act – the act done by the saying. The locutionary act is the act of saying something in a speech situation, and Austin distinguishes three aspects of the act. 'Saying' anything thus involves the following:

(A.*a*) always to perform the act of uttering certain noises (a 'phonetic' act), and the utterance is a phone;

(A.*b*) always to perform the act of uttering certain vocables or words, i.e. noises of certain types belonging to *and as* belonging to a certain vocabulary. . . to a certain grammar, with a certain intonation, &c. This act we may call a 'phatic' act; and the utterance which it is the act of uttering a 'pheme'. . . and

(A.*c*) generally to perform the act of using that pheme or its constituents with a certain more or less definite 'sense' and a more or less definite 'reference' (which together are equivalent to 'meaning'). This act we may call a 'rhetic' act. . .

(Austin 1962: 92–3)

As Austin phrased it, the rhetic act can be taken in two ways, as Bach and Harnish have argued (1979: 19–20), depending on whether the phrase 'certain. . . sense. . . and reference' is seen to identify denotation in utterances in case they are ambiguous, or whether it refers to what the speaker means and refers to in the use of expressions. Given the pervasiveness of ambiguity in natural languages, the phatic and rhetic acts cannot be conflated, especially as referring expressions in a language rarely pick out referents uniquely on the basis of (semantic) meaning alone. As Bach and Harnish state, 'reference at the level of the phatic act does not in general determine reference at the level of the rhetic act' (*ibid*). The locutionary act is an utterance in a language L with the requisite phonetic (phonological) shape and grammar. Sense and denotation as well as determination of speaker reference could be involved when the locution is used in context. The act of saying has also to be distinguished from the utterance act. Two people saying the same thing – using the same locution – will be performing two utterance acts. 'Saying' is thus used in a restricted sense: the physical act of making noises from the mouth of a person does not constitute an act of saying, nor would acts like repeating words and phrases while learning a foreign language, testing a microphone, etc. be, strictly speaking, classified under the locutionary act, in the tripartite form given above, even if linguistic sounds or even grammatical phrases are used.

The illocutionary act is the act done in the saying; in other words, utterances are invested with *illocutionary force* when considered as speech actions. The utterance may name the act performed, as in the 'classic' performative, but it may not, for, as Austin noted, the utterance 'Guilty' performs as effectively as 'I pronounce you guilty'; 'I'll meet you at the station' is as much of a promise as 'I promise to meet you at the station' if the felicity conditions are respected.

The perlocutionary act is the act done by the saying, and relates to the receiver's end of the communicative act. There is a measure of debate about where the illocutionary act ends and the perlocutionary act begins, but generally the perlocutionary effect is that which is related to the intended illocutionary force of the utterance. If the illocutionary act of my utterance is that of a promise, then the recognition of the commitment I make to you through or in my utterance as a promise is the intended perlocutionary effect. As Austin noted, *uptake* has to be secured. You may also be amused by or contemptuous of my promise, but such effects do not normally fall under the heading of the perlocutionary act. To complicate matters further, some acts may not be done in standard performative fashion – persuading, for instance. I cannot persuade you by saying 'I (hereby) persuade you'. I may try or attempt through argument or emotional appeal or some other means to persuade you, but I may not perform it directly as I may 'I promise you'. Similarly, with a verb like *hint*: it is not an action that can be performed directly by naming the verb, explicitly, *in* the saying. We do not say 'I hereby hint. . . ' to hint, although we may describe the action as such when we report it, as in 'It was a hint. . . ' or in second person form, 'What are you hinting at?'

Austin estimated that there were over a thousand verbs in the (English) language and attempted to classify illocutionary forces of utterances according to them, although he confessed he was far from happy with his classification. John Searle (1969, 1976), attempting to systematize Austin, provided five major classes, although he has changed some of the labels in different works:

- *Representatives*, which commit the speaker to the truth of the proposition expressed, as in stating, asserting;
- *Directives*, which attempt to get the interlocutor to do things for the speaker as in requests;
- *Commissives*, which commit the speaker to doing things for the interlocutor, as in promises;
- *Expressives*, which express a psychological state of the speaker as in apologies, laments, etc.; and
- *Declarations*, those speech acts which are backed by institutional authority and effect changes in institutional or public states of affairs, like declaring war, naming ships, etc.

And there are other classifications.

Searle also provided a different framework for the description and explanation of speech acts. Instead of the looser notions of felicity conditions as dimensions along which speech acts may be felicitously performed, and attached to verbs as in Austin, Searle attempted a general theory of illocutionary acts to which his classification is related. The felicity conditions were made constitutive of the acts themselves. And constitutive in Rawls' (1955) sense, where a distinction is made between *regulative* rules and *constitutive* rules. Regulative rules oversee and monitor the performance of activities independent of and pre-existing the rules, as in table manners or traffic codes and so on, whereas constitutive rules construct the activity itself, as in soccer or chess, where the rules *are* the game, so to speak. Activities within the scope of the rules are thus defined in relation to them, whether they are those appropriate to moving pieces on a board in chess or kicking or heading a ball through goal posts. One activity or action *counts as* something else. Searle's speech act schema is constructed in such a way so as to allow for an utterance to count as an act of a certain kind when constituted with respect to conditions in appropriate ways. The conditions that constitute an act are: the propositional content condition, the preparatory condition, sincerity conditions, and the essential condition which captures the sense of 'counts as'.

A speech act, like a request, requires that the propositional content of an utterance refer to a future act A of H; the preparatory conditions state that S (speaker) must believe that H (hearer) is able to do what is requested and that the action requested would not have been undertaken voluntarily by H in the normal course of events. Thus, requesting someone to walk to the moon which would flout the preparatory condition, or to close a window when it is obvious to S that H is about to close the window anyway, would not count as a canonical request. The sincerity condition attaching to requests proposes that S wants H to do A while the essential condition enjoins that the utterance counts as S's attempt to get H to do A. By contrast, a speech act like 'thank' would take a different description. The propositional content refers to a *past* act done by H; the preparatory condition states that act A has benefited S and that S believes this to be the case; the sincerity condition assigns gratitude to S as the proper internal state for thanking, with the essential condition making the utterance count as an expression of gratitude or appreciation (Searle 1969: 66–7).

Various *illocutionary force indicating devices* (IFID) like explicit performative verbs, intonation, etc. provide a degree of transparency in identifying which act is actually being performed in an utterance. Under one interpretation at least, 'I bet. . . ' performs the act of betting if the requisite felicity conditions are met. In communication, however, such transparency is not necessarily guaranteed even when the verb names the act. An utterance like 'I promise to meet you at the station' can accrue extra communicative capital and be emphatic or insistent to some degree about the act of promising precisely by naming the act in this way. Similarly, 'I warn you. . . ' in certain circumstances can intensify into a threat when explicitly performed. Additionally, the phenomenon of *indirect speech acts* reveals that the form of the utterance need not give any direct indication of the force. Even habitual requests like 'Can you pass the salt?' use a question about *ability* in order to perform the speech act of requesting a particular action – the passing of the salt.

Thus, it is not the case that in most daily interactions performative verbs are explicitly named. Most communication is conducted in elliptical and indirect ways: 'I'll meet you at the station' can count as a promise; a statement or prediction like 'The ladder is about to fall' suffices as a warning. Indirectness can be deep enough to divorce completely the illocutionary force of an utterance from its propositional content in overt form. An utterance can also change force with changing contexts: 'The currents are treacherous over there' could count as a warning to someone about to swim in the water referred to but remain only a statement of fact, or opinion, or an assertion, to a non-swimmer. The understanding that the same utterance can be used to do many things and can lend itself to many interpretations is standard in language use. For instance, a simple assertive like 'It is raining outside' can be used to do a multitude of things, as Martin has shown. It can,

> report to the hearer that it is raining outside
> get the hearer to believe correctly that it is raining outside
> get the hearer to believe falsely that it is raining outside [she is lying or mistaken]. . .
> get the hearer to believe that it is Tuesday [because his competence in English is slim and he takes her to be saying that it is Tuesday]
> get the hearer to believe that it is Tuesday [because he believes that it rains only on Tuesday]
> get the hearer to take his umbrella
> get the hearer to stay around awhile
> get the hearer to leave
> get the hearer to think she is stupid

insult the hearer
please the hearer
surprise the hearer
wake the hearer up
cause war to break out in Guatemala [How? I leave
    it to your imagination]
practice her English
practice her lines in a play
see if the microphone she is speaking into is
    turned on
do nothing at all except make the noise [if
    nobody is listening]

(Martin 1989: 83–4)

As if this were not enough, illocutionary forces can also cluster or chain in relation to an utterance: 'Have you cleaned your room?' from a parent to a recalcitrant or truant offspring could function as a request for information, a command and a threat in the sense of 'Have you. . . if not do so immediately, or else. . . ' Others, like questions, refer back to previous speech acts and to the contents of previous utterances: 'Yes' as a reply or answer will be assessed with respect to what has gone before, whether one is agreeing to a proposal of marriage or to pay someone five pounds (Searle 1992b: 140). Speech acts can be embedded in complex constructions, and can also be performed in other than first person, present, active indicative form – 'Passengers are requested not to cross the railway lines' or 'I'm warning you, don't use my car'.

If utterances could be used to mean what they say, to mean other than what they say, and mean more than they say, and less than what they say, how do we communicate at all? If by saying 'It is raining outside' the speaker intends to get the hearer to stay a little longer, how does the hearer interpret 'It is raining outside' to mean 'stay a little longer' in cases where nothing in the utterance via the rules of the grammar, conventionality, compositionality, polysemy, mazes of etymology, ambiguity, indeterminacy, presupposition, entailment, etc. can enable the hearer to interpret the one as the other given that they are two independent and mutually unrelated propositions? If the hearer interprets it as (a) 'war is declared in Guatemala' or (b) 'it is Tuesday' she obviously wouldn't feel it incumbent on her to stay a little longer as required of her, since 'stay a little longer' is still not part of the conventional, etc. meanings of either (a) or (b) and, hence, would not figure in the interpretation – in what is understood by the hearer. Uptake would not be secured, and the communication would fail, even though *some* interpretation can be arrived at on the part of the hearer – that 'war is declared in Guatemala', for instance, or even the fact that 'It is raining outside', and the hearer could well take her umbrella and go, having missed the point of the utterance.

If the form of an utterance can be split from its illocutionary force, and if illocutionary forces can be multiple, and change depending on context, how can communication be achieved? How do hearers hear a question about ability in, for example, 'Can you pass the salt?' and identify it as a request for action? Or interpret an observation about a state of affairs like the currents being treacherous as a warning not to swim in the water when the issue of swimming has not been raised or mentioned at all in the utterance or even a previous utterance? The gap between the locutionary act and the illocutionary act being what it is in these instances, how can the illocutionary force of the utterance be communicated, conveyed, so that the hearer may secure uptake? Without uptake the hearer could hardly proceed even to next turn and dialogue would grind to a halt every time a speaker speaks, or be characterized by repairs which only shifts the problem, since the problem of uptake will surface in attempted repair utterances too. If the illocutionary force of the utterance is a request and action is required on the part of the hearer, the hearer has to understand first what is required before undertaking to do or not to do it. Empirically, although there are instances of misunderstanding, hesitation and bafflement as to what is meant there is understanding as well and turns proceed smoothly, and with split-second timing to boot, as Conversational Analysts have shown. How is the latter achieved?

It is to the work of Paul Grice and Griceans that we turn for a possible explanation. Grice distinguished between causal, *natural meaning* as in 'Those spots mean measles' and *non-natural meaning* or *meaning*nn as intentional *speaker meaning* in communication. Meaningnn is conditioned by voluntariness, intentionality, motivation, on the part of the creature which produces the signs and the kind of meaning this entails is that which is operative in communication. Thus utterances produced in communication are of the kind which are *intended* to achieve an effect of a desired kind in the hearer, and what is more, the hearer should only recognize that the tokens are used with that intention and that the hearer is meant to recognize it. In Grice's formulation,

> 'A meant something by x' is (roughly) equivalent to 'A intended the utterance of x to produce some effect in an audience by means of the recognition of this intention.'

> (Grice 1989: 220)

Strawson has pointed out that there are sub-intentions involved in the above, so that for a speaker to mean something by x, S must intend

(a) S's utterance of x to produce a certain response r in a certain audience A;
(b) A to recognize S's intention (a);
(c) A's recognition of S's intention (a) to function as at least part of A's reasons for A's response r.

(Strawson 1971: 155)

The recognition of the intention with which the utterance is produced is meant to be recognized or communication would fail – if some other intention were imputed instead, like response g, which may be plausible and meaningful in general terms but not related to response r which is what the utterance was designed to be recognized as bringing about. The intention here is of the *reflexive* kind, R-intentions, as it were, with meaning and interpretation tied to speakers and hearers and not to the code, or conventional meaning alone, though the code plays its part.

The notion of speaker meaning makes clear that speakers can use utterances in contexts of communication for various purposes, and the same utterance could be used to achieve different responses, or different utterances used to achieve the same response. There can be gaps, therefore, between what the speaker says and what the speaker means by the use of an utterance in context. Moreover, sentences composing the utterance need not be completed ones either. The linguistic token could be a part of a sentence, elliptical, or just a word or phrase, but whose propositional content is capable of being recovered.

Grice's notion of meaning$_{nn}$ and speaker meaning have been developed along different lines, both semantic and pragmatic (Levinson 1983). For our purposes, we shall pursue its role in the analysis of communication in conversation or interaction.

In his 1957 article on 'Logic and conversation', Grice (1989: Ch. 2) set out the conditions for communication of this kind. Communication is conducted with respect to a kind of inter-personal and social contract, which is also a rational one, which in general terms, he labelled the *Co-operative Principle*, which is deceptively simple in its formulation:

make your contribution such as is required, at the stage at which it occurs, by the accepted purpose or direction of the talk exchange in which you are engaged

(1989: 26)

Grice then distinguished more specific maxims which are related to the general principle. They are, the Maxims of Quality, Quantity, Relevance and Manner.

The Maxim of Quality
try to make your contribution one that is true, specifically,
(i)   do not say what you believe to be false
(ii) do not say that for which you lack adequate evidence
The Maxim of Quantity
(i)   make your contribution as informative as is required for the current purposes of the exchange
(ii) do not make your contribution more informative than is required
The Maxim of Relevance
make your contributions relevant
The Maxim of Manner
be perspicuous, and specifically,
(i)   avoid obscurity
(ii) avoid ambiguity
(iii) be brief
(iv) be orderly

(Levinson 1983: 101–2)

All of the above has been subjected to intense scrutiny, debate, contention and revision. It must be noted, however, that the Co-operative Principle and its Maxims cannot be reified or valorized into a back-slapping affair. Grice contends that communication is a rational activity in the sense that the means used are reckoned to be reasonable ones, and that the Maxims or some such must be seen as overarching assumptions operative in common among participants to govern the conduct of conversation. We do not come *cold*, as it were, into contexts of communication. Maxims and principles are not laws, with a binary either/or; in Grice's framework, they regulate communication both in the observance and in the breach, where the breaches are overtly performed and intended to be recognized as a breach for rational ends. Communication is a co-ordinated affair, and participants are required to co-operate in order to manage and negotiate their attempts at communication, but some common grounds are needed.

According to Grice, participants orientate to requirements like giving information which they either believe is true or have evidence for such a belief, they give as much information as they deem they are required to, speak relevantly, and as clearly as they can without undue prolixity or obfuscation, or incoherence, in order to maximize their communicative efforts and, moreover, expect others to do the same in return. Even where none of the maxims seem to be observed and interlocutors are not ostensibly behaving in the expected manner by talking clearly, etc., participants would still assume that such behaviours are attempts at communication and that they have some point, that there is a reason for it, and that it is up to themselves as hearers to interpret it – i.e. the assumption is that it is rational, reasonable, 'means–end' behaviour on the speaker's part and aimed at communicating, to which hearers respond. Grice's overall framework involves not just the Co-operative Principle and the Maxims, but the mustering of encyclopedic or real-world knowledge and principles of inference which speakers use and speakers expect hearers to use in order to arrive at what speakers mean.

Thus, in cases like the following,

A   What time is it?
B   Eight o'clock.

B has responded to the request for information in A's remark and provided an answer to the question. A, with respect to the assumption that the Co-operative Principle is in force, takes it that the answer is what B believes to be true – that it is indeed eight o'clock, and B is giving the quantity of information required, is speaking relevantly and clearly. If A or B is in doubt at each encounter with another whether the maxims are being observed, whether they can take another's word for anything – the time of the day, or when the next faculty meeting is scheduled to occur – it is difficult to see how life can go on.

On the other hand, interactions of a different kind like the one given below are also possible.

A   What time is it?
B   Well, the postman's been.

Here, B's answer appears to flout the requirement to be relevant and would seem to be performing unco-operatively, but if A assumes that the Co-operative Principle is in force, she would assume a reason for this behaviour and interpret it as relevant in spite of appearances. This overt and ostensive flout of the maxim of relevance, if deemed to be co-operative behaviour, would generate *implicatures*, as Grice termed them, and ostensive flouting of this kind would be interpreted as meant to be understood as such, so that the processes of reasoning can start. Thus A could conclude that B is not sure of the exact time, or she would have given it (with respect to the Maxim of Quantity), and gives information instead which is within her power or evidence (Maxim of Quality), perhaps not as succinctly as she can (Maxim of Manner – in the hesitation in 'Well. . . '), which will enable B to work out the answer: that it is, perhaps just after eight o'clock or thereabouts, depending on encyclopedic beliefs or assumptions which are being drawn on between them; that postmen usually come around eight o'clock; and inferences, that if the postman has come and gone then it must be after eight o'clock.

What is seemingly unco-operative behaviour is not, since B relies on A's capacities of inference to use unstated assumptions from what is taken to be shared encyclopedic information of the way things work outside language – the comings and goings of postmen – to get to an interpretation of what B means, although B does not say it herself. If encyclopedic assumptions stated that postmen come around twelve o'clock, then that is the inference that would go through, that it is after twelve o'clock and not after eight o'clock, as in the other case. If speaker and hearer believed or assumed different things about postmen – the one that they come around eight and the other that they do so about twelve – then miscommunication is achieved because the criterion that background, encyclopedic information should overlap is not operative, and inferences triggered are using different premises to the ones intended. The same utterance, depending on the path of inference and the encyclopedic information mobilized for it to work, will deliver different 'meanings'.

Such contextual inferences are implicatures, specifically *conversational implicatures*, to be distinguished from more semantic or logical relations like *entailment* that attach to propositions and are conventional. There are other kinds of implicatures – *generalized* implicatures as in 'I walked into a house' which generates an implicature to the effect that the house was not mine; or *conventional implicatures* which are not dependent on principles or maxims of the kind dealt with above, but are not truth-conditional either and, therefore, open to pragmatic modes of interpretation (see Levinson 1983: Ch. 3). Maxims can clash, be violated, flouted and exploited, and one could opt out of co-operation altogether. Implicatures are also defeasible or cancellable, or they just drop out if they are not considered to play a role in communication, even if initially assumed to do so.

The concept of implicature is important because it enables us not to restrict a concept of meaning in communication only to the code. The use of contextualized implicatures means that 'meanings' can be created with respect to the particular context and the conditions that obtain within it. Such 'meanings' need not transfer to any other context unless similar intentions and conditions obtain. They could be produced whenever the occasion demands and then they disappear, since they are not coded.

Grice's work has had far-reaching influences on deliberations on the whole issue of meaning and how it may be theorized, and is of a complexity and extent that would not lend itself to adequate review in the present instance. But it has influenced the issue of speech acts, which is where we began. One of the more comprehensive and insightful attempts to wed Grice's ideas to the issues of speech acts comes from Bach and Harnish (1982). Their schema is constructed on the basis of the fact that,

> what is communicated is determined not merely by what is said. The structure and meaning of the expressions used are essential, but so are the speaker's intention and hearer's recognition of it. In our view a communicative intention has the peculiar feature that its fulfilment consists in its recognition. The speaker intends the hearer to recognize the point of his utterance not just through (1) the content and (2) the context but also because (3) the point is intended to be recognized.
>
> (Bach and Harnish 1982: xi)

Bach and Harnish base their schema on an inferential model à la Grice and speaker meaning. Their overall schema is slightly different to that provided by Grice. Instead of Grice's Co-operative Principle they propose (i) a *Linguistic Presumption* which ensures that speakers can identify an expression *e* in Language L because they are members of the same speech community – they share a language in common – i.e. one is not speaking Russian and the other English and neither knows the other language. Participants also share (ii) a *Communicative Presumption* which requires a *mutual belief* in those communicating that communicative tokens issued are used with R-intentions, with an illocutionary intention that is intended to be recognized. And (iii), *Mutual contextual beliefs* (MCPs) are background information and contextually salient, and are involved in the computations of inferencing required in context. And these are 'contextual', since activated by context; 'mutual' because participants interacting need to have them, and what is more 'not only have them, but believe they both have them, and believe the other to believe they both have them' (*ibid.*: 5); and 'beliefs', because they need not be true like knowledge propositions are deemed to be for them to be operative in inference.

What is 'said' by a speaker in a context of communication is generally underdetermined in relation to what is meant so that what is 'said' forms the basis, merely, for the hearer to work out, infer, what the speaker intends by the expression used. As we saw earlier, the process of working out involves the locutionary act as well, since contextually operative meaning has to be inferred. Reference assignment, or delimitation, in relation to what the speaker has in mind has to be undertaken for pronouns, proper names, definite descriptions and slips of the tongue, malapropisms, spoonerisms, and unfamiliar accents or pronunciations of words, which the hearer has to disambiguate as contextually appropriate in relation to what is being said. Where the locutionary act names the illocutionary act, inferencing is still at work, since the hearer is yet to be satisfied that such compatibility is intended, given that naming a performative verb does not guarantee that only the named act is being performed or intended to be performed. Pragmatic judgements are at work even at this level and hearers have to make them in relation to the intention they are supposed to recognize.

Illocutionary intentions are communicative since they are directed at hearers and govern the sort of meaning that is to be understood by them. Not any possible effects, but only those intended to be recognized and identified because intended to be recognized partly on the basis of what is said, are to count as communicative ones. The hearer has work to do, in scrutinizing the speaker's utterance and mobilizing powers of inference with respect to the Communicative Presumption.

Perlocutionary acts are also split between those that are related to illocutionary intents, and other kinds which are not. Since recognition of the kind described is all that is needed for understanding and communication to be effected, intended illocutionary effects when recognized as such achieve communication. How the hearer chooses to deal with the understanding is another matter. But this description of speech acts actually permits a choice for subsequent action in these cases. If the speaker's illocutionary intent in requesting is recognized by the hearer, communication, or 'uptake', is achieved, but the hearer may well, subsequently, decline to do the act requested. The speaker may have failed in getting the action she wanted done by the hearer, but not owing to a failure of understanding, but out of choice or necessity or some such on the hearer's part. It also makes room for some of the more game-playing aspects of communication, since the hearer may have understood only too well what the speaker meant her to recognize (as in the kind of participant structures described in Chapter 2, where the target addressee is not the real addressee, see pp. 30–7), but chooses not to reveal it in her subsequent actions, which holds even if she were the target addressee.

Bach and Harnish's taxonomy of illocutionary acts is different to Searle's, although indebted to it, in that they build in attitudes, more specifically, to illocutionary acts. This is in deference to the Sincerity *Condition*, although communicative success does not depend on personal sincerity (Bach and Harnish 1982: 39). Nor does it require the hearer to form a corresponding attitude, but if she does, then such a perlocutionary effect is achieved in addition to illocutionary 'uptake'. It also allows them to claim different strengths for beliefs, wants, etc., as pertinent to different illocutionary acts, as between insisting and suggesting, for example, which again the hearer may understand but need not share. They divide acts into Communicative and Conventional ones, the former correspond more or less to Searle's categories, while the latter divide into two categories – Effectives and Verdictives – in place of Searle's Declarations.

Communicative acts are of the following types. *Constatives* (assertives, informatives, suppositives, descriptives, etc.), *Directives* (requestives, questions, requirements, prohibitions, permissives, etc.), *Commissives* (promises, offers), *Acknowledgements* (apologies, condolences, congratulations, thanks, greetings, bids, acceptances, rejections). Conventional acts include *Effectives* and *Verdictives*. Effectives bring about changes in institutional states of affairs, like Austin's classic performatives, when issued by the right person by virtue of office and in the right circumstances – hiring or firing an employee, naming ships, etc. Verdictives, too, are tied to institutions, but are judgemental acts and have binding import within the institutions in which they occur, as when a referee calls a player's move on the field a 'foul', or when a natural fact like a death is adjudged to be a 'murder'.

Communicative acts are individuated with respect to some attitude – of the speaker to the propositional content and to the intention that the hearer form a similar attitude, or the strength with which the attitude is held, and so on. Each class includes a list of sub-acts which vary aspects of the main criteria for each of the superordinate categories.

> . . . *constatives* express the speaker's belief and his intention or desire that the hearer have or form a like belief. *Directives* express the speaker's attitude toward some prospective action by the hearer and his intention that his utterance, or the attitude it expresses, be taken as a reason for the hearer's action. *Commissives* express the speaker's intention and belief that his utterance obligates him to do something (perhaps under certain conditions). And *acknowledgments* express feelings regarding the hearer or, in cases where the utterance is clearly perfunctory or formal, the speaker's intention that his utterance satisfy a social expectation to express certain feelings and his belief that it does.
>
> (Bach and Harnish 1982: 41)

Differences between members of either the same class or among different classes are characterized by changes in intention and attitude expressed. Constatives express beliefs with a corresponding intention that H forms (or sustains) a similar belief. Constatives of the Assertive class like 'affirm', 'avow', 'claim, etc. take a description of the following kind:

In uttering *e*, S asserts that P if S expresses:
i. the belief that P, and
ii. the intention that H believe that P.

Predictives, also constatives, like 'forecast', 'prophesy', 'predict', are distinguished from the above in the manner given below.

In uttering *e*, S asserts that P if S expresses:
i. the belief that it will be the case that P, and
ii. the intention that H believe that it will be the case that P.

(*ibid.*: 42–6)

And so on for all the sub-groups of constatives.

Members of the Directive class express attitudes to some prospective action on the part of the hearer, especially the desire or intention that the hearer take the utterance and attitude it expresses as a reason for acting as desired. The description of a member of the Directive class like a requestive ('ask', 'request', 'beseech', 'implore', etc.) is the following:

In uttering *e*, S requests H to A if S expresses:
i. the desire that H do A
ii. the intention that H do A because (at least partly) of S's desire.

(*ibid.*: 47–9)

Commisives are acts in which speakers obligate or commit themselves, or propose to commit themselves (offers) to doing things. A Commissive like a promise can be described thus:

In uttering *e*, S promises H to A if S expresses:
i. the belief that his utterance obligates him to A
ii. the intention to A, and
iii. the intention that H believe that S's utterance obligates S to A and that S intends to A.

(*ibid.*: 50–1)

And finally, *Acknowledgements* (*ibid.*: 51–5), which may require only perfunctory expression of feelings in some instances, given that they are socially prescribed on many occasions, and the members of this class are similarly discriminated and defined. They include social acts like 'thank', 'greet', 'congratulate', etc.

Each class and members of the class are distinguished by differences in attitude – beliefs, wants, desires and intentions. For a speaker to request

A of hearer, is for speaker to express a desire for A and an intention that what is requested is undertaken by H at least partly because of the speaker's desire for it. Thus, although at first glance, it would appear that only the speaker is involved in these acts, their description involves hearers and their rights, too. If a speaker promises, the hearer has a right to believe that a commitment is being undertaken on the part of the speaker to do what is promised; if a speaker requests, the hearer has a right to believe in the desire of the speaker for the thing requested, and that the appeal made to hearer to do it is intended as such by the speaker. Understanding requires not only the grasp of the content of the utterance, of what is said, but of the attitudes – desires, commitments, intentions – that go with them as acts. Recognition of these as intended to be recognized alone is required for communication to take place. Subsequent action is left to the discretion of the hearer.

Both communicative and conventional acts are performed with the intention that the utterance counts as a certain act, but the means are different. Communicative acts are successfully performed when the hearer recognizes the intention with which they are performed; conventional acts are successful if the utterance meets the requirements of the relevant conventions. The intentions are given by convention and do not require the workings of R-intentions. This does not mean that communicative intentions are not necessarily operative in conventional acts. A boss who is a friend may make one redundant but also communicate personal regret. An officer of the law may apprehend you and simultaneously inform you of his or her belief that you are breaking the law. The institutional or conventional act will go through regardless of the communicative act. Conventional acts, moreover, though fact or reality changing by virtue of the power of institutions, can also be challenged, or rendered void by other institutional (conventional) acts, as when marriages are dissolved, or peace declared, or when higher courts overturn verdicts of lower ones and so on. Bach and Harnish (1982) declare mutual beliefs to operate in both types of acts (communicative and conventional) to cover those instances where people take authority on faith, so to speak, since details of some conventions, or legislations, or even that some legislations and their related procedures exist at all, may be obscure but their existence and power is believed in and conventional acts are successful as a consequence.

Bach and Harnish's schema is more complex, discriminating and detailed than the selective abstract given above, but the reliance on mutual contextual beliefs (MCBs), in general, has been criticized as leading into infinite regress owing to the condition of *mutuality* (Sperber and Wilson

1982). In subsequent work, Sperber and Wilson attempt a more cognitive account of communication, and take account of the risks that communication involves. Communication thus becomes, relatively, a more hit-or-miss affair, but not wholly so, since they do not use it in the sense that 'anything goes', but under certain restrictions, which are included in the theory. Details of the theory are still being debated.

In their book on *Relevance* (1986), Sperber and Wilson make a distinction between what they call the code model and the inferential model of communication. Language as a code pairs sounds and meanings via the grammar – i.e. phonetic and semantic representations of sentences. Code models of communication, which have had a long history, propose reconstructions of sender's messages via the signal by the receiver, the physical signal encodes the thoughts, etc. to be communicated. These are then transmitted to and decoded by the receiver. The inferential model assumes a gap between the code and its use, and between thoughts or ideas to be communicated and the means used, but the gap is filled by inference and not by more coding (Sperber and Wilson 1987a: 697).

Utterances, or communicative stimuli, are intentional objects but theorized differently in the Relevance model. Grice's insights regarding what it means for a communicator to mean something by an utterance in terms of intentions and the recognition of intentions is retained but in a slightly different form. The utterance or other communicative stimulus has a double and interrelated function – to inform interlocutors about something but also to inform them of the informative intention, i.e. that there is something to be communicated and that it is intended to be communicated. The first is regarded as an *informative intention*; the second, a *communicative intention*, the latter a second-order intention. Grice's proposal that communication is dependent on general standards of communication – the Co-operative Principle and the maxims – and a common orientation to these standards, the utterance in context, and inferences or implicatures generated in them, is also retained, but given a less speculative rendering and backed by a cognitive model that seeks to explain how this might be and how the gaps in Grice's insights may be plugged.

Orientation to the Co-operative Principle in communication, in Grice, ensured that even flouts of the maxims could be reconciled in terms of the fact that higher order conformity to the Principle can be assumed. Instead of this mode of explanation, that discrimates among various degrees of directness or indirection in communication with respect to the following or flouting of Maxims, Sperber and Wilson (1986, 1987a) propose that in a context of communication, all utterances come with a *presumption of relevance* so that the question of following or flouting Maxims does not arise. We have already noted how a communicative utterance may be invested with the dual character of being both informative and reflexively communicative at the same time. The utterance functions, therefore, as overt verbal means in communication and is an instance of *ostensive-inferential communication* (OIC), a concept which is regarded as basic to communication.

The concept of OIC is backed by the fact that whatever stimuli, verbal or non-verbal, are offered in a context of communication, it is as *manifest* or overt behaviour. It is an ostensive act, and moreover, the fact that it is intended as such must also be manifest. Thus an utterance or any other stimuli – gesture, gaze, movement, etc. as a *communicative act* – is an ostensive act; it is meant to be ostensive, to be noticed and to gain the hearer's attention. Thus, if I were to say that 'The church is in the park', the utterance is an ostensive act and offered for your attention, with a *presumption of relevance* within the interaction. As communication, of course, it is not enough that you should decode the fact that the church is in the park. You should also be aware that I meant to *communicate* to you the information that the church is in the park. In other words, the understanding can be seen as complex on the hearer's part – it is not just the decoded 'The church is in the park', but the elaborated 'Speaker wishes me to be aware that the church is in the park' or, more strictly, 'Speaker wishes to inform me that the church is in the park'. Understanding on the hearer's part has to absorb speaker's use of utterances, which then forms the basis of the response when hearer switches role to that of speaker. The inter-personal dimension, therefore, is constructed at this level – of hearer's assessment of speaker use of utterance – rather than at the level of the code meaning of the utterance alone. With respect to speech acts, in Bach and Harnish's (1982) schema, this would involve considerations of speaker attitudes – thus, 'speaker wants me to close the door' in a request, 'speaker is committing herself to meeting me at the station' in a promise, etc. – rather than the bare understanding of the content of the utterance alone as 'please close the door' or the deictically unreconstructed 'I will meet you at the station', in acts of identical reconstructions of the code.

Utterances are exchanged in contexts and, as we have seen, the notion of context is a complex one. In Sperber and Wilson (1986, 1987a, b), the focus is on the *cognitive* aspects of context and is a psychological construct. Context is described as a set of assumptions that are or can be mentally represented and which can be given semantic representations. Assumptions can be derived from the visual and acoustic channels in the context of situation, from other assumptions already stored in memory, from the utterance or the co-text of previous utterances. We carry around a vast store of assumptions and beliefs about the world, about each other, about events in the past, etc. Information of this kind is stored conceptually at an address in the mind and can be activated if the utterance requires it. Much information, too, is stored in chunks or blocks – the concept of a trial will include all kinds of stereotypic or prototypic information as appropriate to the trial frame or schema. The hearer has to activate and utilize the right context and sets of assumptions or beliefs to arrive at the intended interpretation, and speaker, of course, has to assume that the hearer will activate the right assumptions for communication to succeed. Thus, as Sperber and Wilson note, contexts, in the sense of cognitive contexts, are not given, but selected, activated in the process of communication, and knowledge should not always be assumed to be mutual or shared in advance but is often something whose mutuality comes about as a result or consequence of communication.

The utterance merely provides evidence by drawing something to the hearer's attention as an ostensive act. The hearer forms assumptions on the basis of the evidence of incoming information based on the ostensive act and combines them with existing assumptions in order to yield new assumptions. Thus, inferencing is at work which enables the hearer to arrive at an interpretation, assuming that what is inferred by the hearer is probably what the speaker meant to convey. *Contextual implications* are derived from processing. The new assumptions yielded by the inferencing work are called *contextual effects*, since they are arrived at on a particular basis within the context and the assumptions drawn on within it by those involved. Incoming items of information will produce contextual effects in different ways – (1) they may play a role in the derivation of contextual implications; (2) they may provide more evidence and hence strengthen an existing assumption; (3) they may contradict an existing assumption. When an item has a contextual effect in that environment, it is relevant.

In interaction we also assume some overlap or intersection among our different representations, our assumptions or beliefs about the world in which we live. At any moment an individual has available a set of accessible contexts, the context in which we are involved, etc. An initial context consists of assumptions drawn from the immediate environment, including assumptions based on visual or acoustic information in the shared environment of potential interaction, which, if manifest to us, we may initially assume is manifest to others, i.e. that such information is mutually manifest to participants. Thus, if you and I are in a courtroom, and I see you and you see me, it is manifest to me that you are there, and manifest to you that I am there and it is manifest to both of us that we are there, and the facts can be mentally registered by both of us. *Mutual manifestness* of this kind, in which intersection of assumptions in cognitive environments is presumed, is a weaker requirement than shared knowledge since the latter leaves us with the problem of establishing how we can ascertain that our knowledge is in fact shared. There are also the deductions made from the immediately preceding utterances in the cotext.

The cognitive environment is defined as a set of assumptions which can be mentally represented, and the assumptions can be derived via the visual or acoustic channel from the spatio-temporal context of utterance, from other assumptions, from previous utterances or from memory. The cognitive environment is in a constant state of flux in interaction as assumptions are added or revised or discarded as a consequence of information derived or exchanged or denied in communication. But since communication is always situated discourse, assumptions about the spatio-temporal context, the situation in which participants are involved, who participants are, etc., are all subject to assumption formation.

Utterances in context produce contextual effects and alter the cognitive environment of the audience. Contextual effects are created by combining assumptions made about the ostensive stimuli, with existing assumptions in order to form new assumptions. And these are the product of mental work, even if unconscious and generally at high speed. Thus, the initial context can be expanded by adding other assumptions or by recovering assumptions already held, and so on. Given the fact that at any given moment a wide range of potential assumptions are available, since contexts as sets of assumptions can also include nested contexts and embedded assumptions, the issue of context and assumption selection is important. Initially, the utterance directs attention to something. It is on the basis of attention drawn to something that the process of inferencing and context selection starts. The potentially large set of assumptions which can be activated in communication needs to be controlled. A restriction is introduced to balance the processing costs involved and the cognitive benefits to be gained. The hearer is required to use minimal processing effort in order to achieve optimal contextual effects.

Utterances are underwritten by a presumption of relevance, and if an utterance is relevant in context it will produce contextual effects in that context. An assumption with greater contextual effects will be more relevant than one with less, for the same effort. But it is *optimal* relevance, not *maximal* relevance that is at stake – i.e. a contingent and personally satisfactory level of contextual effects a hearer assesses as needed for interpretation, from the expenditure of minimal processing effort, not all possible effects, in maximal mode. The presumption of relevance is owing to adherence to the Principle of Relevance – that an utterance as ostensive inferential communication communicates the presumption of its own optimal relevance.

If an utterance is deemed to be an act of ostensive-inferential communication, it comes with a guarantee of optimal relevance – that it will yield contextual effects which can be derived by an amount of effort that is not gratuitously higher than is needed to achieve optimal effects. Where this balance is upset, and the kind of effort required is deemed to be higher or greater than anticipated, the interpreter will expect to gain some extra reward – more contextual effects, relevance, or depth of understanding, etc. And although processing can go on for ever in theory, the question of effort or cost controls or can control how far interpreters will go in any one instance in seeking understanding, so that the degree of cost with respect to reward is self-monitoring. Closures are contingently effected by interpreters, in optimal fashion. In written discourse the time at one's disposal is greater than in spoken discourse.

Speakers or communicators have to attend to this fact, too. If they ask for attention, then the fact that processing will require costs of time and effort will be a factor that constrains the means used to communicate by the speaker, who is required to frame utterances in a way so as to use least effort – to use less effort, as far as possible, but, if 'more' is used or intended, then the expectation of rewards has to be satisfied.

The inferential process is defined in relation to one kind of inference – non-demonstrative inference from assumptions to assumptions as an automatic and unconscious process. The reasoning involved is therefore not self-consciously undertaken. An inference is accepted as true or probably true on the strength of other true assumptions. In *demonstrative inference* – All men are mortal/Socrates is a man/Therefore Socrates is a mortal – the truth of the premises guarantees the truth of the conclusions. In *non-demonstrative* inference the truth of the premises makes the truth of the conclusion merely probable. In communication, the latter is operative, since there is no proof offered for the communicator's intentions.

Assumptions are held with different degrees of strength or conviction and could be revised. The initial strength with which an assumption is held can come from different sources – something seen or witnessed can achieve a greater degree of strength; so can the word of respected authority, or the trust in someone's word, or one's confidence in the speaker. The strength of the assumptions derived is dependent on the strength with which the initial assumptions are held. Derived assumptions are only as strong or weak as the strength of the initial premise.

Inferencing processes enable the mind to derive more information from the information it already possesses. Communicants can derive optimal cognitive benefit from much less with which they are supplied by checking the mutual consistency of their assumptions. Assumptions can therefore be weakened in the light of other assumptions, or strengthened, or discarded if newer information causes inconsistency which weakens earlier ones. The cognitive context, therefore, is dynamic. The deductive device takes as input a set of assumptions and systematically deduces as many conclusions as it can.

Communication can, moreover, be strong or weak – the deduced conclusions, may in fact be the ones that are intended and can be determinate ones. On the other hand, they need not be and can be vague – thus, something can be strongly communicated or only vaguely or weakly so. Different degrees of determinacy are possible. An utterance that forces the hearer to supply a very specific premise or conclusion will result in stronger or more determinate communication. Where an utterance permits itself to be read as consistent with the principle of relevance but on varying premises, communication will be vaguer and less determinate; weaker implicatures result and the hearer has less confidence that the premises supplied and conclusions arrived at are the ones intended. Much literary interpretation is arrived at on the basis of weak implicatures generated, which permits greater freedom and variety of interpretation.

All of this takes us a long way from folk beliefs about communication – that a speaker puts a message into the sentence and it flows out at the other end to the hearer in conduit fashion like water from a tap, which passivizes both participants in communication. Both reflexive-intentional and inferential requirements ensure that the hearer, the interpreter, is active; and so is the speaker in orientating to this fact and taking it into account in communication. The utterance, the expression e, can be underdetermined, overdetermined, or adequate, or anything in between. Neither speaker nor hearer are characterized as code dupes searching for meaning in the sentence either synchronically or diachronically but rather as attending to the utterance and utterance requirements and using inferential resources in context as relevant.

Communication, therefore, is not a matter of coding alone. Given the presumption of optimal relevance in any communicative act, as a mutually manifest and ostensive act, the principle of relevance requires that optimal, not maximal, contextual effects are to be derived via minimum processing cost, although neither maximal nor extra processing costs are ruled out. The hearer has to compute the utterance – disambiguate as necessary, etc. and form assumptions and use them with respect to other assumptions to arrive at an interpretation. These other assumptions may well be encyclo-pedic assumptions, and ideological assumptions, cultural assumptions, etc., since there is nothing in the framework to forbid these. And the insertion of such assumptions into the inferencing process is constantly called for. This mode of explanation takes in the risks of communication since much is left to hearer inferencing.

Above all, understanding in communication and interactions is not a matter of scrutinizing others' heads as much as scrutinizing the utterance, and using one's own. Nor are copies of *one* meaning presupposed as *meaning*. Even if there were a copy of speaker's intention lodged via communication in the head of the hearer, there is no way of verifying this. As Bach and Harnish (1982) note, in practice, in context, the assumption that communication has been achieved works on a default basis – in the absence of evidence to the contrary, success is assumed. Sperber and Wilson (1986, 1987a, b), too, stress that there can be no proof. Moreover, Bach and Harnish, who award intentionality a stronger role, write it, not autonomously and individualistically into the speaker's head, but into the inter-personal and social contract that constrains behaviours in communication; the role of intentions figures trans-personally, within the realm of *mutual* beliefs and the Communicative Presumption regarding the use of utterances which is activated in contexts of communication, a point which is sometimes missed when intentions are seen as properties in the heads of speakers alone. Sperber and Wilson are less reliant on the notion, but do not exclude it altogether, and where it does play a role, it is similarly located as pertinent to communicative activity, in trans-personal fashion.

The difference in the role of intention lies in the issue of *uptake*. Whereas Bach and Harnish require that 'uptake' is achieved for commu-nicative success – that illocutionary intents and attitudes of the speakers are grasped by hearers by whatever means – Sperber and Wilson are more tolerant of unintended implicatures going through since they do not see uptake, though important, as a necessary condition for communication (Sperber and Wilson 1987b: 740). This means, as far as one can tell, that the line between understanding and misunderstanding the speaker is not very clear-cut in Relevance theory since it is optimal effects as deduced by the hearer alone, at minimal cost, that are required from ostensive stimuli. With respect to the example given earlier, if 'It is raining' is an ostensive act and the contextual effect derived by the hearer is 'It is Tuesday', when the speaker wishes that the hearer would 'stay a little longer', one would term this miscommunication. On the other hand, the model can cope more easily with instances like the following in which if a speaker were to say 'It is cold in here' when it is mutually manifest to interactants that the window is open and that there is a draught, the hearer takes it as a request for closing the window, and closes it, even if on the speaker's part it was no request at all and only an observation. Even if theoretically this can be classified as a misunderstanding, as it would be in Bach and Harnish's framework, unless some manifest evidence were provided to the contrary, within the discourse context, this could well go through as successful communication, as happens often in everyday uses.

Whereas Bach and Harnish (1982, 1987) work on a notion of strong and full communication, Sperber and Wilson (1986, 1987a, b) allow for partial uptake, fewer effects than those the speaker may have wished to convey, and the like, to count as instances of communication. More shadings are possible. Also, Sperber and Wilson appear to leave it to the participants within the context itself to sort out what counts as understandings or misunderstandings rather than provide general conditions for them. The default condition, it would appear, is more strongly at work in their framework so that unless 'misunderstanding' were made ostensive and mutually manifest within the interaction, i.e. becomes a discourse matter, communication will be assumed to have been effected, which is actually how things work in context.

But the same processes are seen to underwrite both communication and miscommunication, however assessed, literal and non-literal, determinate and vague and, moreover, in particularized, contextualized fashion, since they are dependent on what is adjudged to be contextually manifest and relevant. Particular assumptions and paths of inference are also brought to bear on the utterance on the part of those in interaction. Thus communication leads us from the propositions of the said to those that are meant, and no amount of coding will get us there where the two are unrelated via the code. It is not more coding which is required, but pragmatic inferencing.

POLITENESS PHENOMENA

The mentalistic bias of the two theories dealt with above, the latter more than the former, focus on the 'what' and the 'how' of understanding utterances in communication when the propositional content is inadequate in many ways to whatever is meant, as it inevitably is. But users and uses of language in communication are also subject to social pressures since participants rarely engage with each other only in the discourse roles of speaker and hearer. They confront each other in social roles as well. The rights, responsibilities, taboos, of speech with respect to status, race, gender, age, of the participants affect the way language can be used in contexts of communication. Also, norms of social behaviour require attention since linguistic behaviour in interactions is often assessed socially.

From this perspective, Grice's Co-operative Principle in its rational underpinnings in the Maxims have been supplemented, although the kinds of attempted supplementations have varied. Grice himself was aware that other Maxims may well have to be explored, like politeness, together with the pressures they may bring to bear on communication.

Brown and Levinson (1987) base the concept of politeness on a notion of *face*, which gives rise to different kinds of politeness strategies, with respect to either positive or negative face considerations. *Face*, a concept in its modern renderings initiated by Goffman (1967), is a property negotiated by interactants as social beings, and has been explored at length in pragmatic terms by Brown and Levinson. It relates to the public self-images that are also transacted in social interactions and consists of two associated aspects:

(a) negative face: the basic claim to territories, personal preserves, rights to non-distraction – i.e. to freedom of action and freedom from imposition.

(b) positive face: the positive consistent self-image or 'personality' (crucially including the desire that this self-image be appreciated and approved of) claimed by interactants.

(Brown and Levinson 1987: 61)

Participants orient to face considerations, on the basis that attention to others' face claims ensures attention to one's own given the emotional investment in it, and the vulnerability of face to 'face loss' in dealings with others. Attention to face may only be perfunctory or superficial, as a 'diplomatic declaration of good intentions' (*ibid*.: 62), so that another's face wants may not be wholly satisfied. But in general, it is in everyone's best interests to respect others' 'face' which provides the reciprocity needed for face maintenance in the interests of all, everyone's face being dependent on everybody else's being respected, since face threat could result in counter-threat. In 'positive face' the claim to have one's self-image respected is thus also a want that one's goals and self-image in interaction are positively promoted, while considerations of 'negative face' presuppose the want not to be impeded or imposed upon by others. And these are mutual claims and wants, of course, on the part of those in interaction. But my claims and wants may well conflict with yours, as may yours with mine, hence the need for negotiation and strategic uses of means given these conflicting inter-personal claims or desires with respect to the achieving of goals in interaction.

The means in the framework are rational ones, and directed at ends, and designed with respect to the potential for conflict in the clash of face claims and wants. Speakers as actional, goal-directed agents will, *ceteris paribus*, seek to minimize or eliminate face threat as the most efficient, rational way of fulfilling their goals. Participants will seek to maintain face mutually. Where things are not equal, strategies which run the risk of encountering counter face threats, or challenge in other circumstances, could well be mobilized with impunity.

Given the fact that there are many speech acts which are intrinsically face-threatening to a participant, either on grounds of imposition, or the incurring of debts, or because face enhancement is not relevant for one reason or another, different strategies need to be used. Face strategies take account of the pressures at work in context, like the need to communicate the speech act if an FTA (Face Threatening Act) is used, the want to be efficient with respect to one's goals in choice of means, and the want to minimize face threat (*ibid.*: 68).

An FTA may be strategically performed in different ways. A speaker may go *on record* in instances where it is unambiguously clear what the act and intention is, for instance, 'I (hereby) promise. . . ' which can also give the speaker the appearance of honesty and directness as much as clarity of intent. Or the act may be performed *off record*, indirectly, when there is no single unambiguously attributable intention to which the speaker can be held accountable. Such strategies could be either in the interests of tact or manipulation, since responsibility for subsequent, face-damaging effects, if any, can be avoided by the speaker. All indirect speech acts that rely on inference are involved here, as also figurative uses, understatement, hints, etc. If the act is performed *on record*, it may be delivered either *baldly, without redress* or *with redressive action*. A case of the former would be commands, or other acts which dispense with considerations of face threats to self or other, where the speaker is the more powerful participant; the same applies in an emergency, when the maximally functional or expedient strategy is required. In cases of fire, for instance, I may well yell 'Jump' rather than 'I wonder if you would mind jumping' to preserve your life rather than your 'face' alone.

One may, of course, not perform FTAs at all, but given that even claiming someone's time and attention can be regarded as an imposition, it is difficult to see how inter-personal communication or action can proceed very far if one were to avoid them altogether. Factors that influence the choice of strategies include not only positive and negative face, degrees of redress and the modes of performance listed above, but also the social status of participants, the power balance in force between them, assessed 'pay-offs' among choices and the rankings of impositions as given in a particular culture.

A comprehensive examination of strategies is undertaken in Brown and Levinson's study. Positive politeness involves affirmation of common ground, and the promotion of the view that the participants are co-operators. Relevant strategies include manifestations of interest in H, or H's point of view, needs, wants, etc., and are exaggerated, if necessary; in-group, or solidarity markers in the use of jargon, slang, address forms, dialect, etc.; the avoidance of disagreement, the enhancement of agreement; the giving of deference, sharing or manipulation of presuppositions, etc. Negative politeness can be enhanced by strategies of indirection that leave it to H to decide, i.e. avoidance of coercion; or by mitigatory strategies – for example, the use of hedges like 'sort of', 'as it were', rather than bald assertions; by the communication of awareness of H's wants not to be imposed upon, and the like. Even daily acts like requests are FTAs in that they involve the other in future acts on behalf of oneself, and hence call for negative face redress. Among possible strategies are the following:

- *Be pessimistic* where doubt is expressed explicitly as to whether the right conditions obtain for the appropriateness of the requested act, e.g. 'You couldn't possibly. . . '
- *Minimize imposition* where the intrinsic seriousness of the imposition is diminished, e.g. 'I *just* want. . . ', 'Can I have a minute. . . ?', etc.
- *Give deference* where speakers either humble themselves or raise H's positive face in treating H as superior – in the use of honorifics, in self-deprecation when receiving compliments or minimizing the worth of gifts offered, etc. – 'It isn't much but. . . '
- *Apologize* where speakers, by apologizing for doing the FTA, communicate awareness of infringement of H's space and the fact that it is being taken into account, e.g. 'I know this is a bore, but. . . ' Other strategies along the lines of the recognition of infringement include the *communication of reluctance* – 'I hate to impose but. . . ' – or *impersonalizing* the I–you pronouns, using the passive rather than the active voice, or *nominalizing* – 'Your performance was not as good as expected' as opposed to 'You performed badly'.
- *Point of view distancing* especially in the use of tenses to distance speaker from the hearer and the act being performed in the deictic centre, e.g. 'I was wondering if. . . ', 'I thought I might ask if. . . '

The above is a sample of the many strategies that are discussed by Brown and Levinson (1987), and cross-culturally as well. Positive and negative politeness strategies may operate as 'social accelerator and a social break' (*ibid.*: 231). Strategies may be mixed and matched – a speaker who assesses her own contribution to have been too blunt may redress in next turn, or add on mitigating elements at the end of her turn. If the level of closeness or formality attained is adjudged to be satisfactory, strategies to sustain the level could well be employed, so that the juggling of devices and strategies could form a map or index of the course of the evolving or attained quality of social relationship. Even vagaries of mood could be plotted among interactions if the speaker were expansively oriented to the world at large at some given moment and delivers a host of positive politeness forms, and goes off-colour the next day into coldness or hostility. Moreover, such strategies need not remain fixed along the unit of a sentence, phrase or turn, or be performed as a single act. They may be enacted sequentially along a series of turns. Offers, for instance, often require the participant to be cajoled into acceptance, which could require more than one turn and act.

Leech's *Principles of Pragmatics* (1983) is in many ways similar to Brown and Levinson's in its exploration of politeness issues, but there are also differences. Grice's Co-operative Principle is supplemented with the *Politeness Principle* and both principles work together in various ways as forms of *Inter-personal Rhetoric*, in a goal-oriented, means–ends framework. A notion of rhetoric focuses upon the effective means used to produce some desired effect in the hearer, and the notion of goal is seen as more serviceable than intentions, given the risk of interpreting them as unique and determinate.

Where Grice's Co-operative Principle is concerned, Leech contends that communication and pragmatic force are constrained not only by rational considerations but by social ones. Thus, two kinds of principles are operative – the Co-operative Principle (CP) and the Politeness Principle (PP) – and their complementary workings govern the generation of implicatures in conversation. Whereas the CP provides a framework of reasoning and implicatures, the PP motivates the notion of co-operation as a socially empowered one, and performs a higher regulative function in maintaining friendly relations and social equilibrium as desired social goods. And the PP can be seen to rescue the CP in many instances – as in unostentatious flouts of the Quality Maxim in the issuance of social lies to save face or in the use of indirection in communicating 'impolite' beliefs, which can add social and inter-personal reticence to rational implicatures.

Implicatures get us from what is said to what is meant but with respect not only to communicating illocutionary goals, but also to social goals – of maintaining social comity and equilibrium. Speech acts are re-categorized according to the kind of relationship between the two sets of goals, since, socially speaking, acts are not neutral. Acts like demanding and ordering are *competitive* since the illocutionary goal competes or is in putative conflict with the social goal. In *convivial* acts like inviting or thanking or offering, there is coincidence between the illocutionary and social goals. These two categories are most concerned with politeness. In the competitive category, politeness works to minimize discord and mitigates the intrinsic discourtesy in asking or demanding and has a negative function. In convivial acts intrinsic politeness is enhanced and so this class serves positive politeness functions. The third class, of *collaborative* acts, is indifferent to issues of politeness, and includes acts like asserting and reporting, the 'representatives' in Searle's (1976) taxonomy. In the *conflictive* class of acts like threatening and reprimanding, the social goal is actually negated by the illocutionary goal (Leech 1983: 104–5)

Leech posits various Maxims to regulate politeness – of Tact, Generosity, Approbation, Modesty, Agreement – although the Tact Maxim has received the most attention. The Politeness Principle itself has been characterized in general terms in the following fashion:

• Minimize (other things being equal) the expression of impolite beliefs.

and the Corollary

• Maximize (other things being equal) the expression of polite beliefs.

(*ibid.*: 81)

The maxims, especially of Tact, are in turn constructed on a set of scales of 'cost–benefit to hearer' and degrees of indirectness in the content of the utterance. In the first instance, the greater the benefit to hearer, the more polite an expression. In the following, all directives in imperative form, the politeness increases as benefit to hearer increases, and decreases relative to the degree of imposition on hearer, 3 involving more costs for hearer than 1.

1   Have another sandwich
2   Look at that
3   Peel these potatoes

(*ibid.*: 107)

The other scale employed is that of the degree of indirectness used in the utterance. In the following, the same propositional content is embedded in forms which vary the degree of indirectness. The more indirect the form of the utterance, the more polite it seems.

1   Answer the phone
2   Can you answer the phone?
3   Could you possibly answer the phone?

(ibid.: 108)

Yet degrees of indirection cannot be mapped on to degrees of politeness in a straightforward fashion, as can be exemplified in the different effects rendered in the two modal forms 'Won't you sit down?' as opposed to 'Can't you sit down?' By contrast with 'Sit down' both are indirect, but the 'Can't you. . . ' form triggers an implicature to the effect that hearer can but won't and thus of irritation on the part of the speaker. Thus, indirection in illocutions is related to 'optionality'. Those forms that provide options for the hearer and leave it open for H to choose the course of action are the truly polite uses of indirection. As optionality increases, politeness increases. In the light of the above, the Tact Maxim in its function of regulating comity in interactions is constituted by two sub-maxims:

Minimize cost to H
Maximize benefit to H.

The other maxims examined by Leech work on similar principles of costs and benefits to H. Minimizing cost to H involves negative politeness, while maximizing benefit produces instances of positive politeness. Following the maxims ensures that conflicts are held at bay which is the point of the maxims, and that social life is conducted in 'polite' ways, at least on the surface, and based on mutual acts of inter-personal tact and consideration. Even in instances where speaker may need to break the injunction regarding costs to H, the use of *Irony* ensures that impolite beliefs are expressed politely, even if the Maxim of Quality is broken in the effort. In *Banter*, on the other hand, impolite beliefs expressed openly are read as 'non-serious' and hence not flouting the Tact Maxim, in spite of appearances to the contrary. The various syntactic forms are similarly ordered with respect to the Tact Maxim, imperatives being most costly to H, on the whole, while the interrogative and 'unreal' forms which signify conditional, hypothetical, future states are seen as being more serviceable for polite uses, in the optionalities they offer. Overall, therefore, while the CP ensures that communication and interaction are conducted on a rational basis of means and ends, the PP works to ensure that that very rationality is directed at social ends.

PRAGMATICS AND DRAMA: GENERAL

The above reveals the variety of approaches that are available to an investigation of the pragmatics of dramatic dialogue. Although the programmes outlined deal with a cluster of similar problems and issues, and there is considerable overlap among them, the emphasis is different in each case. Austin (1962) focuses on the *actional*, performative, 'doing' aspects of language use and issues of appropriate contextual conditions that authorize the 'happy' or felicitous performance of acts. Searle (1969, 1979) retains this insight, but is more 'rule-governed' in his approach, with acts also related to issues of meaning and communication. Bach and Harnish (1982) like Sperber and Wilson (1986, 1987a, b) are also primarily concerned with the communicative and cognitive aspects of illocutionary force. The former tie acts to the attitudes of users in a relatively orderly way. They provide, too, directions for understanding or analysing institutionally backed acts, conventional acts, in a way that the others, generally, neglect to do. Sperber and Wilson's cognitive model opens up the drama of understanding itself as an active and particular contextualized process, while Brown and Levinson's (1987) model, like Leech's (1983), steers us into considerations of social use that users must respect if they are to perform as social beings with others similarly identified. Although there is considerable tension among those who are 'mentalistic' and primarily interested in issues of communication, and those who are basically preoccupied with language as a form of social action, the two profiles of pragmatics are not unrelated. Not only is communication involved in issues of action, including social action, but communication itself can be actional in being negotiatory in discourse.

Each of these has something specific to offer in their directed inquests of the field, and the field itself encompasses issues pertinent to language as action as well as those that relate to dramas of communication, which are sometimes dealt with as if they are mutually exclusive. In discourse, dramas of communication, and miscommunication and non-communication, are also actional, given that they are consequential to the communicators, and are enacted via turn-taking, in time. Given that there is no integrated theory of pragmatics, as yet, anywhere in sight, an eclectic approach is favoured for the purposes of attuning the insights gained to the workings of dramatic discourse.

Theories deal with idealized conditions and maximum success; situated performances are alive to contextual contingencies in such a way as to place maximal success as only one among a cline of options, since exigencies or emergencies in context may fail to meet the conditions necessary for maximally successful performance, and these have to be negotiated, or clarified, or put in place via pre-sequences, for instance. But misfires, abuses, infelicitous acts for one reason or another, misdeeds and misdoings are also interactive realities, contextually produced, but the assessment or categorization of them, as such, is generally relative – in relation, that is, to some socially operative notion of felicity which functions as a 'norm' or 'prototype', which theories attempt to capture. Although non-closure and unhappy acts are as probable in contexts as 'happy' ones, communal and inter-personal investments are generally, if not exclusively, in felicitous performance. It is as if the collective desires of societies and individuals were, in fact, for successful performances and harmonious outcomes, notwithstanding ample evidence, in reality, to the contrary. Given inequalities among social groups 'happy' outcomes are often perspectivized, from one participant's rather than the other's point of view, and more widely, the terms of comity or co-operation may favour one group in society rather than another. For our purposes, therefore, both the negative realizations of pragmatic theories as much as positive ones are open to scrutiny, since consequential, failure being as actional in its own way as success.

The application of pragmatics, especially in its speech act version to fictional texts, has been the object of some debate. Austin (1962) claimed that speech acts in plays were etiolated and hollow and parasitic on their real-life uses. Searle in his 'Logical status of fictional discourse' (1979: 58–75) has proposed a macro-speech act in terms of pretence to account for fictional language in general. The divide has been radically questioned in the field of pragmatics as well as outside it, for instance, in Derridean readings (Petrey 1990: 105–6).

For our purposes, the issue is cognitive and social. If we frame activities in a context as fictional our assumptions and expectations regarding practices are changed accordingly. We do not infer that the actor is actually bleeding profusely when an excess of tomato ketchup or whatever is daubed on the clothing or bodies of actors who are ostensibly murdered. We keep the fate of fictional characters and real actors separate in our heads, since framed differently and in complex mode – as theatrical representation of a dramatic fiction. As Elam notes, in Austin only the locutionary act is assigned to actors, the act of uttering the speeches; the illocutionary act potential, and perlocutions, one may add, of those speeches are attributed to the fictional dramatis personae (Elam 1989: 100).

As far as dramatic dialogue is concerned, one crucial effect is that the force of the language/action dichotomy is weakened, a dichotomy sustained by the assumption that action is non-verbal action and to be held in opposition to the verbal. If saying is doing, and words are deeds and, what is more, in interaction, call forth other deeds, dialogue presupposes a network of doings in the sayings, action and counter- or complementary action in the course of its linear progress, via turn-taking, in time. Thus Ross Chambers declared the speech act 'the theatrical act par excellence' (Petrey 1990: 86) in drama – the performative aspects of speech rendering it sympathetic, rather than alien or hostile, to use in the theatre. Not lexis versus praxis, but lexis as praxis, as Keir Elam stated; the action, as Richard Ohmann remarked, 'rides on a train of illocutions' in a play (1973: 83).

But not illocutions alone, since illocutions are one part of a complex trilogy of which speech acts are constituted – viz. the locutionary act, the illocutionary act and the perlocutionary act (which is in turn split into intended perlocutions related to R-intentions of the speaker and unintended ones generally independent of speaker intention). The identification of intentions is arrived at via assumptions and inference with respect to the principle of relevance.

THE INTENTIONAL SELF

The issue of intentionality, too, in speech act theory has caused some embarrassment. In literary studies, one of the more comprehensive attempts to analyse the area is Petrey's (1990) study, but Petrey rules out intention altogether, and regards all acts as conventional in his analysis of speech acts. This does not help us distinguish among those that are strongly institutionally determined, and those like requests which are not. Petrey states that all speech acts are communally authorized, but since there is no linguistic form-illocutionary function identity in many cases, Petrey does not explain how we are supposed to identify speech acts in these cases. There is no way of explaining the phenomenon of indirect speech acts which Petrey does not touch upon.

Thus, it is the classic performative which names the verb in the locution that is relevant to Petrey's analysis. But even here, disambiguation is needed since 'I bet you it will snow tomorrow' need not be an act of betting at all, but speaker may mean something weaker, like 'I feel that it is highly likely that it will snow tomorrow'. Which interpretation is relevant to context – i.e. which inference the speaker intended the hearer to make – is important, since different consequences ensue, even where understanding or the sharing of beliefs alone is required and not action sequels. The fact that listener switches role to that of speaker in turn and delivers responsive speech means that inferring what speaker had in mind, speaker meaning, becomes part of the communicative effort. Understanding includes not only the conventional or coded meaning of the utterance, but also whatever is inferred as speaker wants, desires, beliefs, etc. in the use of utterances in context, pragmatics generally linking language with users, and in dialogue, interactionally and often, inter-personally.

Petrey's embarrassment with intention derives from the idea of it as some internal thing in the head of the speaker which is transmitted via the message to the head of the hearer in conduit fashion and as a copy of itself, but this attitude deracinates the interactionality involved in communication and denudes it of dynamism and risk, as noted above. The code model is not the one involved. The problem is actually broader, since the unease both inside and outside pragmatics relates to the ideology of 'person' or 'self' which intentionality presupposes, which casts the individualistic self as the locus of agency, control and continuity in its actions. Yet, such a notion of the self is only one among many others, as the discussion in Chapter 1 (see pp. 37–47) reveals. And even if intentionality were a basic mark of 'the human', as some have claimed – and child acquisition studies reveal that intentional action indirectly performed is understood by children early in life – the cultural values associated with it can vary widely. Even within cultures self-regimes can vary, as between those of a dandy and a saint, for instance.

The individualistic self with attributes of will, responsibility, agency, etc. for its actions is privileged more highly in the Christian West, as analysts have noted (Rorty 1976a; Philips 1993; Hill and Irvine 1993), but the concept, although not necessarily absent in other cultures, is more marginalized by them, relative to the importance awarded the concept in the West. To the Balinese, for instance, the Western model would be more appropriate to Balinese children, for there is a reversal of the notion in adult affairs, whereas the West retains the concept of a bounded individuality into adult life (Shweder 1993: 13; Geertz 1993: 123–36). Among Samoans, a person's speech actions may be assessed not according to speaker intentions primarily, but with respect to consequences on others (Duranti 1993: 24–47). In general, not all societies are inclined to the same degree to rely on inferences about intentional motivation in talk or action (Philips 1993: 255–6). The moral to be gleaned from the cross-cultural record would seem to be that properties or attributes awarded to the 'self' are not universally homogeneous, but an issue of preferences along a spectrum of possibilities. Cultures privilege different possibilities, with others available but not used as much in communal life since assessed of lower value. The claim to universality of any notion or notions has to take account of how other cultures have calibrated these concepts in the organization of their own affairs (Shweder 1993).

In the West, the notion of intentionality in inter-personal affairs is linked to other notions like responsibility on the part of the self, and liability in relation to others. And as long as a self is made liable for its actions as intended action, in a culture, the concept of intentionality will remain in force as a powerful social factor in the interpretation of actions. Even here, as we have seen, there is variation, since degrees of liability are often awarded to excuse others or oneself from consequences of breaches, and often liability can be negotiated in inter-personal affairs. And if the West does privilege the ideology of the intentional self as a product of its own recent Christian history, then pragmatic rules (for native-speaker English) could hardly fail to take the fact into account in terms of the explanatory power and empirical or descriptive adequacy of the models proposed.

Major analysts in the field, as noted above, like Bach and Harnish (1982), site intentionality within the sphere of the *communicative* contract – as a communicative presumption that is mutually believed to be opera-tive in interactive contexts. In Sperber and Wilson's theory (1986, 1987a, b), too, assumptions about informative and communicative intentions that attach to mutually manifest indicators like utterances are similarly offered as assumptions already in place in a context of communication. The possible wider cultural motivation, however, is not overtly specified in these studies. It is as speaker use of linguistic tokens, in context, as motivated and other-directed use, and relevant to the business in hand, that the concept will be used, in this study. The concept of 'language-in-use' is language used by someone to someone for specific purposes, as the notion of speaker meaning makes clear, and is not just some transcen-dental abstract. The notion of 'goal' is often used instead of intentionality and is equally serviceable. However strongly or weakly the concept is adhered to in any specific instance, it does not affect the procedures, if the notion of speaker meaning and use of utterances forms part of the social and communicative contract among interactants. At any rate, the specific intentions or goals that we ascribe to interlocutors are actually compiled as contextual effects by interpreters and computed on the basis of its relevance in the interaction.

And we impute intentions to each other, as we do desires, wishes, wants and a lot else, and construct subjectivities from the evidence of others' often discontinuous speech and behaviour (Butler 1990b: 271). The identities so constructed are inferential accomplishments on our part in response to ostensive behaviour, and open to change or confirmation or doubt in relation to further evidence. In drama, they are 'compelling illusions' (*ibid.*) and supported only by whatever evidence we feel we have for constructing them, in the interpretation of the dramatic figures' speech and behaviour. Their imputed and interpreted forms of existence are sustained only by our own modes of belief in our constructions.

Subjectivity or identity is thus assembled via contextual effects in discourse – the product of interpretation, even when identity is self-interpreted, though read as cause (Herman 1989). In whatever fashion identity and subjectivity are privately or internally experienced, in interaction it is discoursally and dialogically produced, as an effect of inferences. Some theory or theories of self are usually invoked to underwrite the inferences we make in response to a character's speech and behaviour, which may coalesce a character into the rigidities of trait theory or fragment them into creatures of self-alienation, self-doubt and fissure, or a lot in between. Given that dramatic figures are usually presented, like persons outside the fictional frame are encountered, in situations in gapped or fragmentary mode with time lapses to be accounted for, either between segment and segment, act and act, or scene and scene or even only with respect to lifetime, as it were, presupposed by their entrance on the stage, or page, the stabilizing of the subject as a tensed one, and open to the vicissitudes of time and situation, even where contradiction and not continuity is evident, is something that recipients do.

Moreover, if the subject, as situated subject, is basically constructed within dual metaphors of the self – the theatrical and the legal – as Rorty (1976b) noted, the *performances* of the subject are under the threat of *liability* for its performances, for both word and deed, in its encounters with others. In context, within social activity, intentionality is tied to liability with respect to the other, and to responsibility, in relation to self, since speech and action will be interpreted as one's own whenever there is no manifest evidence to expect, assume or believe otherwise. But these are open to negotiation. In communication, a cultural subject's desires and intentions are assessed with respect to what it may rightfully claim as a *social* subject, and not as a unilateral psychological one since embedded in situations in which respect of others' social rights and the demands made by these socially empowered rights are constraints to be considered. The tension between the two within a given ideology is where the drama, and agonies, and the agonistics, of intentionality as goal-directed behaviour are located.

But in complex mode. For, as Bakhtin notes, subjectivity in discourse is actually in a three-way tension among considerations of I-for-myself, I-for-others, the-other-for-me (Morson and Emerson 1990: 173–230). The inner sense of self is constantly in engagement with the self constructed by others, who, in Bakhtin's view, are needed to complete the idea of a self, to give it form and boundaries. Nor can selfhood be secured by mapping itself on to images offered either by ego or other. The self constructed by others is directed to a speaker's self-in-act in situated fashion, and is always contextualized, partial; while the self constructed by ego is equally unfinalizeable since the self of I-for-myself is projected towards the future and, hence, is self-in-process, at any moment of its action. Equally, in its I-for-others modes, it is enmeshed in the mutuality or asymmetry of the terms of the other-for-me. The self is thus never purely and simply identical with itself in dialogic interaction.

And as for the issue of one goal or intention per utterance, such is not entailed either, when speaker use is regarded as directed use. For, as Sperber and Wilson (1986, 1987a, b) note, communication is risky, and can be both determinate and vague and speaker intentions and goals may well be multiple and also indeterminate. Moreover, communication may be partial and still suffice for the moment. For it is optimal and not maximal success that can be expected in context, in communication. The resistance to agency, goal-directedness, intentionality also relates to contemporary beliefs about 'the nature of language', 'the human', etc. which is generally pessimistic, and militates against the possibility of clarity, determinacy, rationality and communicative potency, which theories appear to promote. But as long as liability for word and deed accrues on the subject, as social subject, in situations, the reading of it as an intentional agent will prevail, even where intentions are obscure or irrelevant, or even where only degrees of responsibility or liability are imposed, and even when, in theory, it is impossible to subscribe to a notion of a subject as endowed with such attributes. The strength of social assumptions and expectations cannot be overridden, in action, by the strength of theories, in abstracted mode, alone. But social life itself may employ plural concepts of selfhood, and strategically in situations, as argued earlier, a fact which may be obscured when the focus is solely on the dominant mode.

In drama, the issue of speaker, goal-directedness in language use, is tied to the degree to which we may assess dramatis personae to be speakers who 'own' their speech, and where the speaking conventions in force in the fictional world presume a world which makes speakers liable and responsible for the effects of their speech. As noted in Chapter 1 (see pp. 30–7), discourse roles of spokespersons, ghostees, etc. would not be open to charges of liability for speech to the same extent that canonical speakers would be. Moreover, the historical dimension needs also to be borne in mind since the dramatic figure can be modelled on different theories of the 'person' in different eras. The dramatic figure as 'person' in the Renaissance derives from a 'humanist' model, revolutionary in its time, which the post-modern dramatic figure has left behind, although not in universalist fashion in every instance. Nostalgias for former models and overlaps are still evident and functional. Popular television plays still reproduce what 'high' art may deem defunct. Different theories of self and the different kinds of identity they make available, in Rorty's taxonomy, and different modes of figure characterization in a play or in plays of a period, also signify diversity. Different dramaturgies and conventions (Szondi 1987; Kennedy 1983) have historically scaled and constrained the importance to be awarded to notions like intentionality, responsibility and liability to speakers as canonical 'persons' in the speech events in which they are involved in a play, whether the styles of speech adopted are naturalistic or not.

LOCUTIONARY ACTS

Assumption formation and disambiguation of indeterminacies in the utterance can proceed smoothly enough to be invisible in dialogue, but the importance of their sub-textual roles in providing the background context for the dramatic action, economically, cannot be minimized, when the fit between speaker goal and hearer interpretation is achieved without a hitch. The unstated pragmatic work can be made visible since, although much is left unstated, inferences made are taken on board in interpretation. In the Wesker extract examined earlier (p.125) Sarah and Harry in the opening exchanges play QA sequences in harmonious fashion: Sarah questions, Harry answers in adjacency pair mode. Pragmatically speaking, Sarah's interrogatives are not just 'questions' – they can be interpreted as speech act requests for information which Harry interprets as such and responds to accordingly. They could also be partly phatic as well, Sarah merely keeping the channel open at this stage. As requests, the focus is on her illocutionary desire to know the information requested, to which Harry responds, which collaboration makes for harmony. In similar vein, Harry's 'answers' invoke the related attitude of belief in what he says, which Sarah accepts as the truth of the case; at this stage, at any rate.

SARAH   You took the children to Lottie's?
HARRY   I took them.
SARAH   They didn't mind?
HARRY   No, they didn't mind.

There are ambiguities in Sarah's first utterance – for the audience, in particular. Does the definite referring term, 'the children', refer to their own or somebody else's children? And who or what is 'Lottie's'?: an intimate associate or relative's home, a gymnasium, restaurant, clothes shop? One economical assumption could be that the referents for the definite referential term 'the children' must be their own children, and that 'Lottie' must be someone in close relation to the interactants, and these would have to suffice for the moment. The characters themselves possess overlapping assumptions about both referents, since there is no manifest problem of disambiguation for them. Once the reader or audience makes assumptions as to how to disambiguate the terms, further assumptions can also be made – the characters are parents, their children are at a trusted person's home, though the reason why is not available. More assumptions are added later on, when the topic of the political march and anticipated violence enters the interaction, which are added to the store of assumptions already in place as the dialogue proceeds so that we could assume that the children are absent for their own safety. The audience is actively involved from the very beginning in creating the necessary information and the off-stage context of the play.

On the other hand, the risks of disambiguation can be used strategically by speakers, since coincidence between the rhetic and phatic acts, in Austin's terminology, cannot be assumed. What is more, natural language ambiguities in the locutionary act can be exploited by recipients since it is up to recipients to co-operate in the communicational endeavour of working out speaker uses of utterances. The excesses that could result from unilateral exploitations of code and inferential possibilities in the utterance can be material for comic episodes, when recipient behaviour is adapted not to speaker delimitations but to the 'dislocationary' potential of the locution itself, as Elam has shown, in Shakespearean comedies. The extract given below is from Shakespeare's *Twelfth Night*, which is only one among Elam's many examples.

SIR ANDREW   Bless you fair shrew.
MARIA   And you too, sir.
SIR TOBY   *Accost*, Sir Andrew, *accost*.
SIR ANDREW   What's that?
SIR TOBY   My niece's chambermaid.

SIR ANDREW   Good Mistress Accost, I desire better acquaintance.
MARIA   My name is Mary, sir.
SIR ANDREW   Good Mistress Mary Accost –
SIR TOBY   You mistake, knight. '*Accost*' is front her, board her, woo her, assail her.
SIR ANDREW   By my troth, I would not undertake her in this company. Is that the meaning of *Accost*?

(Elam 1989: 209, 1.3.43–55)

Punning, lexical misfires as in the above, the refusal to disambiguate, with intentional play on ambiguities substituted instead on the part of recipients, reveal the perils that communicators can face, since they can become the butts of others' comic, irreverent and carnivalesque energy. In Tom Stoppard's *Jumpers* (1972) even the proper noun as name loses its referential stability when Bones the Inspector cannot quite grasp or remember what the name of his interlocutor is and he uses anything that comes to mind as substitutes. Moreover, in the extract given above, the 'misunderstandings' between Sir Toby and Sir Andrew are actually a contest between different possible 'meanings', alternative 'understandings' and not between meaning and non-meaning. Sir Andrew's interpretation of 'Accost' as Maria's name is a legitimate one, given that it is derived from the context via a path of rational inference, but it is not related to Sir Toby's intended meaning which focuses on the verb as act. In the event, it is Sir Toby's meaning and not Sir Andrew's which is made to prevail in context to which Sir Andrew defers, his own understanding being reciprocally cast as 'misunderstanding' *in situ*.

Wrongful disambiguation on someone's part can also be matter for tragedy since mistaken assumptions can be lodged in a character's cognitive environment and believed to be true and 'real', with fateful consequences. This is the case in *Othello* when, as eavesdropper, the 'proof' of Desdemona's infidelity is clinched for Othello when he sees the careless use of the handkerchief, and above all, disambiguates references to 'she' and 'her' as pertinent to Desdemona when in fact the speaker, Cassio, meant Bianca.

Locutionary performance and its uptake can have other sinister effects, as David Birch has argued, and can be socially slanted. Linguistic variation is a cultural and inter-cultural fact but subject to the pressures of power and consequent stereotyping. Thus, accents of dialect speakers, speakers of the dominant language as a second language, foreign speakers, and others, become easy scapegoats for racist and prejudiced displays by the manipulation of the phonic and phatic aspects of the locutionary act.

Birch (1991: 89) cites instances where this is the case and explores the ways by which such stereotyping can be resisted. The examples used are from South African writers who restore to their own dialects inter-personal agencies and communicative and expressive efficiencies and reciprocities in their plays.

The stereotype as a cultural commodity in a group can be used against the consumers, as Noël Coward does in the play *Conversation Piece*. Here, the plan between Paul, an impoverished Englishman, and Melanie, an even more impoverished French girl, is to dupe the credulous English gentry by playing on their stereotypes by presenting Melanie as an aristocrat whose father has been executed by the French revolutionaries, in order to arrange a lucrative marriage; the older male is in command. The device used for this subterfuge and to create the required identity for her is precisely to make her speak either in French or in foreigner English in the presence of others. In Fugard's *Sizwe Bansi is Dead* (1974; quoted by Birch 1991: 140–1) it is the use of translation that turns the stereotype on its head. The context of situation and participant framework used are more complex since the white boss does not speak his workers' language and uses an intermediary. The translator, Styles, who is black, has to relay white speech to his fellow black workers. In the effort, the translation is not only of the white boss's speech but the translator's black identity and solidarity with other workers is instilled into it as well. In the extract given below, the boss gives his orders, and Styles 'translates' in this vein.

> 'Tell the boys, in your language, that this is a very big day in their lives.'
> 'Gentlemen. The old fool say this is a hell of a big day in our lives.'
> The men laughed.
> 'They are very happy to hear that, sir.'

Styles is in the role of the mouthpiece and not the canonical speaker, which white rule does not permit in this situation of utterance and, therefore, he is without the rights of canonical speakers; he does not 'own' the intentionalities of speech, nor even compositional rights to the utterances he mouths. He resists the passive role of functionary of white interests by finding his own voice and agency in the role, and communicative, interactional and political potency for his speech against given conditions as a result. He 'ambiguates' 'speaker–boss' by referencing him as 'the old fool', and the laughter of the men back to the boss as 'very happy' to hear the boss's commands. He embeds a canonical speaker within the role of mouthpiece, to which the other workers respond. The racially motivated blindness and linguistic deafness – the white cannot disambiguate or infer, not knowing the language – in the overall political pathology of the white to blacks is also dramatized by playing the situation in this way. In these latter cases, rule exploitation provides possibilities for different inter-personal situations unlike rule-following in the Wesker instance (see pp. 127–8).

CONVENTIONAL/INSTITUTIONAL ACTS

Conventional acts in Bach and Harnish's (1982: Ch. 6) classification are those that are institutionally constituted with participants in public roles and enacted in public settings via public procedures. Many of Austin's (1962) original 'performative' examples were drawn from this category and served his purposes well, since the role of felicity conditions, procedures, etc. was made more visible in these instances. Among pragmaticists, institutional acts have claimed little interest since their performative power is seen as more automatic and restricted, their workings to be attributed to their place in a public script or a conventional ceremony or ritual, and thus have little to contribute to the understanding of issues of meaning or communication. Socio-pragmaticists, too, have paid less attention to this class of acts and have concentrated more on how social factors influence the performance of communicative acts.

Yet social reality and social life are deeply conditioned by the pervasive control of such acts. Being born is not enough to have a social existence or identity, the fact is conferred on one in different ways as one is categorized, as gendered infant, minor or adult. One is not even properly dead unless institutionally certified as such. Death is not just a natural fact, socially speaking, not only because of the fact of brain death, but also since it has to be further sub-classified as lawful or unlawful death. Boundaries between health and disease, sanity and madness, proper and improper sexuality and the like are also institutionally drawn. The food we eat, the clothes we wear have similarly to be institutionally authorized – as legally possessed and not unlawfully appropriated. Given the many institutions in a society (Bach and Harnish 1982: 112) like hospitals, schools, leisure and interest associations, employing institutions, religious institutions, secret societies, etc., not to mention the written acts that also bedevil us – bills, guarantees, contracts, forms, receipts, statements, etc. from bank, tax office, shops, employers, and other civic and public bodies – the network of institutional acts, practices, rights and obligations in which we live and move and have our being is an immense part of social life. So are the obligations and public identities for individuals this network requires and the liabilities they bring in their wake. Both are so habitual as to be naturalized and taken for granted.

When institutional events and conventional acts enter a play and their workings are dramatized, the-taken-for-granted is defamiliarized, and the wider issues of power and control in public life and their effects on a society and subjectivity are foregrounded as issues appropriate to that world. They are among the world-creating devices that can be used to portray the fictional world, and in a special way, since they point to a pre-existing world of political, corporate or civic life in a society. The issues enacted and outcomes achieved signify the state of the political world and the nature of the forces that are operative in that world since it is in the name of society at large that institutional acts and events achieve their particular, world-changing force.

In speech act theory, the examples given are usually one-liners, which tend to obscure the fact that institutional acts are embedded in institutional events and are enacted in extended fashion within configurated procedures. Moreover, where speech procedures are unscripted, as in trials, the performative competence of the principals and participants in their public roles can influence outcomes. Powerless strategies in power-driven contexts can count against the users of them. The strategic use of given procedures and the performative adequacies or inadequacies of participants in their roles are factors to be taken into account since they can colour otherwise similar events in specific ways and influence outcomes.

The psychological, personal, inward turns into solitude and alienation on the part of characters in modern drama means that the world of public affairs is generally not a central concern nor portrayed in any sustained fashion in plays. This is not the case in earlier drama, especially Renaissance drama, and above all in Shakespeare, where public and political issues are traced on a broad canvas (Alvis and West 1981). The English history plays, in particular, foreground political issues, but similar concerns are to be found in the Greek and Roman plays as well. Even in the romances and comedies, the polis is not too far away from Arcadia, since exile and restitution, both institutional acts, motivate the action and its closures. In the variety of social life these plays include, the afflictions of civic life and the trials of power play a crucial part as characters are made to sustain their public roles and private ambitions with varying degrees of success, and the fit between private disposition and public office, and the links between office and power, are also brought into view. There are inward turns when dramatic speech constructs an internal persona in its private existence, but these are usually presented as foils to, or in tension with, the pressures of the public identity, action and role.

The private and the public intersect, with identity on trial in many cases within the terms of the political formations and their situated demands on the dramatic figures, mostly male, whose fates, by necessity or choice, are embroiled in them. The clash of protagonist and antagonist is also a clash of different ideologies in their struggle for ascendency. As Elam notes (1980: 159), illocutionary conflicts set in motion social, ethical and inter-personal forces in a play; in institutional contexts, the triumph or downfall of a character in a major public role is a social and political defeat as well.

As public figures the dramatis personae, especially when major protagonists or antagonists, are not presented as 'flat', social or political dupes either, but are generally given will, or wilfulness, and calculation in the actions they undertake, especially for the major figures, thus instantiating the Renaissance concept of 'subject'. They are also constructed within a variety of situated contexts in which they are required to perform with respect to the contingencies they face in the deictic contexts of their interactions. And they perform in uneven fashion, since the social, the political and the inter-personal are heterogeneously constructed when contextualized into specificities, with different demands made on the interactants in different contexts, to which they respond with different degrees of adequacy. A homogeneous subjectivity of power or powerlessness, unitary positions of dominance or subordination, or attendant strategies of power or non-power, that repeat in all instances on a binary divide, however constructed, are hard to come by in the dramatic world, given that there are usually reversals of fortune and changes in states of affairs, and various inter-personal and institutional networks of relationships to be attended to as part of the action.

The social world, too, is configured in complex fashion, and the demands of power and its pursuit or exercise are undertaken within the context and network of other activities and inter-relationships which their societies offer (Alvis 1981: 5) – the quest for fulfilment, identity, love or happiness, the joys and betrayals of sexual love, of family association, and friendships for pleasure or profit. These private pursuits are affected by the nexus in which characters are placed and the possibilities and resistances offered by the social milieux they inhabit. The fictional world, even when riven, is a world of transactions with others like or unlike themselves, sharing political regimes for better or for worse, subject to laws and governed by institutions and norms, their lives enmeshed in the bonds of community, convention, opinion, beliefs, taboos, of shared social life, and involving accommodations, alliances or antagonisms of various kinds. Issues of power arise within such complex configurations, but, in critical and global instances, are brought to the forefront in two major sites – the battlefield, and the floor of institutions in public contexts – which are both definitive sites for the trials of power and it is these, therefore, that figure most strongly when the antagonistic forces in the dramatic world are brought into play to change the course of affairs in it. The will to power, in its exercise, rarely remains either a wholly public or a wholly private, personal or homogeneous matter.

One of the earliest applications of speech act theory to drama was Stanley Fish's reading of Shakespeare's *Coriolanus* (Fish 1980b), which uses Searle's (1969) framework. Although protesting that speech act theory has to be applied judiciously to literary works, Fish nevertheless provides a reading which interprets the tragedy within the tension of a transcendental individualism which sets itself above the communally binding claims of the society in which the protagonist lives and which his illocutionary behaviour enacts. Coriolanus' sense of self is founded on his proven merit in battle which he deems sufficient proof of his worth. Yet, to be appointed to the consulship, to which he aspires, he is required to request the votes of his fellow citizens, which he does with barely concealed contempt, and his illocutionary behaviour, in the long run, undoes him. Although he recognizes no obligation to the collective, the collective proves stronger.

Coriolanus must request votes, and the felicity conditions on requests require that he sincerely desire whatever is requested, that he believe that it is in the ability of the hearer to do what is requested, and that the action requested would not have been performed in the normal course of events anyway. Coriolanus flouts such conditions, since it is his own rightness for the post which is displayed as self-evident; at least in his own eyes. Nor will he greet his fellow citizens. Greetings are speech acts which habitually and often phatically enact the reality of community and communality since they are minimal but important initiatory, inter-personal acts at the thresholds of social encounters. His refusal to engage in the activity similarly seeks to express his independence of the community.

Promising is an act to which he is partial, as is refusing. Fish sees both as in character, since promising, although a commitment to do something, is basically an act that involves keeping one's own word, and not incurring a reciprocal obligation to someone else for some action done on one's behalf. Refusals, too, are acts that signify independence since they are acts that say 'I can do (in the fullest sense of agency) without it'. He even refuses others' praise, since his own self-esteem forbids his acceptance of others' evaluation of himself. The citizens banish him, to which Coriolanus responds with a counter 'I banish you', infelicitous, but expressive of a transcendent ego that recognizes no communally instituted authority, of citizenry or state. His subsequent offer of his services to the enemy – the Volscians – carries the self-constituted freedom of individualism into areas where the institutional facts and powers of his world can destroy him. His behaviour is institutionally assessed as treason, ironically when he is attempting to mediate between the two warring camps, and he is put to death.

The play, Fish observes, seems often like an early exemplification of speech act theory. Fish concentrates on the quality and consequences of Coriolanus' illocutionary behaviour which are interpreted in the light of speech act 'rules' provided by Searle and the kind of meanings they produce. As acts, however, they function as forms of social praxis in the fictional world. The monolithic and monologic nature of Coriolanus' speech action function as acts of personal and social disregard for his interlocutors and are at odds with communal requirements. The consequences of this clash are destructive for the protagonist and for all that he signifies.

Fish's focus is generally on one character and the manner in which his speech style constructs his subjectivity, although the analysis makes clear that what fuels the tragedy is the egotistic selfhood which cannot subordinate itself to trans-individual, communal necessities. But *Coriolanus* is also a drama of public life, with the protagonist in a public role. In the political and civic realm, the private acts of an individual take on more than private import, and in public, institutional contexts are subject to interpretation as authorized by the procedures of the institutions in which they are used.

Coriolanus' troubles begin when he leaves the context of war and its practices and conventions and seeks to enter the political realm. He offers himself as *candidate* for election, and although in an institutional role he refuses to conform to the instituted procedures and practices by which elections are conducted and office conferred in his public and civic world. Institutional acts are transacted via procedures and have binding force when successfully executed. They confer changes in status, rights, privileges, and in the play, political power on the individual who falls within their effective or verdictive scope – the election and ratification of the office of consul. His flouting of the procedures sets the terms of the course for his political ambitions and his life.

Illocutionary behaviours in institutional settings rarely stand assured of being read as indicative of individuality alone since they are interpreted within the scope of institutional proceedings and acquire institutional meanings. A defendant's constatives are not assessed with respect to the strength of the individual beliefs that support them. They are re-read with institutional colourings, as institutional acts, as 'witness', 'confession', 'evidence', etc. Coriolanus' illocutionary behaviour – his refusal to reveal his wounds, his refusals to request votes as the convention required – as public behaviour in the role of candidate baffles the citizens and is interpreted as insult since inappropriate to expected, procedural behaviour. His constatives, in expressing his beliefs about the populace during the proceedings in the Senate, are similarly assessed, not only as private beliefs, but as treason, and he is driven into exile. The inertness of procedure in speech act theory is far more dynamic in its workings in practice, since procedural meanings are performative, legal and effective meanings in public contexts. The role played by procedure as a form of public validation of speech is notable, since it functions as political instrument for power in the conflict between the factional interests in the play – the patricians and the citizens as represented by Coriolanus and the tribunes.

In the wider national context of Rome in the play, it is a time of political turmoil with the state engulfed in war and famine. The patricians have appropriated the larger part of the available food and the citizens demand greater rights and shares in the country's resources. Thus, the scope of dominant power is contested, and the power base on which its institutions rest is unstable, with patrician and plebeian in conflict. Some power has already been conceded by the patricians in the installation of the tribunes, Brutus and Sicinius, as representatives of the populace. Coriolanus belongs to the most conservative wing of the patrician fold with a political ideology of class privilege which is manifested in his attitude to the populace, which enjoins that patricians are born to rule and plebeians to be ruled. The tribunes are institutional agents representing the citizens' interests, and in opposition to Coriolanus in particular.

The citizens are represented variously, since the populace, unlike the tribunes, are icons of subjectivized deference to the power of the status quo, but are erratic in their reactions to circumstances. The conflict is focused and enacted, in the immediate instance, between Coriolanus and the tribunes, both institutional agents, but it is wholly political. Coriolanus' attitude to the citizens being what it is, his election to the office of consul poses a threat to the tribunes' own, newly won political clout. But the battle between Coriolanus and the tribunes is also a battle for control and power between two political ideologies which they also represent. The personal animosities are entirely owing to their irreconcilable political interests and affiliations – between them there is no subjectivity or inter-subjectivity external to it. More generally, the conflict is also that of two versions of the state itself, and the global terms of public life it regulates and the manner of regulation, which brings to the forefront issues of government and political life under various possible regimes, since this is a society in transition.

Shakespeare's representation of the terms is actually pessimistic. Within the action of the play, matters of state are sorted out in public contexts but the workings of procedure in public acts become a cover for vested interests which seek to control them, given their world-changing import. The tribunes manoeuvre Coriolanus into a procedural form of election where he is made to seek votes. When their calculations go awry and the citizens give him their votes, the tribunes stage a counter-coup, and seek to get the vote reversed on the grounds of irregularities (plus the threat of civil disorder), thus cynically and astutely invoking other procedures (or violence) to invalidate what procedure had made valid. They trap Coriolanus in a world of institutional protocols which he does not respect nor understand, given the limitations of his patrician ideology. They finally provoke him into the kind of behaviour which can be institutionally outlawed, which he delivers as a point of honour.

Control of the public procedures is sought by both sides since the outcomes are binding. The patricians attempt to tutor Coriolanus in the political arts of hypocrisy and dissembling. Volumnia's advice to her son is a textbook account of how institutional acts in public contexts should be performed: only follow the procedure, defer to the convention, speak the right words at the right time, pay lip-service to sincerity, one is a conventional and not an intentional speaker. In the event, the wrong words are uttered, sincerely and passionately, and Coriolanus is banished. But no particular group or individual comes out of these situations unsullied, given the stakes and the pressures of the deadly political games of means and ends that engulf them all.

If Coriolanus' illocutionary behaviour shows him unable to understand his links to a wider collectivity, it also shows him blind to the political realities of his world which are in flux. A great soul, proven valour, or deserved merit has little chance if it stands alone and cannot play the power game with skill. The constative turn of mind and speech in institutional contexts (as in communicative ones) is his hallmark, and one he favours – he speaks the truth about his feelings for the populace, his contempt for public protocol, for democratic rights, his belief in his own worth, and the patrician right to rule, regardless of circumstance and the political necessity to project an appropriate subjectivity in the role – the requisite thoughts, feelings, etc. in Austin's (1962) terms – which is adjudged a handicap by his supporters and as unfitness for the office he seeks by his political opponents. The tension between the impulses of the private self and the compulsions of the public one, the mismatch between intentional and institutional behaviour when located within a trans-personal and cleft world of political forces in combat undo him, since he is outmanoeuvred by the tribunes who exploit the split.

The use of conventional acts as institutional acts in their discoursal renderings in drama is a way of representing the realities and trials of political power in the fictional world. Such acts are not descriptions of the state, they *are* the state, as Fish (1980b) noted. They index as they enact the realities, whether conflictual or consensual, of power, authority, legislation, control, regulation. The constitutive elements – like agents in appropriate roles, validating protocols and procedures, consequences and sequels, and the process itself when enacted – display the terms of the contention of forces, political and 'social, ethical, inter-personal', in Elam's (1980) terms, of that world. Since institutional facts are created out of the process, the playing of the institutional roles, the uses of procedure and its effects with respect to the conflicting forces in the fictional world, are consequential, since binding, and the balance of power could be tipped in favour of one or the other of the contending parties depending on how the institutions and their verdictive powers, in particular, are made to work by those involved.

The descriptions of conventional acts in speech act theory are generally agnostic in relation to political power, although social power on the part of its agents is assumed. But institutions and the felicity conditions on institutional acts and the workings of institutional events they authorize are stable only insofar as the power base on which their authority rests is secure. The links among the different elements – agents, conventional acts and events, procedures, authority, legitimacy, sequels – can come apart in marked cases like insurrection or revolution (Petrey 1990: 91). Where the dominant power is challenged the authority of the performative utterance as institutional action could also be weakened. In cases of civil strife or invasion, where the contending power is strong, sectional splits can fracture consensus. And if the revolutionary power orders the army, which was at the service of the incumbent power, back to the barracks, *and the army obeys*, the *making* felicitous of a hitherto infelicitous, treasonable, act dramatizes the shift of political allegiance and the reality of the authority of the new power and its base for institutions and their acts.

Such eventualities breed others. Conventional acts of naming confer a new status on persons – the 'king' as 'tyrant' or 'despot'; the erstwhile 'terrorist' of one order becomes the 'hero' or 'heroine' of another. Designations and denotations and their connotations are politically re-perspectivized. Objects or events similarly change their referential stipulations – a blood-stained fragment of pavement or wall becomes a shrine; a day in the calendar, a commemorative day, a holiday. Institutions and their acts remain, but with different agents and revised procedures, and function in the interests of whichever ideology implants or enforces its control; the needle of felicitous performance points to the magnetic north of dominant power.

The power exercised by agents in public, institutional arrangements, is often *de jure*, legitimate power, since ratified as such by the collective, willingly or not. But power may be challenged or abused in little or large measure. The legitimate power may be weak and power actually exercised *de facto* by illegitimate persons or groups. Whatever the state of power in a society, the abstract notion of power dissolves into concrete situations of enactment, when dramatically represented as institutional, discourse events. In them, the tangible course of the exercise, maintenance or challenge of power is transcribed, and the process by which power is made a reality in the dramatic world. Moreover, the interactional course through which the conflicts and engagements of power are enacted also requires that power is not seen only as a static property of persons or groups but as emergent within a process of its exercise or contestation, within the contingencies of the situations in which it is enacted. Thus power, as the product of authority, control, coercion, consensus, manipulation or whatever, is distributed along the interactional course in which it realizes itself. Its distributional and emergent course may enact the consolidating of given power, the sustaining of it, its loss or recovery. When open to the public gaze, in public contexts, as institutional events usually are, such enactments function, too, as enacted spectacle of the dramatization and display of the power (or contingent powerlessness) of power.

In Marlowe's *Edward II* ([*c.* 1591] 1966), Kent, the uncle of the young King Edward, is tried and sentenced to death by the usurper Mortimer. In Keir Elam's analysis of the trial (1989: 159–62), part of the conflict centres around the infelicity of Mortimer's speech acts, as Kent makes clear in his challenges to Mortimer. Mortimer has no right to command or execute anyone, least of all Kent himself. But Kent's challenges to Mortimer fail, as the latter's assumed claim to the rights of procedure and power are successfully sustained. The guards who are ordered by Kent to disobey Mortimer obey Mortimer's bidding, unlawful though it is. The ability to command not only the action but the perlocutionary sequel as well on Mortimer's part makes him the real power, even if his role in the proceedings is not. The interaction dramatizes the fact that usurped power has worked.

Status-wise, Edward is ostensibly the real power as King in this scene but his helplessness is visible in the perlocutionary effects of his speech. He attempts intervention on his uncle's behalf and commands Mortimer – 'My lord, he is my uncle and shall live', a regal command which does not take hold since Mortimer dismisses it. He appeals to Queen Isabella who dares not interfere. Finally, he decides to attempt another strategy – 'and yet methinks I should command; /But seeing I cannot I'll entreat for him'. As Petrey remarks,

> The illocutionary gulf between commanding and entreating is also the sociopolitical gulf between ruling and being deposed. What words do or fail to do *effects* who Marlowe's characters are or fail to be.
>
> (Petrey 1990: 88)

Another variation on the exercise of power in the conduct of public discourse events in drama is to be found in *Richard II*. The King's authority is dramatized in his control of the procedures in the scene. Power in action is power to control consequences of speech, to control the sequels to one's illocutionary acts, and to bend others' actions to one's word and will. The point at issue is treason, and the official designation and referential status of 'traitor' has to devolve publicly on either Mowbray or Bolingbroke (Porter 1979). Accusations made off-stage and unofficially are now to be made official and in the presence of the King and the two antagonists come in the institutional role of 'appellants', and ceremoniously accuse and hurl insults at each other, each calling the other 'traitor'. Only the King can determine to whom the designation can apply, via institutional procedure and the exercise of verdictive authority, and the name hovers, as Porter notes, in search of the right referent and felicity conditions to authorize it.

After the charges and denials have officially been made by Bolingbroke and Mowbray, a date for the trial is requested. Richard, however, attempts to change the rules unilaterally and deflect the course of the proceedings, and tries to play the occasion as a personal dispute between the two men and advises them to make peace. The point of Richard's manoeuvre is to re-define, re-reference, the proceedings in such a way as to turn the public and constitutional issue of treason to something more trivial and domestic – the personal quarrels of men of choler; hence the solution proposed of personal forgiving and forgetting.

K. RICHARD   Wrath-kindled gentlemen, be rul'd by me;
Let's purge this choler without letting blood;
This we prescribe, though no physician;

Deep malice makes too deep incision:
Forget, forgive: conclude and be agreed,
Our doctors say this is no month to bleed.
Good uncle, let this end where it began:
We'll calm the Duke of Norfolk, you your son.

(1.1.152–9)

Richard's illocutionary performance in the role of King is authoritative and composed of power-ridden directives in imperative mode to all concerned. But neither Richard nor Gaunt succeed in getting the antagonists to throw down the other's gage. With many face-saving protestations, both men politely refuse to obey the King's commands. Both plead to be put to the test since their public identities, as men of honour in the eyes of society, are at stake, in life as in death. Their illocutionary performances in return frustrate the intended sequels, even if deferentially and with overt attention to possible threats to the King's 'face'. They invoke their rights to have their claims assessed according to public protocol, thus wresting control of the proceedings back from Richard. Although Richard reminds them that as King 'We were not born to sue but to command', Richard nevertheless sets the required date, converting the fact of the public failure to command as a personal failure to reconcile intractable men.

The interactional and discoursal playing of procedure is very elaborate in the play, since the dialogue reflexively focuses on the institutional nature of the context and the procedural nature of the action. Elaborate contextualizing cues are provided by Richard to ensure that the public and institutional nature of the context and activity is referenced adequately. Richard questions and ascertains that the protocols are in force as necessary. He interrogates Gaunt about procedural details even before the appellants are brought before him, and makes a public spectacle of ensuring that everything is in order as required. He swears oaths of impartiality, especially with respect to his kinsman Bolingbroke. Even Gaunt joins in the game and reminds Bolingbroke that protocol would not allow him to 'bid' twice that the gage be returned. Our first introduction to Richard is thus as a competent king who acts with respect to due processes of law and convention. And Richard proceeds in this vein, controlling the course of the contention competently till the moment when he commands forgiveness and reconciliation, but the arbitrary departure from constitutional protocol does not succeed. The sequel to his commands does not materialize.

The final test by combat which he ratifies here is not carried through since Richard unceremoniously frustrates its completion by decreeing banishment in a later scene, again after much attention to procedure. He aborts the procedure so that the traitor cannot be named; and advisedly, since rumour implicated Richard himself in the unlawful death of Gloucester. When covert attempts to manipulate the proceedings fail, Richard resorts to arbitrary and overt means. The wayward and autocratic exercise of power, evident in the banishment and the later seizure of Bolingbroke's inheritance on the death of Gaunt, is based on an ideology of kingship as divine right which is inviolable in his eyes, but the ideology and the political order over which it presides are already in decline. The later sequels to these acts set events in motion that bring Bolingbroke to the throne and ruin Richard. Ideological beliefs in the power of the role, here, in a divinity that encircles the crown, are no comfort when material power, in the shape of both army and aristocracy, desert the monarch.

The world-changing nature of institutional events and acts and their public powers of legitimization make their performance points of anxiety and contention in plays where public life and its ways are in focus. In spite of their seemingly politically indifferent status they are deeply implicated in issues of power. Their successful performance mediates and authenticates, in the eyes of society at large, the usually ill-gotten power that is desired and achieved, and binds functionary agents in its service and steers consequences towards its own interests. Bolingbroke himself deposes Richard formally, and his control over the illegitimate proceedings ensures his legitimacy. Even a Machiavellian like Richard III leans on procedure and protocol by cynically stage-managing his election as King. And the noble Brutus feels it incumbent upon himself to be seen to be doing things by the book after the treasonable murder of Caesar in allowing Antony to deliver the funeral oration, against the advice of the more politically astute Casca. In all these instances the intentional in the conventional is evident as are bias, manipulation and political self-interest which control the workings of these acts and the course of the procedure. And control of procedure and the public spectacle of effective power in the making or the working makes power, as political power, felicitous and potent.

Infelicitous acts in the public domain, felicitously performed, abound in Shakespeare's and others' political plays when the trials of power are being portrayed. The unauthorized speaker is often in control of procedure, coercing into submission authorized others when the political power base on which the felicity conditions themselves rest is contested, insecure or in transition. Even acts which publicly attest to personal fealty are up for grabs as politically circumspect acts. Oath-making and oath-taking, as commissives, publicly pledge loyalty and bind the speakers to future courses of action with respect to the propositional contents of the pledges given to the person addressed. But the bending of the knee as subjective and sacred token of an objective and public contract with power is as easily unbent when power fades. Bolingbroke in *Richard II* is only one case in point. Broken oaths are as numerous as broken bodies in these plays. Commissive breath and retributive blood flow liberally as the ink of history. The reluctant Hamlet, under private oath to the ghost of the father, is in a different league, as are the Macbeths with their secretly broken oaths and their visions of dagger, spectre and spot.

For time may also extract its dues. Speech acts like 'reminders' punctuate, iterate and insist on the deictic contracts entered into 'then' in the 'now' of speech though far removed in time. The unfulfilled or betrayed speech contract haunts, in time. Bolingbroke as Henry IV is *reminded* by his 'rebels' that they were, denotatively and publicly, 'loyalists' to his cause and ambition. But felicity conditions can be contested, especially the preparatory condition to speech acts. Prospero *reminds* Ariel and Caliban of the commissive debts they owe to him, which Ariel, under protest, accepts but which Caliban sees as no contract at all, since Prospero's claim to reciprocity on him in time is invalid in his view. The public, inter-personal or institutional contracts on which the felicity of speech acts rests is particularly vulnerable in *The Tempest* since it is a world in which no institutions or social contracts get off the ground, and yet issues of rights and power are central to the contests between Caliban and Prospero regarding the island.

Caliban's fealty is to another time, and another order, which pre-dates Prospero. The order to which he belongs descends from Sycorax, his *mother*, but he is held in Prospero's time, but without trans-personal or institutional arrangements of any kind, and thus power and rights and the conditions for felicity are continually at issue between them since beliefs about rights are conflicting. Thus superior force is the only arbiter. The right to the island devolves on himself, in Caliban's view, by blood and inheritance, before the usurper with his European magic powers to inflict cramps swam into his ken from across the unknown of heaven's waters, to accept hospitality, to appropriate knowledge of terrain and its resources, and finally the land itself for his own uses. Prospero's reminders, like his commands, are infelicitous to Caliban who constantly counter-challenges and counter-reminds as to who owes whom a commissive debt, but is made to submit to Prospero's greater, non-linguistic, force.

Only counter-claims, counter-acts, counter-discourses, as it were, on the issue of rights and power exist on the island. The issue itself involves other aspects: rights to subjectivity and sexuality; to resources; rights to evaluate, among other things, the aesthetics of personal, physical appearance since the values in the play are ideologically myopic – solely those of the alien eyes from across the waters; rights to determine appropriateness of behaviour in contexts; to spatial freedoms in the right to movement; to inter-personal freedoms of association; sexual freedom to desire, love or propagate, in reciprocal terms. Denial of these, as is the case in the play by Prospero to Caliban, are markers of enslavement.

There is no 'social life', nor trans-personal conventions, and no institutions regarding impartial powers of adjudication, and no inter-personal conventions that work consensually. The felicity conditions are not consensually authorized for either speaker's speech acts, and their mutual rebuttals of attempted felicity, which is attempted control, contracts their interactions. In the play, matters are concluded only by Prospero's superior force, which is used to coerce Caliban into the sequels required, in master–slave mode, which bears down hard on Caliban, since Caliban is the only agent of truly independent, insubordinate energy, as the untamed 'other' having to be accommodated within Prospero's regime, but in possession of alternative claims and beliefs to counter-rights which motivate challenges to Prospero.

To Ariel, the immaterial spirit-sprite of freedom, whose element is air and not the earth and its ways, the two power regimes of Sycorax and Prospero are much of a muchness and need costly accommodations for survival. Both signify bondage, in differently coloured wrappings. Some negative and resistant acts to Prospero are visible in Ariel's interactions, but he mostly brings his perlocutionary acts into line with Prospero's illocutionary intentions, and carries out the sequels to them as required, as negotiary acts. And inheritance and control of land, and more land and, astutely, heaven, are precisely the powers that expiate the guilt of the past for Henry V who is represented, in panegyric mode, as the politically acceptable King, whose commands are obeyed, who controls and competently completes his institutional procedures, whose intentional acts take hold, who keeps his oaths and gets others to keep theirs, and who even courts and wins his bride bilingually and cross-culturally. Elizabeth I herself was reputed to have seen herself figured in Richard II.

Representatives of power wisely exercised are also available in Shakespeare – the Duke in *Othello*, for instance, in his conduct of the dispute between Brabantio and Othello on Desdemona's elopement. These instances are within a context of uncontested power. The Duke's power is stable and unchallenged; he rules by consensus or at least his authority is supported, it would seem, by members of his community, and there are no challenges to it or negative assessments of it in the dramatic world. He functions as the prototypic, constitutionally figured ideal of consensual, status quo authority, dispensing impartial and humane justice, without coercion, fear or favour, and in the interests of the community, which individual subjects, whether law-abiding or not, subjectively and publicly endorse.

Overall in the conduct of public affairs in drama, the smooth management of the course of institutional discourse events functions as representative of status quo formal authority in action, signifying political power or supremacy – witness, for instance, Lear's conduct of the proceedings of the division of the kingdom, in the conventional role of King, before the unconventional voice of Cordelia disrupts the charade and shows it up for what it is. Challenges and infelicities usually open up more complex issues.

Conventional acts can have wider social and subjective scope, and bring other acts within their jurisdiction. Such is the case in classical Spanish theatre in the controls exercised on speech and behaviour by the conventions of honour, as Myra Gann (1986) has shown. As social praxis, certain proscribed utterances become highly performative. An insult to a wife counts as a challenge and dishonours the (male) co-participant. The wife is not included in the protocols of speech in her own right. An utterance like 'You lie' in certain circumstances would require defence unto death, however extreme this may seem to a modern audience. No referential authority or validity, nor burden of proof, is sought in mitigation, since the convention is sustained only by practice and the consent or coercion of members which underwrites the convention as 'praxis'.

Other aspects of the convention are explored by Margaret Hicks (1986). Social rules forbid challenge of the higher born by the lower-ranked subject, even where the seduction of the latter's wife is at stake, female sexuality intertwined in male notions yet again, without much reference to the female. Thus redress and mitigation have to be sought indirectly by male cunning and subterfuge which actually fuel complicated plots in the plays. Effective counter-speech is negotiated in the guise of madness, or in figurative modes which erase claims to rationality and intentionality. Such conventions and the acts and privileges they authorize are highly biased in favour of specific groups, but pass for universal social norms in the community concerned, when accepted, subjectivized and practised as *honour*. More globally, speech acts have been used to trace the course of political worlds and the issues they raise in Shakespeare's history plays. Porter (1979) analyses the changes in political philosophy effected in the changing fortunes of speech acts from *Richard II*, with its monological enactments, to the more inter-personally interactive kinds favoured by Henry V, as indicative of the change from medieval notions of power to modern, democratic modes.

The speech act vision of plays is not confined to the doings of the mighty either. Interpretations of their acts on the part of others, of equal status, or on the part of social inferiors, are also cues to assess the wider, communal, state of affairs in the fictional world. The whole class of constatives express beliefs of varying strengths; the 'confirmatives' like 'certify', 'conclude', 'corroborate', 'substantiate', 'validate', etc. presuppose greater belief in the propositions expressed than the weaker 'suggestives' like 'conjecture', 'guess', 'speculate', 'hypothesize', suggest. 'Concessives' express a weakened belief in a previously held belief when something is conceded, or concurred with, while in the case of the negative members of the class like 'dissentives' and 'disputatives', where prior claims are contested, it is the production of disbelief in them that is intended (Bach and Harnish 1982: 42–4).

Reports by authorized persons – even humble messengers – presuppose the truth of whatever is expressed, but this can be contested or not even believed by others. And this is the case for all the constatives, where the intention to be believed may be clear but the perlocutionary sequel may not follow. Moreover, the perlocutionary power of gossip and rumour in plays also reveals that even weakly attested 'truths' can function as objects of strong belief. Speech acts which relay beliefs and reactions of the dramatic figures about the world in which they live enable the dramatist to paint a picture of that world via the beliefs, even if conflicting or partial, which are held about it by those who live in it. Those acts that predicate belief in a future state of affairs, like warnings, or prophecy, are also notable, since future events may well make them true – the soothsayer's warnings to Caesar about the Ides of March, John of Gaunt's warnings to Richard II and so on.

Other classes can be similarly mobilized as and when occasion arises in plays. Grievances reveal malfunctions from one perspective about what may seem a satisfactory state of affairs from another, and reminders, as we have seen, hark back to previous states of affairs. Commissives like promises bind speakers to future courses of action and to time, while directives attempt to co-opt others to some course of action, in the present, but to be undertaken in the future. Searle's Expressives overtly manifest emotional states as discourse matters either perfunctorily or profoundly. Different acts and classes of acts offer different perspectives and strengths of attitude on the part of speakers to whatever is expressed and can form a tapestry of cues for interpreters to create the state of affairs in the dramatic world. The sequels to such acts may be similarly assessed, since these occur in time and could either further or frustrate the course of the action. They may function, too, as cohesive links among different segments or even parts of the same segment in plays given the links, in time, between speech actions and their sequels.

INTER-PERSONAL ACTS AND THE TRIALS OF COMMUNICATION

The illocutionary behaviour of a character permits us to impute a subjectivity to a name on a page or script and to furnish it with an inner world of beliefs, assumptions, desires, attitudes, emotions, feelings, etc. as may be inferred by its use of utterances. The transformation of the linguistic sign – a name or equivalent designation – to an extra-linguistic 'person' is accomplished via inferences in assigning whatever mode of subjectivity seems relevant to behaviour. The illocutionary and perlocutionary progress of utterances allows us also to trace the action structure, the proairetic dimension underlying the use of speech (Elam 1980: 157). The pragmatic performativities of utterances enmesh interactants inter-personally, in a world of social obligation, liabilities, rights and privileges, within which individual goals have to be negotiated. Rules of use may be exogenous, given, in the society of which members are a part, but it is their endogenous dynamism within interactions which is of interest, and these are strategic.

Personal goals and the possibilities of their fulfilment are set within the tension of wider, trans-subjective constraints, but not in one-to-one correspondence since global rules do not list contextual strategies, but whatever strategies are used, they are subject to sensitivities of inter-personal and social interpretation in context. Speaker strategies themselves point both ways. They are other-directed in interaction, but simultaneously self-oriented, too, to the speaker's goals, attitudes, desires, etc. in the exchange, which in turn require negotiation given the constraints on behaviour imposed by considerations of 'face'. Strategies used may be safe or risky, and communication itself may succeed or fail, and trace its course via direct, determinate or indirect and ambiguous strategies. The management of the different kinds of tension endemic to self–other exchanges and the symmetries or asymmetries that result may also be analysed in interaction, and interactions themselves may be achievements of communication or of miscommunication, non-communication, estrangement or conflict.

How speech acts operate across a stretch of discourse is still not properly understood. Schiffrin (1994: 45–91) claims that utterances create environments with options for next utterances; Sperber and Wilson (1986) propose the flux in cognitive environments and assumptions, so that assumptions generate assumptions and could motivate next turn; Leech (1983) suggests that macro goals involve micro ones; and Searle (1992a, b) that prediction is not possible. One concurs with Searle, but buttressed by Sperber and Wilson, since how an utterance is understood cannot be predicted except with respect to what is in the cognitive environment at a particular stage and the inferences that are derived from previous utterances which motivate turns. But some formal constraints are indeed operative, via sequencing rules, for instance, and the necessity for uptake and co-operation, but given that these may not be played, and 'noticeable absences' and refusals of intended perlocutionary sequels may occur, it is difficult to see how prediction can be said to hold across the board. One concurs, too, to some extent, with Leech – that overall goals might need contingent ones but the course cannot be predicted, given options which strengthen the unpredictability of the other in interaction. Goals themselves can be multiple and may change in the course of an interaction.

Something is attempted by speakers and something is achieved, even negatively, but there are no 'ideal' speech situations in contextualized interactions. The symmetries of attempts and effects enshrined in the theory dissolve into the contingencies of the events in which speech functions. Variables in speech events are many; spatio-temporal context, role, status, and communicative competence of interactants, etc. and goals and ends of speakers are to be negotiated within the temporalities of evolving turns. The start-up or initiatory conditions for interactions are thus actually *asymmetrical* and have to be negotiated or brought into alignment in interactions. Such conditions motivate the communicational effort in the first place, since if theoretical symmetry is always a practical reality, one need only utter one-liners and perfect understanding can be assured. Symmetries are products of theoretical discourses whose business it is to be unambiguous, comprehensive, fully explanatory, etc. Where symmetries are visible in context, they are products of interactive work, temporally and inter-personally accomplished and within the contingencies of the situation itself. And contingencies can generate interactive work. Interactants may not be able to assume that the preparatory conditions which should be operative for illocutionary performance are in place. These may need to be ascertained or negotiated via speech, in pre-sequences. There may be doubt as to what kind of assumptions one may expect the other to make about some matter, and these, too, may need to be clarified. Inferences made may be the unintended ones, and might need repair, and so on.

Thus, understanding itself can become actional and a process in time, as the example from *Twelfth Night* (see pp. 204–5) reveals, when the initiatory locutionary act serves as barrier to, rather than conveyor of, meaning in communication. Moreover, when meaning is conveyed, the respondent may not respond as desired, or the understanding given may not be the understanding sought, or one's goals may be frustrated, or 'face' may be on the line, and so on. The sphere of the inter-personal invests the canonical speaker with will, want, obligation, desire, belief, intentionality, rationality and inferencing capacities, actionality, social rights, goals, expressivity and expectations in the use of speech, but does not guarantee success on unilateral terms. Moreover, canonical speakers are only one option in the participant framework itself.

In drama, dramaturgies and situations either restrict or maximize the possibilities afforded by the canonical prototype in the use of speech. To Szondi (1987), the history of modern drama is a long and crisis-ridden flight from the terms set by 'the Drama' as he calls Renaissance drama in which the arena of the inter-personal constructed the thematics and carried the action of plays; the sphere of the 'inter-' itself, as the 'between' among the dramatis personae, being the major context for action, at the expense of the intra- and trans-personal. But Szondi's notion of 'the Drama' is both strict and restricted. He rules out Shakespeare's history plays from its scope, for instance, and also discounts speech genres like narratives based on memory as being more 'epic' and isolating rather than 'dramatic' and inter-personal in character, and thus not immediately actional enough, which would not be the case when speech is considered from the point of view of speech events, as the discussion on Dell Hymes' mnemonic of SPEAKING has shown (see pp. 18–19). Different speech genres are permissible and often occur.

From the discourse perspective, it is an issue of strategy and the canonical variables may be calibrated or accented in numerous ways for situations or subjectivities to evolve or to be presented. All kinds of situation are, therefore, open to pragmatic analysis. Subjectivities created via speech use can also alter. Discourse strategies privileged by different dramaturgies can vary considerably, and even overturn the prototype, but from our point of view they remain strategies, nevertheless. The 'inter-personal' itself can be enacted in myriad ways, in ruptured, estranged or mutually collaborative fashion. For the arena of the inter-personal is a varied and often varying one, the sphere of the 'inter-' may trace a wide range of possibilities across the whole spectrum of positive–negative. It is a world of emotions, hopes, desires, fears, memories, etc. but also of the lack of them; it can include intimacies and distances, calculation and co-operation, coercion and manipulation, trust, mistrust, constancies and betrayals, eloquence and muteness, friendships and hostilities, self-protection, self-revelation, evasion, and so on. Different strategies or even the same strategies can be used to provide different effects and consequences, inter-personally.

From the pragmatic perspective, even epic figures who address the audience directly and seem outside the inter-personal exchange of dramatic characters are still under pragmatic ordinance, given that the addressees, the audience, have to impute both belief and relevance to their utterances and take the propositions they express on trust as 'relevant' to the dramatic world. Similarly, the audience has to assess the 'uptake' required by plays like Handke's *Offending the Audience* (1969) when direct address to the audience is involved, and decide how to interpret the action in progress. The discourse context for drama has both a lateral and a projective dimension. The inter-personal speech event of personae is part of the overall stage event and the use of the projective dimension to the audience in communicative or metacommunicative fashion is not to break the complex frame of the stage event, in which speech is embedded, but only to break the constraints of *one*, strongly held, dramatic convention.

Speech use, whether addressed to the audience or to the characters, will function with respect to both contingencies. In the stychomythic 'wit combats' of Elizabethan plays (Kennedy 1983), the inter-personal interest is not absent even if the form is theatre-conventional, since who wins and who loses is still consequential, the aesthetics and efficiency of the individual performances being attributed to the speakers and their control of the rules of the game, within the competitive pressures exerted interactionally on individual performances. The overall goals can be assessed as competitive, in Leech's terminology, to which both participants orientate and collaborate even if the form is conventional. Even listening is a discourse resource and can be enacted in different ways – negatively and positively – as we have seen (see p.36), so that long narrations are not 'outside' speech contexts. Silence, too, is a discourse resource, including the silence of listening or not listening to speech within earshot.

As for the dramatis personae, the analysis of illocutionary styles as indicative of the 'person' of the dramatic figure has been one productive use of the theory, as explored above in Fish's reading of *Coriolanus* (see p. 210). Speech styles, however, as pragmatic strategies adopted by the dramatis personae, also function to create the situations in which they find themselves and in which their performance implicates them, and to construct the quality and tenor of the relationship itself. Lakoff and

Tannen list three major strategies that characters may use. Their analysis is conducted on the television play, *Scenes from a Marriage*. The strategies used to handle their marital situations are the following:

i.   Pragmatic synonymy or paraphrase. They use different linguistic devices to achieve similar ends.
ii. Pragmatic homonymy or ambiguity. They use similar linguistic devices to achieve different ends.
iii. Pragmatic identity. They use the same devices toward the same ends.

(Lakoff and Tannen 1984: 330)

Each of the characters has a broadly typical style. Johann's is distancing, or pontificating, sarcastic, abstract, generalizing, and complex. Marianne's self-deprecating, and by turns, both deferential and comradely, and she uses 'a smokescreen of non-stop verbiage made up of impressionistic romanticism or a flurry of questions' (*ibid.*). Their contrasting styles define their individualities as 'persons', and equip them with differential strategies in their inter-personal trials. But they also use similar strategies at different times but for the same ends (pragmatic identity), whenever it suits them – evasion of an issue by proposing some other form of action, like going to sleep, or suggesting that difficult topics not be aired. Pragmatic synonymy can be seen in their use of different strategies for similar ends – Marianne uses excessive verbiage to deflect confrontation, Johann pontificates. Pragmatic homonymy is evident in the way each of them makes use of similar devices like a barrage of questions for different ends. Marianne uses the device to deflect confronting the problems that beset their relationship or in order to avoid hearing answers to any of her questions. But she also uses questions in order to get replies; Johann uses a stream of questions rhetorically, in order to taunt and provoke. The pragmatic workings of their preferred strategies are examined on a three-level structure. Although at the superficial level they seem similar, they both ask questions; at the level of intent there is conflict, since information-seeking questions invite co-operation, while the rhetorical questions deflect and provoke anger; at the third, deeper level of effect on the other participant (the most inaccessible level), they correspond again, since both are in secret collusion not to communicate, to collaborate in non-communication.

The tri-levelled analysis enables the authors to confront the central paradoxes of the relationship across the whole series: why two such seemingly compatible people separate in the first place, and further, why when conflict is the only mode of interaction open to them they cannot stay apart either. It is the deep complicity of the agreement to disagree that binds them, which gives them the common ground on which their relationship rests. The apparently dissonant, anti-communicative and unsatisfactory state of affairs between them is sustained by the fact that this state of affairs is deeply satisfying to both parties, and thus enacts mutual dependency to sustain it as the truth of their relationship. If harmony were to be profound it would similarly operate at all three levels as would true conflict. The intermediate type is the subtle one for what it tells us of the ways of communication and the complexities involved in the sphere of the inter-personal. But the proffered levels of analysis also posit different modes of calculation and satisfaction on the part of inter-actants, whether in conscious or unconscious fashion, none of which is independent of the others. Interpretations at the third, 'deepest' level are obviously the products of even weaker implicatures than the second or first would make available.

The inter-personal, especially in its exploitation of canonical resources, is also a sphere of change and transformation. Motivated speech strategies, on the part of speakers, intend to affect the other in various ways, and the dynamics of change may be fuelled by personal investments of various kinds in the outcomes of interactions. Motives themselves may be strong, impelling the speaker to direct the course of a desired outcome with powerful strategies, or to generate strong implicatures, or they may be weak, with indifference or ennui evident regarding outcomes and consequences. Strategies, too, may be overbearing with respect to the other, or delicate, in the attempts to co-opt or coerce the other into the desired alignment with self – directly or indirectly, with or without respect to 'face', collaboratively or conflictually. Variation is the norm, as situations are created in their specificities, the course taken, in each instance, structured in accordance with the dynamics of the inter-personal event in progress but responsive to the pressures of the wider, dramatic design, to which specific situations and personae and individual speech events in drama are beholden.

Among the more fragile modes of attempted change are those that focus on belief, or assumptions. As cognitive and internal properties, beliefs and assumptions are hardly actional, yet the process by which change is wrought, or attempted, interactionally, can be. Initial beliefs and assumptions of some kind can be presumed to be available to participants, about each other, the context, the dramatic world in which they exist, social norms, speech behaviour required, etc. Yet both understanding and believing can become processes in their own right as personae attempt to *get the other* to understand or to believe something, and to bring the other in alignment with self. The interactional course makes speech use actional, as changes in cognitive states are attempted, and the initial gap between participant beliefs is bridged and transformed, especially where resistance has to be overcome. The course itself may be slow, as facts are digested or the full implications gradually sink in. Changes in this sphere may or may not lead on to further action, but they do effect changes of perspective on events or persons in the dramatic world. These may be global – the recognition scenes in Shakespeare, when 'the truth' is revealed, retrospectively change the understanding of the events themselves in which personae have been involved. Or they may be local, within some segment or other in plays as part of the global sequence of action.

Persuasion scenes and strategies abound in plays, of whatever dramaturgical complexion, and are enacted across the whole spectrum of success–failure. In *Othello*, the mental drama of assumption formation and belief change is itself part of the dramatic action. Othello often expresses the inferences he makes as the contextual implications of Iago's interactive performances take hold. The play begins with Iago having to persuade Roderigo to change his mind about his own value to Roderigo, under the circumstances of Desdemona's marriage. Iago has obviously, hitherto, been well paid by Roderigo on the understanding that Iago would deliver Desdemona's consent to his suit.

RODERIGO   Tush! Never tell me; I take it much unkindly
That you, Iago, who has had my purse
As if the strings were thine, shouldst know of this.
IAGO   'Sblood, but you will not hear me.
If ever I did dream of such a matter,
Abhor me.
RODERIGO   Thou told'st me thou didst hold him in thy hate.
IAGO   Despise me if I do not. Three great ones of the city,
In personal suit to make me his lieutenant,
Off-capp'd to him. . .

                                                                        (1.1.1–10)

Roderigo's most recent assumptions regarding Iago, as manifested in the opening lines of the play, are highly negative; former trust having been shattered by events, distrust of Iago is evident. The attitudes underlying his illocutionary acts are of *disbelief* – disputatives and dissentives in Bach and Harnish's (1982) terminology. He refutes, speech-act-wise, any prior suggestion of innocence or ignorance on Iago's part and says so quite explicitly in his first turn. The disbelief intensifies into accusation as well. The *in media res* opening signifies that the off-stage level of resistance to

Iago's restitutive attempts has already been high even to the extent of refusing him a hearing, as Iago's first line of speech makes clear. Roderigo just does not believe that Iago did not know of the relationship or secret marriage between Othello and Desdemona, in spite of his protestations to the contrary. And, moreover, he is very put out at the thought that Iago may have known all along. By the end of the interaction, Iago has won over Roderigo and taken control of the action. The strategies he uses are varied, but cumulatively linked and directed towards the same goal; their purpose, to weaken the force of the negative beliefs that Roderigo holds about himself.

In drama, especially Shakespearean drama, different 'projects' are assigned to the interactants (Beckerman 1970). In Hallett and Hallett (1991), the 'propelling' character attempts (in discourse vocabulary 'negotiates'), in persuasion events, to get the consent of the 'resisting' character, but the 'projects' are usually dealt with in terms of mutual independence. In discourse terminology the vertical pattern which often underwrites performance frameworks with respect to actors has to take account of the 'horizontal' mapping of response on to the vertical.

Discourse-wise, Iago, in the first place, ostentatiously invites negative perlocutionary effects, face-threatening and self-denigrating beliefs about himself, in self-debasing mode – but conditionally – 'If. . . Abhor me', 'Despise me if. . . '. He uses conditional concessives, admitting Roderigo's right to his negative beliefs about himself, but in 'irrealis' mode, as a hypothesis, which seeks to absolve him of guilt in the present instance, or at least to delay the final accounting. The explicit illocutionary admission of Roderigo's right to 'abhor' and 'despise' himself 'if. . . ' generates inferences to the effect that the preparatory conditions that authorize responses like abhorring and despising, which must assume some culpable prior act on the part of the other, do not apply in this case. Roderigo is indirectly asked to confront a different 'truth' about the case instead. Iago thus attempts changes in the cognitive context, to sow doubt in the mind of Roderigo to counter the latter's immediately held certainties. This ploy does not succeed since Roderigo continues to display lack of belief at Iago's professions of hate for Othello. The desired alignment in belief between the interactants is not forthcoming.

Iago tries again with a long speech narrating a story of his dispreferment for promotion by Othello in favour of Cassio, whom he abuses and derides, in constative mode, the whole being designed to provide evidence and support the implicature that he has no reason to favour Othello, since he is the injured party in career transactions. The explanatory effort on Iago's part is high and he holds the floor at length.

Roderigo still resists the inferences he is supposed to make, as evident in his reply: 'By heaven, I rather would have been his hangman' with its dissentive illocutionary attitude and evidence of latent suspicion and distrust, which is thrust back at Iago. The reply, however, is ambiguous, since it could also be taken as sympathy on Roderigo's part. Iago, however, appears to respond to the dissentive inference – 'O, sir, content you./I follow him to serve my turn upon him. . . ' Another long and unctuous speech follows about the power of patronage which undermines true merit, as a truth universal, especially in its applicability to himself. Iago uses the constative convention of the whole truth in his speech act of confession which concludes the turn, as he lays bare his reasons, and his soul, so to speak, the 'truth' convention strengthened by the risky nature of the 'truth' he tells, which invites, encloses and binds Roderigo into and within the proffered complicity of the trust presupposed – as preparatory condition – of such acts of intimate, personal revelation and self-disclosure. The general content of Iago's confession is that his outward show of duty to Othello is a mask for his own ends and, further,

> Were I the Moor, I would not be Iago.
> In following him, I follow but myself –
> Heaven is my judge, not I for love and duty,
> But seeming so, for my peculiar end:
> For when my outward action doth demonstrate
> The native act and figure of my heart
> In compliment exter'n,'tis not long after
> But I will wear my heart upon my sleeve
> For daws to peck at: I am not what I am.
>
> (1.1.57–65)

The indirection in former strategies gives way to a direct and risky confession of deep malice towards Othello and an admission of the sinister nature of his own behaviour. And the risk pays off. Iago's performance, backed by canonical truth conventions, of disclosure as that of a 'true', 'internal' self, convinces Roderigo sufficiently for him to take Iago on trust again. He does not reason further and question whether Iago may not be wearing his heart on his sleeve for his own ends in the present encounter, too, since the level of optimal relevance, in Sperber and Wilson's terms, sought by Roderigo from what Iago has said is more limited, to his own particular concerns within the immediate situation. Roderigo's behaviour, based as it is on canonical assumptions regarding speech and person, is no match for the manipulation of these self-same conventions by Iago.

Control of intended perlocutionary effect by display and metacommunicative, reflexive reference in the locutionary act is also used by Desdemona (3.3.1–28). Pragmatic identity in strategy is not complete, however, since she uses it unconditionally. The change attempted is a strengthening of Cassio's shaky belief in the possibility of Othello's pardon for his recent drunken behaviour. Desdemona attempts to get Cassio to share her own belief that all will be well, a contingency the latter has little reason to believe will be the case, given the scale of his disgrace. The initial distance in their mutual assumptions about the possibility of a successful outcome has to be bridged, which is undertaken by Desdemona. The strategy used is to urge on Cassio repeatedly, her own desired perlocutionary effect, and unconditionally, in other-orientated fashion – 'Be assured Cassio. . . ', 'Do not doubt, Cassio. . . ', '. . . be you well assur'd. . . ' Her present assurances, strongly invested with her own belief, are also backed by strong commissives, through which she binds herself to bringing about the promised, future state of affairs – 'I will do/All my abilities. . . ', 'I will have my lord and you again/As friendly as you were', 'He shall in strangeness stand no further off/Than in a politic distance'. Cassio's original, despairing assumptions that change may not be possible are dislodged sufficiently for him to leave matters in her hands. The unconditional commitment, however, is to a future course of affairs which, in effect, she is not able to fulfil owing to the vagaries of time and circumstances beyond her control.

Assumptions may also be so ingrained as to resist change, and the inability to effect change or be changed can also be interactionally and dramatically presented. This is the case with Othello once Iago's poison has taken effect. Seeking further evidence of Desdemona's supposed infidelity, he questions Emilia.

OTHELLO   What, did they never whisper?
EMILIA   Never, my lord.
OTHELLO   Nor send you out o' th' way?
EMILIA   Never.
OTHELLO   To fetch her fan, her gloves, her mask, nor nothing?
EMILIA   Never, my lord.
OTHELLO   That's strange.
EMILIA   I durst, my lord, to wager she is honest,
Lay down my soul at stake. If you think other,
Remove your thought; – it doth abuse your bosom.

If any wretch have put this in your head,
Let heaven requite it with serpent's curse;
For, if she be not honest, chaste, and true,
There is no man happy; the purest of their wives
Is foul as slander.
OTHELLO   Bid her come hither. Go.

[*Exit* EMILIA]

She says enough; yet she's a simple bawd
That cannot say as much. This is a subtle whore,
A closet-lock-and-key of villainous secrets;
And yet she'll kneel and pray; I have seen her do't.

(4.2.6–22)

Each question is a request for information, each item being checked out point by point, in protracted mode. Each piece of information requested is given by Emilia, which adds up cumulatively to a set of facts that radically contradicts Othello's own assumptions, since Emilia emphatically denies that Desdemona was guilty of any of the actions lodged in Othello's enquiries. Denials, as speech acts, link to previous assertions and their illocutionary beliefs, and function as counter-beliefs to weaken the other's stated or inferable beliefs. At the end of this interrogation, Othello's response, 'That's strange', reveals some awareness of the contradiction and conflict in his mind about his present suspicions about Desdemona, as a consequence of the clash between the old and the new information with which he has to contend. He cannot refute Emilia's strong assertions and thus cannot disbelieve them.

Emilia's subsequent unsolicited testimonial should serve to augment his belief in Desdemona's fidelity, as should her advice and plea to him to renounce his train of thought. Othello, however, solves his problem by reasoning that Desdemona must be an even more cunning and subtle whore than he had realized, and that she had deceived a simple Emilia. The strength of the premises of suspicion and distrust overrides any other alternative – even Desdemona's piety seems diabolical to him. He cannot determine, even from the strong evidence he has been given, that he must have been mistaken, which is one obvious conclusion, given the unequivocal belief in Desdemona displayed in Emilia's utterances. Such an inference he cannot countenance, and the enacted rejection allows the audience to gauge the depth of the poison in the mind, to which the mode of reasoning he adopts gives access.

The play of inferences and assumptions in interactions can create ambiguities as to how an utterance is to be taken, but this is to some extent controlled by the notion of optimal relevance as assessed by the inferencer. But the communicant who is called upon to do the inferencing work may take a different path of inference or draw the optimal line differently to the one assumed by the speaker, or not be too sure which level is the optimal level. These eventualities, if displayed and made into a discourse matter, may enact 'misunderstanding' and call for negotiation of meaning. Or the indeterminacies may be passed over in silence so that communication is weak and exactly what is communicated or intended to be communicated may be obscure. On the other hand, the presupposition of optimal relevance could be used strategically in interaction to let pass some inferences, even if assumed to be intended ones, in the interests of others, which are employed instead as more serviceable to immediate or long-term, inter-personal or social goals. In J. B. Priestley's *The Linden Tree* (1948) Mrs Linden wants her Professor husband to retire even though he does not want to. She attempts to get the co-operation of the University Secretary, Mr Lockhart, who duly visits the Linden household, and after a brush with the unexpected Mrs Cotton, 'the woman-of-all-work' in the household, is greeted by Mrs Linden.

MRS LINDEN   Oh – Mr Lockhart, I hope you haven't been waiting long. Poor Mrs Cotton isn't – well – you know – quite –
LOCKHART   No, I gathered that.
MRS LINDEN   Only at times, when things happen to upset her. We've had an accident to the drawing-room ceiling. This house is really in a shocking condition, and Robert won't make a fuss about it to the bursar – it's University property, you know – *your* property.
LOCKHART   Shall I say something to him?

(Priestley 1948: 406–7)

In Lockhart's first turn in this encounter, he gets the unstated inference about the unconventional Mrs Cotton without Mrs Linden having to articulate 'impolite beliefs' about her for him, responsive as he is to the display of hesitations in Mrs Linden's turn. In the next exchange Mrs Linden, although her locutionary acts are all assertions, makes excuses for Mrs Cotton, stating mitigating reasons, stating the accident in the house as evidence, and ends the turn with an indirect accusation to him of University negligence over the house. Of the many inferences that can be responded to – that her husband's indifference to household matters is giving her a hard time, that she would like his sympathy, that she is complaining, that if the house is University property then it is the University's fault, in fact, his own fault as University Secretary – Lockhart chooses to ignore the more face-threatening inferences of personal negligence and chooses to focus on the inferences to be drawn about the husband not talking to the bursar and offers to talk to 'him' which is ambiguous between the two, but could possibly be the bursar under the circumstances. Not only is an 'offer' a socially convivial act, in Leech's (1983) framework, with illocutionary and social goals coinciding, its illocutionary attitude is other-orientated; thus, the inference about sympathy is taken on board, as is her complaint about the state of the house. Also, the underlying assumption to be gleaned is that it is not the University Secretary's business but that of the bursar to look after property, so that he diffuses the face threat, while also passing the buck. The tension generated by the crowding in of possible inferences and consequences is dispersed by the choice of inferences to which the response is geared. The more conflictual path which the interaction could have taken is not pursued, although the excess of inferences does, as it were, hang in the air for a while.

In general, the importance of beliefs, assumptions, inferences, is not confined to the inter-personal sphere, in mutual exclusion of the social, as the debates between socio- and cognitive pragmatists would have us believe. They are involved and play a role in how the social is constructed or made concrete. Moreover, the energies and material resources that are invested in the political and social spheres, to the issue of hearts and minds for ideological ends, should at least give us pause for thought. Collective beliefs in justice, social equality and freedom, the superiority of a race or a religion, or the utopias of consumerism, have been known to topple political regimes or fuel genocide; while personal beliefs on some issue on the part of individuals have also, historically, withstood abuse, torture and martyrdom. In the inter-personal sphere, attempted changes in beliefs can also function as assaults on the mind of one participant by another and as means to power. Given the Renaissance philosophy of 'the human', the mind and its properties may propel courses of action which in turn, in such dramaturgies, can propel other actions.

Beliefs and assumptions are cognitive resources, internal, mental resources nourishing senses of reality and truth, the stability of concepts and selfhood, and the rightness or wrongness of actions in a social world in which individual existence with others is enmeshed. Like existential presuppositions which attach to propositions and function as world-creating devices in drama, pragmatic beliefs construct the reality of the world for characters. But as beliefs they can be violated sufficiently, by others, for the whole internal nexus of thoughts, feelings, emotions, reasonings and motivated actions, etc. to be affected so as to re-perspectivize reality itself as experienced, believed in, or known, and to shatter a sense of self-coherence. Belief changes transacted as a necessary part of social, inter-personal life can also be highly destructive when undertaken in the interests of unilateral power by one character over another. Change can be effected by power-driven coercion, but also more covertly by manipulation and the latter occurs in *Othello*. Iago's target is Othello's mind, as site of belief and source of action and feeling, given the Renaissance mould of subjectivity that underwrites dramatic figure construction. Iago never directly or candidly accuses Desdemona, but plants cues to allow Othello himself to make the kind of inferences and draw the conclusions that insidiously corrode former trust and belief in Desdemona and Cassio, and to act accordingly – to manage his own self-destruction.

Iago's manipulation of Othello's belief structures is invisible, not manifest, in Sperber and Wilson's (1986, 1987a, b) terminology, since his strategies are covert. Contradictory inferences are only possible from ostensive acts from independent sources in the play, and these, limited as they are, Othello does not countenance anyway. Iago splits his own subjectivity so that the 'self' that can be inferred from his illocutionary behaviour is actually at odds with the executive, super-ordinate, goal-directing self which cold-bloodedly and covertly controls and manipulates the contextual effects his victims can derive. Iago's superordinate goals cannot be inferred from the immediate goals that are available from his utterances which his manifest performances make available. Although Othello, status-wise, exogenously, is in the superior position in the asymmetrical social relations between them, inter-personal power, in the endogenous realm of interaction, resides with Iago who bends Othello's mind and behaviour to his will.

The audience, in possession of the missing premises, all along can construct a very different 'selfhood' for Iago and draw more accurate inferences. But 'reality' and 'truth' are characterized as fragile constructions of pragmatic beliefs on the part of the characters, and open to manipulation, and seen as partial, conflicting, perspectivized, contingent and unknown in any totality in the course of the play. Even at the end, Iago's reasons for the scale of destruction over which he presides are never fully available.

Other situations in plays may question the possibility, stability or power of beliefs or goals as active, motivating, personal or inter-personal, communicative or actional resources. In much modern drama, interactions are predicated precisely on the fact of beliefs being weak or contradictory, and motives, obscure. Interactions, at best, generate feeble inferences which are not followed through in next turn, which create either radical indeterminacy, or inhibit inferences from moving purposively along any cohesive or rational path, or from moving not very far at all. In Pinter's *Silence* (1978), analysed earlier from the ethnomethodological point of view (see p. 97), inferential possibilities are either so unconstrained as to be vacuous, so that virtually anything goes as inference or interpretation, or are extremely limited, with little if any stable cues either in the interactions or in context as to how to proceed with inferential work. The speech conventions used inhibit, or make irrelevant, negotiatory inter-personal labour among the characters. The dialogue is constructed in such a way as to leave out such options so that very little interactive work is engaged in among the characters.

Such discourse strategies may serve to construct very different kinds of subjectivities and inter-personal possibilities, but they still are the products of the processes that such strategies make available. The use of speech can either stabilize some set of beliefs about the state of the world or radically undermine such an eventuality. The 'recognition' scenes in Renaissance drama, and the drive towards the 'hidden' truth which is supplied at the end, unify the terms of that world. In modern drama, by contrast, in a Pinter, for instance, there are unmotivated reversals which obstruct attempts to bound a given state of affairs as 'the truth' or the 'reality' of the case.

In *Old Times* (1978), the 'reality' status of much of the action of the play is often interrogated and different strategies are used. At the end of the play, in Kate's long speech, she asserts that she remembers the manifestly 'living' stage Anna to be dead twenty-odd years ago and relates the episode. The truth value to be awarded Kate's constatives is never resolved since the ties between belief and reality and utterance and belief are actionally unravelled.

KATE   [*To* ANNA] But I remember you. I remember you dead.

[*Pause*]

I remember you lying dead. You didn't know I was watching you, I leaned over you. Your face was dirty. You lay dead, your face scrawled with dirt, all kinds of earnest inscriptions, but unblotted, so that they had run, all over your face, down to your throat. Your sheets were immaculate. I was glad. I would have been unhappy if your corpse had lain in an unwholesome sheet. . .

(Pinter 1981: 67–8)

Earlier on, although Anna is ostensibly a stranger to Deeley, he does relate an instance in which he had met Anna at a pub, but the fact status of this 'memory' is uncertain. A similar instance occurs, in fact, in Ibsen's *The*

Master Builder (1958) in which Hilde's claim that Solness had kissed her many years earlier raises issues of the 'truth value' of the incident, even though both of them discuss it and Solness appears to take Hilde's word for it, but the truth of the case is not settled (Kennedy 1983: 204–5). At any rate, appropriate contexts for interactions like these have to be supplied and assumptions built up accordingly, since they contradict and render invalid 'realistic' readings, and so dream, nightmare, hallucination, fantasy are often drawn upon to 'make sense' of such speech transactions.

In Marilyn Cooper's analysis (1987) of Pinter's *Betrayal* (1981), the issue of mutually 'shared knowledge' in the pragmatic framework is shown to be inadequate to explaining the kinds of interactions that appear in the play. The notion of 'shared knowledge' that Cooper takes to task has been questioned in the pragmatic field itself (see Smith 1982), on the grounds of the infinite regress that it can generate, which Cooper's analysis demonstrates on the level of interactive reality among the characters. Robert acts on the assumption that Jerry knows that he knows and Jerry does likewise with Robert, and so on, but this proves to be false and who knows what becomes the topic of interaction itself.

The kind of 'mind' that is dramatized in the play is not the Renaissance mind or an Enlightenment mind or even that of a canonical speaker, with the cognitive context open to semantic representations, with short and long-term memory as resources, and dependability invested in inferential capacities. Much that is open to assumption formation and which the audience notes simply does not register at all on the characters, who behave as if they just cannot remember what they had said earlier and continually contradict themselves or disclaim knowledge or remembrance of their past statements to each other. The mental realm is thus dramatized as unreliable, forgetting or not registering events being more 'normal' than representing and remembering them. Assumptions have to be negotiated and put in place over and over again, but once in place, there is no guarantee that they will remain there to generate other assumptions later on. Similar strategies are to be found in Beckett's *Waiting for Godot* (1955), or *Endgame* (1958), where the congruence of beliefs on the part of characters on what happened, or even what exists, to stabilize events in the universe of discourse of the dramatic world, is not available in many instances.

Many plays of the Absurd challenge our day-to-day, automatized realities and modes of meaning. The dramatic world operates on speech conventions that resemble but do not work like those in the audience world. To the characters themselves their interactions are 'normal', and believable and coherent to themselves in the fictional world, and authorized by the speech conventions in 'their' world. 'Their' speech conventions, however, radically undermine 'ours', as their worlds do, in which their interactions work 'naturally'. The perspective of 'Absurdity' is constructed by the audience, and conceptualized as such to account for the mismatch between the rules of the game in the fictional world and those of the audience world. But the logic and rationality of the Absurd is forged on similar lines to ours, but unfamiliar inferences are forced on us as a consequence of the ways in which the rules of interaction in the play world are played (Sherzer 1978; Gautam and Sharma 1986).

In Ionesco's *Salutations* (1968), the threshold rules of the reciprocal speech acts of greeting are observed but are protracted and combined in ways which undo their social salience while the mode of performance unravels the cultural 'appropriacy' of behaviour in the audience world. An impeccable logic is adopted in following the rules. The three Gentlemen greet each other in strict rotation and exhaust, in fact, all possible, logical permutations, including self-greetings. A similar strategy appears in *Improvisation* where Barts I, II and III perform in like fashion. In *The Lesson* as Paul Simpson has shown (1989: 171–93), the Professor's speech is overloaded with politeness strategies to his pupil, but the strategies far exceed the perfunctory acts of face-saving or face-enhancing habitually engaged in between interactants like these, especially as the power, status-wise, is with the Professor. Face strategies are piled on for no apparent reason, and the pupil, of course, as so often in these plays, does not bat an eyelid in disbelief.

Register rules are the resource in Pinter's *Trouble in the Works* (Short 1989: 156–63) and the transgressive use of the 'limits' familiar in the audience world, as resource, is quite usual in these plays (Sherzer 1978: 269–85). But strategies of defamiliarization involved in carrying through otherwise 'normative' processes beyond audience world appropriacies are also available in earlier plays for comic effects. A similar strategy to Pinter's excessive use of register in parodic fashion is found in an earlier play, Jonson's *The Alchemist* (Kennedy 1983: 146–7). The difference is that in the Restoration play such interactions enter the fictional world as 'other' to the speech rules dominant in that world and take their place as one type among others. The characters themselves, moreover, make it matter for comment, and thus a discourse matter. They perspectivize it. In Pinter, such speech conventions are 'naturalized'; the interactions go through as 'normal' among participants on a default basis. When these strategies are constrained and used as one among other forms of interactions they play a different role to those plays where some particular style is highly restricted and repeated as the only or major possibility available for interactions. The restriction of the use of available speech conventions can universalize some convention(s) as 'the truth' about interactions or language or speech, but such are effects, brought about by the contingencies of use. The social or theatrical metacommentaries that can be inferred from the two types of plays are different. Strategies can cross the boundaries of dramaturgies, but their effects will differ, dependent on their cumulative, co-textual placing.

The range of the inter-personal is extensive, as noted earlier, but whether deep intimacy or open conflict or something in between is at issue, the communicative possibilities realized within the discourse track followed and the pragmatic options used will contour 'situation', 'subjectivity', the 'inter-personal' and 'the social'. Given that communication is a risky affair, convergence, understanding, comity are as much interactional accomplishments as divergence, misunderstanding, conflict. Inter-personal attention may be mutually intense, mutually listless or asymmetrically distributed. Misunderstandings, like conflicts, are interactional achievements and complex events with rules and forms of life of their own and need not be regarded as the dark side of understanding or harmony. Misunderstandings often serve to strengthen comity as much as to disrupt it (Coupland *et al.* 1991; Grimshaw 1990). But they require interactive work, like their opposites, for participants to bring them into being, and to sustain them, or to repair them, and the sources and structures of conflict are multiple. The rules, however, implicate the participants in their interactional attempts, in the doing of their events within the workings of speech as mental and social praxis.

POLITENESS AND POWER

Politeness rules regulate inter-personal relationships so as to ensure that harmony as a social good may prevail. The necessity for rules, however, presupposes the possibility of conflict which the rules seek to neutralize. Even in equal status encounters, therefore, asymmetry of interests and instability can be the social 'givens' which are to be harmonized via the rules. Granted the pressures and necessities of goal fulfilment in interactions, there is incipient friction between intentional and social goals. Politeness rules can be turned in various ways to serve a whole range of functions, inter-personal and dramatic. Precisely because the rules can be superficially observed, mismatches between immediate and superordinate goals can be veiled by the use of politeness. Moreover, the use of politeness strategies does not automatically ensure the achievement of comity or equality.

'Face' and 'pragmatic politeness' considerations fuel politeness strategies, with degrees of indirection calculated on 'face' threat and a cost–benefit scale, to mitigate imposition. But because there is no umbilical cord binding speaker, speech and strategy, politeness strategies and the indirectness they make available can be used for highly coercive ends to act as cover and to silence or mislead the interlocutor as well. Grammatical markers of politeness as in address forms, the use of honorifics, *tu/vous* distinctions, etc. can reference status and social relations, but can also be used to change the level of inter-personal closeness or distance between or among interactants. In Wilde's *The Importance of Being Earnest* ([1896] 1962), initial friendliness is displayed in the change of address forms, mutually agreed upon, from the formal 'Miss Cardew', 'Miss Fairfax' to 'Cecily' and 'Gwendolen'. When antagonism owing to misunderstanding occurs between them, the change in address forms to formality signals distance, while the highly indirect 'polite' methods of disagreement used regarding which of them is actually engaged to Ernest constructs not comity, but an acute frostiness in their relations. Rudeness as banter, on the other hand, creates comity and bonding between the men.

'Rudeness' displayed in banter mode functions as mask for interpersonal anxieties and affectivities, in Terence Rattigan's *In Praise of Love*, the problems of understanding the invisible emotional tremor in the visible, stiff upper lip being the point of many interactions in the cross-cultural household – Estonian, English, American, in this instance – and leading to the denouement of the play. More generally, and culturally, the inter-personal problems engendered by playing one-sidedly, one set of cultural norms as universals is articulated within the household by the *émigrés* in the fictional world, whose politeness codes are not those of the English.

Lydia is the Estonian wife, a resistance worker and concentration camp refugee during the last War and married to the English Sebastian, now writer, who rescued her from the KGB. At the time of the play, Lydia has a terminal illness with a time limit on her life and is in conversation with Mark, an American and a long-standing family friend, to whom alone she can articulate her thoughts and feelings about her past and present condition. English cultural norms and the politeness masks that are needed to be worn, and the silences, suppressions and restrictions they signify in the necessities not to say, to say indirectly, to suppress emotion, or understate, when applied cross-culturally, result in humiliation and alienation for the non-English participant who is, moreover, totally unaware of the norms and uses her own. Lydia describes her first encounter at a party within the cross-cultural politeness scenario, where one person's politeness is another's pain. The following conversation ensues: the participants being cultural exiles in an alien cultural context assess, via experience, the value and costs of 'polite' social practices, when enforced cross-culturally.

LYDIA . . . Back to Sebastian's party. Do you know, Mark, the party started at nine and at eleven there was no one left. No one at all. I'd bored the whole lot out into the night.

MARK Refugee stories?

LYDIA [*indignantly*] I didn't know they were forbidden! I mean, people that night asked me politely about what it had been like being invaded alternatively by the Russians, then by the Germans, and then by the Russians again over six years – and like a bloody idiot I went and told them. All of them. Finally, they were round me in a circle, looking at me so politely – you know those polite English looks – Oh God, how I hate polite English looks. . . !

MARK I hate politeness.

LYDIA [*Aggressively*] You don't. You're the politest man I know –

MARK Yeh, but I don't look it.

LYDIA True. Sebastian's friends did. Glassy-eyed from boredom, of course, but I didn't see that. Sebastian did and tried to stop me, but I wasn't to be stopped. I told them all about myself – All.

MARK Even the Russian General?

LYDIA You bet, the Russian General. . . You see the one thing I was so sure about the English, was that they all had a sense of humour. . . Famous for it. . . So when I told them that a Russian General had selected me from a Labour Camp to be his personal driver because he liked my 'Body-work', oh how I thought they'd roar –

MARK Not a titter?

LYDIA Not a smirk.

MARK Well there wouldn't be, would there? It's a terrible joke.

LYDIA [*Indignantly*] It was the best I could manage under the circumstances –

[*A pause*]

Oh those glassy stares! – Oh God, and how angry Sebastian was!

[*Imitating him*]

'You see, my darling girl, it isn't quite done over here to parade your emotions so publicly. We, as a race, on the whole prefer to – *understate*. Do you understand, my darling?' – I was guilty of bad form, especially as, I think I did, I cried a bit when I told them. . . Oh damn the English! I think that their bad form doesn't just lie in revealing emotions, it's having any at all.

(Rattigan [1978] 1985: 195–6)

In other instances, as in Noël Coward's *Conversation Piece*, conventional politeness strategies and ostensive attention to the other's face could actually function as unilateral strategies for control, dominance and self-interest. Paul's goal is to trap Edward (Lord Sheere) into committing himself to marrying Melanie, an under-class waif, as part of a plan to ensure his own (and her) financial future, although Melanie subverts this master-plan in the end. The means, in the extract quoted, are politeness strategies. Paul's strategies are many, including 'humbling himself' but also deliberately to misunderstand Edward's illocutionary intentions and to make and display the wrong inferences, manifestly, as if on grounds of positive politeness, which enables him to re-reference the situation according to his own plans. When the startled Edward explicitly states his position, we get the following:

EDWARD [*firmly*] I have not proposed marriage to Melanie.

PAUL That does credit both to your upbringing and your personal integrity. I unfortunately am not in a position to put your fears entirely at rest. I cannot tell you for certain whether or not she really loves you, but if you will take the advice of an old man, don't give up hope, don't despair too soon –

([1934] 1979: 219)

Banter, irony, etc. can also turn inter-personal situations around in various ways. But indirection as a social necessity has many uses – for face-saving purposes, but also for power, and as coercive in cross-cultural instances when illocutionary silences or locutionary repressions are extracted unilaterally and one-sidedly without imagination or understanding of the other's needs to speak. But the unsaid can hover. The speaker cannot be made liable for the words which have not been spoken, and even when words are spoken, implicatures, especially unintended ones, can be counter-used to silence a speaker in turn.

In general, inferences can create a rich sub-text in which the power of the utterance resides precisely in what can be inferred because it is not articulated. Implications left to be silently constructed can be as expressive as explicit modes of speech. The expressive power of the not-said, the indirect, the unfinished, the elliptical, the understated is integral to the pragmatic functioning of language. The unsaid can function as weapon and could be used for power, manipulation, deceit, as much as tact, consideration and kindliness, or it can signify just plain emptiness. The point is virtually unexplored in studies of drama especially in the literary sphere. The over-reliance on the code, and on explicit, syntacticically complete, written language forms as 'language', or 'the verbal', and the lack of adequate attention to the pragmatic functioning of language has often led to a kind of death of language claim when confronted with phatic or inexplicit styles as strategies of dramatic speech in plays. As the discussion in this chapter makes clear, from the pragmatic point of view, bounded, determinate propositional forms and contents cannot be confused with 'language' and 'meaning' in communication, since instances where the propositional contents of utterances exhaust 'meaning' via the code can be more the exception rather than the rule.

Chapter 5

Gender and language

WOMEN'S TALK

Linguistic investigations into sex-differentiated language were a late development even within the sociolinguistic field of enquiry, which focuses on the relation between language and society. Sex as a variable was not regarded as significant enough, in contrast to class, age, status, region, ethnicity, etc. which were the major factors seen to influence language use. The fact of linguistic sex differentiation had been noted in linguistic studies as early as 1922 by Otto Jespersen whose *Language: Its Nature, Development and Origin* had a section on 'The Woman', drawn from early twentieth-century anthropological work in non-Western cultures. But there were also foremothers, women like Charlotte Carmichael Stopes (1908) and Elsie C. Parsons (1913), who had drawn attention, even before Jespersen, to the actualities of sex discrimination nearer home in the use of 'man' in law, for instance, and the assumption of male superiority this presupposed.

Jespersen's observations on women's language, which included sex-differentiated speech in Western societies, attempted to identify formal, linguistic features and to account for them functionally and socially, but the explanations offered have been criticized as being based on stereotypes (Thorne *et al.* 1983).

Women were regarded as having a smaller vocabulary than men although they were more fluent, their sentence structure was deemed to be less complex since men used a kind of 'Chinese box' structure, whereas women were supposed to string sentences along with the use of 'and' and similar conjunctions. Women 'instinctively shrank' from the use of coarse expressions and used indirect expressions, and had a refining influence on language, but men were the creative innovators and renovators of language. These and other differences were attributed to a variety of factors – from differences in how men and women were socialized, division of labour between the sexes, to differences in education, and biology, instinct, etc. Such a narrative overlooks others, from which different conclusions can be drawn. As Cameron and Coates observe (1988: 14, 24 n.2), in the eighteenth century women were actually blamed for polluting the English lexicon with new and ephemeral words, whereas men were seen as guardians of the purity of the language because of their linguistic conservatism. Male usage is thus seen as the standard, against which women are assessed negatively.

The 'double bind' operative here against women, that you're damned if you do and damned if you don't, has been noted by Robin Lakoff, whose *Language and Woman's Place* (1975) set the agenda for subsequent, more serious work on sex differentiated language. Lakoff's contention was that discrimination against women was evident in two ways – 'in the way they are taught to use language, and in the way general language use treats them' (1975: 4), the net result being that habitual language use functions to submerge their identities, by denying them the means for strong self-assertion and entrapping them in projecting themselves as hesitant and uncertain in their speech styles and delimiting the scope of their topics and concerns as trivial. Having socialized women into such deferential and powerless 'feminine' modes, with penalties for appearing 'unfeminine', society then blames them for not being on a par with men, and categorizes them as lacking in intelligence, clarity of thought and seriousness of purpose, and worse. Similar to Jespersen, Lakoff catalogued linguistic features regarded as indices of women's style or of the female register. Among the features listed are lexical differences, in the use of elaborated vocabulary related to women's domestic domain or interests – cooking, home decoration, fashion; intensifiers, often empty, like 'gorgeous', 'divine', etc.; propensity for euphemistic and polite phrases, partiality for the expression of emotions like love, grief, but avoidance of anger-ridden terms. Syntactic and pragmatic features include the mitigating use of tag questions which reduces the force of assertions, the use of requests in place of commands, hedging with the use of modals, and items that signal uncertainty, 'more or less', 'sorta', 'kinda', etc.; and phonologically, rising intonation on declaratives instead of the falling one, and a marked preference for 'standard' or 'correct' pronunciations. The method adopted was correlative, linguistic features linked to extra-linguistic variables, here, the variable of sex. Her data, too, were collated via introspection, as she herself makes clear.

Research since has proceeded to test, contest, revise and elaborate upon the scope of these pronouncements. In the attempt, the explanatory potential of such one-to-one correlations between features of the linguistic code and the social variable of sex/gender have been radically questioned. Although the fact of sexual imbalance is accepted, the search for the best forms of explanation takes us well beyond such correlations. Investigations reveal, too, the complexities involved in the whole issue of gender construction and its workings.

Since Lakoff's intervention, the feminist orientation in linguistic research has forked into two main areas – to explore sexism in the linguistic code, and to explore how sex differentiation is mediated and modulated in the uses of the code within the whole complex area of 'language-in-use', where contextual factors of various kinds are taken into account. As far as the linguistic code is concerned, even though grammars are supposed to be uncontextualized, the fact of sexism and misogyny is far too prevalent, but most pervasive at the lexical level. Julia Penelope Stanley (1977) has listed 220 terms for a sexually promiscuous woman as opposed to around 20 for a sexually promiscuous man, in the English language, and this in spite of the fact that male promiscuity has traditionally and historically been tolerated and, consequently, less policed. It is as if the male gaze and male anxiety about female sexuality has, across time, conceptualized and catalogued female 'transgressions' in finely discriminating ways, and often enough for these to be codified into the language itself. At any rate, there is no obvious linguistic rationale for such a difference.

Authoritative sources which standardize and regulate the code fare no better. Nilsen's (1977) study of dictionary words that were semantically marked according to masculinity or femininity ('fraternize', 'man', etc. as opposed to 'actress', 'mother', etc.) and related to prestige/non-prestige connotations revealed a ratio of 3:1 in favour of men, with a higher ratio for prestige words – 6:1. The ratio of words with negative connotations tilted towards women by over 20 per cent (Smith 1989: 36–8). Illustrative sentences in dictionaries, too, relied on stereotypes, with women represented in 'female' settings like fashion, cookery, etc., in dutiful, female roles – mother, hostess, etc. – and in emotional situations. Men were relegated to the realms of business, sport, etc. but were also portrayed in less conscientious guises – as delinquents or rebels.

Educational materials like schoolbooks reinforce such attitudes. Pronominal usage favours males, as Graham found, as do references to men versus women, by a ratio of around 4:1 (1975); and this apart from the use of the generic 'he' which has had the most exposure in work outside linguistics. Practices outside the school could also stabilize and circulate bias – editorial conventions of publishing houses could submerge or erase female identity in their reference to women not in their own right, but in relation to their husbands, as Nilsen notes when she came across women famous in their own right – Charlotte Brontë, Amelia Earhart, Jenny Lind, etc. being 'escorted by a male's name' across the page, since they were identified as Mrs Arthur B. Nicholls, Mrs George Palmer Putnam, Mme. Otto Goldschmidt, respectively' (Nilsen *et al.* 1977: 138, quoted by Smith 1989: 42). Other areas that have been examined include the use of address forms, and naming practices: the use of the diminutive '-ette' for women's personal names, for instance, the practice itself seeming to conceptualize women as derived. Family names are father's or husband's names. Female titles like 'Miss' and 'Mrs' distinguish women according to their sexual availability since there is no corresponding contrast for men. The modern contrast between Miss and Mrs was a late development owing to changes brought in in women's roles by the Industrial Revolution when women achieved a measure of independence as wage labourers. Prior to this, earlier uses distinguished between women and girls not between whether they were married or not (*ibid.*: 41).

But the practice of referring to women as belonging to men is more prevalent in society than the other way round – thus, women are more often referred to as 'John's girlfriend', 'Bill's wife', etc. than as individuals in their own right. Unmarked word order in pairings usually puts the male first – 'husband and wife', 'son and daughter', 'host and hostess', etc., as if the positively evaluated or privileged part of the pair takes priority – as in 'day and night', 'rich and poor', etc. (*ibid.*: 47). Added to this is the fact that terms may undergo 'semantic degeneration', a contingency to which terms associated with women are prone, since they accrue negative, mostly sexual connotations (*ibid.*: 48). Terms addressed to men or boys with female connotations similarly downgrade, as in 'sissy', 'effeminate', etc., while masculine connotations attaching to female terms like 'tomboy' seem more favourable.

That sex and gender are not biologically but socially and ideologically problematical is a truism in gender studies, and the above does lend support to the claim. In fact, modern language-related studies on cognitive skills and related to brain functioning, that attempt to determine whether there *are* biologically based differences or not, tend to favour the female. Such studies are contentious, not only because of the political, social and ethical consequences of beliefs that differentiate among groups on a biological basis, which have already been played out so tragically in Western Europe on issues of race, but also because the experimental procedures used, interpretations of data and the inconclusiveness of the tests themselves advise extreme caution.

These studies (Philips *et al.* 1987: Part III) have pointed to differences which have been attributed to the asymmetrical organization of the brain in the male. Female cerebral functions have been seen to be more evenly organized and less specialized. Cerebral lesions or trauma in the same areas of the brain affect men and women differently – women suffer less speech impairment when the left hemisphere is affected. Boys, it is said, are prone to more 'reading difficulties' than girls. There are differences in developmental or maturation terms, too. In the first few months of their lives, female infants display more spontaneous vocal activity; they also learn to speak earlier and do so more frequently, therefore seeming to acquire language skills sooner and develop them faster. Their vocabulary is larger and they produce two-word 'sentences' earlier than boys. Boys are supposed to display greater spatial skills, which they appear to retain for a longer period of time – into their teens and beyond.

Other differences have also been speculated upon. Linguistic skills are supposed to require linear processing; spatial skills necessitate holistic or Gestalt processing. One cannot, however, construct any global biological structure of gender 'paths' from such studies. For a start, it has been pointed out that there may be different routes to the same goal of linguistic and cognitive 'competence'. Nor is it clear how such differences relate to adult abilities, unless we presuppose an unchanged and unchangeable linear path of progression along given lines, which is generally not the case. Moreover, other factors like 'sinistrality' – right- or left-handedness – hormonal differences, etc. and their influence on brain lateralization may also have to be reckoned with, knowledge of which is, at best, partial, contested and inconclusive.

Such biologically orientated research, although offering no reliable possibility of gendered, pre-given, blueprints, also offers no support to traditional notions of female cognitive and intellectual inferiority and lack of rationality, on the grounds that women had smaller brains – a charge, incidentally, also levelled in the past at non-white races to justify colonial expansion and exploitation. The moral of such tales would seem to be that where there are differences, dualisms and disparities are not far behind, especially in the worlds of human and social affairs, motivated as they are by the will to power. Thus, the notion of difference, whatever its value conceptually, rarely projects social equality or justice, or mutual respect, at least in the Western tradition, constituted as it is within the long reach of its Enlightenment heritage of dichotomies and polarities, of rational/ir-rational, culture/nature, objective/subjective, etc. into which the concept of the female, in its difference from the male, is inevitably drawn (Hekman 1990). The disparate values such dualisms have acquired in verbal, educational, economic, domestic, political and social practice have frozen differences into hierarchies, of superior/inferior, dominated/dominating and the like.

And it is with respect to the social pressures and arrangements of gender that the more productive insights about sex-differentiated language are to be found in the area of 'language-in-use', which takes account of social pressures and the social arrangements of gender. Here, not the code alone, but situational constraints like settings, social rules, roles, expectations, control of interactive resources, and such like, of the kind investigated in the previous chapters, also play their crucial part so that the issue of sex turns out to be far more mediated in relation to both power and patriarchy than the correlative model of a one-to-one link between sex and language would have us believe. From this perspective, then, studies that have scrutinized Lakoff's (1975) features of 'women's style' reveal that her conclusions are too strong. Tag questions, a major syntactic feature associated with women's language, have been shown to have many functions, thus casting doubt on Lakoff's claim that tag questions, unless used as felicitous speech acts of requests for information, are markers of female tentativeness.

Janet Holmes (1984a) provides a more considered analysis when she points out that finer discriminations are needed than those possible in the straight conflation of tags with female weaker social style, in which the one is necessarily seen as evidence for or symptom of the other. The quantitative method is also censured in favour of a more complex framework that includes the various parameters involved in the notion of 'situated' discourse. Given that participants – in the plural, sp-H – are involved in the speech situation, tags could be either speaker-oriented or addressee-oriented – modal or affective in Holmes' (1984a, b) terminology. Modal, speaker-oriented tags are felicitous requests or wants for confirmation or information as indicated by the felicity conditions on such speech acts. Thus, 'You weren't in Paris last August, were you?' under this interpretation would be a request for information owing to uncertainty on the part of the speaker regarding the state of affairs referred to by the proposition in the utterance. On the other hand, an utterance like 'Take this bag, will you?' would be 'affective', i.e. addressee-oriented, the tag 'will you' an addressee-'face'-oriented form, which serves to rescue and transform the 'bald, without redress' FTA signified by the imperative minus tag – functionally, 'softeners' in Holmes. 'Facilitatives' promote 'positive' face since they display a speaker's affiliation with the hearer's positive face wants. Tags, here, have the added function of mobilizing the adjacency pair rule, by inviting the H to take a turn: 'You were in Paris last August, weren't you?' Not all tags, therefore, are covert requests for

approval as Lakoff held; they have more active and positive, inter-
personal and socially facilitative functions.

Holmes' framework provides greater options, and hence possibilities
for socially positive readings in interactional terms, even if distributional
criteria reveal sex-differentiated preferences – women prefer such forms
in contrast to men. However, it is not the *fact* of the distribution alone that
counts, but the interpretation and explanation that is built on the 'facts' –
i.e. on what is concluded from the results in association with the hypothesis encapsulated in the theory or method adopted, and the premises on
which the interpretation is founded. Coates *et al.*'s study (1988) reveals
asymmetries between male and female uses of tags, but leads them to
conclude that 'the use of facilitative tags correlates with conversational
role, rather than with gender *per se*. Where men take on a facilitating role
they are able to produce a large number of facilitative tags' (Coates and
Cameron 1988: 86).

Fishman (1980, 1983), on the other hand, sees women using tags in
facilitative fashion to get information from uncommunicative male interactants, but interprets them as burdened with the work of keeping
interaction in progress. Tag questions may be used to forestall opposition
especially if used in an overbearing manner. In different settings, different
uses of tag questions are evident between men and women. In classroom
settings, both women and men use equal numbers of tag questions. In a
group of engineers and designers, men used more. Between heterosexual
couples at home women used more.

Further, alternative analyses are available that do not tie tags to gender,
but to power, in studies in discourse analysis on 'unequal encounters'
(Coates and Cameron 1988). Tag questions are seen here, as 'Conducive'
question forms – those where a question contains a completed proposition
which constrains the response as agreement, since they take more interactive effort to challenge. In 'It was a good party, wasn't it?', agreement
is presupposed. From this point of view, tag questions can be reanalysed
as 'highly assertive strategies for coercing agreement, and not indications
of tentativeness' (*ibid.*: 87). Powerful interactants favour such forms –
magistrates, for instance (Harris 1984). From this perspective, they function as indices of power not powerlessness as Lakoff claimed. Easy
correlations between linguistic features used by one sex or the other in
terms of power or powerlessness are thus open to question. Diplomats,
too, are frequent users of indirection, thus the style is not confined to either
women or powerless groups. Cross-culturally, indirection can be typified
differently. Keenan's study (1974) of Malagasay women reveals that

indirection is a marker of male speech in this community; women's styles were more direct.

Lakoff's views on intonation have also been challenged. The high rise tone rather than the assertive neutral fall in response to questions is evaluated as hesitant, emotional, etc. but regardless of sex (McConnell-Ginet 1978). But women who used the fall were regarded as sounding more masculine than when they used the high rise tone. Accent, too, complicates the picture; and with it the variable of social class. Female RP speakers are assessed in relation to their class rather than their sex – they are seen as more competent, egotistic, etc. in line with all RP speakers and, significantly, not penalized with unfemininity in relation to dialect speakers (Smith 1989: 86–9).

Other studies refute readings of female characteristics of speech as symptomatic of female powerlessness. O'Barr and Atkins' (1980) study of features of the female register in settings like the courtroom revealed that social and occupational status had a more decisive influence on distribution of such features than gender alone. Also, familiarity with, and understanding and control of, situational norms had a part to play, since experienced witnesses had lower scores for such features even if they were women. Lower-status, blue-collar men and unwaged wives scored highly. Setting, too, could be a determinant. Crosby and Nyquist (1977) used three different settings to test the distribution of 'female' language features – conversations in a laboratory, conversations with male and female attendants at a large convention and in a police station. Although women had higher scores in the laboratory and convention settings, both sexes showed evidence of 'powerless' language in the police setting when interacting with police personnel, the setting and situation being power-laden against them. Women interacting with women showed higher scores than men interacting with men.

Instead of the correlative model, in which certain linguistic features are regarded as indices of female identity and women judged accordingly, an alternative, social network model as developed by Lesley Milroy (1980) and others has proved more useful in explaining the distribution of certain phonological features in women's speech. The method used contrasts with classical studies of the Labovian kind (Labov 1972), where distributional differences in women's speech revealed the phenomenon of 'hypercorrection' – a marked preference for pronunciations that approximated to a standard or prestige version, especially in formal contexts. Such results have been duplicated in many countries and regions. Different explanations were offered – that women, especially older women, were more conservative in the use of forms, or that women were more status-conscious and thus preferred non-stigmatized variants.

Milroy's work offers an alternative explanation as to why women prefer standard to vernacular forms, since she raises the possibility of social networks and their influence on speech. The individual is not regarded as uniquely endowed with certain speech characteristics, and related to sex, but as responsive to the characteristics that are shared within the solidarity network(s) within which the individual is also situated. And male and female networks are different. Close-knit networks serve to preserve and maintain certain kinds of speech – male, working-class networks in Belfast, which were the focus of Milroy's study, preserve the vernacular forms, whereas women who do not share this network have less affiliation with such norms. In other words, women's speech reveals not a greater affiliation with the prestige norms, but a weaker affiliation with the male, working-class, solidarity network norm.

Certain conditions had to be satisfied for network membership along 'density' or 'multiplexity' lines. Thus neighbourhood ties, work ties, family or kinship ties, leisure ties, were all involved. 'Density' refers to a personally, close-knit 'territorially based cluster' with close, internal relationships – groups of either sex who meet on a regular basis for some activity, neighbourhood gangs of boys, or women who meet on a regular basis for tea or coffee, for instance. 'Multiplex' networks require different but overlapping connections or links among different individuals. Members of a network might know each other as workmates, neighbours, friends, etc. Two individuals have to be linked in more than one way for the link to be multiplex. Thus, kinship access to more than one home, sharing a workplace with at least two others from the same area, sharing the same sex with at least two others in the same area, with whom workplace is shared; sharing voluntary, leisure interests or pursuits with others from the same neighbourhood, or workplace; would all enable an individual to score highly on the network score, although criteria like 'workplace' and 'leisure hours' would bias the score in favour of men. Women are part of the labour force, but it is debatable whether they have leisure hours or pursuits outside the home to the same extent (Coates and Cameron 1988: 21).

But there is evidence, however, that the vernacular is used as a marker of masculinity or male solidarity by working-class men. Hence, its retention will be motivated for social reasons in this analysis. But here, too, there are complexities. Jenny Cheshire's (1982) study reveals that different variants can correlate with different sex groups and so different variants can have similar functions for male and female groups. In relation to degrees of adherence to peer group values, boys' variants, like non-standard 'was', 'never', showed greater strength, whereas girls' usage revealed adherence to a different set of non-standard items as norms – past tense 'come', 'aint' as copula. What Cheshire's work also makes clear is that girls' groups do produce their own vernacular, female norms. They do not clutch at the standard. On the other hand, Viv Edwards' (1988) research into the speech of British-born black young adults, whose parents were of West Indian origin, found no significant differences in their speech although she does claim that there is evidence for sex-related patterns. The range of these results is salutary since it enables us to conclude that some women have a weaker affiliation to the vernacular than others depending on peer group pressure and the strength of the network to which they belong, and whether it is open or closed. It is not the case that a preference for the standard is uniformly sex-related.

Another factor to be considered in this question of sex-related varieties is the influence of the labour market and social mobility as Patricia Nichols (1983) found in her study of the speech of two black South Carolina communities. Socioeconomic changes may precipitate shifts in usage as was the case with younger women whose speech favoured standard forms more systematically, whereas older women, like their male counterparts, retained the vernacular. Nichols explains these findings as owing to the kind of job opportunities that were opened up for the younger women, in the service industries, which were also white collar. Older women were usually to be found in the traditional, domestic and agricultural areas, and men in construction jobs. Both these latter groups were established and closed, and had no incentive to acquire the standard which was redundant in their lives. Standard speech was required for the younger women and, therefore, the motivation to acquire it. These wider social and economic forces also exercise leverage on identity, generally, but also gender identity, since gender here is not in the realm of anatomical or psychological necessities, but constructs itself in connection with others with whom one considers one belongs, and the requirements of solidarity behaviours this necessitates. Linguistic markers, like the vernacular, can also be used strategically, as a code-switch, to signal or display, or to make a reality of degrees of closeness, belonging or 'in-groupness' or distance in the use of the standard.

Such research indicates that the analysis of gender in language requires more than one level of investigation since the display of gender identity is governed by complex factors. Situation and situational norms, status, institutional and conversational role, membership in networks, socioeconomic necessities, and such like, may also be crucially involved.

However, gender binds are not completely dissipated by either the multi-functionality of linguistic features or through the constraints of situational factors mentioned above. For such research focuses on speakers, generally. The possibility for greater freedom for gendered self-expression and efficacy that is opened up here is not wholly supported by other factors. For speakers do not unilaterally determine power, powerlessness, solidarity, dominance or subordination, in speech situations. There are the hearers, the recipients, targeted or untargeted – in the realm of the Other – who evaluate a speaker's speech, and the reciprocal, responsive, retaliatory return judgements and assessments they make are crucially conditioned by the societal, ideological assumptions and prescriptions regarding how gendered speakers are supposed to behave, and these are also influential.

For a start there is evidence of gendered 'deafness' in mixed party talk. Women may speak but may not be given a hearing since various strategies are used to silence them, inattentiveness to their speech, or non-listening, being one of them. In conversation, as mentioned earlier, listening is an interactive resource, the attentiveness to another's speech requiring displays of attention. Male styles of response generally do not include or delay the minimal attention markers, like 'mm', 'yeah', nods, etc., which are used to display positive listening, which women generally display in talk (Zimmerman and West 1975). It has been suggested that men and women use such markers differently; men interpret them as agreement, while women regard them as merely facilitative or supportive signals to another's turn. Thus, there is room for misunderstanding as to what is going on interactively. But such non-supportive displays can also be used in gender-consequential ways. In the absence of such markers, women expend a lot of energy in talk, as Fishman (1980) notes, to get ratification for what they say, but they are often unsuccessful.

Men appropriate control, too, of interactional resources, like the floor, as conversation analysts have revealed. They interrupt women more and hog the floor and their turns are longer (Zimmerman and West 1975). Nor is it the case that male contributions are necessarily more effective or persuasive as a result; even in task-oriented settings, where male skills are supposed to be required, male contributions do not substantially control the outcome (Nemeth et al. 1976). It would appear that men are partial to the sound of their own voices, in public settings, regardless of time, turn rights, or point or relevance of their speech, while blithely censuring women for talking too much, which is the stereotype. In personal, domestic settings, too, in wife–husband interactions, women perform as the less dominant partners – they facilitate interactions rather than take the dominant role themselves, allowing the men to do most of the talking (Soskin and John 1963). On the other hand, even when women talked more and raised topics, they did not receive interactional support in the form of minimal responses or acceptance or expansion of their topics; their husbands' 'deafness' or non-interest defeating their interactive attempts (DeFrancisco 1991).

But men behaved in similar ways with other men as they did with women, the general pattern being that a few dominant men would do most of the talking in all-male interactions. Dominance hierarchies of this kind seem to be accepted by men, since, presumably, the right to be competitive is condoned by men, and hence also the rights of challenge. In mixed encounters, dominant men actually mitigate their propensity to full, male dominance with women, relative to men, but not in such a way as to relinquish their hold on the floor or interactive resources in any major way. Both sexes spoke more when the listener was a woman (Markel *et al.* 1976)

The use of the floor – in terms of interruptions, and turn length, in particular – can be deeply manipulated in sexual terms, especially where the (targeted) hearer is a woman and the speaker is a man. The burden of being the target of speech, and in the role of the listener, is placed heavily on the dominated, male or female, in such instances. But where the 'rules' of interaction, in situated discourse, are subordinated deictically to superordinate and gendered power relations, greater pressure devolves on women, given that the right to compete for the gendered floor is a risky, even if not a wholly determined, strategy in social-sexual terms. There is a price to pay for women. Extended turn rights, appropriated with (most often without) ratification, in gender terms, can signify obvious gender privilege, while gendered inattention, or turn lapses on the part of the male, can equally disempower the female in cross-sex interactions.

If speech can be used systematically by men as a dominance strategy, male inexpressiveness, inarticulacy and silence in interactions can also be comparably mobilized, as Jack Sattel (1983) has noted. Male inexpressiveness, especially in personal and emotional matters, has traditionally been viewed as a sexual-cultural trait, and as a consequence of socialization, given that the male domain was the public sphere in which emotional considerations and feelings were required to be suppressed. In all-male talk, too, such displays would be regarded as a sign of weakness, and make men vulnerable to other men. But inexpressiveness and expressiveness can also be used manipulatively, as self-interest or self-defence in the game of sexual politics. In his analysis of a passage of dialogue in Erica Jong's *Fear of Flying*, male inexpressiveness is not, in Sattel's words, 'a deeply socialized inability to respond to the needs of others – the male here is *using* the inexpression to guard his own position. To not say anything in this situation is to say something very important indeed; that the battle we are engaged in is to be *fought* by my rules and when I choose to fight' (*ibid.*: 122). Similarly, in analysing the male character's behaviour in Alan Lelchuk's *American Mischief* Sattel submits that the use of *expressiveness*, on the part of the male, to communicate personal and intimate disclosures to women is, in fact, highly manipulative, since, he 'tells women fifteen minutes after he meets them that he is sexually impotent, but with the clear insinuation that "maybe with you it would be different. . ." In this situation the man's skill at dissembling has less to do with handing a woman a "line" than in displaying his weakness or confidences as a sign of authentic, nonexploitative male interest. . . ' (*ibid.*: 123).

Perception studies reveal, too, the force of social pressures against which women have to contend. Subjects were asked to categorize the responses of a nine-month-old infant to various toys including a jack-in-the-box. Some subjects were told that the child was a girl, others that it was a boy. The child's startled cry at the jack-in-the-box was interpreted as fear by those who thought it was a girl, as anger by those who were told it was a boy (Condry and Condry 1976). Women professors were adjudged by students to be more sympathetic but less competent in their use of co-operative styles.

Although linguistic features of powerlessness, etc. may not be 'sex-saturated', but sometimes 'sex-preferred' or 'sex-imposed', the pressure of others' stereotyped expectations of gendered speaker behaviour is still a force that women have to reckon with. And this is compounded by norms that govern speech behaviour in situations. Powerless styles when used or appropriated by women result in 'double jeopardy', for them, since they are still categorized lower than men who use the same features. Although higher-status women, class-wise, or occupation-wise, are seen to 'upgrade' in relation to lower-class or -status men, it is not the case that situationally 'underprivileged' or disadvantaged men and women are assessed on equal terms. Bradley's (1980) study on 'expert' interactants discovered that there was an insidious hierarchy of evaluations at work – less expert women were penalized more than expert women, predictably, but more, too, than less expert males, the sex factor overriding and unbalancing the equality of 'ground' provided by the disadvantaging 'expert' factor for both sexes in this case. The 'burden of proof' (Preisler 1986: 22) requirement is thus imposed harder on women than on men, the default expectation being that men, in general, are more competent in comparison to women (or, to put it another way, women are less competent because they are women), even though in 'expert' interactional settings, assessments of competence/incompetence are reckoned to be neutral. It is taken for granted that men are competent even if, performance-wise, this is not the case. Thus, status behaviour could be gendered – male styles, strategies, contributions being the unmarked norm in status-infused settings and interactions.

But the complication here is that (white), middle- or upper-class women backed by professional status (in Britain, especially those with RP, or standard English, accents and fluency) may have the edge over unwaged or lower status, working-class men who fulfil the stereotype in their speech and/or behaviour, in institutional settings, even though the latter would be advantaged in contrast to their female class and status counterparts in the same situations. Status alone, however, does not appear to advantage women in interacting with men, at least where floor management is concerned. Research into doctor–patient interactions reveals that, although doctors in general interrupt patients more, female doctors were interrupted more often than their male counterparts when the patient was a (white) man. Similarly, where the 'boss' was a female, she was subjected to more challenge for the floor by her male subordinates than the male bosses were (West 1984a, b; Woods 1989).

Eight factors for dominance formed the basis of the hypotheses in Woods' study – that dominant speakers will be selected to speak, will self-select, will interrupt and overlap, renew speakership rights after a pause, will speak through transition relevance places without a pause, and interrupt and overlap more than non-powerful participants. They will also be interrupted and overlapped less and gain more assent terms as minimal responses than they will give. Not all her hypotheses were supported, but the ones which *were* supported revealed that status does not override the gender differential in all cases. Women bosses were interrupted more than their male counterparts, while their own interruptions were less successful. Females, whether boss or subordinate, generally received fewer assent terms, and male subordinates held the floor longer than the female bosses. Men also spoke through transition relevance places more often, hence closing options for speaker change more frequently while they held the floor. Woods also makes the point that support for such tactics was given more frequently by the women, male dominance of this kind being jointly managed and not male-imposed alone.

This does not detract from the point made regarding the power of the stereotype. It extends it into other areas and mitigates it in gender terms. But it does establish the fact that sex/gender itself is not a unitary category based on biology alone, and that since society itself is multiply stratified on unequal terms – class, race, status, etc. – women may gain or lose, relatively speaking, with respect to other women, as well, according to their insertion into such structures. The other side of this coin is that sex can still function as a disadvantaging factor for women when they are on seemingly equal, social ground with men. 'Privileged' women would still fare worse with 'privileged' men even though they are advantaged in relation to another, class-based asymmetry. And, of course, status does not make them immune to challenge from lower status men. And different composites derived from diversely calibrated calculations of class, sex, status, economic and class security, colour, race, age, religion, sexual preference, area of the planet, etc. would provide evidence of different degrees of advantage or disadvantage, among women, men and women, and men and men.

Non-white feminists, especially those defined as minorities in dominant white cultures, have pointed out that white, feminist theorizing leaves out of account their own specific concerns of racial oppression into which white women are drawn oppositionally, while lesbian feminists have distanced themselves equally from heterosexual theorizing about female sexuality and identity. For our immediate purposes, here, it would seem to be the case that 'underprivileged' women dramatize the inequalities resident in political and social structures in force wholly; inequalities based on the sex division can be re-cast asymmetrically in turn among women themselves according to other biased divisions, like race and class or sexual preference.

Much of the above demonstrates a *deficit* theory of women, which sees them as 'in lack' in relation to men, but this is also partly owing to the kind of mixed-sex contexts in which the research has been conducted and the norms of competence, which they require, which favour the male. When a *difference* theory is adopted and female speech performance can be assessed on its own terms, the negative effects of the deficit perspective disappear. We have already noted how 'female' speech forms like the use of questions or tags need not signify powerlessness or weakness in sexual terms, but may also function in socially empowering and enabling ways. And it is these which operate more normatively as sex-preferred strategies in all-female contexts.

Edelsky (1981) has noted the difference that the kind of floor in force can make to the interactive quality of gendered interactions. In analysing cross-sex university committee meetings she observed that the one-party-talks-at-a-time kind of floor endorsed male interactive modes while a 'free-for-all' kind of floor, where collaboration was needed, was more conducive to female speech. Woods' (1989) however does not wholly support Edelsky's conclusions, since she found that lengthy turn-taking on the part of the men was operative even in the F2 type of collaborative floor. The basic resource of the floor itself and the floor rules that are operative may either promote female linguistic and communicative expressiveness or inhibit it in its congeniality or uncongeniality to the creativities, typicalities and spontaneities of female modes of talk.

Within the female subculture then, the floor and turn-taking are characterized differently since the goals of talk are generally at variance with those of men. Women seem to prefer and display a more collaborative and non-competitive attitude to talk which is reflected in the strategies they use. Dominating practices are generally eschewed in favour of inter-personally attentive ones. Simultaneous and overlapping speech is also much more common among women, and not seen as a threat to the floor rights of a speaker, as it is in mixed-sex conversations. Participatory, 'minimal' responses, as we have seen above, are given more freely. Topic differences, too, have been noted – women speak more often about home and family and personal matters than seems to be the case with men, who favour more impersonal topics like work or leisure pursuits. Topic development shows variation – men preferring abrupt changes of talk, while women sustain each other's topics. The use of so-called 'powerless language' features – tags, questions and the like – reveals a greater regard for the rights and feelings of others given that women among themselves are not, on the whole, plagued by dominance anxieties in interactions.

Female genres of speech, like gossip, have also been shown to have a less derogatory function as trivial and mindless tittle-tattle in which women engage. Not only is gossip not specific to women, since, in general terms, it has informational and socially cohesive functions to perform among women, it is a genre which lubricates social relations among themselves in gender-specific ways within the everyday, social contexts in which women live their lives and in which immediate topics of concern to most women, arising from their traditional responsibilities and affairs – home, husband, children, neighbours, neighbourhood, community, personal experiences, etc. – are shared and ratified on female, interactive terms (Cheshire 1982: 135–40 for discussion). Ritually, too, in certain societies women are the major players in significant social events, their contribution to community life being made invisible when male genres alone are considered. Such is the case in the function of wedding songs in the Gujarati community in Britain which help consolidate an alternative identity in an adopted land, and keep alive skills which are oral but handed down through generations through singing and songs. Such female events thus preserve older, social, symbolic and aesthetic values in the community as it adapts to the alien pressures of a Western context.

Given the different subcultures of male and female and the different interactional normativities evident within them, there is room for considerable misunderstanding as to what is in fact going on in mixed-sex interactions. Coates lists several flashpoints in mixed-sex interactions. Female paralinguistic strategies signal involvement; they look at each other, lean forward, while men lean back and avoid direct or sustained eye contact. Women prefer more equal, participatory floor and turn-taking patterns, men compete for dominance and to establish hierarchies. Women give supportive, minimal responses to ratify floor rights, while men take them to be markers of agreement. Questions have different functions and women use questions as part of interactive work; women may also use rhetorical questions which men often take as requests for information or advice (Coates 1993: 187–95). Women respect links to previous turns, men do not submit to the necessity as much and concentrate on their own goals in conversation. The effects can be seen on topic development, with women collaborating and men moving from topic to topic. Women use more self-disclosure than men, who prefer impersonality instead. Verbal aggressiveness is indulged in more by men than women. Women value listening, which men do not, when they are required to do it; and collaborative modes of simultaneous speech, especially strategies of 'shadowing' another's speech or anticipating another's words, are common among women in contrast to the competitive overlaps and interruptions more common among men.

Difference models of sex and language allow women's skills, competences, preferences and the conditions within which they function best to emerge independently and thus more positively than within the deficit model. The two are, however, complementary and interrelated, since together they reveal the range and complexity of factors that impress themselves upon and modulate any understanding of the category of the woman. Neither model provides the last word on the subject, either. If the difference model reveals female equilibriums and dexterities in their own spaces and on their own terms, the deficit model discloses the prerequisites and circumstances of their discomfiture within the wider patriarchal structures within which they live, move and have their being, and which define them on other terms. Neither supports sex or gender as a given essence, or quintessence – that is, women were not born to speak in powerless tags, though they may well have it thrust on them.

Abstract construals of gender and femininity have thus to be negotiated within specific contexts, and within what Thorne et al. (1983: 16) have called 'the social arrangements of gender', which are varied and moulded historically. In interactional terms, gender has an external, actional life, whatever the nature of its inwardness, and is projected within the constraints of the situations in which women and men find themselves. Gender materializes in situations and in performance and modulates and is modulated by the situation of utterance and its contextualized and contingent demands. The variables are multiple: place, time, setting; and for the speaker, participant role, class, status, race, age and kind of participant(s) addressed; and control of interactional resources. Social normativities, too, have to be enacted within the pressures of the interaction itself. The conceptual staticity of gender is thus dispersed into various social performances within which gender identity is contingently constructed and negotiated.

Given that the context of situation is embedded in a context of culture, cultural assumptions regarding femininity and masculinity can constrain behaviours so that the terms of the negotiation are often asymmetrical, since operational normativities in situations are, generally, androcentric and favour the male. Female norms and normativities are not assessed, as yet, as equal when different. Neither sex, however, is umbilically attached to linguistic forms in terms of power or powerlessness. Exogenous constraints or strictures are not always directly realized endogenously, although address forms, diminutives, titles, etc. may code status or sex directly. But social directives like 'Be polite' are both situationally and strategically constrained with options regarding positive or negative 'face' which, again, are not necessarily uniquely listed as such in the linguistic code. Directives like 'Be feminine' are even more mediated. Power and powerlessness also are emergent realities in interactions, the result of strategies used, with accommodations or resistances enacted as process among participants. Power is not attached to the linguistic form necessarily, but to the sphere of inter-personal relations which are constructed via language use – in the realm of who does, or can do, what to whom, where, when and how, and with what effects.

If gender quiddities dissolve and disperse into differentiated, context-constrained performances, gender relations do not, since based on power differentials, and these remain asymmetrical. In crucial areas of social life they are dominance–subordinate relations, and this skewed structure binds the sexes to each other on terms that qualitatively affect members' experience of their own sex and gender as much as the other's. If 'masculinity' is prototypically assumed to entail control, assertion, dominance, and 'femininity' to be subordinate, passive, affiliative, or predicated on some binary divide with positive and negative values attached to them, preferred strategies would seek to sustain gender predicates in the interests of gender security, given that non-conformity is a risky, sometimes taboo, option. What is more, when individual men and women are assigned to one or other group category, they are heir to whole clusters of predicates so that inequalities and the associated positive and negative values are reproduced and enacted as expressions of gender identity. In daily interactions, the use of categories is a resource which interactants rely on to 'membership' each other, as Sacks (1969–72, 1972) has shown. What is worse, in inter-group relations (Turner 1982), if a category is deemed to be salient, all the characteristics of the category may well be assigned to the person concerned. Similarly, if one categorizes oneself as 'in-group', a whole host of sub-categories or characteristics are assigned to oneself, a move best exemplified in racist relations, but applicable to gender equally. People stereotype others but self-stereotype as well, which bolsters on a daily basis the prejudices and inequalities that are often enshrined in normative categories or directives.

Discourse deliberations about gender of the kind rehearsed above do not, in the main, provide strong possibilities for suturing together sex, society and language in one long unbroken sweep. Gender does not issue forth unproblematically into language from a source like biological sex, or a psychic core. The notion of 'situated discourse' forbids the characterization of men and women as some kinds of sexed naked apes, or psychic centres, devoid of social meaning. In interactions, it is participants who enter the reckoning, and participants in roles – wives, mothers, sisters, daughters, friends, neighbours, colleagues, clients, consumers, drivers, customers, personnel, employers, employees, patients, doctors, professionals, strangers, passers by, etc. Interactional events are both speech events and social events. And the same 'person' can appropriate different roles, and use different strategies in the same role. Identity, including gender identity, is thus assembled in various ways in its performativities *in situ*.

Moreover, if the production level of expression or expressiveness is important, the perceptual and respondent level of interpretation is equally so and the two are not necessarily symmetrically aligned. Gender in performance, as gender-in-act, is simultaneously gender-interpreted, not gender in the raw, so to speak. And stereotypes and social prescriptions on femininity and masculinity do play a significant role here, but are modulated by the contingencies of context and performance in different ways. Powerlessness or power are not only superordinate categories, but are interactively and dynamically achieved; they are also emergent properties within interactions. But social regimes of power condition normativities of behaviour which influence speech strategies. Men more easily appropriate the control aspects of interaction than women, the contexts and processes of interaction often disfavour women, female communicative competences and preferences being underrated and often suppressed in mixed-sex talk. Social assumptions, norms, sanctions and ideologies regarding femininity and masculinity inevitably function as inhibitory factors on the desired equality between the sexes in the conduct of gendered speech.

Within interactional terms, gender has been seen as a project, and more broadly as conceptual device, and thus characterized in both actional and heuristic terms. The projects of gender may be ones of accommodation or resistance to patriarchal normativities, but consequences will vary. Gendered performances are thus distributed along a cline where different forms of femininity can be exercised, and it is the feminine as sociolinguistics, ethnomethodology and pragmatics in relation to its contingencies and particularities which is the focus here, not the feminine in abstract mode as philosophy or theology alone. The abstract, conceptualized, feminine as philosophy enters interactions in the heuristics adopted but the gaps between concept and action, or rule and performance, have also to be taken into account since performance disperses the abstract sufficiencies and necessities and coherences of concepts into the pressures and contingencies of situations with varying demands made on the sufficiency of a given concept itself.

From the pragmatic point of view, on which little work is in evidence, interpretations and understandings of gender are not read off the utterance, or its indicators of power or powerlessness like tags or intonation. Not only are these unreliable by themselves and need more than one dimension to be taken into account, the processes involved in interpretation are not limited to the code, as we have seen in Chapter 4. Inferential processes and the use of assumptions are crucially involved. Start-up assumptions about women and female speech and behaviour in a context of interaction may well be gendered, related as they are to given, stereotypical characteristics or relations. Neither men nor women are immune to the weight or control of cultural stereotypes. Within the effort–benefit payoffs that control inferencing in the Relevance model, the line of least resistance and minimal cost, being normative, may well favour the generation of normative – i.e. male-dominated – assumptions as well. A mode of interpretation which attempts to read against the grain requires change in assumptions and paths of inference, the refusal of the normative, so that other possibilities and insights may be brought to light as ways of reading 'women'.

GENDER AND ITS DISCONTENTS

The protracted bias of asymmetry arising from the dichotomy that defines sexual relations has been traced in various ways by feminists, and the wider issues involved have had a fair amount of attention in areas other than linguistics. The pervasive workings of sex inequalities has led feminists to enquire into the reasons why they are there at all. The concept of 'patriarchy', originally used by Weber (1947) to describe domination relations between older and younger men, has been used by feminists in different ways, but primarily as a cover term to designate all forms of dominance of the female by the male, and the organization of all affairs in the female domain by men which result in female subordination.

There is, however, little consensus among feminists debating the issues. The problem has been approached from many angles, but two major schools of thought in its relation to drama, especially as literature, may be briefly mentioned; those who base both analysis and explanation on social factors, and those who see sexuality as foundational. The social and the sexual are both involved but the debates circle around the question of priority – whether patriarchy is a by-product of overarching, exploitative, economic and social structures and relations, or whether patriarchal dominance can be traced to the male prioritizing itself and upholding male sexual dominance by multiple forms of control, including the threat of violence and violence itself, in some readings, which contaminates all other forms of social and sexual relations. The wider picture, even in this limited review, that emerges regarding the condition of 'the female', in the Western world, from female perspectives, whether empirical or theoretical, serves to interrogate some of the more comfortable universalizing claims, enforced with the help of economic power, made by the West itself in the area of 'human' relations.

Marxist and socialist feminists locate gender issues within more abstract, exploitative, capitalist relations. The areas of investigation are work and pay, and analysis of subordination draws on the different conditions that apply to women in these areas – lower pay, part-time work, women as a cheap, 'reserve army' for capitalists. Domestic work, which has rarely been regarded as work at all, has been championed while notions like 'the family wage' applicable to male workers and seen as a triumph for labour against capital has done little for women, since it reinforced their dependence and confinement in the home.

In Marxist-oriented studies such conditions were related to class conditions, unpaid domestic labour regarded as exploited labour which serviced male workers for capital, on the cheap, but these analyses were regarded as too reductionist, since gender relations were subsumed under class relations and the scope of investigations and explanations offered relied heavily on the kinds of analysis that were used to explicate class relations.

Socialist feminists, like their Marxist counterparts, award significance and importance to wider, hierarchical or exploitative relations in society, but attempt to theorize patriarchal relations as so enmeshed in social and economic relations as to be indistinguishable (Eisenstein 1979a, b; Hartmann 1979, 1981). This perspective with its dual focus has been dubbed 'dual systems' theory. Thus, capitalism itself is seen as patriarchal, and the terms 'capitalist patriarchy' or 'patriarchal capitalism' have been proposed to describe their mutuality. Hierarchical, exploitative, capitalist relations interweave and support the maintenance of sexual hierarchies in the home and at work, since they are mutually supportive, and in Hartmann's work, historically, too. Since sexual hierarchies are upheld by sexual divisions of labour, the entry of women into the marketplace offers possibilities of transformation of such relations. Social relations between the sexes have a material base, to which conflicts between men and women can be assigned. Hartmann also points out that organized labour in the form of trade unions has contributed to the subordination of women in the upholding of pay differentials and job segregation.

Sylvia Walby, in her *Theorizing Patriarchy*, undertakes a more comprehensive approach and has identified six major 'sites' and their structures and practices which are interrelated, but modular, with relative degrees of autonomy for each. To quote Walby,

> Patriarchy needs to be conceptualized at different levels of abstraction. At the most abstract level it exists as a system of social relations. In contemporary Britain this is present in articulation with capitalism, and with racism. However, I do not wish to imply that it is homologous in internal structure with capitalism. At a less abstract level patriarchy is composed of six structures: the patriarchal mode of production, patriarchal relations in paid work, patriarchal relations in the state, male violence, patriarchal relations in sexuality, and patriarchal relations in cultural institutions. More concretely, in relation to each of the structures, it is possible to identify sets of patriarchal practices which are less deeply sedimented. Structures are emergent properties of practices. Any specific empirical instance will embody the effects, not only of patriarchal structures, but also of capitalism and racism.

(1992: 20)

Walby's approach has been criticized by Marianne Hester (1992) as not attending sufficiently to the pervasive role of sexuality. Hester herself speaks forcefully from the Revolutionary Feminist perspective in which eroticized forms of male sexual control, not exempting violent control, are seen to invade all aspects of female lives. And even if this were true, dominance may still take different and more mediated forms and function in different ways within the complexities of social organizations. Power and domination can often be effective in guises that are least like themselves, overt force and violence not being their only instruments; covert modes do the job equally well.

Walby's six 'sites' and structures as deep structures are the following:

- Patriarchal production relations in the home where cohabitees can exploit female labour, women being seen as the producing class here and men the expropriating one.
- Patriarchal relations within paid work where practices of segregation of women in low-paid or part-time work or exclusion from prestige and well-paid work are prevalent.
- The state being both capitalist and racist upholds male (and white) interests in its policies and practices.
- Male violence, seen as a systematic structure, in male–female relations, collusion with which is not unknown by the state, since the state intervenes minimally in practices like wife-battering, rape, sexual harassment and the like.
- Heterosexual relations as compulsory and its double standards.
- Patriarchal cultural institutions, including religion, education which objectify and promote and circulate definitions of female subjectivity as objects of male interests or desires.

One may quarrel with these divisions, but Walby has also stressed that they are interrelated. At work, which is perhaps the seemingly most neutral, apart from 'the state', which is also more abstract, women are embroiled in different forms of patriarchal exploitation, but from the socialist viewpoint, in capital–labour relations, as well. To take one example, women have been used as cheap labour in instances of 'de-skilling' when monopoly capitalists attempt to channel power away from skilled workers, and for profit for themselves, by introducing lower-paid labour into jobs which have been downgraded (Braverman 1974). And the cheap labour is often women, though black men have been employed in the same fashion, especially on night shifts owing to legislation which restricted women on such shifts. This is the case in industries like textiles which have lost their profitability on account of competition from lower-wage Third World countries, so that wages in the industry are very low.

Women's wages are on the whole (in 1986) 74 per cent of men's hourly rates and 66 per cent of the weekly rate (owing to overtime).

In corporations (Kanter 1977), the management ethic is very gender-prejudicial, very male and oriented to other men. Management jobs are defined as requiring male skills; male culture has its own networks and social contacts that include other men but not women, and males sponsor and groom males for promotion. Women's skills are unrecognized, which is a common factor in both salaried and waged work. Women have few resources in such conditions, since there is psychological debilitation, and fewer women models to emulate or show alternative ways. Walby observes that neither capitalism nor patriarchy stands still, and that patriarchal strategies used at the workplace include those of exclusion and of segregation. Overall, however, whatever changes have occurred in relation to state intervention, it is only an issue of swings and roundabouts, since patriarchy recoups in other ways the ground it has lost.

This is especially true for the other major site of patriarchal domination – the home, or the private sphere, of familial, economic, and marital relations, in relation to the public sphere of work. Since the seventeenth century, there has been an intensification of patriarchal power in the home, which decreased when, earlier this century, married women were allowed to work, and women won the right to vote. Whereas women have gained, through legislation, greater control and freedom of their own sexuality, lives and bodies – abortion laws, easier divorce laws, etc. – the flight from fatherhood and family on the part of men, as a consequence of the same laws, often leaves their wives and their mutually produced children in greater poverty, although separation can also be chosen by women; in the more crucial cases, in response to male, marital or partner, violence.

The statistics on rape, sexual child abuse by men and marital violence reveal that sexual violence as a factor in gender relations is not just eccentric or a kind of blowing of the fuse by men. The growth in pornography tells its own tale. Most rape occurs by men known to women, although the juridical bias is towards the deranged stranger-jumping-from-the-bushes type. Child abuse is standardly conducted by family members or family friends. Moreover, the state convicts a very small proportion of rapists, even among the proportion of reported cases, which is itself small. Police and, especially, court procedures are heavily biased against women who report or seek to convict the offenders. Matoesian's (1993) statistics from America offer support for this view. Additionally, his study reveals that the majority of young men who were questioned on date rape admitted that they would rape if they felt they could get away with it.

This does not mean that all men are rapists, child abusers, etc. They obviously are not, although feminists usually speak of men dominating and oppressing or violating women. But it does mean that culturally endorsed concepts of masculinity and femininity to which adult men and women subscribe are fundamentally implicated. The male fraternity in inter-sex instances of this kind are too tolerant of the terms of the 'given', since constructed by them, and they can be made liable, as a consequence, as either perpetrators or apologists. There are sins of commission but sins of omission, too. Male sexuality of this ilk, in violence-erotic relations with women, when normalized and contoured by men into masculinity, and implanted into state practices to boot, leaves something to be desired – and opposed.

State power is often gendered, since it can act primarily in the interests of men, although, as Walby points out (1992: 160), the state is not a monolith and is open to political pressure. Whatever the law says, however, it devolves on its agents to interpret and enforce the law, and slips between cup and lip are not unknown. The changes – the vote, access to education, welfare, divorce laws, abortion laws, laws against sex discrimination, equal pay, etc. – have had only marginal impact on existing states of affairs, and many of the changes were undertaken only as a consequence of female, organized activity. As a consequence of feminist protest, state intervention into practices of male violence is evident, for example the Sexual Offences Amendment Act of 1976 (*ibid.*: 147), in which a woman's sexual history was not to be admitted as evidence, and which provided anonymity for women. But the number of rape convictions remains disgracefully low, and judges treat rapists leniently. Male, ideological assumptions about rape – 'Good girls don't get raped' or 'When women say no they mean yes', 'Boys will be boys', etc. – have their sway over the proceedings. As far as women are concerned, even if power has shifted away from the private, domestic realm it has accreted in the more abstract, public one, and Hartmann (1979, 1981) and Walby note that women may well have given up their private patriarchs to fall into the arms of public ones.

Patriarchal power can be very entrenched, given its longevity, and change resisted owing to its integration with sexual identity, for the two are not unrelated. In her study of the restructuring of compositing in the print industry Cynthia Cockburn (1983; see also Hester 1992: 14–18 for discussion), within a basically economic and class analysis, also examines how patriarchal, sexual considerations become enmeshed with them.

The study focuses on a particular dispute in the printing industry in the 1970s, when computerized photocomposition was to replace the hot metal process of typesetting. The National Graphical Association, the union involved in the dispute at the time of the research, was an old craft union whose traditions bore the marks of its history. And these were very male dominated. As a skilled craft guild in the early days of printing, sons of printers themselves were given priority for apprenticeship, which actually excluded the sons of the illiterate, unskilled sections of the populace, but it completely excluded girls. Induction rituals, 'chapel' customs and rules governing union members' behaviour, etc. were similarly male and part of the working life of members from their entry as apprentices to retirement. Cockburn notes that there need be no formal banning of girls:

> The exclusion is inherent in relations between workers in the workplace and practices that were designed, maintained, and adapted over time precisely to create a close identity of interest among a fraternity of men who defined themselves as masculine, a universe away from women.
> (1983: 19)

When women were occasionally employed, as in the late nineteenth century, and later, men fought hard to remove them from the all-male preserve. Later, during the War, although women were allowed restricted jobs, it was on union conditions that they were removed when there were men to do the jobs. Women were later introduced into the trade nevertheless by employers for various self-interested reasons, with the union itself caught up in changes that affected the classification of their jobs.

Sexual relations are thus not separated from work relations. Nor are sexual considerations. The dispute in the industry was ostensibly about the effect on workers and their jobs attendant upon the 'de-manning' of the industry for capitalist profit, by the introduction of new technology; but in more ways than one. The fight for the retention of the hot metal process which was being replaced was defended not only because it kept more men in jobs than the technologized replacements, but also because the harder physical labour involved in the hot metal process was a marker of the working man's 'manliness' – of sexual identity. The kind of clerical skills required as a consequence of the change were seen as 'women's work' by the men themselves, and Cockburn contends that much of the bitterness and intensity of the dispute was owing to this other, fundamental threat.

Moreover, men had also to confront the fact that the male exclusiveness on which their solidarity was based was under attack in two important ways. Computerization meant that their own, traditional, male skills were not 'skills' after all, and women's skills were not inferior either. The rationale for a proper wage, too, was on the grounds that men are the breadwinners – they earn a 'family wage', they provide for the wife and family. Thus workmates, when they were women, and competing for dwindling jobs, become a threat, like other men – but a double threat, economic and sexual. Moreover, the male subculture was also supported by woman-objectifying talk, sexual expletives, innuendoes and narratives of sexual exploits and fantasies with the compositing room adorned with pictures of women, in 'tits and bums' mode, and with the computer itself being used to produce life-size printouts of naked women. When women researchers entered this realm, elaborate apologies were made (Cockburn 1983: 134). What is interesting, too, in all of this, is the multi-way split of the category 'woman': as wife to be supported; as workmate to be excluded; as interactant to be mollified; and as sexual object to be humiliated. Studies such as these reveal the multiple sources, sites, mechanisms and daily practices by which asymmetrical male–female relations are reproduced and upheld, and the costs to women, even under circumstances of change.

Radical and Revolutionary feminists (Hester 1992), on the other hand, have less interest in accommodations of this kind between patriarchy and other systems and focus on sexuality, male sexuality, instead, as the root cause of dominance. Radical feminists see male and female realities as different, and focus on the personal immediacies of female experiences as known by them within male-dominated society since 'the personal is political'. The emphasis is radically pro-female and founded, not on division in terms of labour, and economic power in its private/public sites, but on divisions based on sexual power.

For Revolutionary feminists, *heterosexual* relations are seen to uphold structures of male dominance through the control of female sexuality, often with violence or the threat of violence, male power dependent on eroticizing and subordinating the female to its desires and control in these instances. And so, the terms of male sexuality are under interrogation in Revolutionary feminist interrogations, as are its definitions and functions in male–female relations. Heterosexuality, as 'compulsory sexuality' (Rich 1980: 631), is seen as a political institution that extends and elaborates its control over women by defining female sexuality in the interests of the male. The consequences are contradictory. Either there is only one gender, as Wittig (1981) states, and that is female, since the male is a universal, or there is only one gender, the male, because it is universal. At any rate, the dominant–subordinate relationships that ensue are seen as founded on the need for power in sexual relationships on the part of the male, and as endemic to male sexuality, since unequal power relations as erotic relations translate into male–male homosexual relations as well (Hester 1992: Ch. 5).

Other, more theory-oriented studies diversify the terms of the social/sexual relation. Lacanian/post-Freudian feminists are also interested in issues of sexuality, but theorize them differently. Among the theoreticians the work of 'the French Feminists', as they are labelled, has been influential, although the aura of a unified stance can be misleading. Julia Kristeva, Luce Irigaray and Hélène Cixous are generally cited as the major figures, the common factors being the influence of psychoanalytic theories of 'the subject' and the psychic construction of identity derived from Jacques Lacan's re-working of Freud.

Briefly, Lacan (1966) claimed that it was with a child's entry into the 'Symbolic' order, with the acquisition of language, that the different journeys of sexual difference are undertaken. But the story actually begins much earlier, in the pre-linguistic stage, when the child in the 'Imaginary' order sees no separation between itself and the world, including the mother, and is a bundle of drives. Lacan uses the pun on '*homelette*', both little man ('*hommelette*') and the broken egg ('*omelette*') to describe the child, its identity flopping over in different directions, with no definite contours. In the 'Mirror stage', however, the child identifies with the unity of the image in the mirror, reading it as 'a self' or 'myself', and thus subjectivity is posited as an imaginary relation via the operation of the gaze, which constructs the self via the object-image. The mechanics are extended to the gaze of the 'Other' or others who confirm a solidity, albeit fictional, for the self.

In this narrative another crucial stage is the Oedipal, the passage through which is different for the two sexes. The male child under the threat of castration by the father is separated from the mother, his gendered identity thus constructed under the Law of the Father, which stands for cultural authority in its variegated modes, and symbolized by the Phallus. Lacan contends that the Phallus is not the penis, since nobody is actually supposed to own the Phallus, but there is some ambivalence here. The male child is required to identify with the Phallus. But the position offered and the identity constructed in the Symbolic order is predicated on primary loss, on interdiction against identification with the body of the mother.

For the girl, identification with the Phallus is not possible, and she is thus constructed in terms of a different mode of 'lack' and identifies with a degree of hostility with the mother. The construction of identity within the Symbolic Order is thus posited on a triangular structure and it is because of such a structure that the dyadic relation between mother and child is broken and the child can take its place in the Symbolic Order. But the loss of the primary, pre-Symbolic unity that ensues on the entry into the Symbolic is responsible for the creation of the Unconscious, with Desire constantly in search of its lost object. The subject is thus split, and Desire is diffused through all symbolically authorized forms of life.

To many, both the phallocentrism and the biologism of Lacan's theories, and the designation of women as 'in lack', have proved problematical. The issues of sexuality and difference have had to be re-read in various ways. Kristeva (1980) locates 'the female' in the pre-Symbolic domain, the 'semiotic' as she terms it, as that which exceeds Symbolic control. Femininity thus becomes the repressed underside of the masculine and its correlates, the Phallus, patriarchy, law, rationality, etc., but endowed with the capacity to disrupt the Symbolic from within. The language of poets especially of the avant-garde is identified as manifesting this basically feminine energy in literature, especially in the pulsing rhythm of sounds. To Irigaray (1977; Moi 1985: 127–49) the female is absence, the unrepresentable, within the signifying economies of the Symbolic, which read the woman as 'in lack' as 'Other', etc. only to uphold the coherence of the male, and as man's negative, reversed, mirror image. Female existence in the signifying chains of the Symbolic is to function as Man's specularized 'Other', which is, in fact, the Same. Whatever the feminine might be 'outside' this arrangement is repressed and unknown, which Irigaray seeks to bring into existence in various ways.

Hélène Cixous, too, appropriates the pre-Symbolic but gives it 'voice' in her notion of 'écriture féminine' (or, more accurately, 'writing said to be feminine') as 'decipherable libidinal femininity' which does not restrict itself to the agonies of the binaries of male/female which generally underwrite the other theoretical positions, since sexuality is seen as 'other bisexuality'. Thus inclusiveness, openness, homogeneity, plurality, transformations are projected as the space of the Mother, as the Realm of 'the Gift' rather than 'the Proper'. Generosity, the openness to differences rather than the boundaries of difference, is theorized as the significant forces in this realm. Cixous' own writing, with its profusion of styles, attempts to give voice to the plenitude she posits as the mark of the Imaginary (Moi 1985: Ch. 6).

Critics on the whole are not convinced that biologism is not integral to the discourse. And much less attention is paid to the fact that 'the Symbolic' even metaphorized as culture at large is stratified on levels other than sexuality. There are only two forms of socialization – one for women, another for men, both homogeneous and unitary categories in 'the Symbolic' and 'language'. The passage through the Oedipal offers one explanation for the initiation of gender difference, but it is debatable whether this could be sustained in one long, unchanging line of separation from its initiation, henceforth, based on biology as it is, or whether this scenario is appropriate to all cultures equally. The emphasis on sexuality in this holistic, uncontextualized fashion generally tends to undermine the importance of other factors. For instance, sexuality may not be implanted into the social in uniform fashion for all women regardless of contexts, or the kinds of limits differentially imposed on them in a stratified social order. This last hierarchizes women in relation to each other as well, according to other asymmetries – race, class, age, etc. Nor is the role of language within 'the Symbolic' clear, since a kind of strong Whorfianism seems to ghost the discourse. What happens to bilinguals or multilinguals? Or to minority languages and their subcultures in society? Are female speakers of immigrant languages and heir to other cultures within another 'Symbolic' and subjectivity? And if so, are they even more 'in lack', sexually, than their patrial counterparts, given that minority languages and cultures are socially underprivileged, power-wise, with respect to the dominant? And from whose perspective?

Women and men, and their offspring, are also distributed 'vertically' so to speak, so that sexed identities are simultaneously other identities, with different possibilities in 'the Symbolic' open to them, as socio-linguistic-economic-class-race-age-gender identities, which function differently in different contexts, within different identities (in action) being called for, the variables being what they are. Thus the sexual is re-traced in different ways according to class, status, race, etc., and is re-inscribed far more conflictually, and indeterminately, even for women, in 'the Symbolic'.

Entry into a given 'symbolic' via language(s) is also entry into the economic advantage or disadvantage, minority/majority, race advantage or disadvantage, status/class advantage or disadvantage, in which the sex division is enmeshed. Subsequent paths could take different forms because culture or society itself is not a monolith of uniformity. This does not mean that the sexual division can be collapsed into these other divisions any more than these separate divisions can be collapsed into each other. Issues of sexuality will be subjected to different risks and pressures given the unequal distribution of power. It also means that the sexual division has to take note of its imbrication in these other divisions, since sex-divided females in relation to males are among themselves also socially stratified, with respect to power, in socially, racially and sub-culturally differentiated ways.

And women can profit or lose in relation to other women as much as men in socially relative ways: for instance, in class-based, upstairs–downstairs societies; in racist, memsahib structures in Colonialist India; the mistress–servant relations in white apartheid societies, or in black–white relations in America, as an effect of exploiter–exploited relations. It also means that solidarity or mutual affiliation among different constituencies of women is something that cannot be taken for granted on grounds of sex alone under these circumstances, and is that which has to be undertaken, produced and earned, negotiated mutually, against the seductions and dissipating threats of other, sectional, self-interests. Thus, what is shared as sexual oppression (and much is) as a common factor on the male–female divide can also be a matter of degree, and forms of oppression can be multiple when they are brought to bear on different sorts and conditions of women, a fact that a female politics cannot afford to forget.

The post-structuralists and cultural materialists pose other problems in attempting to adapt or modify or apply the work of Derrida, Foucault or Lacan to sexual issues. The problems related to the essentializing of concepts like 'femininity' or 'woman' or 'patriarchy' are crucial in these frameworks, since the Derridean imperative enjoins that the binary constitution of concepts in relation to their opposite in negative/positive terms is bound to fail, and that 'displacement' and 'différence' forever elide the closure of meaning, including the category of 'the female'. Foucault (1978), too, locates sexuality not in ontologies but within practices and regimes of power that organize sex in binary fashion, so that gender becomes an effect of such practices and not the cause, as it is usually reckoned to be in accounts of sexuality. But the challenge to foundationalism has also been seen as destabilizing the very categories that are needed and have been relied on to get feminist projects as political projects off the ground. Deconstructionists, and post-modernists of whatever orientation, as anti-foundationalists refuse notions of origins, unitariness of concepts, including the 'feminine' or 'woman', 'subject', etc. and the priorities that binaries inevitably generate, but have had to grapple with the problem of reversals and the impossibility of escape from priorities, or to defend both theory and practice against charges of triviality, or determinism, if a political programme is to be forged at all (Butler 1990a; Hekman 1990; Weed 1989). There is also the problem of contradiction and regress which such discourses can generate. Theories, arguments and discourses that purport to deny foundations are still, paradoxically, founded on the foundational axiom or premise that 'there are no foundations'.

And finally, Third World and 'black' feminists project their own points of departure, circumscribing any incipient hegemonic tendencies or dispositions to universalism that may lurk in white, Western feminist theories, of the kind detailed above. In the event some of the limitations are also opened up for scrutiny. In Mohanty's (1991a, b) critique, the binary divisions, male/female, dominated/subordinate, on which Western feminists theorize their positions are seen to lead to a uniformity and totality and homogeneity about women that is inadequate to the different sorts and conditions of women's lives which are heterogeneous. The constituency of 'women' becomes an 'already constituted, coherent group with identical interests and desires, regardless of class, ethnic or racial location, or contradictions', which implies 'a notion of gender or sexual difference or even patriarchy which can be applied universally and cross-culturally'. The reduction of all female experiences, cognition, interests and forms of life to the category of the 'oppressed', without respect to the specificities of their construction in different societies or to the specific conditions of oppression, necessarily erases the different meanings and dynamics of the term and the different relations that produce it.

The methodology that sustains this viewpoint is also criticized since analysis is directed at finding as many examples as possible to support the original premise. Whichever framework is used – sociological, legal, religious, economic, etc. – the original, binary division is mapped on to the descriptive material which then functions as explanation. A confusion thus results between the explanatory level and the descriptive level of the analysis. An 'elision' is also evident between the discursively produced 'woman' as a unified category, and the 'women' who are the subjects of their own materially produced histories, with the former standing in for the latter.

The category of 'third world women', constructed in contra-distinction to 'first world women', is subjected along similar lines 'to multiple distortions'. The category globalizes the different nationalities, different histories, and different kinds of resistance to colonialism, different religions and cultural practices and values into the category of the 'oppressed' in relation to men and patriarchy, while specificities are completely erased. Religion, which has a very different function in different Third World contexts, is given no attention outside its role as an instrument of patriarchy. Islam, for instance, is reduced to a single, patriarchal ideology, buttressed by male, Muslim power which 'Muslim women' internalize, which ensures the stability of the system (Mohanty 1991b: 62–3). The fact that 'Muslim women' are distributed across many countries and continents and that the term 'Muslim' itself has Arab, non-Arab, African, Asian, European, etc. contexts, with their own internal configurations, oppositions, social practices, differential regulations, etc. is eradicated.

Practices like the wearing of the veil lose their historical, national and

changing functions and become symptomatic, unilaterally, of male patriarchal oppression in uniform terms. Iranian women who never wore the
veil before the revolution assumed the veil as a sign of solidarity but then
had to wear it compulsorily. The changing relations and cultural meanings
and values associated with wearing the veil even in one national context
cannot be captured in the Western feminist terms of analysis. As for
religion, so also other aspects like the sexual division of labour, reproduction, family, patriarchy, marriage, etc. The values various practices and
relations acquire in context, national and cultural, become invisible.

White, Western female self-presentations become the norms that define 'third world women' in their writings. The 'oppressed' woman
category when applied to 'third world women' makes Western feminists
the true 'subjects' of female counter-history. Other women become 'objects' of various forms of victimization in their own cultures. Institutional,
family and other structures are assessed according to Western standards.
The 'third world difference', grounded as it is on the uneven power and
economic advantage that constructs the relationship between the two
'worlds', is conceptualized in terms of 'development', which includes all
phenomena – culture, religion, values, family, etc., as much as economics
– without respect to the fact that the Western may be only one mode of
development and that other societies have other histories of development,
which the pre-supposed Western line of development, as 'DEVELOP-
MENT', again tends to negate. The 'third world' is thus denied its own
history on its own terms, even though time never stands still in the Third
World either. Third World women are interpreted in this structure of
argument in colonial fashion. Thus,

> . . . third world women as a group or category are automatically and
> necessarily defined as religious (read 'not progressive'), family-
> oriented (read 'traditional'), legal minors (read 'they are still not
> conscious of their rights'), illiterate (read 'ignorant'), domestic (read
> 'backward'), and sometimes revolutionary (read 'their-country-is-in-
> a-state-of-war; they-must-fight!'). This is how the 'third world
> difference' is produced.
>
> (Mohanty 1991b: 72)

Universalized images bereft of history or culture are produced and
circulated in Western feminist discourses, of 'the veiled woman, the
powerful mother, the chaste virgin, the obedient wife, etc.' (*ibid*.: 73), via
which codings the First World–Third World differences are maintained.
Western feminist discourse and its terms, when it functions as a 'master-
discourse' about 'women', is seen as highly detrimental to others. Lesbian

and black feminists, too, have attempted to circumscribe and delimit the scope of these theories and the terms of their construction of women. For non-white constituencies of women, even in the West, they are seen as oppressive, since being spoken for in this way deprives them of agency and articulation in their own concerns.

Priorities, too, vary, as Angela Gilliam (1991), an African-American, has stated. On global and international terms, the issue of 'oppression' as it plays itself out in many 'third world' societies when invested in 'men' allows the 'elitist' Western women who are often the spokespersons and agents for first world policies to escape responsibility for the long reach of Western capitalism and its effects in which they are implicated. The issue of sexuality, too, cannot be seen independently of the social and political since embroiled in wider forces – including access to the world's resources, goods and services – which affect 'women' differently.

Differences can be considerable and dependent on whether 'women' are inscribed within the majority, class and race-wise, or whether they are minorities in the West; or whether they are in non-Western contexts with access scaled variously. The major split in Western feminist thinking between those who prioritize issues of sexual identity and sexuality, and those who focus on economic conditions and politics, cannot hold for those who are not in the privileged Western, white, middle-class position. The issue posed, as one of choice as to whether women's struggle is about 'increasing their access to and control over the world's resources' or 'access to and control over orgasms' (*ibid*.: 217), is a false one. The wider notion of 'women's struggle' includes 'women's identity' and 'sexuality' but not as independent terms, since such a focus can be productive of narcissism and undermine what should be plural, collective and shared concerns across the differentiated conditions of women's lives. The poor and working-class women in America, according to Gilliam, 'identify survival issues to be food, housing, health care, and employment, not sexuality' (*ibid*.: 218).

Issues of identity cannot be collapsed into sexuality alone, or to the consciousness of monolingual, monocultural females. The 'mestiza consciousness' (Anzaldua 1987) of cross-culturally located women, as heir to different cultural and historical memories, is 'a borderland consciousness', of necessity, a multiple consciousness that has to grapple with and often attempts to negotiate and integrate opposing values, knowledges and frames of reference, rather than locate itself in oppositional fashion on a simple binary of the white/male:female kind. And depending on the specificity of the borderland – American/Mexican in Anzaldua's case – the negotiation of the meanings of 'racism, colonialism, sexualities and class' will vary. The attempt to 'heal the split' of borderland consciousness also involves

> a recentring of these knowledges – from the ability to see ambiguities and contradictions clearly, and to act with moral conviction. Consciousness is thus both singular and plural, located in a theorization of being 'on the border'. . . Thus, unlike a Western, post-modernist notion of agency and consciousness which often announces the splintering of the subject, and privileges multiplicity in the abstract, this is a notion of agency born of history and geography. It is the theorization of the materiality and the politics of the everyday struggles of the Chicanas.
>
> (Anzaldua 1987, quoted by Mohanty 1991a: 36–7)

The different concerns and issues, some conflictual, some complementary, which have been rehearsed above should not be seen as the onset of the death of feminism. To be sure, especially in literary studies, contentious voices are often raised. Conflicting claims and counter-claims – as to the value of theory, or whose position is 'essentialist' or not, whether 'theory' is male and should have no place in feminism, and the like – are heard over and over again. The issues are serious and difficult ones and many more 'conversations' may have to be undertaken before productive relations among these various positions can be forged. No theory or position or analysis, by itself, is adequate to all the issues generated, a contingency that is true of many disciplines and explorations. The will to power in contemporary literary-critical theories can sometimes inhibit attention to the fact that theories usually delimit the phenomenon to be investigated, and that the modes of explanation offered are not necessarily adequate to all of the data, and in relation to all issues, for all time. Issues of what theories are supposed to do are never actually debated or adequately confronted in the field. But plurality is not necessarily a problem since such a variety of issues could only be articulated by women and for women within the space that feminism has claimed as its own.

GENDER AND DRAMATIC DISCOURSE

Feminist concerns relating to the production of 'woman' as a cultural sign have also been explored in those areas where representations of female sexuality and images of women are constructed, commercialized and circulated – in the 'high' arts like literature and drama, in high prestige educational spheres or in popular domains as in romantic fiction, advertisements, film, television, and the like. From the point of view of this study, gender in drama is gender as it is actively and interactionally produced *in situ*. Gender identity is constructed from the inferences derived from a character's linguistic, situational, pragmatic, paralinguistic and other cues which function as cultural cues as well as within the constraints of face-to-face interaction. Behaviours can vary as situations unfold through the course of a play. Situations project, but are also produced by behaviours within them. The reality effects they generate are multiply constrained by various discourse parameters and inferential procedures.

In both the deficit and difference models of gender it was clear that variables of context like the sex composition of the interactants – mixed-sex or single sex – and spatio-temporal setting, institutional (public) or non-institutional (private, domestic) can make a difference as to how gendered interactions can be conducted and understood. 'Roles' – both discourse roles of speaker–hearer, and social roles of the interactants – also exert their influence since they may instantiate differentials of power. Interactive styles vary: women use sites of interaction, especially inter-personal ones, to realize mutual accommodation, and reciprocal empowerment through speech rather than dominance. Speech repertoires are thus mobilized differently and for different ends in interaction. Sex-preferred strategies are evident, but sex-preferred modes of talk can become sex-imposed in mixed-sex talk, owing to the costs to gender and cultural security that society can extract. Where gender dues are paid in these terms, suppression and negative assessments of women's speech as 'powerless' may also follow.

Within Hymes' mnemonic of SPEAKING (see pp. 17–18), therefore, gendered differences are apparent. The spatio-temporal context can be gendered, but participant roles allied to social power will mitigate notions of blanket disadvantage. Gendered identities are also simultaneously, socially and racially stratified, and women characters are encountered in different roles – sister, wife, friend, lover, servant, lady-of-the-house, mother, colleague, stranger, neighbour, professional, colleague, client, traveller, etc. – and roles may change with different interactants. Impediments exist on gendered terms for the realization of goals, since control of interactive resources is usually appropriated by men. 'Keys' vary, with women prototypically enlisted at the 'emotional' rather than the 'rational' or executive grades of the spectrum; instrumentalities vary, too, given that alternatives to speech – ritualized songs, chants, etc. – are mobilized by women, and speech genres like gossip or personal narratives can be gendered, too, given that they can be typically associated with one or other sex. Speech norms as universals in a culture, in mixed-sex contexts, generally favour the male.

The context of culture, too, provides its more general directives about sexuality and femininity which inevitably influence issues of gender behaviour, power, and security in both self, and other-assessments of femininity and masculinity in interactions. Racial and cultural readings of the two terms and their relations also vary. Even if different discourses of the self and subjectivity are available which posit the notion itself to be a divided or diversified one, the self, as a subject of social liability, has also to be considered, which enforces responsibility for the actions and words of an (adult) subject – no matter how divided theoretically – as his or her own. Yet liability devolves differently on the male and female on sexual and behavioural matters, but the power differential can devolve unequally along other axes like race, and colour and class, which do not always map on to the sex division in neat or equivalent fashion.

Interpretation is dependent on cultural assumptions about female behaviour, in general. But gender construction is also dependent on the particular inferences generated and the assessments made about particular female behaviours within the situations in which the dramatic figures are absorbed. No figure arrives on-stage or on the page devoid of initial, assumption-inducing cues. These may be bare or full depending on the descriptions given via names, type, or role in the list of dramatis personae on the page, or their sexed and clothed, unclothed, costumed, or cross-dressed appearance on-stage. Assumptions are set up which may be flouted or furthered in whatever follows.

Dramatic representations, like representations overall, are produced, are synthetic, but have to be authenticated, by others, often within the constraints of a culture's ideological overdeterminations. It is very easy to confuse the representation and its reality or referent, and treat them as the same. In representation as realism the deputizing act can be conflated with the act of reflecting a given real world, and representations in literature can be mistaken for the 'truth' about women as lived in the 'real' world. And the issue of representation is also linked to notions of discursive formations, ideology, etc. where it is difficult to accept simple relations of correspondence and transparence. And, as Turner (see pp. 7–8) noted, they have metasocial functions to perform.

Representation, however, is built on a relation between something and something else. The linkages are actually very numerous as the variety of lexical resources in the (English) language, its vocabulary for representations, makes clear. Thus, representative relations can be authority-backed deputizing or proxy relations, typifying relations, incarnatory relations, impersonatory or personifying relations, illustrative, symbolic and likeness relations, etc., and encompass objects as different as maps, blueprints, mugshots, photographs, silhouettes, fingerprints, mimicry, role-players, insignias, crowns, scarecrows, popes and parliamentarians as enlisted in any standard thesaurus. The relations manifested by 'misrepresentation' are equally enlightening – falsehood, exaggeration, dissimilarity, distortion, injustice, parody, botch, etc. – so that acts of 'representation' would appear to bring with them an offer of 'good faith' with respect to the justice, balance, proportion or truth of their presentations of the 'other' to which they are conceptually linked. But the 'offer' is no guarantee.

Female dramatic figures are constructions which are assembled via strategic linguistic use, and their representational modes of construction are open to scrutiny. They are ever assembled out of the contingencies of their performances *in situ*. The abstract constitution of gender in discourses may enact themselves in multiple ways since there is no one-to-one correspondence between speech and sexuality or speech and power, or even the biological female and some concept of 'the female', since concepts regarding the female, like identity and person, are multiple. Gender cannot be read off one dimension of analysis, either. And there may well be tensions among the different dimensions along which gender may be constructed.

Moreover, binary modes of conceptualization and the signifier/signified relation are not held to with the same force in linguistic investigations as in literary theories, since the Saussurean and structuralist paradigm has given way to post-Chomskyan ones. Prototype theories, schema theories and relevance theory, not to mention the different frameworks examined in this book, do not privilege the code in the way, or to the extent, that structuralist and post-structuralist theories generally do. The latter would appear still to be within the same structuralist problematic, even when in opposition to it. The start-up assumptions in any context of interpretation are those that are accessed within that context. But the possible range of assumptions about any particular event, activity or behaviour can be enormous and even contradictory. Assumptions can be derived from the immediate situation or from memory, but are open to ideological and cultural influences. The path of inference is not a given, either. Meaning and interpretation are far more contingent and constructed matters than is the business of mapping analytical categories or attributes as produced in some theoretical discourse on to biological females. The net effect has been to deprive the concept of 'the female' (even as a universal) of agency of any kind in her own affairs, and close all possibilities of resistance to a given order, or of change (Butler 1990a). The status of the biological female in interaction is that of a gendered participant; via relevance theory she would figure as an ostensive or manifest subject in her self-presentations. 'Femininity', 'sexuality' and other aspects of 'gender' could be accessed via the visual and acoustic channels in face-to-face interaction as much as the linguistic one. The rest is the work of assumptions and inferences on aspects of the subject's self-presentation, within the context of interaction, and constructed by respondents or observers, and conducted within the risks of communication and understanding.

The relationship between the social constitution of things and the linguistic is not one-to-one either in every instance. Language has its own processes and modes of existence. So do social systems. Ideologies of male and female, and the asymmetries of power as lived relations between the sexes in a society, are constantly produced and reproduced in contexts in different ways, as forms of action. In his study of rape trials, Matoesian (1993) analyses the ways in which patriarchal power as the patriarchal and social enters the institutional context of the trial and invades the contingencies of talk. Neither talk nor context in the courtroom is initially gendered, but made so when women are embroiled in the courtroom setting and its activities and transactions.

The structure of turns of talk – the turn-taking system – in courtrooms is pre-given and turns are pre-allocated to participants, thus distributing the opportunities for talk asymmetrically. The arrangement itself signals the pre-existing, differential rights that structure courtroom talk, and reproduces the systematic asymmetries of power as organized in society. Discourse options, and hence, the power to direct the trajectory of talk, is in the hands of the defense attorney (DA). The use of selective categorizations to give substantive content to what is happening – referential devices, interrogation devices, etc. – is unevenly distributed. Often, in rape trials, these are drawn upon to silence alternative readings of the rape act especially from the female victim's point of view. The DA regularly uses the protocols of the proceedings to promote one view, usually male, of the event in question.

Various strategies are mobilized. Greater and greater warrantability is demanded from the victim with respect to anything she says about the rape; conducive questions limit her answers to 'Yes' or 'No'. Devices like the 'poetic' or rhetorical structuring of a series of questions with the 'punch-line' at the end are used to lead the woman into undermining her own version of events gradually and surely. Resistance on her part, in the form of repairs or elaborations of talk, are quickly quashed since the control of the course of the interaction is in the DA's power.

Above all, the inferential techniques used, and the *cultural-inferential* logic that emerges in the questioning, are designed to produce the conclusion of guilt on the part of the female victim and these strongly evoke normative, male assumptions of how women *should* behave, and this last is wholly patriarchal. Thus, questions about how the victim met the man, whether the woman knew his last name or not, how and why she got into the car, and wasn't she having a good time with him previously, and the like, are directed at instilling the kind of assumptions into the proceedings that would classify her as asking for or inviting the rape, which is also in the process of being re-categorized, re-referenced, as 'normal, sexual intercourse'.

The power-ridden structure and practices of the courtroom are thus used to normalize male violence by managing the interaction in such a way so as to produce conclusions that the victim was responsible for her injuries and also, given the context, to decriminalize the act of rape by simultaneously categorizing it as a 'normal' act. The battle is for meaning, to make one categorization and referencing of events rather than another to prevail. The cohesive nature of the talk devices used, the control of talk, and the direction in which it is propelled within the sub-sections of the courtroom event *produce* the meaning structures with which to interpret the content (as to what it all 'means' or signifies) and these are radically slanted away from the female and her version and meaning of events. The substantive content given to what is said in the events of the trial via the structures of talk are actually invaded and infused with male power, male assumptions, male justifications, although never once mentioned or *named* as such.

Matoesian, like Walby, favours a 'modular' description of social structure in which structure is seen not as a homogeneous or uniform 'whole' but as composed of different sub-systems with their own distinctive set of practices and qualities, but capable of interacting with other sub-modules. The specific processes and problems generated by the modular programme as initiated by Fodor in *The Modularity of Mind* are still under investigation and the translation of Fodor's insights to social modules needs greater investigation and explanation. Assuming, for the moment, the value of the notion of modularity as an explanatory resource in cultural affairs, domination does not have a single source or a single set of practices and the practices or properties of sub-modules can interrelate. The practices of domination for race and class could well differ in some respects from those of sex. And the practices of the module of race – unlike class, its schemas and its assumptions – are yet to be fully exposed in Western contexts as they work in public and private contexts.

The courtroom is embedded within the module of the law, and has its own distinct procedures and discourse practices which are independent of sexuality, but as a patriarchal sub-module the legal processes and discourse practices interact with modules like violence and sexuality and draw on patriarchal ideologies. Not only are rigid disciplinary practices inflicted on courtroom participants, the epistemologies and ontologies that are *produced, in situ*, as a consequence of *discourse* practices in this context are installed as the truth and nothing but the truth of the case.

What the above discussion makes clear is that the constitution of gender can change with changing contexts since the kind of practices and forms of behaviour and the liabilities that are extracted from women are not uniform from situation to situation on the grounds of biological sex alone or in relation to some abstract concept of the female or even in relation to a given 'place' in a pre-given social structure. Neither structures, nor concepts, nor pre-given places in pre-existing structures do anything, as Matoesian observes. It is members of a society who do (*ibid.*: 197). The 'image' of social structure that takes its rise from Durkheim's 'social facts' in which social agents are pre-located structurally and placed in relational systems, is reductionist, in Matoesian's view, since social structure is made to precede action chronologically and independently influences it, so that 'action is treated as epiphenomenal, as a residual concept, which to varying degrees is dissolved into structure' (*ibid.*).

Instead, a two-way traffic, 'a mutuality and simultaneous elaboration' between structure and practices, structure and action is proposed, in line with recent thinking in discourse studies, so that structure itself becomes actional, structural-social relations being made to happen and interpreted and put into place and constantly reproduced in everyday practices and everyday contexts by those participating. The production and reproduction of social relations are those produced by members for each other and with each other as processes in time and open to interpretation via the *performance* of knowledge as 'practical consciousness' rather than as abstract, analytic concept or determination alone.

As far as gender is concerned, the interest lies in how 'women' are made to happen, so to speak, how specific forms of gender are brought into being, within their situated, interactional performances, and in relation to the modes of 'authentication' that are drawn upon in interpretation, the strategies of power, and the 'normalizing' and normativizing closures and categories that are used to make them happen in specific ways. Precisely because there is no one-to-one relation between the representation and the reality to which it purports to refer, activity frames, assumptions and inferences are needed to make such representations into 'realities', since synthetically produced. From the pragmatic point of view, meaning and interpretation are built on assumptions and built up with respect to them as well. They are not coded into the 'utterance' or ostensive stimuli, necessarily, nor exhausted by them. It is possible, therefore, to read in line 'with' a normative grain, and to take normative inferences on board in constructing meanings and interpretations, or to read 'against' such a grain by changing assumptions and paths of inference accordingly, or by mixing the two. There are options, but the social and ideological and patriarchal assumptions drawn upon play their crucial role in constructing 'the female' in question.

The different frameworks that have been analysed in previous sections are relevant to the analysis of gender in interactive discourse. Two specific and contrasting instances will be examined, both from Shakespeare, as exemplary economically, politically and culturally powerful Western productions. As an example of a 'passive' or 'powerless' type, Ophelia in *Hamlet* could be regarded as a suitable candidate and the strategies that construct her as such can be analysed. Goneril in *King Lear* is taken as exemplifying gender in 'powerful' mode.

The contexts of situation in which Ophelia is inscribed are mostly family ones, before her madness, and placed in the home, or with her family in a public place like the palace for the performance of the play within the play. The 'places' of speech are all interiors. In Elizabethan times, drawing on the family 'module' from social structure, and the associated 'schema' or sets of knowledge or assumptions about 'the family', would invoke, too, the asymmetries built into patriarchal family relations on grounds of gender, and with respect to age and marital status which discourse resources used seek to materialize. The roles Ophelia has to perform, in reciprocal fashion to the men, who are her major interactants, are those of sister to Laertes, daughter to Polonius, possible bride-to-be to Hamlet. To the King and Queen she has no particular status in her own right; only as she is defined by the men in her family or via her association with Hamlet. All her social roles are highly male-subordinated ones, which are intensified by her youth and unmarried status.

Ophelia's first appearance (1.3) is in a family role, as sister, within her own home, to her brother Laertes, prior to his departure to renew his studies. Interactive strategies used construct the brother–sister roles, which are enacted via speech. Given the asymmetry in the roles, the interactive styles are typical, gender-imposed ones, as described in gender studies. Laertes uses 'male' strategies, takes the lead, initiates and controls topics, gives unsolicited advice in imperative mode, hogs the floor by taking long turns and pays no reciprocal attention to what his sister has to say. Ophelia, for her part, generally behaves as the exemplary 'female' respondent, especially in having to bear the burden of facilitative listenership. She uses short turns by contrast to her brother's long ones and provides no challenge for the floor. Only at the end of the interaction does she counter-advise Laertes to practise in his own life what he has preached to her in a longer turn than she has used hitherto, but mitigates it first with a promise to take his advice to heart and follow it to the letter, in other-orientated fashion. At other times she uses questions as indirect strategy to make her own assertions, as a form of resistance, but she gets no hearing.

The interlocking of these basic strategies as turns unfold across the interaction shows Ophelia's subordinate status to be not a 'pure' and direct reflection of given gender identity, or as unilaterally or uniformly constructed as a cultural expression of sex, but as actively produced – inter-produced – within the terms of the interaction. Ophelia's playing of her role as sister is often also resistant and oppositional to Laertes, but her interactional rights are overridden. Thus, her 'silencing' and subordination are not in the fact that she cannot speak or control language, but that she is not listened to or given *interactional* equality. Her intentionalities in the use of speech are ignored or evaded by Laertes with impunity.

Laertes' topics are not related to his own life but to hers, and her sexuality, in particular. He is the 'expert' speaker on the ways of men and categorizes her relationship with Hamlet in male terms, asserting the 'truth' of Hamlet's designs on herself, which are to trifle with her affections, for his own temporary amusement. Ophelia's response to this mode of referencing her affairs is a question – 'No more but so?' – not an assent form, or a token of reassurance or even facilitative. In fact, of her three responses in this episode, two are questions, neither of them requests for information. In the first instance, her reply to Laertes' injunction that she keep in touch is an other-supportive 'Do you doubt that?', as an indirect assertion of certainty – 'How can you doubt it/Don't doubt it'. The indirect 'No more but so?' is of a different order, since the implicatures generated are of *dissent* with Laertes' point of view, and invested with an illocutionary attitude, in Bach and Harnish mode, of disbelief on her part – interpreted as 'Is that all you think?' or 'Do you really think that is all there is to it?' which may even be ironic. Laertes provides no 'uptake' of her implicatures: he merely re-asserts his own position – 'Think it no more' – and her dissenting point of view has no interactive life and is submerged into silence.

Laertes' next turn is a very long one, with hosts of directives to her about what she should believe, what Hamlet is 'really' up to, what she must fear – in short, the loss of her chastity. The burden of listening is extracted from Ophelia without preamble, apology or mitigation. And

Ophelia responds as a co-operative listener, and other-orientates again –
'I shall the effect of this good lesson keep/As watchman to my heart ...'
But once she takes the floor she holds it and ends her turn with a spirited
counter-lesson, a counter-directive in imperative form ('Do not. . . '), her
speech style moving into more directly assertive mode, in complex
syntactic form to match his own, and draws on worldly and poetic similes
and metaphors, judicious alliteration, and lexical and semantic contrasts,
to make her point.

> But, good my brother,
> Do not, as some ungracious pastors do,
> Show me the steep and thorny way to heaven,
> Whiles, like a puff'd and reckless libertine,
> Himself the primrose path of dalliance treads
> And recks not his own rede.
>
> (1.3.46–51)

Laertes' response is a one-liner, for the first time, when his own
sexuality is on the line, which contrasts radically with the amount of
speech time he has spent on hers. But again he offers no more interactive
space since the point of her speech is dismissed as irrelevant to himself –
'O, fear me not!'

Other discourse resources are similarly used to diminish her in this
scene. Our first introduction to Ophelia is in a farewell sequence, the
leave-taking itself being accomplished by Laertes in the very first line of
speech – 'My necessaries are embark'd. Farewell.' The rest of the interaction, in fact, falls into the 'unfinished business' slot which sequencing
rules permit for conversational closures, which his turn enacts. The next
line of his first speech begins 'And sister. . .', which assigns her and her
affairs to the status of an after-thought. The main matter which has been
attended to off-stage is male business, to do with Laertes.

Moreover, she is placed metaphorically, and possibly literally, on the
threshold of two spaces, two worlds, the internal world of domestic duties
and the home, which is her domain, which confines her, and the external,
outside world of study, travel, new relationships, sexual freedom, work,
adventure and leisure to which Laertes and not she has access. It is only
in madness that she is free to cross over, with impunity, into the outside
world, or wander where she will, unchaperoned, in internal or external
spaces, or make bawdy jokes and raise taboo topics. In madness, too, she
interrupts Gertrude and holds long turns when she will, and carries on with
her own topics and is deaf to those initiated by others which she overrides,

in a reversal, in mirror-image fashion, of her inter-personal behaviour with Laertes.

The restricted mode of representation is reinforced by the social network possibilities which are open to her in the course of the play. No multiplexity is possible, where 'multiplexity' is defined in adapted mode as associations outside immediate, family ones. Even density possibilities are restricted. Family relations and association with the royals, on varying levels of formality, are evident, but she is cast in weak roles of sister and daughter. She has no access to them on her own terms, except in madness. No confidant nor friend of equal status is available, nor links with other females in the role of mother or sister; only a world of men who are both blind and deaf to her concerns. This contrasts, in fact, with Gertrude, who is wife, mother and Queen in a public role, and also in semi-informal roles with others as part of her 'job' as Queen or in the role of wife and mother. Gertrude has access to contexts and relations that are multiplex. Polonius seems to be more than a courtier and subject and also some kind of family intimate, who is close enough with her own family to be permitted to hide behind the arras in her bedroom to eavesdrop on her conversation with her son. Rosencrantz and Guildenstern, too, are dually cast – as Hamlet's fellow students but also spies and emissaries for Claudius and, to some extent, Gertrude. The Queen has access to the whole world of the court and affairs of the realm in a way Ophelia does not have.

Other speech events in which Ophelia is cast as interactant include those with Polonius, with Polonius and the King, and with Hamlet. The style of interaction with her father follows the course already seen with Laertes. Polonius similarly makes the topic of her sexuality and relationship with Hamlet his business and his topic. But his strategies are far more power-laden; the role of 'father' is played autocratically, and often insensitively. Whereas Laertes' appropriation of the topic of Ophelia's emotions and sexuality was characterized, even in imperative mode, by speech acts like warnings and advice, Polonius' speech style is marked by commands and interdictions, the consistent denials of her propositions, and dismissals and displays of disbelief in what she has to say. This leaves Ophelia with little option as to what course she should follow in her own emotional affairs, which are hardly hers any longer.

Polonius is highly intrusive in his interrogation of Ophelia, and more overtly dismissive of her opinions and scornful about her evaluations of Hamlet and her own affairs. The strategy he uses is to repeat what she has said and re-reference it with negative connotations. Interactive attention, when given, is thus deflected against her. Her beliefs and evaluations of

her relationship with Hamlet are subsequently never developed or taken
seriously.

> OPHELIA   He hath, my lord, of late made many tenders
> Of his affection to me.
> POLONIUS   Affection! Pooh! You speak like a green girl. . .
> Do you believe his tenders, as you call them?
>
> (1.3.99–103)

Polonius' demeaning play on 'tenders' continues into the next speech.
And later, the following transpires:

> OPHELIA   My lord, he hath importun'd me with love
> In honourable fashion.
> POLONIUS   Ay, fashion you may call it; go to, go to.
> OPHELIA   And hath given countenance to his speech, my lord,
> With almost all the holy vows of heaven.
> POLONIUS   Ay, springes to catch woodcocks!. . .
>
> (1.3.110–15)

Ophelia resists, but with delicate strategies of indirection to begin with,
and then by holding her own by turn skipping Polonius' turn and perspective on herself and Hamlet and reinforcing her own, thus contradicting
Polonius. But her turn gets no inter-personal support or hearing. Polonius
denigrates and explicitly undermines her perspective and scoffs at her
beliefs, launching into a long turn that silences her by blocking any further
access to the floor. Instead of responding to the displayed intentionalities
in her own speech, her beliefs, her propositional attitudes to her own life
and lover, Polonius, like Laertes, behaves as if she is endowed with none
of these, and evokes and exerts patriarchal power and commands explicitly that she has nothing more to do with Hamlet. The exogenous terms of
the patriarchal contract, as power of the father, is endogenously internal-
ized and realized in her explicitly named speech act, 'I shall obey, my lord'
– obedience extracted by command.

In the later scene (3.1) when she is made to act as bait to Hamlet, the
asymmetry between the men and herself is intensified. She is denied even
the normative rights of the canonical participant framework, since another
one including eavesdroppers is substituted, which forms the context of her
speech. The intentionalities of her speech are hardly her own. She scripts
the rejection of Hamlet with her own speech and finds her own interactive
strategies within the awful contingencies of talk with Hamlet at this stage,
but its goals and outcomes have already been prescribed by the patriarchal
chain of command, with herself at the coal-face, so to speak, and the

persons of the King and father in the executive position and present, if invisible, in this most personal and crucial moment of her life. The abuse from Hamlet she gets in return only overburdens the excessive weight of male power with which she has to contend, which is all that the play has made available.

She begins the scene with *herself* taking the initiative to open and conduct interaction with Hamlet, the invisible male directive and power impelling and carrying her through to doing as she is bid. Her strategies are stronger, more independent. Her ripostes to Hamlet's denials of giving her 'remembrances' are firm and felt, and she invokes 'the noble mind', usually male, of the Renaissance, as her own, to whom 'Rich gifts wax poor when givers prove unkind'. She debates the issue of the relationship between 'beauty' and 'honesty', using her former questioning strategy to assert her own opinion, but without effect.

As Hamlet's verbal violence increases with the 'nunnery' speech, his turns get longer, forcing her to be the mute recipient of his abuse. She switches key and genre, and unilaterally changes, for once, the nature and terms of the speech event itself, away from the interactive speech modes whose rules the men control and to the genre of 'prayer', in a very personal and emotionally expressive key that provides the release for her speech on her own terms. She does the same later, in madness, when songs are used. She thus feminizes the speech event and its terms for herself. She does not counter-abuse; she 'prays' in the face of yet another verbal assault on her, and her sexuality.

After the 'nunnery' speech from Hamlet and the demand as to the whereabouts of her father, her response to the violence in Hamlet is a one-liner – 'O, help him, you sweet heavens!' – while the abuse that follows is responded to with 'O heavenly powers, restore him!' Hamlet rants in between in long turns, but her speech interactant is elsewhere, in the heavens, with Hamlet and his violence sidelined, lateralized, in the use of the third person 'him' to his face. With yet another round of abuse and the command that Ophelia go to the nunnery, Hamlet exits and Ophelia, 'alone' and rid of the responsibility to carry out others' commands, breathes one of the most-quoted speeches in the play, this time from the mouth of a very abused woman.

> O, what a noble mind is here o'er-thrown!
> The courtier's, soldier's, scholar's, eye, tongue, sword;
> Th' expectancy and rose of the fair state,
> The glass of fashion and the mould of form,
> Th' observ'd of all observers – quite, quite down!

And I, of ladies most deject and wretched,
That suck'd the honey of his music vows,
Now see that noble and most sovereign reason,
Like sweet bells jangled, out of tune and harsh;
That unmatch'd form and feature of blown youth
Blasted with ecstasy. O, woe is me
T' have seen what I have seen, see what I see!

(3.1.150–61)

The topic of the turn may, at first glance, appear to focus on Hamlet, but it is herself and her own blocked emotions which are actually expressed. The description of Hamlet forms only one part of the turn, and functions as foil to her own sense of loss. The illocutionary force of the speech is that of a lament – an expressive, of felt loss – which the syntactic cues in the exclamatory forms used, which are pervasive in this speech, emphasize.

The King and Polonius re-enter after this speech and focus on Hamlet's performance, which is the topic. They continue to address each other. Nobody bothers with Ophelia, although she is present in the context of situation. She is not addressed; turn-taking controlled by the men bypasses her. Ophelia's state of mind and her emotions, visibly and audibly dramatized and enacted as co-text, have been invisible to them, the reality of her life in this situation just does not register as worth attention, concerned as they are with their own plans. After they have arranged future plans for Hamlet, her father turns to her with a jocular 'How now, Ophelia!/You need not tell us what Lord Hamlet said; /We heard it all'. No turn is permitted her after this address, since he reverts to the King as his addressee. Ophelia is thus marginalized in the new speech context, her after-thought status dramatized in her cursory embedding in a more important interaction between the men.

The silencing is total and it has been achieved by male actions; she merits no 'personhood', so she remains a non-person, the lack of mental as much as verbal attention on their part erases her, physically present though she is. The men acknowledge no speech or interactive rights on her part – about her sexuality, her opinions about her own emotional life, her 'face' needs, her wants and desires in her speech acts for herself. Their strategies cast her as someone having no internal life, no feelings worth their attention, no 'self' or identity of her own, and without rights even to emotional space or privacy, and this in a play where so many opportunities are given to the male hero to display precisely these privileges. Her interactive role is confined to services to themselves, to listening and obeying and deferring, which are imposed on her. Any other mode she attempts is not heard, is dismissed, undermined, scoffed at or subjected to threats and penalties or abuse by the men, including her erstwhile lover, Hamlet.

Ophelia's own speech strategies display some of the properties of Lakoff's female register, especially in her use of indirection, and later, in the-play-within-the-play-scene, other-oriented, mitigating or facilitative strategies, in response to Hamlet's ribald talk with her. But she mostly uses a variety of strategies. Her indirect rebukes to Hamlet, her diffusions of the possible consequences in public of the speech liberties that Hamlet takes in relation to herself, her control of her own personal and social position in this scene, reveals her as anything but passive. And she is the one who has been observant enough to notice the beginning of the King's flight from the scene. Her speech failures are actually constructed not on the production, but the *reception* dimension where the power of the men resides. And there are different degrees of power that she is cast against – brother, father, father and King, lover. Ophelia's relatively long speeches – hers are never as long as the men's to her – to Laertes, and to Polonius, in the description of the 'mad' Hamlet and his antics, and the final speech in the nunnery scene, reveal her as possessing verbal re-sources, conceptual sophistication, stylistic complexities and poetic qualities to match Hamlet's own. But they are given no context in which to find expression or to function on her own terms, except in a 'feminized' speech context, and one without the usual male interlocutors.

Sexuality becomes a central issue in a specific way because it invades the verbal interaction, from the mouths of the males, but it is actually dialogically structured. There are two points of view, Ophelia's and the males'. Moreover, sexuality is not represented as sexuality per se, but that constructed within the interaction, within sexual relations as family rela-tions and as affective relations, inter-personally. To the men, whatever their inter-personal status with her, her young, virginal sexuality is the focus of obsession, control or verbal abuse – in the mouths of father, brother and lover. The version of sexuality they articulate and read at or into her is the normative male one. Each of the men virtually accuses her of being a real or potential 'whore' on the basis of a peculiar male fallacy, which enjoins that the sexuality of a young, unmarried female being the object of predatory, male lust in the order of things, it is the woman's responsibility to safeguard it for male pleasures and purposes. Liability for virginity devolves on the woman, but not equivalently on the men. The contradiction is articulated by Ophelia, in her counter-advice to Laertes, but it does not enter the accounting, as Laertes' dismissive one-liner to

Ophelia makes clear, when she raises the issue. And, of course, the discrepancy is not lost on Ophelia, who instils it into the discourse; but it gets no hearing. And so, they lecture her rather than each other, and enact the mould of asymmetrical arrangements regarding sexuality in their world in their interactions.

To Ophelia herself, her sexuality is not at issue except within the assaults of male discourses and descriptions, for she just does not *believe* their versions of sex relations; they do not figure subjectively in her own pragmatic beliefs as 'the truth' of her relationship with Hamlet. She attempts again and again to re-reference the general, male descriptions and dynamics of sexuality, as power-ridden, predatory lust, as inadequate, and tries to re-categorize it, in terms of affective reciprocity, but she is scoffed at or ignored in return. The male point of view prevails, as 'reality', to which she is made to subscribe – 'obey' – as proper to her role and identity as daughter or sister.

In the wider context of culture, in the historical context of early modern England, the tenor of sexual relations as enacted in the play could well have evoked a cultural logic which was different to modern ones, and which would normalize the modes of dominance to which Ophelia is subjected, as appropriate to women. The 'activity frame' evoked regarding the family would be highly patriarchal, as Jankowski (1992) has argued, with even the state being imaged as a family, with the King as father to his subjects. Women's identities were constructed in relation to men, as daughters or wives, with marriage playing a central part, the control of the father being transferred after marriage to the husband. Women were not allowed legally to buy or sell property, or make wills or initiate law suits. Women's chastity was embroiled in male anxieties regarding the legitimacy of heirs and the descent of property. Discourses on virginity, marriage, chastity, etc. were often contradictory given that the period itself was a transitional one – from late medieval feudalism to early modern pre-capitalism, and from Catholicism to Protestantism.

In spite of the Protestant, Puritan emphasis on reciprocal affections and companionship in marriage, the policing of women and female behaviour took many forms, even in marriage. 'Unruly' women, as 'scolds', 'shrews', those who violated acceptable protocols, were subjected to many forms of social and public correction: shrews' bridles, cucking, carting, skimmington, for instance, which involved, respectively, the public display of the offenders wearing metal gags to restrain the tongue, being strapped in a chair to be pelted or jeered at, being paraded in a cart, or being immersed in water several times. Skimmington punished the men as well for not keeping their wives in order.

Normative assumptions regarding 'proper' female behaviour would thus be derived from cultural practices which defined and enforced them and would colour appropriately the cultural logic evoked by the interactions. The inferences generated by the manner and course of talk unify Ophelia as a type of the normative daughter and sister in her relations with her family members, thus reproducing and circulating and automatizing a highly power-inflected set of gender relations which materialize in the talk and which the interactions enact. With Hamlet, the inferences are not quite so stabilized, since Ophelia is represented as innocent of his accusations, but Hamlet's talk does draw on general male assumptions about female sexuality as threat, which are applied to Ophelia indiscriminately.

The emphasis on sexuality in this way is not based on the fact of Ophelia being a female, alone, in the abstract. Other dimensions, like the age factor and her unmarried status, are also involved, since marriage was the crucial event in the passage of control of female sexuality – virginity to chastity – from father or brother to husband, which intensify her vulnerability. The asymmetry constructed by the talk silently indexes gender relations as control relations and as 'normal' within the 'family' schema evoked, which the talk itself constructs in actional form, as activity and within the terms of the activity types it evokes as appropriate to it. Its power is thus reproduced and circulated and normalized in representation. The talk constructs sexuality and gender relations within the contingencies of the speech event contexts of the play – in the leave-taking with Laertes, in the baiting of Hamlet, etc. – with respect to dramatic matters, too, so that the sterner mode of sexual power enacted contributes to the specificities of the problematics of sexuality as thematic within the play. Father–daughter relations and lover–lover relations display the more brutal possibilities within patriarchal relations to which Ophelia has to submit. The male–female talk transactions rely heavily on the 'deficit' model imposed by the men.

At the other end of the scale, a character like Goneril in *King Lear* would be an illustration of a powerful woman in Shakespeare, and the discourse resources used change accordingly. Like Ophelia she is in the role of a daughter and sister, but Goneril is awarded other roles. She is also wife and a woman of property 'in her own right' thanks to the division of Lear's kingdom. The social networks in which she is involved are both private, density ones and public and semi-public multiplexity ones. Her interactants are varied – Lear, Regan, Albany, Cornwall, Oswald, Gloucester, Edmund, the Fool, the disguised Kent, sundry servants and functionaries. Relations with them are both symmetrical and equal, status-wise, or asymmetrical, with herself in the dominant position. Only in the first scene is she in an inferior position to Lear, but that is short-lived.

The spatial freedom she enjoys, too, far exceeds anything awarded to Ophelia. The spatial contexts of her speech events include all the major residences in the play to which she has rightful access – Lear's in the first scene (which is the exception), her own, Regan and Cornwall's castle and Gloucester's – either via status, as in Gloucester's castle, or as a consequence of family ties with Regan and, hence, on equal ground. And if these are all interiors, the men with power also inhabit them till their fortunes turn, and they are privileged interiors. The outhouse, heath, hovel and the cliffs of Dover are the spaces of the powerless. And she can travel and cross spaces independently: she arrives at Regan's castle to forestall any damage that Lear might inflict after his flight from her own home, and she returns independently. And she is present in the military setting of the English camp near Dover for the battle with Cordelia and her French forces, and its aftermath.

If the contextual components of the situation of utterance like the 'spatio-temporal context' and 'participant' in the SPEAKING framework (see pp. 18–19) favour Goneril, the other components are equally under her control. The discourse strategies she adopts in her interactions (with respect to ENDS, ACT SEQUENCE, KEY, INSTRUMENTALITIES, NORMS, GENRES) are varied, and effective on the whole, and she can adapt the rules to her own advantage and to the pursuit of her own goals. In the division of the kingdom scene, she is the dutiful and deferential daughter, bending her responsive speech to her father's commands in highly 'obedient', co-operative fashion – she gives the information requested, fully, clearly, directly, and even truthfully to all appearances. Once in power, the tenor of her interactions is varied – she can be commanding, collusive, dismissive, seductive, courteous, competitive, conniving, compliant, challenging, etc. as situations and her stakes in interactional outcomes demand.

Unlike Ophelia, she never has to change instrumentalities or genre for personal space. Her element is speech, and the given, normative resources of speech use over which she has an impressive amount of control. Turn-taking strategies are in her control, and pragmatic speech strategies can be both direct and subtle; bald, on-record strategies, as well as indirect ones, are all included in her repertoire, and mixed and matched as required, and used as instruments of power.

For instance, in the quarrel with Lear over the supposed riotous behaviour of his knights (1.4.187–349), her overall goal is to bend Lear to her own will, and she uses the claim of unacceptable behaviour of his retinue as the pretext. From the very beginning of the encounter she implants her own authority. There is no return of Lear's greeting to her, nor does she respond in like key to his jocular 'What makes that/frontlet on? You are too much of late i'th' frown'. After the Fool's pertinent observations, Goneril launches into a long turn, without any preparatory preamble given the nature of the face-threatening acts she is to perform. She takes the initiative and goes on the attack, but she manipulates rules in order to square her public performance with her private goals.

First, she initiates a complaint, a speech act with preparatory conditions that attempt to put the other at risk, as pretext, about Lear's knights who are insultingly, and without mitigation, described as 'your insolent retinue' who 'hourly carp and quarrel, breaking forth/In rank and not-to-be-endured riots'. The description itself functions as preparatory condition in speech act mode, and as pre-sequence in ethnomethodological fashion, which she uses to instal assumptions of her right to a grievance, the ostensive illocutionary attitude being desire for redress. Then another complaint which in fact transforms into an indirect accusation that Lear has not responded to an earlier complaint and controlled his knights, which spills over into the accusation that he seems to encourage them. And then a warning of the course of action she would be forced to take, which, even if in the normal course of events would seem reprehensible, 'necessity/Will call discreet proceeding' in the present circumstances. Her illocutionary acts are all powerful ones, since she appropriates rights to complain, accuse, warn, reprimand, threaten and the right to reciprocal redress. Across the speech the illocutionary forces and attitudes that can be inferred also change from a speaker-centred, weaker desire for redress to stronger, other-directed, hearer-centred acts requiring sequels of Lear, as acts of power.

Cumulatively, her message to him is that he himself is to blame for the course of action she would reluctantly have to take, if he does not conform to her will. There are disclaimers and mitigatory devices and circumlocutions in her speech, but these are designed to save her own face and publicly absolve herself from blame, rather than to protect his. She gives 'reasons', rather than 'overwhelming ones', and thus provides perfunctory evidence of politeness. But the balance between her politeness markers and the 'impolite' propositions is delicately maintained so that the ground conceded with some mitigation or indirection is negated by the tenor of the rest of the proposition which is often bald, without redress, face threat. Thus, her warning is couched in the following manner:

I had thought, by making this well known unto you,
To have found a safe redress; but now grow fearful,
By what yourself too late have spoke and done,
That you protect this course, and put it on
By your allowance. . .

(1.4.203–7)

The mitigatory 'I had thought. . . but now grow fearful', played as if the sentiments expressed are only a matter of her own belief and hopes, does not mitigate the direct accusation that follows.

Lear's turn in response is a one-liner, heavy with disbelief and sarcasm which are communicated indirectly – 'Are you our daughter?' Goneril does not bother to reply, lets the implicature pass by in silence and continues with her own goals and keeps the interaction on the path in which she has set it. She changes tack, however, and delivers seemingly face-enhancing, positive politeness tokens, but with the usual sting. She begins with positive politeness strategies, compliments, with which she also ends, but embeds directly face-threatening acts into her speech which carry her punch. Her overall directive, with indicators of indirection to him, is to come into line with her own wishes. Thus the seeming, illocutionary attitude of desire on her part for a course of action from him becomes, in fact, a necessity for him to conform.

GONERIL   I would you would make use of your good wisdom,
Whereof I know you are fraught, and put away
These dispositions which of late transport you
From what you rightly are.

(1.4.219–20)

The mitigatory 'I would you would. . . ', 'I know. . . ', 'you rightly are' contrast with the bald 'put away/These dispositions which. . . transport you'.

Lear cannot counter these tactics. Whatever he tries, in usually displaced indirect modes, like sarcasm, does not work as attempted power strategies because she gives them no space nor any possibility for interactive life on his terms. She sticks to her own pre-planned course, changing her speech strategies as necessary to keep the upper hand. Lear responds in indirect mode.

Does anyone here know me? This is not Lear.
Does Lear walk thus? speak thus? Where are his eyes?
Either his notion weakens, or his discernings

Are lethargied – Ha! waking? 'Tis not so –
Who is it that can tell me who I am?

(1.4.225–9)

The Fool interjects 'Lear's shadow' in answer, and there is a brief exchange between them which focuses on the sub-text of the power struggle, between father and daughter, in chorus fashion. Lear addresses Goneril with an ostentatious question which is no request for information.

Your name, fair gentlewoman?

Goneril's response does not rise to the bait; she ignores his implicatures and the intentionality of his utterance. Instead, she directly spells out to Lear what she expects him to understand. Her referential strategies re-designate his performance, as 'pranks' in negative mode, thus deflating any interactive advantage he may have gained. She answers no questions, she engages with no negative implicatures generated by Lear about herself. And she reiterates her original stand, and sticks to her own topic, but keeps the minimum of politeness in place, especially in the strong rebuke, and her final stark threat. Redress tokens used are thus cancelled by the bald and on-record strategies that follow. Politeness markers are used perfunctorily, but both indirection and politeness are strategic, to sustain publicly the appearance of deference to her father, but she gives Lear no choice.

This admiration, sir, is much o' th' savour
Of other your new pranks. I do beseech you
To understand my purposes aright.
As you are old and reverend, should be wise.
Here do you keep a hundred knights and squires;
Men so disorder'd, so debosh'd and bold,
That this our court, infected with their manners,
Shows like a riotous inn. Epicurism and lust
Makes it more like a tavern or a brothel
Than a grac'd palace. The shame itself doth speak
For instant remedy. Be then desir'd
By her that else will take the thing she begs
A little to disquantity your train;
And the remainders that shall still depend
To be such as men as may besort your age,
Which know themselves and you.

(1.4.236–57)

Lear calls for his horses to leave after inflicting the first of his terrible curses and he invokes supernatural powers in ritual mode with Goneril as the indirect addressee, as Ophelia had done, and changes instrumentalities, in gender terms a 'difference' model, and a powerless strategy. Unlike the compassion that Ophelia expressed, here is primitive and elemental sexual hate and violence. In his curses, Lear's verbal assaults are on her sexuality, her womb in particular, as a vicious mode of redress which remains an ineffective mark of attempted equalization, in context. As with Hamlet, verbal or actional violence is the last resort to counter female threat.

Goneril's strategies in most interactions are adept, for she maintains her own point of view and her own interests in the variety of circumstances in which she is cast. Moreover, she is also revealed as an arch-planner in her speech, instigating Oswald to discomfit Lear, or foreseeing coming events and taking measures accordingly – by briefing Regan of Lear's arrival with her own version of events, and by attempting to counteract a possible sexual alliance between Edmund, whom she desires, and Regan, whose recent widowhood she sees as an advantage over herself. Her speech strategies reveal her as analytical, practical, calculating, with a good grasp of means and ends, and capable of taking initiatives on her own behalf, and carrying a course of action through, ruthlessly, if need be; there is lucidity and stylistic complexity but little 'feminine' emotional expressiveness in her speech. Emotions she evinces are more likely to be impatience and irritation, especially with Albany, or anger. She is capable of feelings, with Edmund, but even here she is more practical than emotional. There is no eloquence in her as in Ophelia when turbulent. And she is aware of her sexual needs and can initiate and enjoy the pleasures of adultery or lust on a par with any man in her world.

Goneril's 'gendering' in the play via her speech is at odds with prototypic assumptions regarding her 'sex' and appropriate gender behaviour. Her speech resources are canonical ones which she uses with flexibility and skill. On the responsive dimension, too, nobody lectures her on her sexuality even if she is cursed by Lear. Albany's attempted reprimands are dismissed contemptuously. Nobody exhibits 'deafness' in her presence; in fact, she often delivers it herself, instead. As respondent herself, she can be dismissive and coercive of others. Both status and speech competence give her power but there is a perception problem as a consequence, which is part of a wider problem regarding women and power. She uses power and enjoys it, but the terms of power are patriarchal.

It is hard to conceptualize a society with 'female power' which does not share crucial or critical aspects of 'male' power as 'power', given the latter's long history. Given power as patriarchal, Goneril's very competence in its ways distances her from normative assumptions of 'the feminine' and gender identities as appropriate to it. The actions that result from power – the humiliation of Lear, the blinding of Gloucester – reprehensible as they are when conducted by either sex, make her peculiarly prone as a woman to the aggravated jeopardy that accrues on her unconventional gender-transgressive ways, even though her own actions are no worse than those of many male protagonists, including the male cohorts in the play, and she is far less Machiavellian than, say, Richard III, or even Edmund. The cruelty with Gloucester is at least in keeping with legalized modes of brutal torture and punishment, especially on the poor and women, as employed by the state and amply evident in Elizabethan times, like hanging, drawing and quartering, or the burning of witches and other such horrors. And Gloucester is seen as culpable, not of stealing sheep or game, but of treason by her camp.

The extra negative load that accrues on Goneril (and Regan) is due to the fact that it is *women* who initiate and carry through the more terrible acts in the play, making them 'monstrous' given their distance from standard assumptions regarding what females *should* be like. The assumptions, inferences and the cultural logic invoked are patriarchal, normative ones. Shakespeare's history plays and tragedies are, of course, not innocent of horrible acts undertaken by men, although none is actually performed on-stage, but none of these appears to offend sensibilities to the same degree as the women's actions do. And unlike Lady Macbeth, Goneril shows no consciousness of gender split in her actions. She makes no bid for sympathy from the audience, or anybody else, in terms of profound and conflicting emotions or thoughts or haunting dreams or hallucinations of spots in her eyes regarding her world, her condition or actions. Even her death is self-willed in its self-infliction. She acts on her own behalf, without apology, she directs consequences, and chooses them when they are out of her control, as at the end. Her confidence is supreme. Paradoxically, like Ophelia who claims the terms of the 'noble mind' of the Renaissance as her own, and attempts also to instil the newer terms of sex relations as equal and affective relations as hers, Goneril enacts the terms of willed, actional, individualistic, Renaissance personhood (usually appropriated by men) as her own.

In our terms, although 'placed' or 'interpellated' in gender terms within the structure and limitations of the 'deficit' model, normatively speaking, no deficit devolves on Goneril in her actions. Deficit, in fact, accrues on the men, like father and husband instead. The static structure and relevant 'positions' are overturned within the situated contingencies of context and action.

At one level of interpretation, Shakespeare's portrayal of women in power in this play is a pessimistic one, since nothing changes structurally or substantially, and this conclusion resonates with its own contemporary force in our own time whether directed at the East or the West. The power of power and its seductions remain whatever the sex of its agents, or incumbents, and power is always and only patriarchal, even in gender-reversed, mirror-image terms. Goneril in the roles of sister, daughter and wife fractures and shatters, in her actions, the containments and prescriptions of 'discourses' about women of the kind mentioned earlier, and the implanted assumptions about 'proper' female behaviour, and kicks over the traces of her 'interpellations' into normative social structures. She abandons all the dutiful female roles and imposed patterns of behaviour, of daughter, wife and sister with impunity. She fulfils no gate-keeping roles for society's pieties and moralities which are imposed one-sidedly on women; and she has no traffic with the double standards on morality and sexuality as played out on Ophelia, for instance.

In so doing, however, she enters the terms and practices of power. The intersection between discourses on femininity and those of power is problematical, as Jankowski (1992) has argued. Unlike the king as ruler who integrated 'the two bodies' of the natural body and the body politic as father of the state, there was no real place for the female body which was generally excluded in all discourses of power. The one cannot be included or mapped on to the other without tensions, so that the resulting product seems at best an anomaly, and at worst 'unnatural', to the normative gaze.

If the cultural assumptions and logics invoked generate inferences of a 'monstrous' world as a consequence, then the terms of that logic are also open to scrutiny. One metasocial inference to be read from the representation would seem to be that chaos is come again when women abandon their traditional posts and duties, their 'finer feelings', their 'powerless' interactive strategies, and the like, and propelled by new forms of female desire join the male world, on its terms because they cannot beat it, as the only available option. The 'monstrous' world that results is predicated on the fear of powerful female presences as much as its corollary, gendered absences in a patriarchal order of things.

And it is a world where there are no proscribed, abused Ophelias to stand as society's, perfunctory after-thoughts on the thresholds of worlds of freedom and duty, to nourish and preserve finer feelings and accept thankless obligations for 'the good of society', and still maintain their sanity. An alternative logic would read the message back into 'society' and require a different 'uptake' so that 'society' itself is enjoined to attend properly to the terms of the 'given' for the maintenance of so-called 'collective' and 'social' values. It would focus, in effect, on the untenability of the division of labour between ethics and power, conscience and coercion, freedom and duty, the fine and the gross, etc. on sexed lines.

The inference of *female* 'monstrosity', too, is questionable on gendered lines, since the 'monstrosities', then as now, are always in place, as invisible and automatized realities of power in force. The scandal is that given brutalities of power can be passed over as normal in most instances, as appropriate and rationalizable to a male order of things, but whose appalling hues can only be highlighted and foregrounded when displaced and contoured into a female body and cross-dressed.

At any rate, no projected options involving women and power work in the play and power devolves on the *son-in-law*, in a lateral move, into a less autocratic, reconstructed male, tolerant and unaggressive – to Albany, who is male, nevertheless, and heir to the traditional patriarchal inheritance, but capable of accommodations. Although the female intervention has brought about changes power reverts to the males once the order has changed. A simultaneous, double movement is evident. While Goneril acquires and uses 'male' competences and power within a given order, a new male order and fraternity is already in the making, out of focus but out there on the heath, or in the corridors or castles of power, which inexorably outdates and displaces the 'competences' of the one in which she has achieved power and, with its fall, there are no women anywhere in sight – no rulers, mothers, daughters, sisters, wives, lovers or friends. Patriarchally endowed daughters, interpellated into patriarchal positions of power, confined to patriarchal strategies, and playing patriarchal games, seem to spell endgame for all women. The male ethic, fraternity and culture, in 'reformed' mode, inherits and prevails. And the female wheel has to be re-invented all over again. The double bind hardly disintegrates once women are in power given the mechanics and genealogy of power – here, the autocratic, arbitrary and wilful heritage of a Lear.

The present situation in Women's drama is one of experimentation and exploration of the new issues and energies that have been released as a consequence of the Women's Movement, even if few female dramatists would classify themselves overtly as feminist (Keyssar 1984; Wandor 1987). Not only are the forgotten or erased female contributions to drama being recovered, experimentation and newer modes of drama are also in evidence. And these draw on all the discourse resources mentioned above in the interests of women. The 'difference' model is far more in evidence as women dramatists seek to explore the possibilities of alternatives to the traditional 'deficit' one.

The spatio-temporal context of situation in which female participants are placed is one significant dimension that inscribes constraints on women. In fact, women dramatists have explored the restrictions and possibilities of place by using the traditional domestic space as a central place in the lives of women. In Shelagh Delaney's *A Taste of Honey* (1975) the home is the site for the struggle of their lives and the mundane realities usually dismissed as trivial become central to the dialogue. Thus, their interactions are 'mediated by food, clothes, cleaning, sleeping, health' as concerns of women in the domestic realm (Keyssar 1984: 40). In public, male places like inns, as in John Arden's *Sergeant Musgrave's Dance* (1960), women become servers of food and sex to the men. By contrast, the women in Caryl Churchill's *Top Girls* (1982) are located in public places with other women as working women running their own employment agency.

Roles have been the object of change as well, since much feminist drama refuses the stability and closure of traditional roles and has provided plays in which continuous transformations, different role possibilities, are offered instead. The roles in Megan Terry's *Comings and Goings* (1967) can be played by either men or women or combinations of them. The play focuses on the relationships between role, gender and behaviour by varying the power differential. In a restaurant scene, the roles of waitress and customer engaged in the typical action of ordering food are varied in such a way that at one point the waitress is at the mercy of the customer; at another, the situation is the other way round. In Caryl Churchill's *Cloud Nine* (1979) gender, physical appearance and role are fractured so that a woman character, Betty, is played by a man; her son is played by a woman; and the black servant is played by a white man. Marsha Norman's *Getting Out* (1980) splits the protagonist female role into two – Arlie/Arlene – as the 'bad' and 'good' aspects of the same persona, to be played by two actresses.

New roles have made their appearance in the more traditional plays written by women so that, instead of the motherless waifs in Shakespeare, mother–daughter relationships are explored by the likes of Shelagh Delaney and Megan Terry. Black women playwrights like Alice Childress re-design the traditional black female role of deference to the white in terms of challenge. In *Trouble in the Mind* (1971), an ageing black actress cast as a servant in a play within a play to a white Southern family becomes increasingly uneasy with the stereotypes including the black one she is supposed to portray, and she finally challenges the director about the 'truths' being enacted. Lesbian roles and relationships, too, are being explored. A whole range of roles, both scarred and enduring, as appropriate to the modern landscape, are also evident – abused girls, abandoned children, single mothers, career women, friends and colleagues, delinquents, prostitutes, both happy and unhappy, speak and act themselves into existence. Attention to the gendered nature of the audience in the performance of plays has also become a point of awareness.

Participant configurations, too, have been changed, as have interactive styles and notions of feminine 'competences' in the acts, goals, ends of speech in these contexts, since women talking, intensely or wittily, acerbically or poetically, women laughing, singing, working, quarrelling with other women as a matter of course, are more in evidence, by contrast with women escorted by men in traditional drama. Instrumentalities and genres have been mobilized in the use of song, stories, etc. in plays by women, and by different voices, black and white, in the use of dialects and other speech textures and styles as appropriate are evident. Different 'floors' have been attempted, of simultaneous speech, of choral speech, of floors that attend to listening as much as to speaking with women cast as interactive 'subjects', as among the wider projects of gender. Women's intentionalities in speech and action are given greater rein when men are removed from the scene, since they are often in these plays only referenced but do not have a participant role. The productivities of female 'norms' are thus being explored. How 'difference' models would cope with 'power', and what resources would be engendered, mono-culturally and cross-culturally, is an open question, although the issue invades contemporary, inter-personal, private and public relationships in societies; but the goal of 'empowerment' rather than 'power' is yet to become a norm in drama, as in life.

Bibliography

Adorno, T.W. (1974). *Minima Moralia: Reflections From Damaged Life*. Trans. E.F.N. Jephcott. London: New Left Books.

Albee, E. (1962, repr. 1989). *Who's Afraid of Virginia Woolf?* Harmondsworth, Middlesex: Penguin.

Allan, K. (1986). *Linguistic Meaning*, vols. 1 and 2. London: Routledge and Kegan Paul.

Alter, J. (1979). 'Coding dramatic efficiency in plays: from text to play'. *Semiotica* 28, 1/2, 247–58.

Alvis, J. (1981). 'Introductory: Shakespearean poetry and politics'. In J. Alvis and T.G. West (eds) *Shakespeare as Political Thinker*. Durham, NC: Carolina Academic Press, 3–26.

Alvis, J. and T.G. West (eds) (1981). *Shakespeare as Political Thinker*. Durham, NC: Carolina Academic Press.

Anderson, J. (ed.) (1989). *Communication Yearbook, Vol. 12*. Newbury Park: Sage.

Anzaldua, G. (1987). *Borderlands/La Frontera*. San Francisco: Spinsters/Aunt Lute.

Arden, J. (1960, repr. 1966). *Sergeant Musgrave's Dance*. London: Methuen.

Aries, E. (1976). 'Interaction patterns and themes in male, female and mixed groups'. *Small Group Behaviour* 7, 1, 7–18.

Atkinson, J. M. and J. Heritage (eds) (1984). *Structures of Social Action: Studies in Conversation Analysis*. Cambridge: Cambridge University Press.

Auer, P. (1992). 'Introduction: John Gumperz' approach to contextualization'. In P. Auer and A. Di Luzio (eds) *The Contextualization of Language*. Amsterdam/Philadelphia: John Benjamins, 1–38.

Auer, P. and A. Di Luzio (eds) (1992). *The Contextualization of Language*. Amsterdam/Philadelphia: John Benjamins (Pragmatics and Beyond New Series 22).

Austin, G. (1990). *Feminist Theories for Dramatic Criticism*. Ann Arbor: The University of Michigan Press.

Austin, J.L. (1962). *How to Do Things with Words*. Oxford: Clarendon Press.

Bach, K. and M. Harnish (1979, repr. 1982). *Linguistic Communication and Speech Acts*. Massachusetts: MIT Press.

—— (1987). 'Relevant questions'. *Behavioural and Brain Sciences* 10, 711–12.

Bakhtin, M.M. (1981, repr. 1985). *The Dialogic Imagination: Four Essays*. Ed.

M. Holquist. Trans. C. Emerson and M. Holquist. Austin, TX: University of Texas Press.

Barker, R. (ed.) (1963). *The Stream of Behaviour*. New York: Appleton-Century-Crofts.

Bauman, R. and J. Sherzer (eds) (1974). *Explorations in the Ethnography of Speaking*. Cambridge: Cambridge University Press.

Beckerman, B. (1970). *The Dynamics of Drama: Theory and Method of Analysis*. New York: Alfred A. Knopf.

Beckett, S. (1955, repr. 1965). *Waiting for Godot*. London: Faber and Faber.

—— (1958, repr. 1988). *Endgame*. London: Faber and Faber.

Belsey, C. (1985). *The Subject of Tragedy: Identity and Difference in Renaissance Drama*. London: Methuen.

Ben-Amos, D. and K.S. Goldstein (eds) (1975). *Folklore: Performance and Communication*. The Hague: Mouton.

Bennett, D.C. (1975). *Spatial and Temporal Uses of English Prepositions: An Essay in Stratificational Semantics*. London: Longman.

Bentley, E. (1965). *The Life of Drama*. London: Methuen.

Beaugrande, R. de and W. Dressler (1981). *Introduction to Text Linguistics*. London: Longman.

Birch, D. (1991). *The Language of Drama: Critical Theory and Practice*. London: Macmillan.

Blakemore, D. (1992). *Understanding Utterances: An Introduction to Pragmatics*. Oxford: Blackwell.

Boden, D. and D.H. Zimmerman (eds) (1991). *Talk and Social Structure*. Cambridge: Polity.

Bolinger, D. (1961). 'Syntactic blends and other matters'. *Language* 37, 3, 366–81.

Bond, E. (1965, repr. 1977). *Saved*. London: Methuen.

Bradley, P.H. (1980). 'Sex, competence and opinion deviation: an expectation states approach'. *Communication Monographs* 47, 101–10.

Braverman, H. (1974). *Labor and Monopoly Capital: The Degradation of Work in the Twentieth Century*. New York: Monthly Review Press.

Brennan, A. (1986, repr. 1988). *Shakespeare's Dramatic Structures*. London: Routledge.

Brown, G. and G. Yule (1983). *Discourse Analysis*. Cambridge: Cambridge University Press.

Brown, P. and S.C. Levinson (1987). *Politeness: Universals in Language Usage*. Cambridge: Cambridge University Press.

Buber, M. (1923, repr. 1937). *I and Thou*. Edinburgh: Edinburgh University Press.

Buhler, K. (1934). *Sprachtheorie*. Jena: Fischer.

—— (1982). 'Deictic field of action and deictic words?' In R. Jarvella and W. Klein (eds) *Speech, Place, and Action*. London: John Wiley and Sons, 9–30.

Burns, E. (1972). *Theatricality: A Study of Convention in the Theatre and in Social Life*. London: Longman.

Burton, D. (1980). *Dialogue and Discourse: A Sociolinguistic Approach to Modern Drama Dialogue and Naturally Occurring Conversation*. London: Routledge and Kegan Paul.

Butler, J. (1990a). *Gender Trouble: Feminism and the Subversion of Identity*. London: Routledge.

——(1990b). 'Performative acts and gender constitution: an essay in phenomeno-logy and feminist theory'. In S. Case (ed.) *Performing Feminisms: Feminist Critical Theory and Theatre*. Baltimore: Johns Hopkins University Press, 270–82.

Button, G. and J.R.E. Lee (eds) (1987). *Talk and Social Organization*. Clevedon, PA: Multilingual Matters.

Calderwood, J.E. and H.E. Tolliver (1968). *Perspectives on Drama*. Oxford: Oxford University Press.

Cameron, D. (1985, repr. 1988). *Feminism and Linguistic Theory*. London: Macmillan.

Cameron, D. and J. Coates (1988). 'Some problems in the sociolinguistic expla-nation of sex differences'. In J. Coates and D. Cameron (eds) *Women in Their Speech Communities: New Perspectives on Language and Sex*. London: Long-man, 13–26.

Cameron, D., F. McAlindin and K. O'Leary (1988). 'Lakoff in context: the social and linguistic functions of tag questions'. In J. Coates and D. Cameron (eds) *Women in Their Speech Communities: New Perspectives on Language and Sex*. London: Longman, 74–93.

Carter, R.A. and P. Simpson (eds) (1989). *Language, Discourse and Literature: An Introductory Reader in Discourse Stylistics*. London: Unwin Hyman.

Case, S. (ed.) (1990). *Performing Feminisms: Feminist Critical Theory and Theatre*. Baltimore: Johns Hopkins University Press.

Chafe, W. (1985). 'Some reasons for hesitating'. In D. Tannen and M. Saville-Troika (eds) *Perspectives on Silence*. Norwood, NJ: Ablex, 77–93.

Chambers, R. (1980). 'Le masque et le miroir: vers une théorie relationnelle du théâtre'. *Études littéraires* 13, 3, 397–412.

Chatman, S. (ed.) (1971). *Literary Style*. London: Oxford University Press.

—— (1973). *Approaches to Poetics*. New York: Columbia University Press.

Chekhov, A. (1923, repr. 1971). *Four Great Plays*. Trans. Constance Garnett. New York: Bantam.

Cheshire, J. (1982). *Variation in an English Dialect*. Cambridge: Cambridge University Press.

Childress, A. (1971). *Trouble in the Mind*. In L. Patterson (ed.) *Black Theatre: A Twentieth-Century Collection of the Work of its Best Playwrights*. New York: Dodd Mead.

Churchill, C. (1979). *Cloud Nine*. London: Pluto Press.

—— (1982). *Top Girls*. London: Methuen.

Cicourel, A. (1973). *Cognitive Sociology*. London: Macmillan.

Clark, H. (1973). 'Space, time, semantics and the child'. In T.E. Moore (ed.) *Cognitive Development and the Development of Language*. New York: Aca-demic Press, 28–64.

Clegg, S. (1989). *Frameworks of Power*. Newbury Park: Sage.

Coates, J. (1986, repr. 1993). *Women, Men and Language: A Sociolinguistic Account of Gender Differences in Language*. London: Longman.

—— (1988). 'Gossip revisted: language in all-female groups'. In J. Coates and D. Cameron (eds) *Women in Their Speech Communities: New Perspectives on Language and Sex*. London: Longman, 94–121.

Coates, J. and D. Cameron (eds) (1988). *Women in Their Speech Communities: New Perspectives on Language and Sex*. London: Longman.

Cockburn, C. (1983). *Brothers: Male Dominance and Technological Change*. London: Pluto Press.

Cody, M.J. and M.L. McLaughlin (1985). 'Models for the sequential construction of accounting episodes: situational and interactional constraints on message selection and evaluation'. In R.L. Street and J.N. Cappella (eds) *Sequence and Pattern in Communicative Behaviour*. London: Edward Arnold, 50–69.

Cole, P. and J.L. Morgan (eds) (1975). *Syntax and Semantics, Vol. 3: Speech Acts*. New York: Academic Press.

Comrie, B. (1976). *Aspect*. Cambridge: Cambridge University Press.

—— (1985). *Tense*. Cambridge: Cambridge University Press.

Condry, J. and S. Condry (1976). 'Sex differences: a study in the eye of the beholder'. *Child Development* 47, 812–19.

Cooper, M.M. (1987). 'Shared knowledge and *Betrayal*'. *Semiotica* 64, 1/2, 99–117.

Coulmas, F. (1981). *Conversational Routine*. The Hague: Walter de Gruyter.

Coulthard, M. (1986). *An Introduction to Discourse Analysis*. London: Longman.

Coupland, N.G., H. Giles and J.M. Wiemann (eds) (1991). *'Miscommunication' and Problematic Talk*. London: Sage.

Coward, N. (1979, repr. 1983). *Plays: Three*. London: Eyre Methuen.

Craig, R.T. and K. Tracy (eds) (1983). *Conversational Coherence: Form, Structure, and Strategy*. London: Sage (Sage Series in Interpersonal Communication: Vol. 2).

Crosby, F. and L. Nyquist (1977). 'The female register: an empirical study of Lakoff's hypotheses'. *Language in Society* 6, 313–22.

Davidson, J. (1984). 'Subsequent versions of invitations, offers, requests and proposals dealing with potential or actual rejection'. In J.M. Atkinson and J. Heritage (eds) *Structures of Social Action: Studies in Conversation Analysis*. Cambridge: Cambridge University Press, 102–28.

DeFrancisco, V.L. (1991). 'The sounds of silence: how men silence women in marital relations'. *Discourse and Society* 2, 4, 413–24.

Delaney, S. (1975). *A Taste of Honey*. London: Methuen.

Derrida, J. (1976). *Of Grammatology*. Trans. G. Spivak. Baltimore: Johns Hopkins University Press.

Dindia, K. (1985). 'A functional approach to self-disclosure'. In R.L. Street and J.N. Cappella (eds) *Sequence and Pattern in Communicative Behaviour*. London: Edward Arnold, 142–60.

Dodd, W. (1981). 'Conversation, dialogue and exposition'. *Strumenti Critici* 15, 171–91.

Dollimore, J. and A. Sinfield (eds) (1985). *Political Shakespeare: New Essays in Cultural Materialism*. Ithaca, NY: Cornell University Press.

Drew, P. (1991). 'Asymmetries of knowledge in conversational interactions'. In I. Markova and K. Foppa (eds) *Asymmetries in Dialogue*. Hemel Hempstead: Harvester Wheatsheaf, 21–48.

Drew, P. and A. Wootton (eds) (1988). *Erving Goffman: Exploring the Interaction Order*. Cambridge: Polity.

Du Bois, J.W. (1993). 'Meaning without intention: lessons from divination'. In J.H. Hill and J.T. Irvine (eds) *Responsibility and Evidence in Oral Discourse*. Cambridge: Cambridge University Press, 48–71.

Dubois, B.L. and I. Crouch (1975). 'The question of tag questions in women's speech: they don't really use more of them, do they?' *Language in Society* 4, 289–94.

—— (eds) (1976) *The Sociology of the Languages of American Women.* Papers in Southwest English IV, San Antonio, TX: Trinity University Press.

Duncan, S. and D.W. Fiske (1977). *Face-to-face Interaction: Research, Methods and Theory.* Hillsdale, NJ: Lawrence Erlbaum Associates.

—— (1985). *Structure and Strategy in Social Interaction.* Cambridge: Cambridge University Press.

Duranti, A. (1985). 'Sociocultural dimensions of discourse'. In Teun A. Van Dijk (ed.) *Handbook of Discourse Analysis, Vol. 1: Disciplines of Discourse.* London: Academic Press, 193–230.

—— (1993). 'Intentions, self, and responsibility: an essay in Samoan ethnopragmatics'. In J.H. Hill and J.T. Irvine (eds) *Responsibility and Evidence in Oral Discourse.* Cambridge: Cambridge University Press, 24–47.

Duranti, A. and C. Goodwin (eds) (1992). *Rethinking Context: Language as an Interactive Phenomenon.* Cambridge: Cambridge University Press (Studies in the Social and Cultural Foundations of Language 11).

Eakins, B. and G. Eakins (1976). 'Verbal turn-taking and exchanges in faculty dialogue'. In B.L. Dubois and I. Crouch (eds) *The Sociology of the Languages of American Women.* Papers in Southwest English IV, San Antonio, TX: Trinity University Press.

—— (1978). *Sex Differences in Human Communication.* Boston: Houghton Mifflin.

Eco, U. (1977). 'Semiotics of theatrical performance'. *Drama Review* 21, 1, 107–17.

Edelsky, C. (1981). 'Who's got the floor?' *Language in Society* 10, 383–421.

Edmondson, W. (1981). *Spoken Discourse: A Model for Analysis.* London: Longman.

Edwards, V. (1988). 'The speech of British Black women in Dudley, West Midlands'. In J. Coates and D. Cameron (eds) *Women in Their Speech Communities: New Perspectives on Language and Sex.* London: Longman, 33–50.

Edwards, V. and S. Katbamna (1988). 'The wedding songs of British Gujerati women'. In J. Coates and D. Cameron (eds) *Women in Their Speech Communities: New Perspectives on Language and Sex.* London: Longman, 159–74.

Eisenstein, Z.R. (ed.) (1979a). *Capitalist Patriarchy.* New York: Monthly Review Press.

—— (1979b). 'Developing a theory of capitalist patriarchy and socialist feminism'. In Z.R. Eisenstein (ed.) *Capitalist Patriarchy.* New York: Monthly Review Press.

Elam, K. (1980). *The Semiotics of Theatre and Drama.* London: Methuen.

—— (1984, repr. 1989). *Shakespeare's Universe of Discourse.* Cambridge: Cambridge University Press.

Eliot, T.S. (1935, repr. 1938). *Murder in the Cathedral.* London: Faber and Faber.

Ervin-Tripp, S. and C. Mitchell-Kernan (eds) (1977). *Child Discourse.* New York: Academic Press.

Esslin, M. (1978). *The Anatomy of Drama.* London: Sphere Books.

Fillmore, C. (1983). 'How to know whether you're coming or going'. In G. Rauh (ed.) *Essays on Deixis.* Tübingen: Gunter-Naar Verlag, 219–228.

Fischer-Lichte, E. (1984). 'The dramatic dialogue – oral or literary communication'. In H. Schmid and A. van Kesteren (eds) *Semiotics of Drama and Theatre: New Perspectives in the Theory of Drama and Theatre*. Amsterdam: John Benjamins, 137–73.

Fish, S. (1980a). *Is There a Text in This Class?* Cambridge: Harvard University Press.

—— (1980b). 'How to do things with Austin and Searle: speech act theory and literary criticism'. In S. Fish (1980) *Is There a Text in This Class?* Cambridge: Harvard University Press, 197–245.

Fishman, P.M. (1980). 'Interactional shitwork'. *Heresies* 2, 99–101.

—— (1983). 'Interaction: the work women do'. In B. Thorne, C. Kramarae and N. Henley (eds) *Language, Gender and Society*. Rowley, MA: Newbury House, 89–101.

Foucault, M. (1978). *The History of Sexuality, Vol. 1*. Trans. Robert Hurley. New York: Random House.

—— (1988). 'Technologies of the self'. In L.H. Martin, H. Gutman and P. Hutton (eds) *Technologies of the Self: A Seminar with Michel Foucault*. London: Tavistock Publications, 16–49.

Fowler, R. (1981). *Literature as Social Discourse*. London: Batsford.

—— (1986). *Linguistic Criticism*. Oxford: Oxford University Press.

Fugard, A. (1974). *Statements*. Cape Town: Oxford University Press.

Fugard, A., J. Kani and W. Ntshona (1974). 'Sizwe Bansi is dead'. In A. Fugard *Statements*. Cape Town: Oxford University Press.

Gadamer, H.J. (1986a). 'Man and language'. In H.J. Gadamer *Philosophical Hermeneutics*. Ed. and trans. D.E. Linge. Berkeley: University of California Press.

—— (1986b). *Philosophical Hermeneutics*. Ed. and trans. D.E. Linge. Berkeley: University of California Press.

Gann, M.S. (1986). 'The performative status of verbal offenses in *A secreto agravio, secreta venganza*'. In E.L. Rivers (ed.) *Things Done with Words: Speech Acts in Hispanic Drama*. Newark, DE: Juan de la Cuesta, 39–50.

Gautam, K. (1987). 'Pinter's *The Caretaker*: a study in conversational analysis'. *Journal of Pragmatics* 11, 49–59.

Gautam, K. and M. Sharma (1986). 'Dialogue in *Waiting for Godot* and Grice's concept of implicature'. *Modern Drama* 29, 580–6.

Geertz, C. (1993). '"From the native's point of view": on the nature of anthropological understanding'. In R.A. Shweder and R.A. LeVine (eds) *Culture Theory: Essays on Mind, Self and Emotion*. Cambridge: Cambridge University Press, 123–36.

Gershuny, J.L. (1977). 'Sexism in dictionaries and texts'. In A.P. Nilsen, H. Bosmajian, J.L. Gershuny and J.P. Stanley (eds) *Sexism and Language*. Urbana, IL: National Council of Teachers of English, 143–59.

Giddens, A and J. Turner (eds) (1987). *Social Theory Today*. Stanford: Stanford University Press.

Gilliam, A. (1991). 'Women's equality and national liberation'. In C.T. Mohanty, A. Russo and L. Torres (eds) *Third World Women and the Politics of Feminism*. Bloomington, IN: Indiana University Press, 215–36.

Goffman, E. (1967). *Interaction Ritual: Essays on Face-to-face Behaviour*. New York: Doubleday Anchor.

—— (1979). 'Footing'. *Semiotica* 25, 1–29.

—— (1983a) 'The interaction order'. *American Sociological Review* 48, 1, 1–17.

—— (1983b). 'Felicity's condition'. *American Journal of Sociology* 89, 1, 1–53.

Graddol, D. and J. Swan (1989). *Gender Voices*. Oxford: Basil Blackwell.

Graham, A. (1975). 'The making of a non-sexist dictionary'. In B. Thorne and N. Henley (eds) *Language and Sex: Difference and Dominance*. Rowley, MA: Newbury House, 57–63.

Greenberg, J. (ed.) (1979). *Universals of Human Language, Vol. 3: Word Structure*. Stanford: Stanford University Press.

Grice, H.P. (1975). 'Logic and conversation'. In P. Cole and J.L. Morgan (eds) *Syntax and Semantics, Vol. 3: Speech Acts*. New York: Academic Press, 41–5.

—— (1989). *Studies in the Way of Words*. Cambridge, MA: Harvard University Press.

Grimshaw, A.D. (1981). *Language as a Social Resource*. Stanford: Stanford University Press.

—— (1990). *Conflict Talk: Sociolinguistic Investigations of Arguments in Conversation*. Cambridge: Cambridge University Press.

Gumperz, J. (1977). 'Sociocultural knowledge in conversational inference'. In M. Saville-Troika (ed.) *Linguistics and Anthropology*. Washington, DC: Georgetown University Press, 191–212.

—— (1982). *Discourse Strategies*. Cambridge: Cambridge University Press.

—— (1992). 'Contextualization revisited'. In P. Auer and A. Di Luzio (eds) *The Contextualization of Language*. Amsterdam/Philadelphia: John Benjamins, 39–54.

Gumperz, J.J. and D. Hymes (eds) (1972). *Directions in Sociolinguistics: The Ethnography of Communication*. New York: Holt, Rinehart and Winston.

Hallett, Charles A. and E.S. Hallett (1991). *Analyzing Shakespeare's Action: Scene Versus Sequence*. Cambridge: Cambridge University Press.

Halliday, M.A.K. and R. Hasan (1976). *Cohesion in English*. London: Longman.

—— (1985, repr. 1989). *Language, Context, and Text: Aspects of Language in a Social-Semiotic Perspective*. Oxford: Oxford University Press.

Handke, P. (1967, repr. 1972). *Kaspar*. London: Eyre Methuen.

—— (1969, repr. 1971). *Offending the Audience*. London: Methuen.

Harris, S. (1984). 'Questions as a mode of control in magistrates' courts'. *International Journal of the Sociology of Language* 49.

Hartmann, H. (1979). 'Capitalism, patriarchy and job segregation by sex'. In Z.R. Eisenstein (ed.) *Capitalist Patriarchy*. New York: Monthly Review Press.

—— (1981). 'The family as the locus of gender, class and political struggle: the example of housework'. *Signs* 6, 3, 366–94.

Hekman, S.J. (1990). *Gender and Knowledge: Elements of a Postmodern Feminism*. Cambridge: Polity.

Heritage, John (1984, repr. 1992). *Garfinkel and Ethnomethodology*. Cambridge: Polity.

Herman, V. (1983). 'Introduction: literariness and linguistics'. *Prose Studies* 6, 2, 99–122.

—— (1989). 'Subject construction as stylistic strategy in Gerard Manley Hopkins'. In R.A. Carter and P. Simpson (eds) *Language, Discourse and Literature: An Introductory Reader in Discourse Stylistics*. London: Unwin Hyman, 213–34.

—— (1991). 'Dramatic discourse and the systematics of turn-taking'. *Semiotica* 83, 1/2, 97–121.

Herman, V. and P. Dodd (eds) (1983). *Prose Studies* 6, 2.

Herskovits, A. (1986). *Language and Spatial Cognition: An Interdisciplinary Study of Prepositions in English.* Cambridge: Cambridge University Press.

Hester, M. (1992). *Lewd Women and Wicked Witches: A Study of the Dynamics of Male Domination.* London: Routledge.

Hicks, M.R. (1986). 'Strategies of ambiguity: the honour conflict in *La Batalla de honor*'. In E.L. Rivers (ed.) *Things Done with Words: Speech Acts in Hispanic Drama.* Newark, DE: Juan de la Cuesta, 15–28.

Hill, C. (1982). 'Up/down, front/back, left/right. A contrastive study of Hausa and English'. In J. Weissenborn and W. Klein (eds) *Here and There: Cross-Linguistic Studies on Deixis and Demonstration.* Amsterdam/Philadelphia: John Benjamins, 13–42.

Hill, J.H. and J.T. Irvine (eds) (1992, repr. 1993). *Responsibility and Evidence in Oral Discourse.* Cambridge: Cambridge University Press (Studies in the Social and Cultural Foundations of Language 15).

Holmes, J. (1984a). 'Hedging your bets and sitting on the fence: some evidence for hedges as support structures'. *Te Reo* 27, 47–62.

—— (1984b). 'Modifying illocutionary force'. *Journal of Pragmatics* 8, 345–65.

—— (1993). 'New Zealand women are good to talk to: an analysis of politeness strategies in interaction'. *Journal of Pragmatics* 20, 91–116.

Holquist, M. (1990). *Dialogism: Bakhtin and His World.* London: Routledge.

Honzl, J. (1940). 'The hierarchy of dramatic devices'. In L. Matejka and I.R. Titunik (eds) (1976) *Semiotics of Art: Prague School Contributions.* Cambridge, MA: MIT Press, 118–26.

Hymes, D. (1972). 'Models of the interaction of language and social life'. In J. Gumperz and D. Hymes (eds) *Directions in Sociolinguistics: The Ethnography of Communication.* New York: Holt, Rinehart and Winston, 35–71.

—— (1975). 'Breakthrough into performance'. In D. Ben-Amos and K.S. Goldstein (eds) *Folklore: Performance and Communication.* The Hague: Mouton.

Ibsen, H. (1958) *The Master Builder and Other Plays.* Trans. Una Ellis-Fermor. Harmondsworth: Penguin.

Ionesco, E. (1958, repr. 1965). *Plays: Vol. 1.* Trans. Donald Watson. London: John Calder.

—— (1968). *Plays: Vol. 7.* Trans. Donald Watson. London: Calder and Boyars.

—— (1970). *Plays: Vol. 3.* Trans. Donald Watson. London: Calder and Boyars.

Irigaray, L. (1977). *Ce Sexe qui n'en est pas un.* Paris: Minuit.

Issacharoff, M. (1989). *Discourse as Performance.* Stanford: Stanford University Press.

Jakobson, R. (1960). 'Closing statement: linguistics and poetics'. In T.A. Sebeok (ed.) *Style in Language.* Cambridge, MA: MIT Press, 350–77.

Jankowski, T.A. (1992). *Women in Power in the Early Modern Drama.* Urbana/Chicago: University of Illinois Press.

Jarvella, Robert J. and Wolfgang Klein (eds) (1982). *Speech, Place, and Action: Studies in Deixis and Related Topics.* London: John Wiley & Sons.

Jaworski, A. (1993). *The Power of Silence: Social and Pragmatic Perspectives.* London: Sage.

Jefferson, G. (1972). 'Side sequences'. In D. Sudnow (ed.) *Studies in Social Interaction*. New York: Free Press, 294–338.

—— (1984). 'On stepwise transition from talk about a trouble to inappropriately next-positioned matters'. In J.M. Atkinson and J. Heritage (eds) *Structures of Social Action: Studies in Conversational Analysis*. Cambridge: Cambridge University Press, 191–222.

Jefferson, G. and J. Schenkein (1978). 'Some sequential negotiations in conversation: Unexpanded and expanded versions of projected action sequences'. In J. Schenkein (ed.) *Studies in the Organization of Conversational Interaction*. New York: Academic Press, 155–72.

Jefferson, G., H. Sacks and E.A. Schegloff (1987). 'Notes on laughter in pursuit of intimacy'. In G. Button and J.R.E. Lee (eds) *Talk and Social Organization*. Clevedon, PA: Multilingual Matters, 152–205.

Jespersen, O. (1922). *Language: Its Nature, Development and Origin*. London: Allen and Unwin.

Johnstone, B. (1987). 'An introduction'. In B. Johnstone (ed.) *Perspectives on Repetition*, special issue, *Text* 7, 3, 205–14.

Kalcik, S. (1975). '. . . like Ann's gynaecologist or the time I was almost raped – personal narratives in women's rape groups'. *Journal of American Folklore* 88, 3–11.

Kanter, R.M. (1977). *Men and Women of the Corporation*. New York: Basic Books.

Keenan, E. (1974). 'Norm-makers; norm-breakers: uses of speech by women in a Malagasay community'. In R. Bauman and J. Sherzer (eds) *Explorations in the Ethnography of Speaking*. Cambridge: Cambridge University Press, 125–43.

—— (1977). 'Making it last: repetition in children's discourse'. In S. Ervin-Tripp and C. Mitchell-Kernan (eds) *Child Discourse*. New York: Academic Press, 125–38.

Kehler, Dorothea and Susan Baker (eds) (1991). *In Another Country: Feminist Perspectives on Renaissance Drama*. Metuchen, NJ: Scarecrow Press.

Kennedy, A.K. (1983). *Dramatic Dialogue: The Duologue of Personal Encounter*. Cambridge: Cambridge University Press.

Keyssar, K. (1984). *Feminist Theatre: An Introduction to Plays of Contemporary British and American Women*. London: Macmillan.

Kristeva, J. (1974). *La Révolution du langage poétique*. Paris: Seuil.

—— (1980). *Revolution in Poetic Language: A Semiotic Approach to Literature and Art*. Ed. L.S Roudiez. Trans. T. Gorz, A. Jardine and L.S. Roudiez. New York: Columbia University Press.

Labov, W. (1972). *Sociolinguistic Patterns*. Philadelphia: University of Pennsylvania Press.

Labov, W. and D. Fanshel (1977). *Therapeutic Discourse: Psychotherapy as Conversation*. New York: Academic Press.

Lacan, J. (1966, trans. 1977). *Écrits: A Selection*. Trans. Alan Sheridan. London: Tavistock.

Lakoff, R. (1975). *Language and Woman's Place*. New York: Harper and Row.

Lakoff, R. and D. Tannen (1984). 'Conversational strategy and metastrategy in a pragmatic theory: the example of *Scenes from a Marriage*'. *Semiotica* 49, 3/4, 323–46.

Leech, G. (1983). *Principles of Pragmatics*. London: Longman.
Leech, G. and J. Svartvik (1975). *A Communicative Grammar of English*. London: Longman.
Levinson, S.C. (1983). *Pragmatics*. Cambridge: Cambridge University Press.
—— (1988). 'Putting linguistics on a proper footing: explorations in Goffman's concepts of participation'. In P. Drew and A. Wootton (eds) *Erving Goffman: Exploring the Interaction Order*. Cambridge: Polity, 161–227.
—— (1992). 'Primer for the field investigation of spatial description and conception'. *Pragmatics* 2, 1, 5–48.
Lewis, D. (1969). *Convention*. Cambridge, MA: Harvard University Press.
Lipman-Blumen, J. (1984). *Gender Roles and Power*. Englewood Cliffs: Prentice-Hall.
Linde, C. and W. Labov (1975). 'Spatial networks as a site for the study of language and thought'. *Language* 51, 924–39.
Lyons, John (1977). *Semantics*, Vols 1 and 2. Cambridge: Cambridge University Press.
MacAloon, J.J. (ed.) (1984). *Rite, Drama, Festival, Spectacle: Rehearsals Toward a Theory of Cultural Performance*. Philadelphia: Institute for the Study of Human Issues.
McConnell-Ginet, S. (1978). 'Intonation in a man's world'. *Signs: Journal of Women in Culture and Society* 3, 3, 541–9.
McConnell-Ginet, S., R. Barker and N. Furman (eds) (1980). *Women and Language in Literature and Society*. New York: Praeger.
McKeever, W.F. (1988). 'Cerebral organization and sex: interesting but complex'. In S.U. Philips, S. Steele and C. Tanz (eds) *Language, Gender and Sex in Comparative Perspective*. Cambridge: Cambridge University Press, 268–77.
Malinowski, B. (1923). 'The problem of meaning in primitive languages'. In C.K. Ogden and I.A. Richards *The Meaning of Meaning*. London: Routledge and Kegan Paul, 296–336.
Markel, N.N., J.F. Long and T.J. Saine (1976). 'Sex differences in conversational interaction: another look at male dominance'. *Human Communication Research* 2, 356–64.
Markova, I. and K. Foppa (eds) (1990). *The Dynamics of Dialogue*. London: Harvester Wheatsheaf.
—— (1991). *Asymmetries in Dialogue*. Hemel Hempstead: Harvester Wheatsheaf.
Marlowe, C. (1966). *Complete Plays*. London: Oxford University Press.
Martin, L.H., H. Gutman and P. Hutton (eds) (1988). *Technologies of the Self: A Seminar with Michel Foucault*. London: Tavistock Publications.
Martin, R.M. (1987, repr. 1989). *The Meaning of Language*. Cambridge, MA: MIT Press.
Matejka, L. and I.R. Titunik (eds) (1976). *Semiotics of Art: Prague School Contributions*. Cambridge, MA: MIT Press.
Matoesian, G.M. (1993). *Reproducing Rape: Domination Through Talk in the Courtroom*. Cambridge: Polity.
Mey, J.L. (1993). *Pragmatics: An Introduction*. Oxford: Blackwell.
Miller, N. (ed.) (1986). *The Poetics of Gender*. New York: Columbia University Press.

Mills, S., L. Pearce, S. Spaull and E. Millard (eds) (1989). *Feminist Readings/Feminists Reading*. Hemel Hempstead: Harvester Wheatsheaf.

Milroy, L. (1980). *Language and Social Networks*. Oxford: Basil Blackwell.

Mohanty, C.T. (1991a). 'Cartographies of struggle: third world women and the politics of feminism'. In C.T. Mohanty, A. Russo and L. Torres (eds) *Third World Women and the Politics of Feminism*. Bloomington, IN: Indiana University Press, 1–47.

—— (1991b) 'Under western eyes'. In C.T. Mohanty, A. Russo and L. Torres (eds) *Third World Women and the Politics of Feminism*. Bloomington, IN: Indiana University Press, 51–80.

Mohanty, C.T., A. Russo and L. Torres (eds) (1991). *Third World Women and the Politics of Feminism*. Bloomington, IN: Indiana University Press.

Moi, T. (1985). *Sexual/Textual Politics: Feminist Literary Theory*. London: Routledge (New Accents).

Moore, T.E. (ed.) (1973). *Cognitive Development and the Development of Language*. New York: Academic Press.

Morris, C.W. (1938). 'Foundations of the theory of signs'. In O. Neurath, R. Carnap and C. Morris (eds) *International Encyclopaedia of Unified Science*. Chicago: University of Chicago Press, 77–138.

Morris, G.H. (1985). 'The remedial episode as a negotiation of rules'. In R.L. Street and J.N. Cappella (eds) *Sequence and Pattern in Communicative Behaviour*. London: Edward Arnold.

Morson, G.S. and C. Emerson (1990). *Mikhail Bakhtin: Creation of a Prosaics*. Stanford: Stanford University Press.

Nemeth, C., J. Endicott and J. Watchler (1976). 'From the '50s to the '70s: women in jury deliberations'. *Sociometry* 39, 293–304.

Neurath, O., R. Carnap and C. Morris (eds) (1938). *International Encyclopaedia of Unified Science*. Chicago: University of Chicago Press.

The New Penguin English Dictionary (1986). London: Penguin Books, in association with Longman Group Limited.

Newmayer, F.J. (ed.) (1988). *Linguistics: The Cambridge Survey, Vol. 4: Language: The Socio-Cultural Context*. Cambridge: Cambridge University Press.

Nichols, P.C. (1983). 'Linguistic options and choices for Black women in the rural south'. In B. Thorne, C. Kramarae and N. Henley (eds) *Language, Gender and Society*. Rowley, MA: Newbury House, 54–68.

Nicoll, A. (1968). 'Dramatic dialogue'. In J.L. Calderwood and H.E. Tolliver; *Perspectives on Drama*. Oxford: Oxford University Press.

Nilsen, A.P. (1977). 'Linguistic sexism as a social issue'. In A.P. Nilsen, H. Bosmajian, J.L. Gershuny and J.P. Stanley (eds) *Sexism and Language*. Urbana, IL: National Council of Teachers of English, 1–26.

Nilsen, A.P., H. Bosmajian, J.L. Gershuny and J.P. Stanley (eds) (1977). *Sexism and Language*. Urbana, IL: National Council of Teachers of English.

Norman, M. (1980). *Getting Out*. New York: Dramatists Play Service.

Norrick, N.R. (1987). 'Function of repetition in conversation'. *Text* 7, 3, 245–64.

O'Barr, W. and B. Atkins (1980). '"Women's language" or "powerless language"?' In S. McConnell-Ginet, R. Barker and N. Furman (eds) *Women and Language in Literature and Society*. New York: Praeger, 93–110.

Ogden, C.K. and I.A. Richards (1923). *The Meaning of Meaning*. London: Routledge and Kegan Paul.

Ohmann, R. (1971). 'Speech, action and style'. In S. Chatman (ed.) *Literary Style.* London: Oxford University Press, 241–54.

—— (1973). 'Literature as act'. In S. Chatman (ed.) *Approaches to Poetics.* New York: Columbia University Press, 81–107.

Osborne, J. (1957). *Look Back in Anger.* London: Faber and Faber.

Parsons, E.C. (1913). *The Ole-Fashioned Woman: Primitive Fancies about the Sex.* New York: G.P.Putnam's Sons.

Patterson, L. (ed.) (1971). *Black Theatre: A Twentieth-Century Collection of the Work of its Best Playwrights.* New York: Dodd Mead.

Petrey, S. (1990). *Speech Acts and Literary Theory.* London: Routledge.

Pfister, M. (1988). *The Theory and Analysis of Drama.* Cambridge: Cambridge University Press.

Philips, S.U. (1985). 'Interaction structured through talk and interaction structured through silence'. In D. Tannen and M. Saville-Troika (eds) *Perspectives on Silence.* Norwood, NJ: Ablex, 205–14.

—— (1988). 'Introduction: The interaction of social and biological processes in women's and men's speech'. In S.U. Philips, S. Steele and C. Tanz (eds) *Language, Gender and Sex in Comparative Perspective.* Cambridge: Cambridge University Press, 1–14.

—— (1993). 'Evidentiary standards for American trials: just the facts'. In J.H. Hill and J.T. Irvine (eds) *Responsibility and Evidence in Oral Discourse.* Cambridge: Cambridge University Press, 248–59.

Philips, S.U., S. Steele and C. Tanz (eds) (1987, repr. 1988). *Language, Gender and Sex in Comparative Perspective.* Cambridge: Cambridge University Press (Studies in the Social and Cultural Foundations of Language 4).

Pinter, H. (1976, repr. 1980). *Plays: One.* London: Eyre Methuen.

—— (1978). *Plays: Three.* London: Eyre Methuen.

—— (1981, repr. 1986). *Plays: Four.* London: Eyre Methuen.

Pomerantz, A.M. (1978). 'Compliment responses: notes on the co-operation of multiple constraints'. In J.N. Schenkein (ed.) *Studies in the Organization of Conversational Interaction.* New York: Academic Press, 79–112.

—— (1984). 'Pursuing a response'. In J.M. Atkinson and J. Heritage (eds) *Structures of Social Action: Studies in Conversational Analysis.* Cambridge: Cambridge University Press, 152–63.

Porter, J.A. (1979). *The Drama of Speech Acts: Shakespeare's Lancastrian Tetralogy.* Berkeley: University of California Press.

Potegal, M. (ed.) (1982). *Spatial Abilities: Development and Physiological Foundations.* New York: Academic Press.

Potter, J. and S. Reicher (1987). 'Discourses of community and conflict: the organization of social categories in accounts of a "riot"'. *British Journal of Social Psychology* 26.

Potter, J. and M. Wetherell (1987, repr. 1989). *Discourse and Social Psychology.* London: Sage.

Poynton, C. (1990). 'The privileging of representation and the marginalising of the inter-personal: a metaphor (and more) for contemporary gender relations'. In T. Threadgold and A. Cranny-Francis (eds) *Feminine Masculine and Representation.* Sydney: Allen and Unwin, 231–55.

Preisler, B. (1986). *Linguistic Sex Roles in Conversation: Social Variation in the*

Expression of Tentativeness in English. Berlin: Mouton de Gruyter (Contributions to the Sociology of Language, 45).

Priestley, J.B. (1948). *The Plays of J.B. Priestley. Vol. 1*. London: William Heinemann.

Psathas, G. (ed.) (1979). *Everyday Language: Studies in Ethnomethodology*. New York: Irvington.

Rattigan, T. (1973, repr. 1985). *Plays: Two*. London: Methuen.

Rauh, G. (ed.) (1983). *Essays on Deixis*. Tübingen: Gunter-Naar Verlag.

Rawls, J. (1955). 'Two concepts of rules'. *Philosophical Review* 64, 3–32.

Rich, A. (1980). 'Compulsory heterosexuality and lesbian existence'. *Signs: Journal of Women in Culture and Society* 5, 4, 631–60.

Rivers, E.L. (ed.) (1986). *Things Done with Words: Speech Acts in Hispanic Drama*. Newark, DE: Juan de la Cuesta.

Rorty, A.O. (ed.) (1976a). *The Identity of Persons*. Berkeley: University of California Press.

—— (1976b). 'A literary postscript: characters, persons, selves, individuals'. In A.O. Rorty (ed.) *The Identity of Persons*. Berkeley: University of California Press, 301–23.

Rosaldo, M. (1982). 'Ilongot speech acts and speech act theory'. *Language and Society* 11, 2, 203–37.

Sacks, H. (1967–72). Lecture notes. Mimeo. Department of Sociology, University of California, Irvine.

—— (1972). 'On the analysability of stories by children'. In J.J. Gumperz and D. Hymes (eds) *Directions in Sociolinguistics: The Ethnography of Communication*. New York: Holt, Rinehart and Winston, 325–45.

—— (1974). 'An analysis of the course of a joke's telling in conversation'. In R. Bauman and J. Sherzer (eds) *Explorations in the Ethnography of Speaking*. Cambridge: Cambridge University Press, 337–53.

Sacks, H., E.A. Schegloff and G. Jefferson (1978). 'A simplest systematics for the organization of turn taking in conversation'. In J.N. Schenkein (ed.) *Studies in the Organization of Conversational Interaction*. New York: Academic Press, 7–55.

Sargent, L. (ed.) (1981). *Women and Revolution*. London: Pluto Press.

Sattel, J.W. (1983). 'Men, inexpressiveness and power'. In B. Thorne, C. Kramarae and N. Henley (eds) *Language, Gender and Society*. Rowley, MA: Newbury House, 119–24.

Saville-Troika, M. (1982, repr. 1984). *The Ethnography of Communication: An Introduction*. Oxford: Basil Blackwell.

—— (1985). 'The place of silence in an integrated theory of communication'. In D. Tannen and M. Saville-Troika (eds) *Perspectives on Silence*. Norwood, NJ: Ablex, 3–20.

Schegloff, E.A. (1972). 'Sequencing in conversational openings'. In J.J. Gumperz and D. Hymes (eds) *Directions in Sociolinguistics: The Ethnography of Communication*. New York: Holt, Rinehart and Winston, 346–80.

—— (1979). 'Identification and recognition in telephone conversation openings'. In G. Psathas (ed.) *Everyday Language: Studies in Ethnomethodology*. New York: Irvington, 23–78.

—— (1988). 'Goffman and the analysis of conversation'. In P. Drew and A.

Wootton (eds) *Erving Goffman: Exploring the Interaction Order*. Cambridge: Polity, 89–135

Schegloff, E.A. and H. Sacks (1973). 'Opening up closings'. *Semiotica*, 7, 4, 289–327.

Schegloff, E.A., G. Jefferson and H. Sacks (1977). 'The preference for self-correction in the organization of repair in conversation'. *Language* 53, 361–82.

Schenkein, J. (ed.) (1978). *Studies in the Organization of Conversational Interaction*. New York: Academic Press.

Schiffrin, D. (1994). *Approaches to Discourse*. Oxford: Blackwell.

Schmid, H. and A. van Kesteren (eds) (1984). *Semiotics of Drama and Theatre: New Perspectives in the Theory of Drama and Theatre*. Amsterdam: John Benjamins.

Searle, J.R. (1969, repr. 1974). *Speech Acts*. Cambridge: Cambridge University Press.

—— (1976). 'The classification of illocutionary acts'. *Language and Society* 5, 1–24.

—— (1979). *Expression and Meaning*. Cambridge: Cambridge University Press.

—— (1992a). 'Conversation'. In J.R. Searle *et al.* (eds) *(On) Searle on Conversation*. Amsterdam/Philadelphia: John Benjamins, 7–30.

—— (1992b). 'Conversation reconsidered'. In J.R. Searle *et al.* (eds) *(On) Searle on Conversation*. Amsterdam/Philadelphia: John Benjamins, 137–48.

Searle, J.R. *et al.* (eds) (1992). *(On) Searle on Conversation*. Amsterdam/Philadelphia: John Benjamins.

Sebeok, T.A. (ed.) (1960). *Style in Language*. Cambridge, MA: MIT Press.

Shakespeare, W. (1994). *Complete Works of William Shakespeare*. London: HarperCollins.

Shaw, G.B. (1898, repr. 1984). *Plays Pleasant*. Harmondsworth, Middlesex: Penguin Books.

Sherzer, D. (1978). 'Dialogic incongruities in the theatre of the Absurd'. *Semiotica* 22, 3/4, 269–85.

Shores, D.L. and C.P. Hines (eds) (1977). *Papers in Language Variation*. Birmingham: University of Alabama Press.

Short, M. (1989). 'Discourse analysis and drama'. In R. Carter and P. Simpson (eds) *Language, Discourse and Literature*. London: Unwin Hyman, 139–70.

Shucard, D.W., J.L. Shucard and D.G. Thomas (1988). 'Sex differences in the patterns of scalp-recorded electrophysiological activity in infancy: possible developments in language development'. In S.U. Philips, S. Steele and C. Tanz (eds) *Language, Gender and Sex in Comparative Perspective*. Cambridge: Cambridge University Press, 278–96.

Shweder, R. (1993). 'Preview: a colloquy of culture theorists'. In R.A. Shweder and R.A. LeVine (eds) *Culture Theory: Essays on Mind, Self and Emotion*. Cambridge: Cambridge University Press, 1–24.

Shweder, R.A. and R.A. LeVine (eds) (1984, repr. 1993). *Culture Theory: Essays on Mind, Self and Emotion*. Cambridge: Cambridge University Press.

Silverstein, M. (1992). 'The indeterminacy of contextualization. When is enough enough?' In P. Auer and A. Di Luzio (eds) *The Contextualization of Language*. Amsterdam/Philadelphia: John Benjamins, 55–76.

Simpson, P. (1989). 'Politeness phenomena in Ionesco's *The Lesson*'. In R. Carter and P. Simpson (eds) *Language, Discourse and Literature: An Introductory Reader in Discourse Stylistics*. London: Unwin Hyman, 171–93.

Sinclair, J.M. and R.M. Coulthard (1975). *Towards an Analysis of Discourse: The English Used by Teachers and Pupils*. London: Oxford University Press.

Smith, N. (ed.) (1982). *Mutual Knowledge*. London: Academic Press.

Smith, P.M. (1985, repr. 1989). *Language, the Sexes and Society*. Oxford: Basil Blackwell.

Soskin, W.F. and V.P. John (1963). 'The study of spontaneous talk'. In R. Barker (ed.) *The Stream of Behaviour*. New York: Appleton-Century-Crofts, 228–81.

Sperber, D. and D. Wilson (1982). 'Mutual knowledge and relevance in theories of comprehension'. In N. Smith (ed.) *Mutual Knowledge*. London: Academic Press, 61–85.

—— (1986). *Relevance: Communication and Cognition*. Oxford: Basil Blackwell.

—— (1987a). 'Précis of *Relevance: Communication and Cognition*'. In *Behavioural and Brain Sciences* 10, 697–710.

—— (1987b). 'Authors' response: presumptions of relevance'. *Behavioural and Brain Sciences* 10, 736–54.

Stanley, J.P. (1977). 'Paradigmatic woman: the prostitute'. in D.L. Shores and C.P. Hines (eds) *Papers in Language Variation*. Birmingham: University of Alabama Press, 303–21.

Steele, S. (1988). 'Introduction'. In S. Philips, S. Steele and C. Tanz (eds) *Language, Gender and Sex in Comparative Perspective*. Cambridge: Cambridge University Press, 263–7.

Stopes, C.C. (1908). *The Sphere of 'Man': In Relation to that of 'Woman' in the Constitution*. London: T. Fisher Unwin.

Stoppard, T (1972). *Jumpers*. London: Faber and Faber.

Strawson, P.F. (ed.) (1968). *Studies in the Philosophy of Thought and Action*. Oxford: Oxford University Press.

—— (1971). *Logico-Linguistic Papers*. London: Methuen.

Street, R.L. and J.N. Cappella (eds) (1985). *Sequence and Pattern in Communicative Behaviour*. London: Edward Arnold.

Stubbs, M. (1983). *Discourse Analysis: The Sociolinguistic Analysis of Natural Language*. Oxford: Basil Blackwell.

Styan, J.L. (1971, repr. 1987). *Shakespeare's Stagecraft*. Cambridge: Cambridge University Press.

—— (1975). *Drama, Stage and Audience*. Cambridge: Cambridge University Press.

Sudnow, D. (ed.) (1972). *Studies in Social Interaction*. New York: Free Press.

Synge, J.M. (1968, repr. 1980). *Plays*. London: Oxford University Press.

Szondi, P. (1965, trans. 1987). *Theory of the Modern Drama*. Cambridge: Polity, in association with Basil Blackwell, Oxford.

Tajfel, H. (ed.) (1982). *Differentiation Between Social Groups*. London: Academic Press.

Tannen, D. (1985).'Silence: anything but'. In D.Tannen and M.Saville-Troika (eds) *Perspectives on Silence*. Norwood, NJ: Ablex, 93–112.

—— (1989). *Talking Voices*. Cambridge: Cambridge University Press.

—— (1990). 'Silence as conflict management in fiction and drama. Pinter's *Betrayal* and a short story "Great Wits"'. In A.D. Grimshaw (ed.) *Conflict Talk:*

Sociolinguistic Investigations of Arguments in Conversation. Cambridge: Cambridge University Press, 260–79.

Tannen, D and M.Saville-Troika (eds) (1985). *Perspectives on Silence.* Norwood, NJ: Ablex.

Tennenhouse, L. (1986). *Power on Display: The Politics of Shakespeare's Genres.* London/New York: Methuen.

Terry, M. (1967). *Four Plays: Viet Rock*; *Comings and Goings*; Keep Tightly Closed in a Cool Dry Place; The Gloaming, Oh My Darling. New York: Simon and Schuster.

Thomas, B. (1988). 'Differences of sex and sects: linguistic variation and social networks in a Welsh mining village'. In J. Coates and D. Cameron (eds) *Women in Their Speech Communities: New Perspectives on Language and Sex.* London: Longman, 51–60.

Thorne, B. and N. Henley (eds) (1975). *Language and Sex: Difference and Dominance.* Rowley, MA: Newbury House.

Thorne, B., C. Kramarae and N. Henley (eds) (1983). *Language, Gender and Society.* Rowley, MA: Newbury House.

Threadgold, T. (1990). 'Introduction'. In T. Threadgold and A. Cranny-Francis (eds) *Feminine Masculine and Representation.* Sydney: Allen and Unwin.

Threadgold, T. and A. Cranny-Francis (eds) (1990). *Feminine Masculine and Representation.* Sydney: Allen and Unwin.

Todorov, T. (1984). *Mikhail Bakhtin: The Dialogical Principle.* Trans. Wlad Godzich. Manchester: Manchester University Press.

Traugott, E. C. (1979). 'On the expression of spatio-temporal relations in language'. In J. Greenberg (ed.) *Universals of Human Language, Vol. 3: Word Structure.* Stanford: Stanford University Press, 369–400.

Trilling, L. (1974). *Sincerity and Authenticity.* London: Oxford University Press.

Tsui, Amy (1987). 'Aspects of the classification of illocutionary acts and the notion of the perlocutionary act'. *Semiotica* 66, 4, 359–77.

Turner, J.C. (1982). 'Towards a cognitive redefinition of the social group'. In H. Tajfel (ed.) *Differentiation Between Social Groups.* London: Academic Press, 15–40.

Turner, V. (1984). 'Liminality and the performance genres'. In J.J. MacAloon (ed.) *Rite, Drama, Festival, Spectacle: Rehearsals Toward a Theory of Performance.* Philadelphia: Institute for the Study of Human Issues.

Van Dijk, T. (1985). *Handbook of Discourse Analysis, Vol. 3: Discourse and Dialogue.* New York: Academic Press.

—— (1989). 'Structures of discourse and structures of power'. In J. Anderson (ed.) *Communication Yearbook, Vol. 12.* Newbury Park: Sage, 18–59.

Veltrusky, J. (1941). 'Dramatic text as component of theatre'. In L. Matejka and I.R. Titunik (eds) (1976). *Semiotics of Art: Prague School Contributions.* Cambridge, MA: MIT Press.

Voloshinov, V. (1973). *Marxism and the Philosophy of Language.* New York: Seminar Press.

Walby, S. (1990, repr. 1992). *Theorizing Patriarchy.* Oxford: Blackwell.

Walker, A.G. (1985). 'The two faces of silence: the effect of witness hesitancy on lawyers' impressions'. In D. Tannen and M. Saville-Troika (eds) *Perspectives on Silence.* Norwood, NJ: Ablex. 55–76.

Wandor, M. (1987). *Look Back in Gender: Sexuality and the Post-War British Drama*. London: Methuen.

Weber, M. (1947). *The Theory of Social and Economic Organization*. New York: Free Press.

Weed, E. (ed.) (1989). *Coming to Terms: Feminism, Theory, Politics*. London: Routledge.

Weissenborn, J. and W. Klein (eds) (1982). *Here and There: Cross-Linguistic Studies on Deixis and Demonstration*. Amsterdam/Philadelphia: John Benjamins.

Wesker, A. (1964, repr. 1985). *The Wesker Trilogy: Chicken Soup with Barley/Roots/I'm Talking About Jerusalem*. Harmondsworth, Middlesex: Penguin. First published in 1960 by Jonathan Cape.

West, C. (1984a). *Routine Complications: Troubles with Talk Between Doctors and Patients*. Bloomington, IN: Indiana University Press.

—— (1984b). 'When the doctor is a "lady": power, status and gender in physician–patient encounters'. *Symbolic Interaction* 7, 87–106.

West, C. and D.H. Zimmerman (1983). 'Small insults: a study of interruptions in cross-sex conversations between unacquainted persons'. In B. Thorne, C. Kramarae and N. Henley (eds) *Language, Gender and Society*. Rowley, MA: Newbury House, 103–118.

Wilde, O. (1896, repr. 1962). *The Importance of Being Earnest*. In *The Norton Anthology of English Literature*. Fifth edition, Vol. 2. General Editor, M.H. Abrams. New York: W.W. Norton and Company.

Wilder, T. (1962, repr. 1982). *Our Town and Other Plays*. Harmondsworth, Middlesex: Penguin.

Wittig, M. (1981). 'One is not born a woman'. *Feminist Issues* 1, 2.

—— (1986). 'The mark of gender'. In N. Miller (ed.) *The Poetics of Gender*. New York: Columbia University Press, 63–73.

Woods, N. (1989). 'Talking shop: sex and status as determinants of floor apportionment in a work setting'. In J. Coates and D. Cameron (eds) *Women in Their Speech Communities: New Perspectives on Language and Sex*. London: Longman, 141–57.

Yell, S. (1990). 'Gender, class and power: text, process and production in Strindberg's *Miss Julie*'. In T. Threadgold and A. Cranny-Francis (eds) *Feminine Masculine and Representation*. Sydney: Allen and Unwin, 190–210.

Zimmerman, D.H. and C. West (1975). 'Sex roles, interruptions and silences in conversation'. In B. Thorne and N. Henley (eds) *Language and Sex: Difference and Dominance*. Rowley, MA: Newbury House.

Index